GREAT GUITARISTS

FACTS ON FILE

GREAT
GUITARISTS

RICH KIENZLE

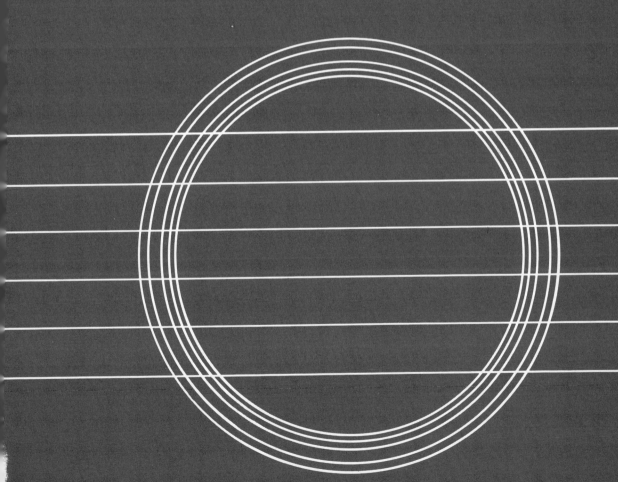

GREAT GUITARISTS

Copyright © 1985 by Rich Kienzle

Library of Congress Cataloging in Publication Data

Kienzle, Richard.
  Great guitarists.

  Includes index.
    1. Guitarists—Biography.   I. Title.
ML399.K53 1985   787.6′1′0922 [B]   83-16609
ISBN 0-8160-1029-3
ISBN 0-8160-1033-1 (pbk)

British Library Cataloguing in Publication Data

Kienzle, Rich
Great guitarists: the most influential players
in jazz, country, blues and rock.
1. Guitar—Methods—History
I. Title
787.6′1′0714   MT582

Printed in the United States of America
10 9 8 7 6 5 4 3 2 1

For my parents

ACKNOWLEDGMENTS

The following are specially thanked for their contributions to this book: my editor, James Warren, who provided encouragement and enthusiasm and who, regardless of the problem, demonstrated the patience of Job; and, my agents, Joyce Frommer and Diana Price, who performed their tasks with complete dedication, conscientiousness and enthusiasm above and beyond the call of duty. Grateful appreciation is also extended to: Peter Guralnick for his encouragement throughout; Charles K. Wolfe for his generous counsel and assistance, often on a moment's notice; Frank Scott and Jeff Richardson for encouragement on the blues section and assistance in obtaining needed recordings; Bob Oermann for sharing materials relevant to Grady Martin; and Jon Chelsted and Joe Niedzalkoski for sharing needed recordings not in my own collection. Jim Laffey put all his resources at my disposal throughout. Kyle Young and Kayce Cawthon of the Country Music Foundation proved enormously helpful with the photos for the country section. My thanks also go to Bob Allen, Keith Kolby, James Burton, Charlie McCardell, Tom Wheeler of *Guitar Player* Magazine, Harold Bradley, Michael Bane, John Morthland, Ellen Findley of Concord Jazz Records, CBS Records, Sidney A. Seidenberg Management, Frank Driggs, Polygram Records, Gregg Geller at RCA Victor Records and Judith Linn.

R. K.

Photo Credits

All photographs of country guitarists courtesy Country Music Foundation, Inc., except Eldon Shamblin, courtesy of David Stallings. Les Paul, courtesy of Gibson Guitar; Scrapper Blackwell, Blind Blake, Wes Montgomery, Lonnie Johnson, Eddie Lang, Jimmy Raney, Django Reinhardt, George Van Eps, Jimmy Page, Jimmy Hendrix, courtesy of the Frank Driggs Collection; T-Bone Walker, courtesy of the Bob Schneiders Collection; Elmore James, Otis Rush, courtesy of *Living Blues* magazine; Barney Kessel, courtesy Abby Hoffer Enterprises; James Burton, courtesy Jamilou Music Productions; Duane Allman, Jeff Beck, Chuck Berry, Mike Bloomfield, Charlie Christian, Freddy King, courtesy of Music Division, the New York Public Library at Lincoln Center, Astor, Lenox, Tilden Foundations; Carl Perkins, courtesy of Carl Perkins Music Museum.

CONTENTS

INTRODUCTION

W hat is a great guitarist? What makes a great guitarist? Actually, it can't be pinned down to just one factor. Many fine players can momentarily excite an audience, but have no lasting impact beyond that. Their styles may be flashy, but they lack originality or creative vision. They may be imitating a musician whom they admire, and though they do it well, it's still mimicry. There's a vast difference between using another's style as a starting point for original musical ideas and simply regurgitating those licks verbatim. Such players may indeed be impressive. Few, however, make a lasting contribution.

And yet many great guitarists began as imitators. As their careers progressed, it was not enough for them to simply echo another's virtuosity. They forged ahead, developing their own concepts and style along the way. Wes Montgomery may have begun his career playing Charlie Christian solos verbatim, but that was at the beginning. His original ideas and his highly creative approach eventually allowed him to transcend Christian's influence. Wes evolved his own style. Echoes of Chris-

tian surely remained, but the final result was his alone. Jimi Hendrix may have started out playing rhythm and blues in bar bands, but he was not content to simply repeat the music of others, even that of his idols, B.B. King and T-Bone Walker. In the end, what came from his Stratocaster was Hendrix, with obvious roots in the past, but moving far into the future.

Great guitarists listen to other great guitarists, and not just those in their own field. Charlie Byrd, the elegant, classically-trained virtuoso of Brazilian jazz has long been a fan of Joe Maphis, the rapid-fire country guitar virtuoso who developed his lead style in an attempt to emulate the fiddlers he backed at western Maryland hoedowns. The late Duane Allman, best known for his lyrical, soulful slide guitar, an extension of the style of Elmore James, also admired Hank Garland, the country/jazz guitar virtuoso who dominated the Nashville studios in the 1950s. George Benson, a jazz virtuoso who was sidetracked into commercial r&b schmaltz in the 1970s, was inspired to play jazz by, of all people, Hank Garland. Garland, while playing in the hardcore country bands of Cowboy Copas and Eddy Arnold in the late 1940s, was spending hour upon hour drinking in the brilliant Belgian gypsy jazz guitar of Django Reinhardt. B.B. King also found inspiration in Django's playing. Django, for his part, was an admirer of jazz guitar pioneer Eddie Lang, who admired Andres Segovia.

But the greatest guitarists' listening habits often extend to the music of instrumental greats in musical genres other than their own. Many jazz guitarists have drawn upon the music of jazz trumpeters like Louis Armstrong, Dizzy Gillespie and Clifford Brown, as well as saxophonists Lester Young, Charlie Parker and Johnny Hodges. They absorb it all, and through such eclectic listening enhance their own talents, making the difference in their developments.

The guitarists profiled in this book are, for the sake of practical reference, categorized into rock, blues, jazz and country. Yet the similarities in these musicians are almost as striking as the differences. Virtually everyone here began playing at a relatively young age; they became obsessed with their instruments, practicing for hours at a clip. And to some extent those habits never really ended. Chet Atkins, in the conclusion to his 1974 autobiography *Country Gentleman*, confided that "I go home every night and get my guitar and practice until I go to sleep with it in my lap, as I have always done." While serving in the army, Jimi Hendrix was considered weird by his fellow soldiers because he talked to his guitar. But to other musicians this may not seem so unusual, for many of them feel that one's instrument is an extension of the mind and body.

Great Guitarists has been written in a way that combines objective research with subjective critical judgments. Criteria for inclusion was, as you may suspect, the most subjective area.

I looked at people who had, for one reason or another, left a profound impact on the guitar's development, both musical and technological (Les Paul has surely done the latter). Those who furthered their instrument's role in a given field—such as Chet Atkins, who es-

tablished the country guitarist as a credible musician with great depth—were included. Those whose music proved influential on other guitarists, or whose styles were fountainheads—such as Merle Travis, T-Bone Walker, James Burton and Eddie Lang—were included without reservation.

Yet those were not the only criteria. Players who have moved, impressed or inspired me at one time or another were also included, even if they were never "stars" as such. In music, as with the other arts, some of the greatest voices often fail to achieve mass recognition though their influence was massive. George Van Eps, a "musician's musician" and veteran Los Angeles studio guitarist single-handedly founded the school of seven-string jazz guitarists dominated today by the better-known Bucky Pizzarelli. Lonnie Mack had but one major hit—an instrumental version of Chuck Berry's "Memphis"—but rock players from Ted Nugent to Stevie Ray Vaughan cite him as an influence. Jimmy Nolen, who played on James Brown's classic records of the '60s, had a driving rhythm guitar technique that rubbed off on players who never knew his name (and plenty who did).

Subjectivity also figured in the selection of guitarists in the primary essays. The most legendary guitar players are examined in essays that combine biographical information with critical judgements, drawing upon the players' recorded legacies to trace their musical developments, and biographical details to connect life and art. You will not find all well-known players here, either, because, despite the obvious commercial advantage of their inclusion, I simply didn't care for their work or felt their impact was less substantive than other critics might believe. Readers will inevitably say "Yeah, but why didn't you include...?" It's all a matter of opinion, and mine certainly isn't the last word. Give 50 music fans the chance to list their favorite guitarists; some will be on everyone's list, but not all.

Classical guitar is not included here because, firstly, I do not follow it extensively; secondly, a major work on the great classical players from Segovia through Julian Bream and beyond should be written by one qualified to do so.

On the other hand, those of you who admire certain lesser-known players may find them in the secondary essays. These briefly examine the careers of guitarists who may have had limited careers, or who excelled in one particular sound that had limited, but still noteworthy influence on others. Steve Cropper, for example, was primarily a rhythm guitar player (with Booker T and the MG's), but created some of the most memorable—and economical—backup guitar ever played. His licks remain important touchstones for today's players, though Cropper himself was no Hendrix or Duane Allman.

It has been said that books like these are usually written by frustrated musicians. In my case, nothing could be closer to the truth. I began playing guitar in 1964, just as the Beatles hit these shores. I learned every George Harrison lick I could, later going on to play sloppy imitations of B.B. and Albert King as well as Merle Travis. I never had the spark to bear down and woodshed in either rock, blues or country and gradually decided to chuck the whole thing, though I still have my '65 Tele and Fender amp in storage in the unlikely event I change my mind.

But I've never lost my love for guitar music, and continued to research and listen. The music of one player would lead to the music of another. Noting that Hank Garland was a Tal Farlow fan led me to Farlow's music, and the conclusion that much of Hank's later jazz efforts—and playing style—were based on Tal's sound. In the process, I became an admirer of Farlow, whose music I'd barely heard before. Such is the musicologist's lot, and the way I learned to appreciate players across the board. Rock guitarists who ignore jazz, and country or jazz guitarists who ignore rock, are cheating themselves—particularly if they ever aspire to turn professional. As I've said, virtually all the players listed in this book listened to a wide variety of music, and the benefits were theirs.

To me at least, the music of the guitarists profiled here has worn well. For the most part, it will still sound good half a century down the line, as all great music usually does. Such players deserve homage, and that, in the end, is the real reason for this book.

Rich Kienzle
Greensburg, Pa.
June, 1985

BLUES

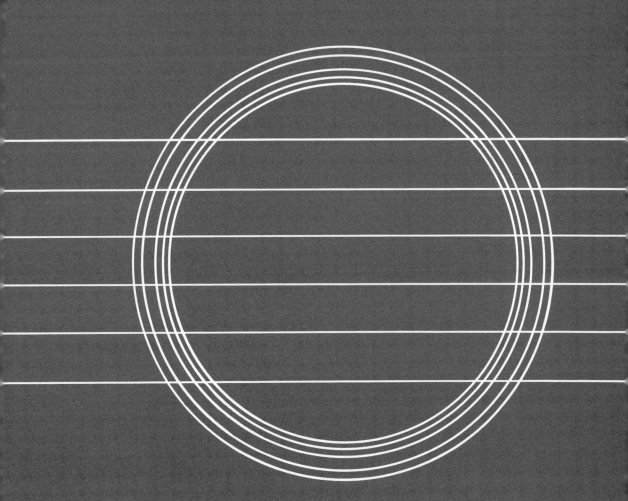

SCRAPPER BLACKWELL

Besides Lonnie Johnson, Scrapper Blackwell was one of the most formidable blues guitar instrumentalists of the late 1920s and the mid '30s. Though he first came to attention through his outstanding series of recordings with singer/songwriter/pianist Leroy Carr, Blackwell also made his reputation with an articulate, often acerbic, guitar style of his own, in debt to but not imitative of Lonnie Johnson.

There are considerable differences between the two. While Johnson's playing acquired an elegance and polish that permitted him to record with a variety of jazz and pop artists as well as bluesmen, Blackwell remained within the blues context through his entire career. He did not record with jazz musicians, or orchestras, but stayed with cruder contexts—both with Carr and maintaining the rough edges in his own solo work. However, Blackwell was more technically skilled and less sloppy than many other bluesmen, which shows on his recordings, and undoubtedly helped make him one of the more admired blues guitarists of his time.

Like many bluesmen, Blackwell's career was interrupted for many years by neglect and changing fashions. Leroy Carr's death had a devastating effect on him, and without question caused him to lose much of his zest for playing. He did resurface in the early '60s, still playing well and having the kind of appeal that could have made him a favorite on the folk club circuit of that period. But a senseless shooting in 1962 in his native Indianapolis, Indiana left Blackwell dead at age fifty-nine, just as he may have been renewing his career.

Francis Hillman Blackwell was born February 21, 1903, probably in Syracuse, South Carolina, one of sixteen children, all of whom were musical. His father Payton Blackwell played fiddle. Francis got the "Scrapper" moniker from his grandmother for being ornery and roughhousing with his brother. In 1906 the Blackwells moved to Indianapolis; Scrapper was but six years old when he built a "guitar" out of a mandolin neck and a cigar box, and began playing for his own enjoyment.

That was the only role the guitar had in

Scrapper Blackwell's life until 1928. He'd been a full-time moonshiner through Prohibition and built himself a profitable business. He'd met Carr through a local music promoter named Gurnsey, yet Blackwell had no real interest in making records, and it took considerable persuasion on Carr's part to get him to record. But in June 1928, due to Scrapper's reluctance to leave town, the pair recorded in WFBM in Indianapolis using portable equipment.

They cut two numbers—"How Long Blues" and "My Own Lonesome Blues"—both of which, released on the Vocalion label, were phenomenal successes in black communities around America. The empathy and understanding the pair had for each other's music created a tight, cohesive sound that would set the standards for such other guitar/piano duets as Tampa Red with Big Maceo, or Georgia Tom Dorsey, and Blind Blake with Charlie Spand. The sound of Carr and Blackwell was the basis for what they all did.

In August 1928 Scrapper recorded on his own for Vocalion. Obviously there were echoes of Lonnie Johnson in what he did, but Blackwell's sound was rougher. Though he played a hard, basic chord accompaniment on "Mr. Scrapper's Blues," he would pause between vocals to add impressive little single-string touches. The record was not outstanding, and its flipside, "Down and Out Blues," was distinguished only by a different set of lyrics. Far better was the February 1929 recording of "Non-Skid Treat," which featured Blackwell, Carr, blues singer Bertha "Chippie" Hill and a kazoo player named Roy Palmer. While Carr vamped, Blackwell, not terribly audible, played complex single string counterpoint. Even better was "Be-Da-Da-Dum," a duet number on which Blackwell, not Carr, handled the lead vocal. He sang boisterously as Carr laid down the rhythmic foundation on the piano. On the chorus, Scrapper scat-sang lines that sounded surprisingly similar to what he spun out on his guitar.

One point made by Blackwell's solo recordings was that his musical relationship with Carr was something very special. Scrapper rarely played as well or with as much authority alone. He did some creditable guitar work with Georgia Tom Dorsey on "Mean Baby Blues," including a terse, nicely phrased solo. But even half a century later, the Blackwell/Carr team has a telepathy, mutual admiration and depth readily heard on its records.

On their best duets, "Barrelhouse Woman," for example, Blackwell plays superbly. His arpeggios sparkle behind his ebullient vocals, economically, sparely commenting at the end of each line, permitting him to play a finely crafted solo on the bridge. Blackwell's attack was hard and percussive. Likewise, "Midnight Hour Blues" features a stunning instrumental introduction by Blackwell, sharp and clear. As Carr provides encouragement ("Lay it on, boy; lay it down, son") Blackwell solos, picking each string with equal force, snapping them for extra volume. Blackwell apparently was not a flatpicker, but plucked the single notes with his fingers, pulling up on the strings as he picked them.

Blackwell's obligotti got repetitive at times, but his flawless counterpoint to Carr's piano and vocals alleviates any annoyance. On "Mean Mistreater Mama" he adds an appealing vibrato as he plays behind Carr. He plays a fine solo on "Big Four Blues," which also features another guitarist: Josh White, then a bluesman, later a folk star. More entertaining is "It's Too Short," an uptempo blues in which the notes from Blackwell's guitar spew diamond-hard, allying with Carr's piano and again abetted by Josh White's second guitar. "Bobo Stomp" is a stunning showpiece for Blackwell. As Carr shouts/sings throwaway lyrics, Scrapper's thrilling improvisations dominate the song, though he does slip into some of his usual patterns.

Throughout the Blackwell-Carr partnership, Scrapper recorded on his own for several labels, including Bluebird. He recorded two hard-edged blues in February 1935. "D Blues" (actually in G) and "A Blues" (in the key of D) were both merely adequate (and occasionally sloppy), as though Scrapper lost his gusto without Carr's effervescent piano.

Unfortunately, Blackwell soon had to work alone permanently. Both he and Carr were prodigious drinkers, but by 1935 Carr had all but destroyed his health by consuming up to three quarts of whiskey per day. The two men had a disagreement on the evening of April 28, 1935, and later that night Carr went into a seizure. The next morning he died of nephritis caused by his alcoholism.

Blackwell recorded two poignant tributes to his friend that day: "My Old Pal" and the cautionary "Bad Liquor Blues," also backing singer Amos "Bumble Bee Slim" Easton on his fictionalized song "The Death of Leroy Carr." Scrapper did other sessions throughout 1935, but Carr's death had killed something within him, and he had largely given up music by the late '30s, only rarely playing. He worked in an asphalt plant full-time, until 1958, after more than twenty-five years of inactivity, he was rediscovered by folklorist Art Rosenbaum. Blackwell began recording again, his skills surprisingly unimpaired. He did credible records for Prestige's Bluesville label and the British "77" label, and accompanied vocalist Brooksie Perry on a Bluesville LP. He did a few club dates, and appeared to be on a comeback.

But Scrapper Blackwell was shot to death in an Indianapolis back alley in 1962. His career's regeneration never came to pass.

Nonetheless, Blackwell was, without question and alongside Lonnie Johnson, one of the first *serious* blues lead guitarists. His strong rhythmic sense and stinging, powerful, fluent lines may have lacked Johnson's sophisticated polish, but became integral to the music that formed the foundation of urban blues guitar. T-Bone Walker, B.B. King and every other exponent of single-string lead guitar owe almost as much to Blackwell as to Lonnie Johnson. Where Johnson played the blues with style, Blackwell's playing came from his guts, as the best blues always does.

Scrapper Blackwell has not received the attention other bluesmen have, but in the music of delta blues legend Johnny Shines and the late T-Bone Walker, the father of modern amplified blues guitar, Blackwell's influence is unmistakable. Blackwell extended the single-string lead style in a wholly different way than did Lonnie Johnson. While Johnson acquired both smoothness and grace, Blackwell managed to create his own sound: more animated and raw, but still precise and thoroughly musical. To many, he was a moderately important figure in the blues, but his impact on the development of blues guitar, if narrow, was nonetheless profound.

DISCOGRAPHY

Three Scrapper Blackwell albums are currently available. *The Virtuoso Guitar of Scrapper Blackwell* (Yazoo) is an outstanding sampler of his work as an accompanist to Leroy Carr and other artists. *Blues Before Sunrise* (77) includes some of his recordings after being rediscovered, while *Blues That Make Me Cry* is an outstanding collection of some of his solo recordings (the others comprise the Yazoo set).

Leroy Carr Volumes One and Two, on Collector's Classics, the excellent *Naptown Blues* (Yazoo) and *Singing the Blues* (Biograph) include Scrapper's accompaniment to Leroy Carr's singing. They were a formidable team, as any of the albums will reveal.

BLIND BLAKE

Blind Blake was one of the leading exemplars of the ragtime-influenced black dance music that was popular in the southeast. Where blues featured "blue" notes and simplicity much of the time, the music of Blake and others, such as Mississippi John Hurt, had a less doleful approach with its roots in the minstrel and medicine shows and in pre-blues black dance music of the nineteenth century. The guitar playing was more complex, oriented toward self-contained fingerpicking, with a syncopated bass accompaniment.

Despite his extensive recording career in the 1920s and early '30s, very little is known about Blind Blake. His copyrights show his name as "Arthur Blake," while other evidence suggests his real name was Arthur Phelps. He was blind, and was born sometime in the 1890s, possibly in Jacksonville, Florida. Who influenced him is unclear. He may have lived in Georgia and also may have sung with road gangs in Virginia in the early 1920s.

His reputation as a skilled fingerpicker—indeed, one of the idiom's pioneers—was clear enough by the mid-'20s, for in 1926 he began recording for the Paramount label of Wisconsin. The sessions were done in Chicago, where he lived during that period. Through 1930 he recorded about seventy titles for Paramount, most of them featuring his nasal, melodic vocals (with some excellent scatsinging) and his complex guitar lines, which influenced everyone from Josh White and Big Bill Broonzy to folk performers like Dave Von Ronk and Leon Redbone, a true disciple who can recreate, often brilliantly, the Blake guitar style today.

Many aspects of Blake's playing later surfaced in the country music approach known as "Travis picking." Blake employed a syncopated accompaniment with his thumb on the bass strings while fingering complex figures on the treble strings. It was a technique that permitted him to inspire dancers anywhere, playing with a relaxed self-confidence and without the heavy-handedness of some blues stylists. Indeed, the roots of the southeastern blues school, which includes Blind Boy Fuller,

Reverend Gary Davis and Buddy Moss, can be heard in Blake.

Blake could accompany himself simply with fingerpicked phrases, such as the repetitive run he uses throughout his 1930 "Playing Policy Blues," but more often than not he efforted more difficult melodic accompaniments, such as the backing to "That Will Never Happen No More," one of his most memorable numbers. "Righteous Blues," also recorded in '30, features some finely syncopated picking behind the vocal and demonstrates his understanding of harmony in the descending chord passage on his solo break.

To have recorded seventy titles when many legendary bluesmen recorded far less is an indication of Blake's popularity, as is his ability to sing risque numbers or slip outrageous comments into his songs, such as his satirical reference to homosexuals in "Righteous Blues." Even the blues numbers he recorded have an almost airy feel to them.

What finally happened to Arthur Blake (or Phelps) is undiscovered. Several accounts of his death have surfaced. One has him killed in a 1941 Atlanta streetcar mishap; another story, from Big Bill Broonzy, describes his murder on the streets of Joliet, Illinois, in 1932. We may never know for sure what his fate was.

But Blind Blake's way with a guitar has gone far beyond the blues, into folk country and even into rockabilly (the Travis style was important in the music of Elvis Presley). It does not sound in any way dated, but has a freshness and joy that sustain both the style itself, and Blake's own old recordings, in an era of synthesizers and electronics.

DISCOGRAPHY

Though little hard information is available on Blind Blake's life, there are five albums worth of his material on the Biograph reissue label, including *Bootleg Rum Dum Blues, Search Warrant Blues, No Dough Blues, Rope Stretchin' Blues* and *The Lovin' I Crave.*

ELMORE JAMES

On the surface it's fairly easy to perceive Elmore James as a guitarist dogged by stylistic limitations. Many of his recordings were virtual clones of his classic 1952 version of Robert Johnson's "Dust My Broom." Elmore's slide guitar adaptation of Johnson's guitar riff on that song punctuated many of his records, making them sound even more like "Broom."

But that is a gross oversimplification, for what Elmore James did was to take the slide guitar concept—a technique involving the use of a metal glass or even bone object (such as a penknife, pipe or bottle-neck) to fret the strings to create a languid, or whining, sound—and put it into a hard-driving, rocking and, most importantly, *amplified* context. Muddy Waters and others were playing electric slide in the '40s, but they phrased in a way so that the guitar took on characteristics of speech. James, on the other hand, defined his rhythm with the guitar as well as using it as a lead instrument.

Elmore James' impact on both blues and rock music has been considerable. The "Dust

My Broom" riff that Johnson created in 1936 has become a stock lick in the repertoires of everyone from B.B. King to Duane Allman. Elmore's screaming, articulate, driving slide has inspired a multiplicity of Chicago bluesmen, including his cousin Homesick James Williamson, J.B. Hutto, Hound Dog Taylor and Earl Hooker as well as rock players like Peter Green, Allman, Eric Clapton, Johnny Winter and George Thorogood. Fleetwood Mac founding member Jeremy Spencer appeared to be obsessed with James' playing in the late '60s.

Critics have often minimized the importance of Elmore's searing, intense vocals, which beautifully complemented his guitar work. His voice, passionate and fraught with tension, was as important to his recordings as his guitar work, and it was his combination of voice and guitar that made his recordings so memorable. Also, like many bluesmen, James, did not use the best equipment; his tone was derived from a modest amplifier, and a hollowbody acoustic "dreadnaught" model guitar with a pickup attached to its top.

It is ironic that rock guitarists have used comparatively expensive Fenders and Gibsons to get a sound Elmore (and other great blues guitarists) obtained from bargain-basement gear.

As he often drew upon the original material of others, Elmore was essential in bringing delta blues into an amplified, postwar era. He did not initially do so in Chicago, but came there after his success with "Dust My Broom" in '52. His career had its up and down periods, but he managed to make consistently fine records until he died in 1963 of a heart attack, the culmination of years of cardiac problems exacerbated by his drinking.

Elmore James was born to Leola Brooks and Joe Willie James January 27, 1918 in Richland, Mississippi. His parents moved around to various plantations through the Delta, and by the time he was twelve he was toying around with a homemade instrument that he kept through his adolescence. He was nineteen years old and living in Belzoni, Mississippi with his family, developing a distinct distaste for sharecropping or plantation work when he married, bought himself a $20 National guitar and started playing in the local juke joints.

It was at this point that his style began to take shape, for he teamed up with two of the delta's real heavyweights: Robert Johnson and harmonica-blowing Sonny Boy Williamson (Rice Miller). Johnson's use of the slide was a revelation for Elmore, who began trying to copy him. Their association must have been short, however, for Johnson was poisoned in August 1938. James did some plantation work through the late '30s, but preferred playing music as much as possible. His direction was set.

Inducted into the U.S. Navy in 1943, he spent two years in the South Pacific and returned to the delta in 1945. He spent much of the next two years working on plantations, and during this time his heart problems were diagnosed. He married again in 1947 and continued to work outside of music until he started making appearances on Sonny Boy's famous King Biscuit Time radio show over KFFA in West Helena, Arkansas. The pair teamed up to do a radio show in Belzoni for a local drug store, advertising a tonic known as Talaho. From there Elmore began moving around the region, working with pianist Willie Love, then with Sonny Boy again over KWEM in West Memphis, Arkansas.

James played on several of Sonny Boy's early Trumpet recording sessions, including his regional hit "Eyesight to the Blind," though he had a largely subordinate role. But his version of "Dust My Broom"—which he would not record—impressed everyone. Finally, while he was running through it at another Williamson session, the tapes were rolling as Sonny Boy and drummer Frock O'Dell backed him. The mix was primitive, but Elmore's slide cut through. As Sonny Boy's warbling harp and O'Dell's steady rhythm pushed him, he shouted out the lyrics and invoked his adaptation of the Robert Johnson guitar riff.

Much to everyone's surprise, Trumpet released it as a record, and it wound up in the national rhythm and blues top ten. This "Dust My Broom" was more exuberant than Johnson's original, and Elmore's guitar accounted for much of the excitement. He did nothing more for a time, then was enticed to go to Chicago to record for Joe Bihari's Meteor label. Actually, he'd recorded "Lost Woman Blues," built around the "Dust My Broom" motif with a slightly larger backing group, in Mississippi in '52 on portable equipment. That October he cut the magnificent "I Believe" in Chicago, yet another variation on "Dust My Broom." Early in '53 he did some recording for the Checker label, a subsidiary of Chess, moving to Modern Records' Flair label in fall, where he recorded the stomping "My Best Friend" and "Hawaiian Boogie," a powerful instrumental that featured some of his most stinging slide. The fluent "Dark and Dreary" also was waxed during this time.

Though Elmore himself was a consistently excellent artist, some of the contexts in which he was recorded did not do him justice. He cut some fine music in New Orleans in May 1955, including "Dust My Blues" (a remake of you-know-what), and some raw lead guitar at the opening of "I Was a Fool" so hard-driving one can hear his pick clicking against the strings. On the slow "Goodbye Baby," he plays a clean, articulate opening before launching into a declamatory vocal backed by an odd vocal group. But the remainder of the 1955 material is, at best, inappropriate. He went to Modern Records' Culver City, California, studio facility to record with the slick r & b band of Maxwell Davis. Try as the musicians did, Elmore was simply too down home for their smooth backing, and the results are a study in incompatability, though his guitar and vocal work are beyond criticism. One of the weakest numbers is "No Love in My Heart," an abortive attempt at emulating B.B. King's "Woke Up This Morning," a hit two years before and wholly dysfunctional in Elmore's style. He ended his stay with Modern on a stronger note, however. "Wild About You Baby," recorded in January 1956, was yet another variant on "Broom" with apocalyptic slide guitar work on the bridge.

By 1957 he was recording for Chief Records, and came up with some impressive material. "Coming Home" was another "Dust My Broom" clone, yet an unusual one. Elmore's slide playing was great, and the backing guitars of Eddie Taylor and Homesick James Williamson melded together cohesively. The reason, according to Mike Rowe's book *Chicago Blues*, was simple: the three were sharing one amplifier. On "It Hurts Me, Too," a remake of slide guitarist Tampa Red's 1940s composition, Elmore plays sharp single-string slide, though the three-in-one amp arrangement doesn't project it well. Far better was the instrumental "Elmore's Contribution to Jazz," a jarring, razor-edged tune with some chilling chords and slashing single-note slide work.

Some of James' best work was done for the New York-based Fire Records, including his still-powerful 1959 ballad "The Sky Is Crying," in which his voice and guitar complement each other brilliantly. In 1961 came the jumping "Done Somebody Wrong," which featured a throat-wrenching vocal and some strategically placed, rhythmic guitar figures. Elmore adds the sort of shimmering slide break that Duane Allman must have committed to memory.

In '61 James returned to Mississippi and recorded there with a slightly more down home flavor, including a version of "Look On Yonder's Wall," on which he returned to the original Robert Johnson "Dust My Broom" riff that had inspired him in the '30s. "Shake Your Moneymaker" was a rocker with surging slide; both Paul Butterfield's '65 version and Fleetwood Mac's '68 cover are most likely based on this one.

Though his health was growing increasingly precarious in the early '60s, James continued to do excellent work for Fire and Enjoy, including "Can't Stop Loving My Baby," with an infectious, light slide riff recurring throughout the song; "Something Inside Me," another compelling ballad, as strong or stronger than "The Sky Is Crying," comprising one of his finest slide solos on record, and "I Need You," another ballad, nearly as good. "Person to Person" was a modern shuffle arrangement with spare slide riffs that worked more percussively. "Pickin' the Blues," a pragmatic if unimaginative title, featured Elmore doing just that over a "Dust My Broom" rhythm in what may have been an in-studio jam. His version of "Everyday I Have the Blues" was tasteful, but something was missing: his spark and enthusiasm weren't there.

The problem was his health. Though his heart condition was worsening, and he was living in Jackson due to problems with the Chicago musicians' union, Elmore was doing little to help himself, considering his heavy drinking. Finally friends in Chicago were able to unknot his problems with the union and in the spring of 1963 he was able to return. He moved in with Homesick James and waited for the last bit of red tape to be cut so he could return to the clubs. He had done one come back performance at Big Bill Hill's Copacabana just after arriving back in town. He was to start performing on a Friday.

That evening, May 24, 1963, James was getting dressed for his formal re-emergence when he suffered a fatal heart attack. He was buried in Durant, Mississippi.

It is interesting to speculate on what might have been for Elmore James. When he died the blues revival was just beginning, and there was already considerable interest in him among European blues fanatics. He had a style of blues and guitar playing that, as with Merle Travis in country or Jimi Hendrix in rock, was clearly identifiable as his own. He was imitated by other bluesmen, as well. J.B. Hutto, Hound Dog Taylor and Homesick James, Elmore's cousin, all continued to mine his vein after his death.

Today slide guitar shows up in TV themes (the CBS show Simon & Simon is one noteworthy example), commercial jingles and film soundtracks. Undoubtedly it became a part of mainstream music because of its use by rock guitarists. Nonetheless, without Elmore James, who refiied the slide for everyone, this probably would not have happened at all. Unfortunate as his early demise was, his legacy remains. Most of his records are still in print; his name is one of the most revered among blues guitar aficionados. Too bad that James himself isn't around to see what he hath wrought.

DISCOGRAPHY

Elmore James has been well-represented on reissues. His first recording of "Dust My Broom" is on *One Way Out* (Charly) with other material from the variety of labels he recorded for. *Got to Move* (Charly) comes from that same variety of labels. *The Best of Elmore James* covers much of the material he recorded for the Bihari Brothers, as does *King of the Slide Guitar. Whose Muddy Shoes* (French Chess) compiles many of his Chess sides with those by Chicago bluesman John Brim. Many more of the Bihari sides are available on three budget-priced United LPs: *Original Folk Blues, Legend of Elmore James* and *The Resurrection of Elmore James.*

LONNIE JOHNSON

Calling Lonnie Johnson the Louis Armstrong of the blues guitar could not be an overstatement, for Johnson was the single most important figure in establishing blues guitar as a credible instrumental style. No single musician did more to create a clear-cut identity for the blues guitarist. His influence was deep and long-lasting, carrying over from the country blues and early jazz recordings on which he worked as an accompanist (and occasional soloist) through his own successful solo career in the late 1930s into the urban blues movement that developed following World War II. Even in the music of Lowell Fulson and B.B. King--and in their followers' playing--the runs, riffs and precision that exemplified Johnson can still be heard.

Johnson almost singlehandedly created a highly defined playing style, executed with a clear, articulated polish that set the standard by which other guitarists were measured. Perhaps the fact that, unlike many early bluesmen, Johnson was also a professional, full-time performer was a factor contributing to his preeminence. Lonnie Johnson's style

was peculiarly his own. He had no musical antecedents and made his own rules.

And yet success was a fleeting thing for Johnson. After an initial run of popularity as both a recording artist and accompanist, he was briefly eclipsed by the more uptown styles of the mid-1930s, although he managed to revive himself before the end of the decade by stressing his vocals and playing amplified guitar. A hit recording came his way in 1948 with "Tomorrow Night," which boosted his visibility. Rock and roll again put him into an eclipse, during which he left music. But before his death in 1970, he was rediscovered and enjoyed several more years of popularity among audiences who'd begun to understand his huge contributions to the blues idiom.

So many classic blues guitar licks can be traced to Johnson that a book could be written about them alone, and there is no question of his impact on every other blues singer and guitarist during his periods of greatest popularity.

Even the legendary Robert Johnson, who

laid the foundations for the Chicago blues sounds of the 1940s and recorded some of the most moving, powerful Delta blues of all time, was clearly influenced by Lonnie. He would even tell people they were related—a measure of how much he identified with the older musician.

Yet Johnson cannot be strictly classified as a bluesman. Some have characterized him as an important jazz guitar innovator, though he was undoubtedly more of an influence on jazzmen like Charlie Christian and Eddie Lang than an actual jazz guitarist himself. Nonetheless, he alone brought the blues elements into jazz guitar that have remained there ever since. His stunning guitar duets with Eddie Lang, whose influence on jazz equaled Johnson's on the blues, demonstrated far more depth and skill than the average blues guitarist of the period. Much of this is traceable to his finesse on the instrument and his appreciation of different musical styles. Yet, though he was a far smoother player than a rough-hewn country bluesman like Charley Patton, he never lost the blues feeling in his music. Even at his most refined, there was nothing ersatz about Lonnie Johnson.

Lonnie Johnson was born in New Orleans on February 8th, no one knows the exact year, but it was probably sometime between 1889 and 1894. He grew up in the heart of the New Orleans jazz district of Rampart Street, where he was able to drink in all the musical legends of that period firsthand. He started working on the streets with members of his family around 1912, playing guitar behind his father's violin. But this group was more versatile than mere street performers, and appeared at indoor social events like weddings and dinners. Lonnie had apparently developed a style of his own even early on, for New Orleans bassist Pops Foster told British blues researcher Paul Oliver that at this early time, "Lonnie was the only guy we had around New Orleans who could play jazz guitar."

Johnson wound up in a theater troupe entertaining the Allied soldiers during World War I, which gave him further experience, but he returned in 1919 to a tragedy. An influenza epidemic killed 13 members of the Johnson family, leaving only one survivor: his brother James, a pianist. It was a staggering loss, and in 1920 Lonnie left New Orleans—alone—and moved to St. Louis, where he played in theaters and on the excursion boats that traveled the Mississippi. Working with Charlie Creath's Jazz-O-Manics and with jazzman Fate Marable into 1922 and performing as a solo artist in theaters developed his abilities as both musician and entertainer.

In 1925 he got his first significant break when he won a blues contest at the Booker T. Washington Theater in St. Louis, and wound up with an OKeh Records contract. Actually, Johnson had recorded previously with the Creath band, but the OKeh contract was his own. He began recording tunes, playing fiddle, guitar, piano or the harmonium, backed by pianists (including his brother James) on occasion. He did well, and became so popular with black record buyers that OKeh was putting out Johnson releases every six weeks. He also accompanied on guitar a variety of blues singers contracted to OKeh. Finally around 1927 he settled on the guitar, and it was then that he began his most valuable work.

During this period he used both six and 12-string, demonstrating a surprisingly assertive style on the latter, an instrument difficult to fret (the string tension on the neck is doubled, requiring added pressure on the strings) and keep in tune. From 1927 through 1928 he did some extraordinary solo recordings using the 12 string, including "Go Back to Your No Good Man," which features him punctuating each stanza with lean, easy-flowing phrases. "Away Down In The Alley Blues," played on a 6-string, is loaded with instrumental phrases later appropriated by Robert Johnson and other Delta bluesmen. Every note and doublestop is clearly articulated. While many bluesmen, even some of the greats, slurred notes and occasionally hit a wild one, Johnson used his precision and clean playing as a trademark that made him instantly identifiable.

A second guitarist, such as Lazy Harris, could only accompany Johnson on recordings like "Four Hands Are Better Than Two," a strutting 6-string solo replete with bent notes and a strong rhythmic bass. "Stomping 'Em Along Slow" featured a similar strongly articulated solo with some interesting, sustained single-note bass work under parts of his solo, a kind of simplification of the fingerpicking styles of the time. "Woke Up With The Blues In My Fingers" featured a slower tempo with ringing arpeggios and perfectly placed bass notes. Another impressive tune from late 1927 was his "6/88 Glide," a tune featuring a rock-solid pianist (John Erby) in the background. Though the tune had a ragtime feel and more jazz than blues, Lonnie's use of a single bent note was an unusual idea for that period. Considering the jazz guitar was still virtually unknown, it was an innovative idea for the time and maybe a bit too much so; it remained unissued until the late 1970s when it wound up on a Time-Life Records jazz guitar anthology.

Johnson also began recording with jazzmen by that time. In December 1927 he recorded with Louis Armstrong's Hot Five, playing a sparkling counterpoint to Armstrong's scat-sung vocal on "Hotter Than That," which worked into a delightful call and response with an ending featuring Johnson's fleet guitar. In 1928 Johnson was featured on "The Mooche" with Duke Ellington's orchestra, then in their famous "Jungle Period." Ellington was still using banjoist Fred Guy, and Johnson used a steel-bodied resonator guitar to cut through. He played a superb, bluesy counterpoint to Baby Cox's vocal. In October 1928 he recorded "Paducah," a blues tune, with the Chocolate Dandies, on which he played a fine 12-string solo containing many of his trademark riffs.

Johnson did his first recordings with Eddie Lang in November (discussed in the Lang essay). Whether or not he actually can be called a jazz guitarist or not (and there are convincing arguments on both sides), there was no doubt that he exerted a formidable influence on Lang's blues playing. The recordings the two did as a team remain the first substantial jazz guitar duets on record, and enhanced the reputation of both men.

While all this was going on Lonnie was becoming a star on the black theater circuit. He had married Mary Smith, a blues singer, in 1925, and the pair remained together until 1932. That was not a good year for Johnson, for OKeh had fallen on hard times (though it later became part of the American Recording Company). His work fell off, though he still did studio sessions (including an unissued session behind singer/actress Martha Raye). After a brief period with the Putney Dandridge Orchestra in Cleveland, he left music for a number of years, working in a railroad tie plant in Illinois, playing only at night.

It wasn't until 1937 that things began to improve for him, when he began working in a Chicago nightclub and hitting the thriving club circuit in town. He did some Decca recordings that year. Then in 1939, he went to the Bluebird label where he began to emphasize his singing. With a spare sound of only piano and bass, the guitar was relegated to a supporting role, though Johnson suffered no deterioration in his skills. Touring the Midwest and the West Coast took up much of his time through World War II, his biting, acerbic vocal style proving to be as effective as his playing.

By 1946 he had recorded a dozen songs for the New York-based Disc label including the graceful "My Last Lover," which featured a fine complex solo. Shortly afterward, he changed not only record companies but instruments as well. Electric guitars had been established by then in the jazz and rhythm and blues idiom, and Johnson finally began playing amplified guitar on his Aladdin recording sessions in June of 1947. Amplification didn't change the essential elements of his style, but it did give his playing a more modern edge. Later in 1947 Johnson signed a contract with the Cincinnati-based King Records, then one of the top independent country and rhythm and blues labels in the country.

The association with King brought him the sort of commercial success he hadn't had since the 1920s. And his guitar playing took on a harsher tone, more biting than before. It accentuated his string choking and cut through the sparse rhythm accompaniment with ease. But on his biggest hit with King, "Tomorrow Night," recorded in late '47 and released in late February 1948, Johnson, playing acoustic, found the sort of success that transcended race. The song, a plaintive pop ballad, had little to do with blues (though he played bluesy runs throughout) and became the tune most associated with him. His 1948 recording of "I Know It's Love" featured his sharper electric guitar. He had another hit in 1948 with "Pleasing You," and still another in early '49 with "So Tired." There were also other fine shuffles like "She's So Sweet" and "You Take Romance." In 1950 he had one final hit with "Confused."

By 1952 Lonnie was on a lengthy British tour, but musical trends and declining record sales ended the relationship with King after four years. A few other releases came on smaller labels, but his career was on the downhill slide again. By 1953 he was living in Philadelphia and took a job as a maintenance man at the Benjamin Franklin Hotel. It might have remained like that had it not been for jazz authority Chris Albertson, then a disc jockey in Philadelphia. One night in 1960 he dug out some old Johnson recordings and was musing aloud on the air as to Lonnie's whereabouts. It surprised him to receive a call from a janitor at the Franklin Hotel who told him of a fellow janitor there named Lonnie Johnson, who took pains to protect his hands with gloves while working.

The next day Albertson went to the hotel and immediately recognized Johnson. He arranged a recording contract for him with the jazz-oriented Prestige label, and soon Johnson was doing club dates for fees far above what he made at the hotel. But he found a radical change in his audiences, which were now overwhelmingly white and interested in him as an influential folk bluesman. The massive blues revival in Europe was some years away, but he found young white audiences there as well. It renewed his musical career, for he was playing as well as ever.

But Lonnie lacked something that younger white blues enthusiasts were beginning to favor: the manic, primitive edge of the country bluesmen like Son House, Skip James and Sleepy John Estes. Johnson's slickness and pop orientation became a liability among his young admirers, to whom Mississippi Delta bluesmen became almost magical. The crowds at his shows began to falter in the late 1960s. He found he still commanded respect in Canada, however, and moved to Toronto in 1965. He was still performing there in 1969 when he was struck by a car that jumped onto the sidewalk where he was standing. It appeared he'd recover, then a stroke paralyzed his left side, all but ending his career.

He managed one final appearance in 1970. On June 16th he died in his Toronto apartment. At that time, single-string blues guitar was one of the most marketable commodities on the contemporary music scene. But the man who virtually founded the idiom was gone, and his passing received relatively little notice, except among the most avid jazz and blues fans.

Lonnie Johnson, of course, cannot be cast as a completely neglected musician, considering his periodic fame and the number of reissue albums that are currently available. But in the understandable rush to praise B.B. King, Albert King and other great blues players, Lonnie Johnson's impact upon the blues guitar-playing idiom--great as it was--has often been undervalued by music critics and historians.

DISCOGRAPHY

Lonnie Johnson's recorded legacy has been fairly well handled by reissuers. In addition to two albums on the Australian Swaggie label, *The Blues of Lonnie Johnson* and *Eddie Lang & Lonnie Johnson Volumes 1 & 2*, there is another fine blues album of forties and fifties material on the Swedish Blues Boy label, *The Originator of Modern Guitar Blues*, with outstanding notes and discographical data.

Domestically, there are numerous early recordings on *Woke Up This Morning, Blues In My Fingers* (OJL), including four previously unissued sides from 1927 to 1932 when he was at his peak. Gusto Records, which owns the King label, has *Tomorrow Night*, with Johnson's big hits of the late 1940s and other material from the King period, on two LPs.

Collectors' Classics' *Lonnie Johnson* includes sixteen 1928-1934 sides, and several of Johnson's jazz performances with Louis Armstrong, Duke Ellington and others are available on Time-Life Records' *The Guitarists*, a superb three-record anthology with extensive annotations (Time-Life Records, Time-Life Building, Chicago IL 60611).

ROBERT JOHNSON

ore than 45 years after his death, Robert Johnson, perhaps the greatest of the Mississippi delta blues singers and songwriters, generates far more mythology and noteriety than he ever did when he was alive. Rock stars have sung about him, had hits with raunched-up versions of his songs and still pore over his music as a religious fundamentalist would study the Bible, drinking in every nuance and searching for hidden meaning and metaphor.

Writers and blues scholars do likewise, sifting through rumors and anecdotes, apocryphal and otherwise, to find the "real" Robert Johnson. The few surviving photographs of him have been jealously guarded by their finders, and seen by very few people. What is it about Robert Johnson, who lived only some twenty-seven years before being poisoned by the jealous husband of a woman he was seeing, that makes him such a figure of obsession, the Mississippi delta's own James Dean?

Certainly the gothic delta imagery of his lyrics, exemplified by songs like "Cross Road

Blues," "Hell Hound on My Trail" and "Come On in My Kitchen" have much to do with it. So does his taut, high-pitched and convoluted vocal style, which gives the impression that he was on the edge, near to selling his soul to the Devil—an image that shows up in his recordings.

Johnson the guitarist was not so much an innovator as a skillful synthesizer of styles and riffs forged by other, more established blues artists he heard both on record and in person. Lonnie Johnson and Scrapper Blackwell were unquestionably influences, as were two of the delta's greatest bluesmen, the team of Son House and Willie Brown. Johnson was also well-versed in other musical forms, including hillbilly and pop formats, though he never recorded any of that material. Bluesman Johnny Shines, a friend and traveling companion of Johnson, recalled him as a master at playing polkas. Yet at least part of Johnson's appeal and impact as a guitarist came from his skillful use of the instrument as a frame for his vocals.

His licks, secondhand or not, became an integral part of the postwar Chicago blues guitar styles as exemplified by Muddy Waters, Elmore James, Robert Nighthawk, Robert Junior Lockwood (whom Johnson taught) and, of course, Johnny Shines. The famous driving guitar riff that opens Elmore James' "Dust My Broom" (itself a Johnson composition) was lifted directly from Johnson's recording, altered a bit and played through an amplifier until it became a cliche, sometimes used well, sometimes not.

Johnson has already inspired two books (one of them a novel) and a third, by folklorist Mack McCormick, will probably be the definitive biography. This essay will concentrate on Johnson's considerable influence as a guitarist, not his vocal style or songwriting.

The best estimate of Johnson's birthdate is May 8, 1911 in Hazlehurst, Mississippi; he was the son of Charles and Julia Dodds. He spent his early childhood with his stepfather in Memphis before returning to the delta, where his mother lived. By the time he was a teenager he'd become interested in playing harmonica. By age 15 he'd married (his wife died in childbirth), and started fooling around with a guitar. He began hanging around the house parties and other events in the Robinsonville, Mississippi area where he met the legendary team of Son House and Willie Brown. So eager was Robert to play that when House and Brown would take a break he'd pick up one of their guitars and try to emulate them.

His success was marginal. House later told folk musician/critic Julius Lester that "...such another racket you never heard! It'd make the people mad, you know. They'd come out and say, 'Why don't you go in and get that guitar away from that boy? He's running people crazy with it!...'" Johnson was probably in his late teens when he went away for about a year to another area of the delta. When he came back to Robinsonville, he showed up at another Son House/Willie Brown performance and asked to sit in. The two were skeptical, but House handed over his guitar, and was awed by Johnson's much-improved playing. From that day on Johnson made his living with music.

Johnson moved around Mississippi, then into the Memphis area, and soon he was on the road all over the South, Midwest and Northeast. He often traveled with Johnny Shines, who remains today amazed by Robert's proficiency on the guitar. They made money on the streets or in clubs or house parties, playing whatever music people wanted to hear, whether it was Tin Pan Alley pieces, Lonnie Johnson hits or Jimmie Rodgers tunes. Shines recalls that Robert could imitate most of the great blues guitarists of the period (a fact borne out by the influences discernable on his records).

It was 1936 when he got his chance at recording through Henry C. Speir, a Jackson, Mississippi music store owner who'd brought Son House, delta blues founding father Charley Patton, Skip James and other Mississippi bluesmen to the attention of record companies with whom he dealt. The American Recording Company (ARC) expressed interest and in November, 1936 an ARC employee offered Johnson a recording session in San Antonio, Texas. Johnson accepted, and traveled there with ARC employee Ernie Oertle, who brought him to a hotel room equipped with portable recording apparatus. The session was handled by a & r man Art Satherley, the man responsible for sessions by Roy Acuff, Bob Wills and Gene Autry in the country field as well as countless blues recordings.

These first performances show Johnson's synthesis of guitar styles had considerable durability. "I Believe I'll Dust My Broom" and "Sweet Home Chicago" both became important and popular tunes in the repertoires of many postwar Chicago bluesmen, the former becoming a huge hit for Elmore James in 1952. Both songs were structured similarly; Johnson apparently used his thumb to maintain a rhythmic bass line. Johnson's riff (which James later made his trademark), was a rapidly strummed rhythmic chord not played with a slide (as James later did it). On "Sweet Home Chicago" Johnson played very similarly; according to Peter Guralnick's essay on Johnson in *Living Blues* magazine, it was based on bluesman Kokomo Arnold's "Old Original Kokomo Blues."

"Terraplane Blues" displayed Johnson's

sleek slide guitar, played with the commonly used open G tuning. He bears down with the slide in the opening figure, hitting it four times before beginning the alternating chord figure that countered his vocal throughout the song. Occasionally, however, he would drift into imitation; "If I Had Possession Over Judgment Day" features guitar playing clearly lifted from Hambone Willie Newburn's 1929 recording of "Roll and Tumble Blues" (better known as "Rollin' and Tumblin'").

Johnson could also make amazing sound effects with his guitar. On "Come On In My Kitchen," one of his most brilliant and enduring compositions, Johnson hums in unison with his sharp, upper-register slide playing, then slides along with his vocal, all the while keeping a single note bass going with his thumb. He interjects, "Can't you hear that wind howlin'" then evokes the howling wind with a slide figure. It remains a chilling performance, with thoroughly appropriate accompaniment. On "Walking Blues" he created a moving bass with his slide, hitting quivering treble notes at the end of each stanza. "Last Fair Deal Gone Down" is uptempo and rhythmic, with rolling bass accompaniment and interjected slide phrases in unison with his vocal, as in "Come On in My Kitchen"—from slide to sharp chords and back to slide. When he sings "That ding-dong keep ringin' so soon," he interjects perfectly executed chimes.

"Terraplane Blues" sold respectably enough to justify a second recording session in June 1937 in a Dallas warehouse. Johnson fell back on some formulas, invoking "Roll and Tumble Blues" in his "Traveling Riverside Blues," with the same slide riffs. "Me and the Devil Blues," features masterful lyrics, but musically is in the same mold as "Kindhearted Woman Blues," recorded in the 1936 session. "Hellhound On My Trail," one of his masterpieces, features relatively restrained guitar, no fancy figures, but simple chords and a steady bass accompaniment. "Drunken Hearted Man" and "Malted Milk," however, were less than earthshaking, and vocally and instrumentally were clearly cribbed from the style of Lonnie Johnson, though Robert was

unable to evoke Lonnie's polished single-string work. Both are weak numbers compared to his other work.

Johnson occasionally revealed his versatility, most notably with the 1936 "They're Red Hot," an insignificant lyric, but played in a buoyant, ragtime guitar style more likely associated with Blind Blake than a delta bluesman. If the idea of Johnson playing country and pop numbers seems implausible, "Red Hot" clearly reveals those facets of his musical persona.

Following the '37 sessions Johnson continued to travel with Johnny Sheins. During that year they appeared on a Detroit radio show known as the Elder Moten Hour, and worked around the delta clubs and juke houses with Rice Miller (Sonny Boy Williamson II), Elmore James, whom he influenced immensely and Chester Burnett, who was a year older than Robert and later became known as the Howlin' Wolf.

In August 1938 Johnson was playing a juke joint in the tiny hamlet of Three Forks, Mississippi, not far from the larger town of Greenwood. He'd been involved with a married woman there, and when her husband discovered the infidelity, he arranged to poison Johnson—who enjoyed his whiskey as he played—by contaminating his drinks. It worked. Johnson became ill and was removed to Greenwood, where he lingered several days before dying on August 16. He was interred in an unmarked grave at a church near the nearby village of Morgan City, Mississippi. Johnson's attraction to women had led to his downfall.

Robert Johnson's influence on guitarists has been considerable. Though he was one of the founding fathers of the delta-based style that contained the seeds of the Chicago blues of the postwar years, he also became a profound influence on later rock musicians who drew from the blues for inspiration. Eric Clapton sang Johnson's "Ramblin' On My Mind" on John Mayall's *Bluesbreakers* album; Duane Allman's slide work, particularly on acoustic guitar, had strong Johnson overtones; Johnny Winter could also evoke Johnson in his playing, and even in the guitar of Jimi Hendrix, particularly on "Red House," the influence of Johnson is present, for the song is based on some of the chord structures and the Chicago blues sounds Johnson inspired.

Interest in Robert Johnson's life and work will probably never end. But though Robert Johnson was in many ways a derivative guitarist, the style he melded from all his early influences has gone far—certainly further than Johnson himself would ever have expected.

DISCOGRAPHY
The total recordings of Robert Johnson can be found on two Columbia albums: *King of the Delta Blues Singers* and *King of the Delta Blues Singers Volume 2*.

ALBERT KING

After B.B. King, Albert King was among the first blues singer/guitarists who was embraced by the younger rock audiences of the '60s. His influence, particularly between 1968 and 1970, was nearly as formidable—if not more so—than that of B.B. himself. Eric Clapton constantly invoked the style of Albert King during his tenure with Cream. His voicelike solo on "Strange Brew" was taken straight from any number of Albert King solos; even the most cursory listening to both guitarists' late '60s recordings will substantiate this.

Albert's playing style is in many ways closer to the slashing, spare guitar styles of '60s rockers than B.B.'s. He is, like B.B., not given to the extensive use of chords. But where B.B. plays fairly elaborate single-string solos, Albert merely sketches them, playing with great economy and creating tension with his legendary bent notes. He can create the impression of a sob or moan merely by grabbing one string (usually an E or B) and choking it several steps above its actual pitch.

Much of his sparse yet pungent style comes from his unorthodox approach to the guitar itself. Like Jimi Hendrix, he plays left-handed; unlike Hendrix, who restrung his guitars with the strings in the correct order (E-B-G-D-A-E from top to bottom) Albert uses a normally-strung instrument "upside down." Likewise, his use of the fleshy part of his left thumb to pick contributes much to his lean, astringent tone. The result is a style of playing so clear that among any group of blues guitarists, Albert's music will be instantly recognizable.

The attention that came to bluesmen in the late '60s revitalized Albert's career as well. His February 1, 1968, appearance at the Fillmore Auditorium in San Francisco, billed with British bluesman John Mayall and Jimi Hendrix (whom King had known when he was still scuffling in Nashville in the early '60s), was a turning point in Albert's career, signaling his escape from the confines of the chitlin circuit and taking of more lucrative engagements. It afforded him the opportunity to do things unthinkable years before. In 1969, he even got to perform with the St. Louis Symphony.

One of Albert's greatest assets as a modern

bluesman has been his musical flexibility. At a time when the musical structures of urban blues (shuffles, medium and fast, slow blues and little else) were relatively set, he managed to successfully move into the context of Memphis rhythm and blues of the mid-'60s without any real compromise. Indeed, most of his most enduring recordings were done for the Memphis-based Stax Records, home of Booker T. and the MGs, Eddie Floyd, Carla Thomas, Sam and Dave and other contemporary r & b acts. Working with Booker T & The MG's and the Memphis Horns, King managed to streamline his sound without impairing its blues content. Records like "Born Under a Bad Sign," "Cross Cut Saw" and "Oh, Pretty Woman" are devastating in their directness.

Aside from their obvious quality, these recordings proved to have the strongest influence on younger musicians. Paul Butterfield, for example, covered "Born Under a Bad Sign" in 1967 on his *Resurrection of Pigboy Crabshaw* album, which introduced his new brass section; Cream covered it in 1968 on *Wheels of Fire*. John Mayall picked up "Oh, Pretty Woman" the same year on his *Crusade* album with Mick Taylor on lead guitar. And in every case, the guitarists—Elvin Bishop with Butterfield, Clapton and Taylor—were using Albert's singing guitar style as a take off point.

Albert Nelson was born April 25, 1923, in Indianola, Mississippi. Though he stated throughout the '60s that he was B.B. King's half-brother, there is no evidence to support this other than that their birthplaces were relatively close. Albert's stepfather Will Nelson was a preacher who had a guitar. Albert tried to play it, but later contented himself, as did many young blacks (and whites) unable to afford guitars, with creating a homemade instrument.

He was fortunate, however, in getting to hear some of the greatest country bluesmen early in his youth. He saw Blind Lemon Jefferson in Forest City, Arkansas, and was taken by his singing and playing. Albert worked around the plantations and got his first guitar in the late '30s. He kept his hand in music,

working some roadhouses and playing with a gospel quartet, another experience he and B.B. had in common. But music as a profession was beyond King's reach though he did work with a group known as the In The Groove Boys around Osceola, Arkansas, in the late '40s.

Around 1951 Albert moved north, first to Benton Harbor, Michigan, then to Gary, Indiana, where he picked up his musical career as a drummer for bluesman Jimmy Reed. It was good experience, but Reed's constant problems with the bottle were rough on a sideman. So late in 1953 he decided to try recording himself, and auditioned for Parrot Records president Al Benson, who recorded one single "Bad Luck Blues" b/w "Be on Your Merry Way." The record turned out to be a hit—or, enough of a hit for Albert to begin playing full time in the Chicago area, and also back in Arkansas.

St. Louis became his new home base in the late '50s, where he did additional recording for the Bobbin label from 1959 into the early '60s, including the outstanding "I'm a Lonely Man." Some sessions for King Records followed, and one in 1965 for the Country label that yielded another early lassic "You Threw Your Love on Me Too Strong," which has all the elements of Albert's mature style. His husky vocals, followed by superb, economical guitar responses, created a hypnotic combination. His solo, a series of choked notes, was amazingly voicelike, but totally unlike either B.B. or Freddy King's sounds. That Albert was inspired by B.B. is clear, but his direction was his own.

In 1966 he signed with Stax Records of Memphis, and it was there that Albert found his most sympathetic surroundings, largely in the work of Steve Cropper and Al Jackson, Booker T. and the MG's guitarist and drummer, respectively. Jackson handled much of the actual production, and managed to place King totally within the characteristic Stax sound, which was lean, austere and based around the rhythm section (usually Jackson and bassist Duck Dunn)—not an inappropriate context for Albert King. Shuffle rhythms weren't used often; Stax's bare-bones, two-four beat marked the label's best material (such as "Hold On, I'm Coming" by Sam and Dave or Eddie Floyd's "Knock on Wood"). The Memphis Horns did not moan in the background as horn sections normally did on blues records, but instead punched out the same, tough, riffs they would play behind any other soul artist. The result was gratifying. *Born Under a Bad Sign*, Albert's first Stax LP, was a study in tension. As the band vamped behind him (Steve Cropper playing the song's recurring riff), Albert and his guitar were out front. He eased guitar licks around his vocal that sliced through the rhythm like a knife through warm butter. Better yet was "Cross Cut Saw," which opened with a powerful blast from Albert's guitar over a vaguely latin-styled rhythm. His vocals were low-keyed, and his guitar solo (which Clapton appropriated nearly note-for-note on Cream's "Strange Brew") was infectious, and as totally harsh as any rock guitarist played at the time. King held one note so long it is difficult to imagine the string surviving, choked by his massive right hand. Even the shuffle tune, "Kansas City," was effected with far more subtlety than such tunes usually were, and even as the Memphis Horns riffed over the top of his guitar, it still came through loud and clear.

"Oh, Pretty Woman" was built around a strong riff that pervaded the number, just as "Born Under a Bad Sign" was. The fact that Albert played virtually the same guitar solo that he'd played on "Cross Cut Saw," changing only the key, didn't matter; the performance was overwhelming. "The Hunter" used a musical foundation similar to that of Booker T.'s "Green Onions," with macho lyrics and more excellent guitar. Undoubtedly the shrill tone on this and several of the other numbers was attributable to King's use of his thumb, which almost snapped the strings on occasion. "Laundromat Blues" was a superb example of his voice/guitar partnership, as he responds to every verse he sings with a lick of equal power.

The result of this new approach was that,

unlike B.B. King in the '60s, Albert got a fair amount of airplay on black radio stations, the Stax/Volt production values adding a sufficiently contemporary edge to make his music palatable to younger audiences, while maintaining his credibility among older blues fans as well.

He did a number of other compelling records for the label in this period, later released by Atlantic on the album *King of the Blues Guitar*. Though it repeated some of the tracks on *Born Under a Bad Sign*, it also featured some outstanding material formerly available only on singles. The wrenching blues "You're Gonna Need Me" was a particularly outstanding track, again with voice and guitar acting as a formidable team. Two instrumentals, "Cold Feet" and "I Love Lucy" (Albert refers to his guitar by this not totally original name), were well done, though the humor on the latter tune is a bit forced. "You Sure Drive a Hard Bargain" boasts some of his best guitar work on record, with Booker T.'s sustained organ chords driving him along. Another instrumental, "Overall Junction," has obvious hints of Freddy King, while "Funk-Shun," a lengthy, medium tempo blues instrumental, shows both Albert's stylistic strengths and his tendency to repeat himself.

A 1968 appearance at San Francisco's Fillmore Auditorium was recorded, with the best excerpts released as *Live Wire Blues Power*. Backed by a small combo (organ, rhythm guitar, bass and drums), it spotlighted Albert's guitar in concert atmosphere. He was able to loosen up onstage, playing with a fury and intensity that rock guitarists were sweating blood to emulate. "Blues Power" in particular displays these strengths. His spontaneity and casualness made the entire album highly worthwhile, and perhaps his best guitar-oriented release.

Another fine studio album followed: *Years Gone By*, which features more excellent singing and playing, a fantastic version of Elmore James' "The Sky Is Crying" and a driving instrumental version of Willie Cobbs' "You Don't Love Me." More albums have come since then, including in 1972 King's *I'll Play* the Blues for You and his appearance in the movie *Wattstax*. His later albums have sometimes been overproduced, but recently Albert has returned to somewhat simpler backup arrangements.

Albert King defined himself nearly twenty years ago, and has managed to continue his lucrative career through the '70s and into the '80s, still respected for his past achievements and his formidable playing. Several of his musical mannerisms, including his famous string-choking, have become standard for the blues guitar, and will remain so long after he is gone.

DISCOGRAPHY
Most of Albert King's earliest recordings are out of print, though some were reissued on

Chess a while ago. Many of his best Stax sides are on the two - LP *Masterpieces* on Atlantic. *Born Under a Bad Sign* is available as a Japanese Atlantic import from Down Home Music. Edsel Records of England recently released a superb single-LP collection, *Laundromat Blues*, which contains all of his best late '60s Stax material. *I'll Play the Blues for You* compiles other material from Stax, and has recently been reissued by Fantasy. But Albert's best album in recent years is *San Francisco '83*, which recaptures the spirit of his old Stax sessions.

B.B. KING

If T-Bone Walker conceived and established the basic style of amplified single-string blues guitar, B.B. King took it to heights Walker himself never could have dreamed of when he started. Coming from the blues-rich Mississippi delta, King went his own way with his music, drinking in a variety of disparate influences to create his own guitar style, combining the sounds of his delta heritage with those of Charlie Christian, Django Reinhardt, T-Bone Walker and Lonnie Johnson.

Certainly King himself never expected to become an American treasure whose appeal transcends economic and racial barriers, the recipient of honorary degrees and more acclaim in the span of a few years than most great musicians would receive in two lifetimes. He has taken the blues from the parochial confines of the chitlin circuit into the best show rooms in America, never compromising onstage (though he's often done so on later records), and playing much the same music he's always played.

King's influence on the entire direction of blues, pop and rock guitar is immense. All the blues-based rock guitarists of the '60s and '70s—Bloomfield, Bishop, Clapton, Allman, Mick Taylor, Peter Green, Johnny Winter, Jimi Hendrix, and countless others—as well as an entire school of black bluesmen—Freddy King, Magic Sam, Little Milton, Albert King, Otis Rush, Albert Collins and Buddy Guy—have absorbed B.B's sound into their own playing.

King's development came through his conscious study of a variety of musical styles, blues and otherwise. Unlike Lonnie Johnson and T-Bone Walker, who had to make their own rules and their own directions, he learned much from both. Even today, though his guitar style is fully developed, their playing is at the heart of what he does. His diverse influences, including Lester Young, Charlie Christian, Louis Jordan, Nat "King" Cole and other jazz/blues artists, give King's music a breadth and depth that goes beyond the blues. Yet he's not content to play slick, urbanized blues with no allusions to the past. Indeed, his admiration for his cousin, pre-war delta singer/slide guitarist Bukka White, and for other pre-war bluesmen (like Blind Lemon Jefferson) led B.B. to make an effort to incorporate the feeling—if not the rough edges—of that music in his own playing. King has even added elements of gospel music in his vocal style, stretching syllables over several beats.

B.B. King's guitar mastery did not develop right away. It took him several years to perfect the fragmented, voicelike guitar identity that's become his trademark; his singing was his greatest strength in his salad days. But by the time he'd had his first hits in the early '50s that began to change. The guitar became as crucial to his musical persona as his voice, becoming in fact a second voice, answering his vocals, commenting upon the lyrics and adding its own dimensions to a song.

One fundamental difference between King and T-Bone Walker is in their use of chords. T-Bone frequently punctuated his songs with chords and arpeggios, B.B. does so far less, preferring instead single-string phrases and using occasional chords for a percussive effect. Walker did this, too, but he played lengthy, linear solos, where B.B. goes in for brief, jagged riffs as he finishes singing a line. On solos he also offers less smoothness, trying to create a vocal quality through his phrasing and use of such devices as his famous vibrato, played with his left hand, or his constant string-choking, which permits him to mimic conversation. He sometimes sustains single notes, or plays furious flurries of notes followed by silence, the better to approximate the pace of human speech.

B.B.'s phrasing also produces a far different tone than T-Bone's. His tone is shrill and at times even slightly distorted, a sound produced by several factors, including his aggressive, percussive picking. B.B. was not one to overdrive his amplifier, as did many of the Memphis and Chicago bluesmen of the post-war era, but he always has a sharp edge on his tone. Though changes in technology pertaining to guitar amplification and recording techniques have refined his sound over the years, B.B.'s basic technique remains unchanged.

That so many rock guitarists of the '60s found their own styles by learning B.B.'s is a tribute to both him and their own understanding of his brilliance on the instrument. Even

some of the most "psychedelic" bands of that era featured guitar solos that were often flat-out steals of B.B's licks, strung together and played at high volume. The best musicians simply use this as a stepping stone to more original concepts, but the string bending and vibrato techniques taken from King's playing are employed today more than ever.

B.B. King brought blues guitar into mainstream American music from the juke joints of the south and the theaters of the ghetto. Forget his singing and his compositions for a moment. Blues guitar licks in his basic style show up in commercials, on movie soundtracks, and even as theme music for TV shows. B.B. himself supplied the music for the short-lived late '70s ABC comedy series "The Associates," and for several film soundtracks as well. Before he became recognized in the late '60s, the idea of using such an overtly ethnic musical form in presentations designed for mass appeal was unthinkable.

Riley B. King was born in a sharecropper's cabin between Itta Bena and Indianola, in the Mississippi delta, on September 16, 1925. His parents, Albert and Nora Ella King, stayed together four years after Riley's birth, Albert eking out a living as a tractor driver. Around 1929 Nora King left her husband for another man and sent Riley to live with his grandmother near Kilmichael, Mississippi. Riley's mother died in 1935 and he stayed with his grandmother, going to school and working in the cotton fields the rest of the time.

His first interest in music came through the Holiness Church which he attended, not far from Kilmichael. The minister was the Reverend Archie Fair, his aunt's brother, who led the congregation with raucous, driving gospel music, accompanied by pianos and guitars. It was there that Riley King first began singing. After services Fair occasionally visited with his in-laws, and when Riley was present he would fool around with Fair's guitar. When the preacher noted his interest, he taught the youth to play three chords. That was King's introduction to the guitar.

He stayed with his grandmother, working in the fields and singing in an amateur gospel group, until 1940 when she died. He returned to his father for two years, then he moved back to Kilmichael, he got a job doing farm work for a time, then in spring of 1943 moved into the delta heartlands where he got a job driving a tractor on a plantation near Indianola. He'd heard records by various bluesmen by this time, and since he was old enough to get into some of the local joints, he was able to hear such top musicians of the area as Sonny Boy Williamson. In 1944 a motion picture gave Riley his first taste of the music of jazz guitar pioneer Charlie Christian, who by then had been dead for two years.

His tractor driving job was considered essential labor during World War II, he was exempted from the draft, and continued driving until 1946. He'd been playing guitar and singing gospel music throughout this time, hearing songs on the radio and through friends. One friend of Riley's named Willie Dotson brought back some Django Reinhardt records he'd obtained in Paris while serving in the U.S. Army; the phrasing and fire of Django's playing moved King deeply, for his musical sophistication had sufficiently developed by then that he knew brilliance when he heard it.

His interest in a musical career was clearcut by now, and he felt a need to move on, so in 1946 he packed up and went north to Memphis, Tennessee, where he felt he'd have a greater chance of achieving his aim. He moved in with his cousin, the bluesman Booker T. Washington "Bukka" White. White, who'd spent time in prison for murder, was a primitive musician and master of slide guitar. Riley played with him, and tried unsuccessfully to imitate his slide playing and chilling vibrato. He wasn't able to, so he created his own style of vibrato, played by using his left hand fingers. It became a keystone of his style. A brief return to Mississippi followed in 1947 before he came back to Memphis in '48, ready to take a serious stab at professional music.

He got his first break sooner than he'd expected. Having met Sonny Boy Williamson back in the delta, Kng auditioned for him, performed on Sonny Boy's KWEM radio show in West Memphis, Arkansas, and got a regular club job all within a day or so of his arrival. His spirits high, he walked into WDIA, the all-black radio station in Memphis, and walked out as the unpaid host of a ten-minute radio show for a booze-laced tonic known as Pepticon. For one just in from the delta, it was a phenomenal run of luck.

Nor did it stop there. King soon had his own full-fledged radio show on WDIA. Dubbed the "Blues Boy from Beale Street" (shortened to B.B.), he became a local favorite, and he soon had offers to expand his club dates. He formed a small band of his own. However, he was still extremely rough as a guitarist, and unaccustomed to playing with other musicians. Today, this seems hard to believe: B.B. is the master, capable of working with nearly any performer. But it was a very real problem back then. One who had a big part in helping him iron out his weaknesses was Robert Jr. Lockwood, Sonny Boy Williamson's former guitarist who'd originally learned guitar from Robert Johnson, a friend of his mother's. Lockwood, who was well versed in jazz, tried to polish B.B.'s rough edges.

However, his limitations as a guitarist were apparent on his first recording for the Nashville-based Bullet label late in 1949. "Miss Martha King," dedicated to his wife, features a clumsy opening intro on electric guitar, still as rough as a delta bluesman would have played it. Another disadvantage (though King later made this work for him) was his inability to play and sing simultaneously. His shouting vocal on the track is actually much better than any of his guitar work, and certainly reflects more confidence. He played almost the same intro on the record's flipside, "When Your Baby Packs Up and Goes," only he kicked the tempo up a bit.

Obviously B.B. was well aware of these flaws. On "My Baby's Gone," recorded in Sam Phillips' Sun studios for the RPM label in January 1951, he shows a bit more confidence and less clumsiness, and his brief solo is adequate. Nonetheless, he continued to concentrate on his singing when he recorded. B.B.'s brief guitar on "Hard Working Woman" is rhythmic, though it owes much to T-Bone Walker.

But his confidence on the instrument was

growing. Later in 1951, at the Memphis YMCA with a larger band, he recorded "Three O'Clock Blues," which featured his characteristic guitar phrases tagged on to each verse. No longer did the saxophone take the leads. B.B. played a chopping, searing solo, shouting encouragement to himself as he squeezed note after note out of his Gibson. Whether this all mattered or not is moot, but by early 1952 "Three O'Clock Blues" had become a massive success on the national rhythm and blues charts, remaining number one for 15 weeks. It was the song that took B.B. into the top black venues of the country.

He also began using figures surprisingly close to slide guitar licks, such as his opening to the 1952 "Some Day Somewhere," which sounds rather close to some of Muddy Waters' characteristic slide guitar patterns from the same period. B.B.'s harsh opening to the jump number "Shake It Up and Go" (a variant on the old "Step It Up and Go") featured some sharp rhythm guitar behind sax solos before he stepped out with a fleet, strutting break of his own. He coaxed snapping, snarling lines from his instrument on "Gotta Find My Baby" a medium-tempo blues shuffle, like the rest of these also recorded at the Sun studio where Elvis Presley would make his first record two years down the road.

King was touring the country, playing clubs and exploiting his success; in the meantime more excellent material emerged from RPM. Still, his guitar was minimized on several of his hits, including "You Know I Love You," his second number one score in 1952. His '53 effort "Woke Up in the Morning" began with a bit of guitar, and though it was actually a variant of his '51 recording "My Baby's Gone," which didn't sell, the new recording hit number five on the r&b charts. "Please Love Me," a number two r&b hit right behind the latter, opened with the familiar Elmore James "Dust My Broom" riff, which King played with his fingers, and repeated on his solo break. His solo was shaky, even compared to "Three O'Clock Blues." But his improvement continued. His 1954 "When My Heart Beats Like a Hammer," possesses, at least partially, the unmistakable B.B. King style, with sputtering

riffs after each verse. His guitar, not a saxophone, handles the solo break. His self-confidence has increased dramatically. His roughness and awkward fingerings are in the past. This record didn't sell, but "You Upset Me, Baby" did, and it, too, featured a harsh, quivering solo with some of the earliest evidence of his finger vibrato. "Everyday I Have the Blues" was also laced with excellent embellishments and a fine solo with T-Bone Walker overtones in B.B.'s lines.

By 1956 B.B. King LPs were appearing on the Crown label, part of the RPM/Crown/Kent operation run by the Bihari Brothers. One of B.B.'s non-hits that appeared on these albums (later reissued on the United-Superior label) is worth examining. Among the few instrumentals he did back then was "House Rocker." It was a straightforward boogie instrumental on which he builds a solo as T-Bone Walker did. For once he is maintaining unrelenting momentum as the horns riff rhythmically behind him. The phrasing is pure B.B., but he shows with this one number just how his abilities have expanded, playing with the fire of Charlie Christian, though not with Christian's sophisticated harmonic awareness. It is a little-known, but phenomenally effective number.

"Sweet Little Angel," which hit number six on the r&b charts in 1956, was dominated by guitar, much of it played in the upper register, with a note glissed up the neck and a fully-formed solo that could have come from nobody else. B.B. now had a guitar style as instantly recognizable as his singing. From here on, the guitar would be a truly integral part of his music, not just something to riff on at the beginning and end of a number.

The instrument had always been important to King. He had, after all, begun naming his guitars Lucille back in 1949, as he's often explained with his story about playing a club in Twist, Arkansas. Two men got into a fight over a woman named Lucille. A large heater overturned and the club caught fire. B.B. ran out, realized he'd forgotten his guitar and ran back in to retrieve it. He nearly killed himself and started dubbing his instruments Lucille as a reminder of such folly.

Unfortunately, by the late '50s King was in a quandary of sorts. His audience was aging; the new r&b groups were a generation ahead of him, and he was not a rock and roller. Younger blacks began looking upon the blues with disdain, and at times B.B. found himself being booed when he played package shows around the country with rock and roll acts. It was not a pleasant experience.

Yet his hits had not fallen off totally. In 1960 came the cathartic six-minute "Sweet Sixteen," which stretched to two sides of a single (RPM had given way to the Crown label). Again, the track was guitar-laden, with Lucille commenting on King's lyrics in the responsive tradition that had begun with Lonnie Johnson and Scrapper Blackwell.

The early '60s were not good times for B.B. King. His attempts to adapt to current trends of the day were both sad and laughable. Titles like "Hully Gully (Twist)," "Mashed Potato Twist," "Three O'Clock Stomp," and "Mashing the Popeye," all issued in 1962 on Kent, pretty much say it all. He was at his peak, but unable to take advantage of it.

That same year he moved to ABC Paramount Records, the label on which Ray Charles had recorded some of his biggest successes. This had its advantages, as the label had excellent distribution. Unfortunately, its producers had their own philosophy about what B.B. King should sound like. The RPM/Kent sides, except for the twist tunes, were generally excellent. ABC smothered him in orchestrations, and the results weren't good.

There was, however, a notable exception. Though his career was static, on November 21, 1964 he recorded a live album at Chicago's Regal Theater, released as Live at the Regal the following year, that stands as one of his finest—if not the finest—example of his impact on an enthusiastic audience. Guitar and voice have achieved equal partnership, each projecting the same emotions in distinctively different ways, working the crowd to a fever pitch. Hearing B.B. outside the sterile atmosphere of the studio is a revelation, as the crowd responds and an outstanding band backs him, with restraint, letting him control the dynamics onstage.

His medley of "Sweet Little Angel," "It's My Own Fault," and "How Blue Can You Get" remains one of his most masterful single performances, with his guitar bridging each of the three numbers to provide a sense of unity. Throughout the album were case studies of virtually every B.B. King guitar idea. He changed his tone, going from a deep, bassy sound to a shrill timbre that cut to the bone. The album so captures the essence of his blues that it remains in print today.

Nonetheless, through 1966 his fortunes seemed stagnant. B.B. had problems with the IRS; his second marriage fell apart, and his future looked less than encouraging. His touring bus was stolen, mere insult added to injury by that point. Even a number two hit on the r&b charts, "Don't Answer the Door," meant little to him then. He recorded another unbelievably compelling live album that November, also in Chicago, at a smaller club. In this more intimate atmosphere and with his own small touring group, Blues Is King was a superb followup to Live at the Regal. He played brilliantly throughout the program, with a particularly intense solo on, of all things, Willie Nelson's "Night Life."

Frustration, nonetheless, was wearing him down, and things continued to look bleak until 1968 when B.B. found himself booked into the Fillmore Auditorium in San Francisco. This was nothing new; it had been part of the chitlin circuit for years. But the clientele had changed, and now consisted of white audiences drawn to the new rock music of San Francisco. After an effusive introduction by Michael Bloomfield, who paid tribute to King's influence on him, he found himself facing a standing ovation that left him emotionally moved.

King's recordings changed little. In 1968 came a studio set Blues on Top of Blues, like Blues Is King, recorded for BluesWay, an ABC subsidiary. It was a fine album with a Basie-styled big band. But B.B.'s bookings were beginning to change; he was playing rock clubs and rock festivals, enjoying the adulation from his new white audiences. He met Johnny Winter, a Texas-born albino whom he'd once reluctantly permitted to sit in at a gig only to find him a surprisingly effective blues guitarist. Winter's lucrative Columbia recording contract, the result of a 1968 *Rolling Stone* article on musicians in Texas, was one more measure of the sudden marketability of blues.

King's next album, *Lucille*, was built around his guitar. The title track was a lengthy, informal recitation about the origin of the name "Lucille" with some interesting autobiographical comments and moderately corny monologue ("Sing for me, Lucille..."), though B.B. plays much fine guitar. With top-flight r&b veterans like pianist Lloyd Glenn and drummer Jesse Sailes, the groove was loose and unforced. *His Best—The Electric B.B. King* was a misnomer. The album certainly wasn't his best, with too many James Brown rhythms that just didn't fit ("The B.B. Jones" is almost as bad as those 1962 twist numbers).

But 1970 brought something that would have been almost unthinkable just three years earlier: a B.B. King blues at the upper end of the pop music charts. The song was "The Thrill Is Gone," a smoldering minor-keyed Roy Hawkins number featuring effective, spare guitar work, which made it to number 15 on the pop charts and number three on the black charts, giving B.B. the mass exposure he'd only been able to fantasize about.

Suddenly B.B. King albums were loading up bins across the country. The old Crown and Kent albums were repackaged in a variety of ways, making some of his best material available to everyone. He also began experimenting with his music. In 1970 *Indianola, Mississippi Seeds* was released, featuring him in collaboration with some of the top names in rock, including Leon Russell, Carole King and Joe Walsh, and a Los Angeles rhythm section. The results were mixed, some tracks successful, others sounding forced. *In London*, a 1971 effort, picked up a then-popular concept of putting blues legends with some of the rock musicians they'd influenced. Again, the results were generally off the mark.

Through the '70s, however, B.B.'s acceptance grew. He did network TV constantly, it seemed. His 1970 *Live at Cook County Jail* album was excellent, and underscored his interest in providing musical assistance to inmates, a philanthropic endeavor that he had the clout to initiate. His albums were of inconsistent quality through this period, but his stage appearances were rarely less than brilliant. His insistence on giving his audience his best has been almost an obsession. After a 1961 car crash that left his right arm severely injured, he still managed to do a show, fretting with just his good left hand (an old T-Bone Walker trick).

Opportunities for Las Vegas (and later Atlantic City) casino appearances came his way, and B.B. made Las Vegas his residence after years of living in Memphis. Today, B.B. King isn't a wealthy man but he is quite comfortable, paying his musicians well and studying music seriously. His interest in the blues has never waned, and he takes a miniature blues library on the road with him, listening to tapes that include everyone from Robert Johnson and T-Bone Walker to Blind Lemon Jefferson.

B.B. King has become an American institution and one of the most influential guitarists of all time. Like Bob Hope or Count Basie, it is difficult to imagine his *not* being there. He refuses to compromise the integrity of his music; his insistence on keeping the spirit of the early blues greats who inspired him in his music is a tribute to that integrity. He speaks with pride of the debt he owes to them, just as Bloomfield, Clapton and others have spoken of their debt to him. As he continues to spend most of his time on the road, the message of his guitar has remained constant—and perennially fulfilling. American popular music—not just blues—would not be what it is without B.B. King.

DISCOGRAPHY

The B.B. King discography is, as you might expect, huge, so this will be a very selected discography. *The Rarest King* (Blues Boy), reissues his first Bullet Recordings and a number of hard-to-find recordings from Modern in a beautiful package. *The Best of B.B. King* (Chiswick/Ace) reissues B.B.'s first album.

There are also a variety (too many to list here) of budget-priced United LPs all taken from the Kent-Modern period.

From MCA are a variety of albums, including the classic *Live at the Regal, Live in Cook County Jail, The Best of B.B. King, B.B. King and Bobby Bland, Now Appearing at Ole Miss* and many more by this time.

FREDDY KING

As a guitarist, Freddie King can be considered somewhere between B.B. and Albert King. His tone was rougher than B.B.'s, his attack far less graceful. At the same time, he played lengthier solo lines than Albert. But perhaps the fundamental difference was that Freddie was far more involved in the post-war Chicago blues scene than either B.B. or Albert, though there are questions as to just how prominent his contributions were in this area. But certainly Chicago influenced him, for his approach to playing always retained the rough urban edge.

While B.B. can be heard in Freddie's playing, equally evident are such Chicago guitar legends as Jimmy Rogers, Hubert Sumlin and, of course, Muddy Waters. Freddie made his name with his instrumentals, and gained popularity when Eric Clapton, Peter Green and Mick Taylor started performing King staples like "Hideaway," "The Stumble" and "Driving Sideways" during their respective tenures with John Mayall. In every case their versions are identical to King's. Guitarist Stan Webb of the 1960's British blues band

Chicken Shack was also so won over by King that he included Freddie's songs on the band's first two LPs.

Like B.B. and Albert, Freddie enjoyed a resurgence of popularity in the late '60s. One of the first signs of this (aside from the Mayall covers) was an enthusiastic appreciation by Bugsy Maugh, then bassist with the Paul Butterfield Blues Band, that appeared in a 1968 issue of *Rolling Stone*. King wound up doing new recordings that showed him beginning to lean toward a more rock-oriented sound. Under the aegis of Leon Russell his recording career was revitalized on Denny Cordell's Shelter Records. Freddie toured extensively and continued recording until his untimely death in 1976 at age forty-two.

Freddie King was born in 1934 in Gilmer, Texas. Since both his mother and uncle were guitarists, he picked the instrument up early, at age six. Texas, one of the most fertile areas in the country for blues, provided him with a wealth of fine influences, among them T-Bone Walker, Muddy Waters and Lightnin' Sam Hopkins. The idea of playing music was attractive to King and at age 16 he packed up his guitar and moved to Chicago.

He started hanging around the Chicago clubs where Muddy, Howlin' Wolf and the others worked, and in 1952 formed a band, the Every Hour Blues Boys, to work the clubs himself. He did his first recording in 1953 as a sideman with Sonny Cooper's group for the local Parrot label, and a year later recorded again, as a sideman with Earlee Payton's Blues Cats, also for Parrot. It was 1956 before King got his own date with the Chicago-based El-Bee label; he did a second (unissued) session for Cobra the following year.

His style had begun to coalesce by that time. Muddy Waters' longtime second guitarist Jimmy Rogers, a superb singer and player in his own right, showed King a different approach from his usual flatpicking, using a metal fingerpick and plastic thumbpick on his right hand. King had become close with Rogers and Chicagoan Eddie Taylor (the lead guitarist on most of Jimmy Reed's classic Vee-Jay sides). Their tutelage changed Freddie's entire sound, giving him dexterity and fluidity while helping him to maintain the rough-edged, hard attack that characterized his playing.

In 1960 Freddie joined Cincinnati-based King Records. He was part of a new generation of bluesmen exemplified by Otis Rush, Buddy Guy, Magic Sam and Luther Allison, all of whose playing reconciled the T-Bone Walker/B.B. King styles with the less polished sounds of Muddy and Wolf. Freddie did his first session in Cincinnati on August 25, 1960, playing a song he'd learned from slide guitarist Hound Dog Taylor that he titled "Hideaway."

"Hideaway" was not his first release. King's subsidiary label for r&b, Federal, first featured him with "You've Got to Love Her with a Feeling," a gutsy blues featuring his smoky voice and some raw guitar work. But it was "Hideaway," released in March 1961, that brought King serious attention. The song showed the strengths of his style. He handled the hammer-ons effortlessly, thanks at least partly to the fingerpicks, and muted the bass strings with his right hand to play a loping fig-

ure before cutting back into the lead with a flurry of chords. More lead and a muted-string quote from "Peter Gunn," then Freddie returned to his main theme to finish out the number. It hit number 29 on Billboard's pop charts, unusual for a blues instrumental at the time. But there were just enough rock ele ments, including humor and a catchy lead line, to make the tune work.

Naturally, King was interested in putting out more product, and his next session, on April 5, 1961, yielded excellent material, including his thick-toned "The Stumble," another catchy number with a loping beat similar to "Hideaway's" stiletto-sharp runs and ripping chords played so harshly his pick sounds came through the amp. "The Stumble" had it all—the Chicago raunch and a rock and roll feel. His next instrumental, "San-Ho-Zay," became something of a hit and featured more superb, harsh lead guitar. It was, if anything, more gritty than "Hideaway," which may well explain why it was less successful at a time when Frankie Avalon and other teeny-crooners held sway over the charts. Freddie was, one might say, an attractive alternative.

He hit the road after the success of "Hideaway," but spent the bulk of his time in Chicago's clubs and blues studios, still recording for King. Freddie's releases included the slow "Christmas Tears," a holiday blues with some great supporting guitar in a B.B. King mold. "Side Tracked," a 1962 release, fea tured him hammering on the bass strings and a hard, distorted sound that came from Freddie's guitar rather than any "tricks" or high volume recording levels.

Freddie's 1962 composition "Hi-Rise" was appropriated by Lonnie Mack a couple of years later for his excellent "Jam and Butter." Hearing both records leaves no question in the listener's mind as to their similarities. King crafted other excellent instrumentals in this period, such as the easy-going, after-hours "Swooshy," "Sen-Sa-Shun" (Sonny Thompson, listed as composer on many of these tracks, clearly had a flair for phonetic spellings and syllables). Freddy fleetly picked his muted bass strings on this last, demonstrating how strong his thumb had become. His music began to take a more overtly rock and roll feel with songs like "You Can't Hide," sung with Lulu Reed. "Now I've Got A Woman," despite its rock and roll beat, had strong echoes of King's Chicago colleague Otis Rush, particularly in its minor-keyed theme and Freddie's beautifully controlled vocal. The lyrics aren't much, but, like Rush, he manages to transcend them with his voice and guitar.

Some of King's best later instrumentals were cut in Cincinnati in 1963, including his churning "Manhole," a number that sold little but was nonetheless masterful, taking changes from Booker T's "Green Onions" as the harmonic basis for the song. "The Sad Nite Owl" was slower and bluesier. Freddie played in close harmony with the pianist (probably Sonny Thompson) to create a new sound (one they should have experimented with further). But it was "Remington Ride," a steel guitar showcase written in 1949 by western swing bandleader Hank Penny and his steel player, Herb Remington, that stands as one of Freddie's finest recorded moments of these years.

Freddie's more than six-minute workout was far superior to the version Penny and Remington had recorded (also for King). Freddie slowed down the tempo to a medium shuffle. Though he began by remaining close to the theme, he took off on some hair-raising improvisations, choking the strings, running up the neck and returning to the melody before cutting loose again with even more exciting, bluesy excursions that gave the song its new dimension. His slurs were perfectly placed. The overall effect was exhilarating. It could have become boring, had he not touched base with the melody; by doing so he maintained the song's identity while making it his own. Another six-minute number, "Hi Tide," was less successful but boasted some excellent playing.

In 1963 King moved to Dallas, which he made his home. By 1966 he was popular enough to travel to England, probably on the strength of the interest generated by Mayall and Clapton. By 1968 the blues revival had begun in earnest in America as well, and

Freddie found his fortunes rising. He had ended his relationship with King in 1966, and had no recording contract. But in 1969 he began recording for Cotillion Records, an Atlantic subsidiary. The excellence of his playing had brought him the new white audience; fans were snapping up his older albums like *Freddy King Sings, Freddy King Goes Surfin'* and *A Bonanza of Instrumentals* as well as his old Federal singles, so new recordings were appropriate. *Freddie King Is a Blues Master*, issued in 1969, was a credible effort, though less focused than his King recordings.

He met Leon Russell in 1971; Russell, then one of America's top rock stars after years as a Hollywood studio musician, signed Freddie to the Shelter label. King tried to move into a rock context with Shelter, and though he was young enough to pull it off, and his guitar playing fit with the times, it's dubious this effort was effective. Freddie sang more than he had before, but the band Leon Russell led behind him was not as well suited to his style as it had been to Rita Coolidge's and Joe Cocker's.

Not all of King's Shelter work was bad, however. His shuffle version of John Fogerty's "Lodi," with both his voice and guitar in top form, was powerful. Other numbers simply didn't work out, and many of the strongest numbers he recorded for Shelter were old blues like Lowell Fulson's "Reconsider Baby" and Willie Dixon's "I'm Ready." During his tenure with Shelter, King also brought his early benefactor Jimmy Rogers back into the studio for the first time in years.

RSO Records, owned by Robert Stigwood (Eric Clapton's manager and the man behind the Bee Gees and Saturday Night Fever) signed King up in 1975. Clapton, as a long-time admirer and disciple of Freddie's playing, undoubtedly had something to do with this. King cut two albums, *Burglar* and *Larger than Life*, but after extensive touring through 1976, he became ill at a Christmas night concert. He was admitted to Dallas Presbyterian Hospital with hepatitis. Complications set in, and he died on December 28, 1976. He was buried in Dallas.

That Freddie King's career ended so

abruptly is tragic, for like Elmore James he was still playing at the top of his form when he died. The only thing that softens the tragedy is the inspiring music King left behind. As his later recordings were less well focused, his King/Federal sides remain his most enduring legacy. If nothing else, Freddie King, at least experienced the adulation and abiding respect from a broad audience that so many other bluesmen missed.

DISCOGRAPHY

Though King released two of Freddie's best albums in the original covers a few years ago, they are currently out of print. However, *17 Original Greatest Hits* (Gusto) and *Hideaway* (Gusto), a double album, reissue much of his best material. WEA, Atlantic's French outlet, has reissued both Cotillion albums *(Freddie King Is a Blues Master* and *My Feeling for the Blues*). And MCA/Shelter still has *The Best of Freddie King* available as a budget set. One new reissue of King material (Crosscut) includes unissued numbers.

OTIS RUSH

At the time Otis Rush appeared on the Chicago blues scene in the early '50s, the Mississippi delta-based blues of Muddy Waters, Little Walter, Howlin' Wolf and Jimmy Reed dominated the clubs and the recording industry. At the same time B.B. King was beginning to make a huge impact with his smoother, urbanized, gospel-influenced blues and his T-Bone Walker-inspired guitar playing, though it was some time before his guitar work matched the excellence of his singing.

Rush was one of the first of the Chicago bluesmen to move away from the delta styles toward the newer sounds of King, creating a style of Chicago blues that emerged from that city's west side (as opposed to the south side, where the delta-based music held sway). Today Otis' style is heard in much Chicago blues, epitomized by such brilliant singer/guitarists as Buddy Guy, Luther Allison and Son Seals. In many ways Otis is the best of both worlds—he has the raw emotion and intensity of the delta men and the stinging, razor-sharp guitar and smoother arrangements of the urban blues professionals. The blues has evolved somewhat since then, but its basic aspects remain unchanged, though rock and r&b aspects appear more often. Like Albert King, Rush is a left-handed player, and their tones are quite similar.

Otis Rush remains one of the most powerful and emotional artists of his generation. His guitar work has a raw, unbridled fury and chilling, intense edge that influenced Mike Bloomfield, Johnny Winter, Eric Clapton and Stevie Ray Vaughan, among others. His compelling vocals have influenced Paul Butterfield and John Mayall. Indeed, of all the bluesmen of his milieu, Otis Rush has relied the most on emotion and feeling, seldom falling back on flashy showmanship or other showbiz tricks.

This has not been totally beneficial to Rush, though his greatness has been long acknowledged by other bluesmen and authorities, including Robert Palmer, who in his excellent book *Deep Blues* describes a Rush performance: "His grainy-gospelish singing carried the weight of so much passion and frustration, it sounded like the words were being torn from his throat, and his guitar playing hit heights I didn't think any musician was capable of—notes bent and twisted so delicately and immaculately they seemed to form actual words, phrases that cascaded up the neck, hung suspended over the rhythm and fell suddenly, hunching at the bottom in anguished paroxysms."

Despite such lofty praise, Rush's career has been plagued by bad luck—particularly in his recording career. Even when admirers like Bloomfield and Nick Gravenites went out of their way to place him in a stronger commercial position, Rush hasn't achieved the mass sales of any of the Kings, or of Muddy Waters before his death. It has made Otis bitter, which hasn't helped matters, though his frustration is quite understandable.

Otis Rush was born in Philadelphia, Mississippi, on April 29, 1934, one of seven children. He taught himself guitar when he was eight, but fooled more with harmonica as he grew into adolescence. In 1948 he moved to Chicago, where he absorbed the city's blues scene. Too young to get into the clubs, he listened to Muddy, Wolf, John Lee Hooker and the rest on records and the radio. Harmonica was still his main instrument when he began playing with a youthful drummer he'd met working in the Chicago stockyards. It wasn't until 1954 that Rush returned to the guitar seriously, billing himself as "Little Otis" as he started at the clubs, initially aping Muddy, Wolf and others of the older generation. That changed when Rush heard B.B. King on guitar. He took lessons briefly from guitarist Reggie Boyd (but quit in order to teach himself) and listened to jazz guitarists as well as blues stars.

Although his guitar skills were still developing, by 1956 his reputation had earned him a recording contract with the new Cobra label. He did his first sessions that summer with a band that included harp master Walter Horton, pianist Lafayette Leake, bassist/composer Willie Dixon and blues/r&b

guitarist Wayne Bennett, who later became famous for his work with Bobby "Blue" Bland. Rush's guitar work on Dixon's "I Can't Quit You, Baby" is a bit busy and overeager (typical of neophyte lead players), but the raw power of his vocal made the song; he took no solo break. "Sit Down Baby," recorded at the same session, was a rocking, if inconsequential, number. Despite Rush's relative inexperience, "I Can't Quit You" became a substantial regional hit.

This set a pattern of sorts: an unadulterated blues number on one side of a release, a lightweight rocker or even a ballad on the other. Rush's second release, in the fall of '56, was true to form. "My Love Will Never Die" was a wrenching, cathartic, minor-keyed blues, on which Otis answered his lyrics with simple guitar licks. He was not ready for strong solo work yet, though he was clearly improving as an instrumentalist. His vocal, as with "I Can't Quit You," was unadorned but moving. "Violent Love," the flipside, was a piece of junk with heavy Tin Pan Alley/Brill Building overtones. Even Otis' considerable vocal ability couldn't overcome material this bad.

Early in 1957 he went into the studio again for Cobra, this time with the great Little Walter on harmonica. "Groaning the Blues" had more of a delta feeling than the earlier tracks, but featured another excellent vocal, and somewhat improved guitar work, including a solo that begins strongly but peters out at the end. "If You Were Mine" was another rhythm number with delta overtones and a tepid guitar solo. He returned to the studios in midyear with the same band (except for Little Brother Montgomery replacing Lafayette Leake on piano), waxing "Love That Woman," an outstanding blues resembling Muddy Waters "Hoochie Koochie Man," and another rhythm tune, "Jump Sister Bessie" which featured a spare but better-conceived guitar solo.

Rush's playing was far more confident by the time of his last 1957 session. With his teacher, Reggie Boyd, also on the session, he opens with a well-conceived line, and plays carefully placed, barbed little guitar fills and a pungent solo. "She's a Good 'Un" had a similar, loping beat; though the words had little substance, Otis' Elmore James-styled opening and snarling riffs introduced a highly danceable rhythmic groove, enhanced by a malevolent guitar break. Guitarist Reggie Boyd's steady rhythm effects deserve recognition, too, and their rhythm work as the song fades is an unexpected surprise.

"Checking on My Baby," recorded in 1958, was a harsh blues with a fine vocal featuring Rush's keening falsetto and crackling guitar fills that seem to jump out of nowhere. "It Takes Time" is an upbeat shuffle with a searing solo that deteriorates into repetitive rhythm playing before he sings again. Neither cut was anywhere near his next magnificent series of recordings, done that same year. "Double Trouble" remains a chilling blues, replete with the imagery of total hopelessness. Otis' sparse lead guitar lines, falling roughly as fills between his unforced, riveting vocals, is equally as emotional. Rush plays shattering, quivering notes, not always precisely, but executing with great power.

"All Your Love" was another minor-key masterpiece, with tough guitar and another inspired vocal. Rush's solo here is a measure of how far he has come; he begins with a cold riff, which Eric Clapton copied note for note on the 1966 John Mayall performance of this song, before breaking into a shuffle, shooting uninhibited machine gun bursts of notes and then returning to his original theme.

Rush's guitar technique had come far in just two years. He was by now a master in his own right, playing a style clearly influenced by B.B. King, but with his own stamp on it: his raw, unrefined tone and his more economic approach alternating with rapidly picked phrases was quite different than B.B.'s. Rush's string bending was always effective, creating tense drama comparable to (and at times exceeding) that of Albert King. He played left-handed, as Albert did, but that was the only real resemblance. Rush used even stronger vibrato than did B.B., which added still more tension.

By 1958 Otis' association with Cobra had ended, and he was doing some touring, but still working mostly in the Chicago clubs. In 1960 he made a superb recording for Chess. "So Many Roads, So Many Trains" was another frightening number on a par with "Double Trouble" or "I Can't Quit You". Rush's next move, to the Houston-based Duke Records in 1962, was far less successful. Though he was playing incredibly well, he was tied up with the label several years and only one single was ever released. Chicago continued to be his home base.

Then in 1965 blues lover Sam Charters went to Chicago to compile a multi-volume sampler of that city's contemporary blues for the Vanguard label. Since folk music labels had gravitated toward folk blues performers like Big Bill Broonzy and Mississippi John Hurt, Charter's concept was quite a departure (and a timely one; Paul Butterfield's debut album on Elektra came that same year). Otis Rush was included in the sessions, and since Vanguard's three-volume set, Chicago/The Blues/Today! was directed at a white audience, it gained Rush an entirely new group of devotees.

The five tracks he recorded (they were released on volume two,) although not profound, were relaxed and unforced. "Everything's Going to Turn Out Alright," an instrumental, was unusual for its country music flavor. His version of Little Walter's "Mean Old World" contained more polished (though not slick) guitar with tight, economical solo work. "I Can't Quit You Baby" was nearly as good as the original Cobra version, Otis' obvious musical maturity giving it a true sense of completeness. His wonderfully expressive vocal reflected greater authority, and his solo was positively stunning. He added more of those furious fills between his vocal phrases which kept the tension high. "Rock," an uptempo jazz-tinged instrumental, was built around roaring, well-articulated leads and ferociously picked muted strings. His version of B.B. King's "My Own Fault" invoked B.B. in places, as if Rush was paying tribute to King.

Rush's performances were some of the strongest material on the entire Vanguard set, and he won a number of white devotees as a result. Rush followed up by touring Europe in 1966, where he recorded again.

Two white aficionados who knew Rush's style well—and firsthand—were Mike Bloomfield and Nick Gravenites, recently of the Electric Flag. They so admired Otis that they got the bluesman an excellent deal: a contract with their own manager, Albert Grossman (who represented Bob Dylan and Janis Joplin as well) and an advance from Cotillion Records, a subsidiary of Atlantic. Bloomfield and Gravenites took Rush to Muscle Shoals to record, and for the first time the guitarist was making substantial money. But the resulting album, *Mourning in the Morning*, released in 1969, was a classic example of good intentions gone astray. Bloomfield and Gravenites were trying to surround him with a more commercial sound, but Rush, firmly entrenched in his own music, wasn't able to adapt. And overproduction negated the album's real value.

Still, Otis was able to break out of the Chicago club circuit and begin performing at blues festivals and rock halls. In November 1970 Grossman negotiated a lucrative contract with Capitol Records for him. He went into the studios again, with Gravenites producing, and created what must be considered his best album: *Right Place, Wrong Time*. Despite its excellence, however, Capitol wouldn't release it, and it wasn't until the independent Bullfrog label leased the rights and issued it in 1976 that the world finally had the chance to hear Otis Rush right.

This time Gravenites didn't repeat his past mistakes. A band that included a number of San Francisco musicians, including ex-Paul Butterfield keyboard player Mark Naftalin on piano, played well-rehearsed arrangements behind Otis. The selection of material was flawless, and the album displayed Rush's true gifts as no other had. Everything—voice, guitar, attitude—were firmly in place. Throughout the album, Rush sang and played like a man possessed, spinning out twisting, complex guitar riffs with ease. His singing on "Right Place" was forceful and impassioned. The arrangements were true to his style, which, when competently engineered,

sounded as contemporary as anything else then being issued.

Rush's guitar was prominent on instrumentals like "Easy Go," where his extended improvisations showed how deep a guitarist he'd become. And even "Rainy Night in Georgia," a song substantially different from his conventional style, became quite respectable, largely because of Otis' singing. He played all over the guitar's neck on "Natural Ball," slurring up and down and invoking that voicelike vibrato. The final track, "Take a Look Behind," a song of regret and guilt, delivered still more outstanding guitar work. *Right Place, Wrong Time* remains Rush's finest moments on record.

Through the early '70s he remained on the road, recording again for the French Black and Blue label in '74, and touring Japan in '75, where some decent live recordings were produced and released on the Delmark label in America as *So Many Roads*. Throughout the '70s Otis used pickup bands of whatever musicians he could get in the towns where he performed. He has been somewhat inconsistent in recent years, depending on his moods—he is an intensely private and somewhat suspicious person—and the quality of his backup. He's done no recording in recent years, and one guesses that his lack of financial rewards despite his general acclaim have profoundly frustrated him.

But Otis Rush is still a relatively young bluesman, and now that the blues has become a better organized industry (albeit a modest one when compared to the rest of the pop music business), one hopes that there is still a chance for his magnificent, intense voice and guitar to achieve the broad acceptance it deserves. It is difficult to imagine him doing movie soundtracks à la B.B. King, but Rush's modern approach had much to do with the revitalization of Chicago blues by younger performers like Lurrie Bell and Son Seals. As a pioneer who is still a dynamic artist, Otis deserves better. Whether he will ever get it is something to ponder.

DISCOGRAPHY

Rush's earliest Cobra recordings, including some alternate takes, can be heard on *Groaning The Blues* (Flyright). Added alternate takes, as well as some by Magic/Sam are on *The Other Takes* (Flyright). Both are British imports. The incredible *Right Place, Wrong Time* (Bullfrog), his crowning effort, is also still available. *So Many Roads* (Delmark) is adequate, while *Cold Day in Hell* (Delmark) shows him in less than perfect circumstances.

T-BONE WALKER

The advent of electric amplification during the 1940s opened up new vistas to the blues guitarist. For strictly practical purposes, it increased volume so the guitar could be heard over noisy crowds in clubs. When played in a larger band, the guitar could project over the horns and rhythm section. But amplification also made possible an entirely new approach. Because of the expanded tonal capabilities, a guitarist could phrase like a trumpeter or a saxophonist, playing with authority and creativity unheard of before. A guitarist could use the wonders of electric amplification to augment and enhance his playing.

T-Bone Walker was the first blues guitarist to exploit those possibilities; he set the precedents for virtually everything that happened in modern blues guitar after him. He created a sharp, lyrical single-string guitar style unlike anything else at the time. Along with Floyd Smith, Eddie Durham and Charlie Christian, Walker was undoubtedly one of the pioneer electric guitarists in America.

And so, Walker was an important bridge between the earlier single-string guitar styles of Lonnie Johnson and Scrapper Blackwell and the smooth, urban blues guitar of B.B. King, Albert King, Freddy King, Pee Wee Crayton, Lowell Fulson, Gatemouth Brown and everyone who followed in their footsteps. Without T-Bone Walker the face of postwar blues guitar would have been very different. He was the fountainhead, the founder of an entire school of blues guitar.

Even today, when a new generation of blues guitarists (including Son Seals and Luther Allison) are rising, T-Bone's playing remains the foundation of what they do. Their rhythms are more modern, yet what comes from their guitars still has the flavor of adventure Walker pioneered nearly half a century ago. And the current masters of the idiom—B.B. and Albert King as well as Otis Rush and Lowell Fulson—have all drawn deeply from Walker's music.

Moreover, T-Bone Walker set the stage for much of what later happened in rock music. Long before Jimi Hendrix was born, Walker was the archetypal electric guitar showman.

His stage act was unbelievably wild for the period. He played the guitar behind his back; he did the "splits" and played behind his back simultaneously; he flipped his Gibson electric out in front of him face up, as if he was playing a dobro or steel guitar. It's not unlikely that Hendrix himself, a sideman on the r&b club circuit during the early '60s, was directly inspired by Walker's antics.

Of course, the entire guitar style he pioneered was at the basis of the blues-influenced rock guitar styles of the 1960s. Several major rock guitarists were inveterate T-Bone fans. Steve Miller, for example, the son of a physician, had the advantage of learning from Walker himself when T-Bone was a patient of his father's. Chuck Berry, Johnny Winter, Doug Sahm, Michael Bloomfield, Eric Clapton, Peter Green, Mick Taylor, Jeff Beck and Jimmy Page are but a few of the rock guitarists who took some inspiration from him.

One can hear the roots of earlier players in Walker's playing style, particularly those of Lonnie Johnson and Scrapper Blackwell (he was particularly taken with the records Blackwell recorded with pianist Leroy Carr in the late '20s and early '30s). Indeed, Johnson and Blackwell's tendency to answer each stanza of a song with a guitar figure became an integral part of Walker's style on vocals, exclusive of his soloing.

But Walker was ultimately his own man. He played far more rhythmically than Johnson, bearing down on each note with his pick. He built a solo, a concept Johnson had perfected, each of his choruses picking up in volume and emotional intensity. Occasionally he would go into doubletime when he soloed, increasing the excitement still further. At times, with the volume up, he would fret notes with his left hand alone (something Hendrix also learned to do). The thick tone Walker used had a sharper edge than Charlie Christian's, most likely due to the difference in Walker's pick attack and touch.

Aaron Thibeaux Walker was born May 28, 1910 in Linden, Texas. His parents, Rance and Movelia Walker, both played music. When Aaron was just two the Walkers moved to Dallas. Aaron's interest in music came early. Marco Washington, his stepfather, sang with him at local root beer stands around town. When he was about age ten he became close to a friend of his family, the legendary blues singer Blind Lemon Jefferson. For a time Aaron was his lead boy, guiding Jefferson around the streets of Dallas while he played and sang. By the time Aaron was thirteen he was beginning to play guitar locally, and at fifteen he became a performer with the Breeding Medicine Show around Texas. He also continued working on the streets with his stepfather.

By the late 1920s, the recordings of Leroy Carr and Scrapper Blackwell and Lonnie Johnson were readily available in Texas, and Aaron began taking ideas from them, building his own style. By the end of the decade he'd become so well-known that a Columbia Records team recorded him. On December 5, 1929, he waxed "Wichita Falls Blues" and "Trinity River Blues," both of which were issued under the pseudonym "Oak Cliff T-Bone," the "T-Bone" coming from a play on his middle name of Thibeaux. "Wichita Falls Blues" is not an awe-inspiring record. It presents a talented young man, singing and playing much like his heroes, who had yet to completely develop his own ideas. His voice is more audible than his guitar, but his playing has obvious references to Johnson and Blackwell. Sales weren't impressive, and T-Bone would not record for the label again.

Still, he was making progress. He won first prize at a Dallas amateur show sponsored by bandleader Cab Calloway in 1930, and appeared briefly with Calloway's orchestra around Dallas. He spent the next several years working with a host of bands, most of them obscure, though he performed in Texas once with the legendary blues vocalist Ma Rainey. Among the bands he spent time with was the Dallas-based Lawson Brooks Orchestra. When he moved to Los Angeles in 1934, T-Bone turned the guitarist's chair over to Charlie Christian, then a teenager.

By 1935 Walker was leading small groups in L.A. clubs, and here we run into one of those disputes, perhaps unresolvable, regarding Walker's use of an electric guitar. Electric steel guitars had been available since 1931. However, Gibson did not introduce its famous ES-150 until 1936. Walker always insisted that he was the first to play an electric guitar, in 1935.

It is not impossible that Walker used some sort of makeshift amplification system. A company known as Volu-Tone was making an electric pickup and amplifier by '35. In fact, steel guitarist Bob Dunn of the seminal western swing band Milton Brown and his Musical Brownies was using such a set-up then having attached it to a Martin guitar. It is possible that Walker, too had a Volu-Tone set up of some sort, so his insistence that he was playing electric before Charlie Christian is quite plausible, if questionable. But because he didn't record again until 1939, it is difficult to pin down when he first plugged in.

In 1939 T-Bone made a move that would spread his reputation around the country when he joined Les Hite's Los Angeles-based Cotton Club Orchestra in 1939. He became a featured part of the Hite organization. The band also had another fine guitarist in Frank Paseley, but it was T-Bone who managed to steal the show with his onstage flamboyance. He'd joined the Hite band on a visit to Dallas, and became an integral part of their stage show. In 1940, he recorded his first significant recording for the Varsity label with the Hite Band: "T-Bone Blues." The recording was a huge success, and in 1941 T-Bone struck out on his own.

Still working out of Los Angeles, he formed his own groups, touring and working locally as well in places like the Little Harlem Club in Los Angeles when he wasn't on the road. In 1942 he began recording for Capitol, doing his first session in July 1942 as part of a band led by boogie-woogie pianist Freddie Slack. "I Got A Break, Baby" opens with a lengthy guitar solo, fluent and enthralling. T-Bone begins with single-string passages, moving to a hard, rhythmic chord passage before leading into the vocal with more single-string work, tagging perceptive little phrases onto the end of his vocal lines, some of them briefly doubling the tempo.

Likewise, "Mean Old World," recorded at the same session, begins with a descending chord passage before moving into cleanly articulated soloing, at one point sounding hauntingly like those Scrapper Blackwell played on his records with Leroy Carr. His vocals on this session, fraught with tension, place him among the finest blues singers of the time, his brilliant guitar work notwithstanding.

That same year, 1942, T-Bone began working at the Rhumboogie Club in Chicago, playing with Billy Eckstine and other major names in jazz. By 1945 a record label had been spawned by the club's success, and in May, T-Bone recorded for the label, backed by the Marl Young Orchestra. His guitar was in fine form for these tracks. He played a stinging solo on "Sail On Boogie." "I'm Still In Love with You," a ballad, clearly shows the vocal influence of Billy Eckstine (also engaged by the Rhumboogie); Walker played a wonderfully fluent solo with hard, driving chord punctuations on the track. "T-Bone Boogie" was a superb boogie, built upon his guitar and the shouted lyrics of countless old blues numbers. He played a stabbing solo, getting into the sort of riff-oriented groove, with the band answering him, that one would have associated with Count Basie. He sang a deep, dark, minor-keyed version of the classic "Evening" with a solo to match. He skillfully doubletimes the opening of "You Don't Love Me Blues" before returning to the medium tempo. He also doubletimes his solo break, the band falling in behind him before reverting to the original pace.

T-Bone was back in Hollywood in 1946, recording for the Black & White label. Among his more interesting tracks were the witty "Bobby Sox Blues." In mid 1947 he did a superb session, featuring "I Know Your Wig Is Gone," with a raffish, jivey opening break that has him playing in unison with the small band. With the sassy trumpet of Teddy Buckner and Lloyd Glenn's flawless piano backing him, T-Bone produced not only the rocking, explosive instrumental "T-Bone Jumps Again," but also "Call It Stormy Monday," his most enduring song.

"Stormy Monday" is a carefully paced number. Surprisingly, his guitar doesn't open it; after a brief horn figure T-Bone goes right into the vocal, playing chords and brief single-string figures behind himself for effect. His vocal is up front, and his guitar break is superbly controlled; every note is perfectly placed—no doubletiming or other effects here. It is a classic performance, more than 35 years after it was recorded. The song became an enormous hit, bringing Walker the fame he'd deserved. Sadly, he wasn't able to realize a great profit at first due to a snafu over the composer royalties (it was a Walker original).

"Stormy Monday" made T-Bone the dominant blues singer/guitarist of the time. In November 1947 he documented some other fine materials including "That's Better for Me," which featured guitar phrases that later showed up in the playing of Chuck Berry. At that series of sessions he also recorded the classic "T-Bone Shuffle," one of his best-known numbers after "Stormy Monday." He stayed with the Black & White label for the remainder of the decade, turning out consistently high quality music, most of it in the groove with which he felt most comfortable, with occasional departures such as the Eckstine-esque "Don't Give Me the Runaround."

By 1950 Walker had stepped up from Black & White to the larger Imperial label. With a far larger concern now behind him, he commenced a five year association that yielded 56 recordings, none of them smash hits but all reflecting excellent production, top-flight vocals and, of course, plenty of outstanding guitar, (such as his smooth, flowing work on the 1950 "I Walked Away"). He did some recording in 1953 with the excellent New Orleans r&b band led by trumpeter Dave Bartholomew that included many of the same musicians who backed Fats Domino.

By 1955, with over 20 years of near non-stop traveling under his belt, T-Bone's health was giving out. Severe ulcers necessitated a major operation during which a substantial part of his stomach was removed. It was around this same time (probably just before his illness) that Walker began a contract with Atlantic Records that would last from 1955 to 1959. Subsequent Chicago sessions included

blues harmonica master Junior Wells, while his L.A. sessions included Barney Kessel, jazz guitarist and one of the area's top studio men. Much of this material was included on the outstanding 1975 Atlantic package *T-Bone Blues*, one of his last truly excellent albums.

He stayed on the road, playing to increasingly older audiences, through the '50s and into the '60s. Like B.B. King, T-Bone's fans were still there, but younger blacks were gravitating to the newer forms of rhythm and blues. He continued to record intermittently, but the records weren't strong sellers. In the late sixties he joined ABC's BluesWay label, where he recorded *Stormy Monday Blues* and *Funky Town*, two respectable, if overly slick, records.

But he found new audiences among the young whites who'd come to the blues through Bloomfield, Clapton, Winter and even Hendrix. Walker began playing rock halls and the popular blues festivals of the late '60s. L.A. rhythm and blues bandleader/promoter/preservationist Johnny Otis featured him extensively with his touring revue in the early '70s, and Walker worked often in Europe as well. He continued recording, doing sessions for labels like BluesTime, Reprise and Polydor, though it became clear by the early '70s that his health was increasingly precarious. His ulcer problem flared up again, and he was often in considerable pain onstage.

In 1974 he entered a Los Angeles hospital, and on December 31 he suffered a stroke. He died on March 16, 1975, of bronchial pneumonia. He was buried in Inglewood, California. A memorial concert was held in Los Angeles later that year.

It's sad that T-Bone Walker died when interest in the electric guitar blues he founded was burgeoning. He did, however, live long enough to see that interest grew through the mass acclaim B.B. King received from the late '60s on. And B.B. has never hesitated to credit Walker as a major source of inspiration. Like Charlie Christian, Walker was an original, and as long as electric guitarists play the blues, T-Bone's music will live on.

DISCOGRAPHY

There is much fine T-Bone Walker material on the market right now. His first recording, as well as many of his rare 1940s singles, are available on *The Inventory of Electric Guitar Blues* (Blues Boy). Many of the Black & White and Capitol sides on which his reputation is based are included on two albums: *T-Bone Jumps Again* and *The Natural Blues* (Charly). From his Imperial period comes the two-LP *T-Bone Walker* (Blue Note). French Atlantic has reissued the fantastic *T-Bone Blues*, while *Well Done* (Home Cooking) includes later '60s recordings.

SECONDARY ESSAYS

Albert Collins

Primarily a guitarist as opposed to singer/guitarists like B.B. King and T-Bone Walker, Albert Collins is a member of the Texas school exemplified by Clarence "Gatemouth" Brown, (though certainly King and Walker were also influences). Collins is best known for his snapping, hard-driving instrumentals, such as "Sno-Cone" and "The Freeze," which feature a biting, lean picking technique and masterful string-bending, earning him a reputation among both blues fans and rock guitarists. One of his disciples is J. Geils of the J. Geils Band, which recorded two Collins instrumentals on the band's first Atlantic album in 1971.

Born in Leona, Texas on October 3, 1932, Collins grew up in Houston, where he studied piano and guitar in school. He listened extensively to blues, particularly to Gatemouth Brown and T-Bone Walker, as well as Lightnin' Hopkins, and by the time he was 16, he was already starting to play bars in the area. In 1949 he formed his own band, the Rhythm Rockers, and hit the Houston club circuit. By 1952 or 1953 he was playing a Fender Es-

quire (a single-pickup Telecaster), beginning an association with Fender that continues to this day. He went on to record his first instrumental, "The Freeze," for the Kangaroo label in 1958. He had another major hit in 1962 with "Frosty."

Interaction with other musicians helped shape Collins' style, particularly his jamming with guitarists like Albert King on the road. But Collins did not come to the attention of mass audiences until the late Bob Hite, lead singer of Canned Heat and a formidable blues authority, brought him to Los Angeles and helped him get a contract with Imperial Records in 1968. He recorded three albums for the label, all respectable, then moved on to the Tumbleweed label in 1971. He didn't record for several years after that, concentrating on touring. In 1978, he cut what still remains his finest album: *Ice Pickin'*, on Bruce Iglauer's Chicago-based Alligator Records; several other fine albums for the label have followed.

Like Albert King and Freddy King, Collins relies little on the standard flatpick. He primarily uses the flesh of his fingers to play, no flatpick, as does Albert; like Freddy, Collins does his picking with his thumb and index finger, which helps him achieve his biting tone. He also relies on stage showmanship to put his music across. Yet there is much substance in his playing, and though his earliest work isn't available, the quality of his material that is—particularly on Alligator—is enough to more than uphold his reputation.

DISCOGRAPHY
Albert Collins' records are generally available, particularly his late '60s and '70s albums. But

his early, reputation-making sides from 1962-63 are now available on *Frosty* (Brylen). Among the strongest examples are *Albert "Blues" Collins* (Japanese Imperial), an anthology of his work for Imperial Records. Five sets on the Chicago-based Alligator label, *Ice Pickin', Frostbite, Frozen Alive!, Don't Lose Your Cool,* and *Albert Collins and the Icebreakers Live in Japan* all spotlight his talents well.

Blind Boy Fuller

Blind Boy Fuller, one of a Southeastern school of blues men, had a vigorous, lusty guitar style clearly influenced by the ragtime of Blind Blake. But unlike Blake, whose music and guitar work had a light touch, Fuller tore the notes from his resonator guitar, fingerpicking in a hard-edged, rocking style that complemented his vibrant vocals. His music was strongly oriented toward dancers, but his effervescent personality came through on record as well.

Born Fulton Allen in Wadesboro, North Carolina, he began losing his sight in 1926, when he was just 18. By the time he was 20 he was totally blind. His earliest influence aside from Blake was Gary Davis (later the Reverend Gary Davis), a highly regarded singer-guitarist who had a profound impact on the entire North Carolina generation of blues artists. Fuller wandered around North Carolina, singing on the streets through the '30s, and was discovered by the American Recording Company in that decade. He recorded a

number of outstanding songs for the label, and his reputation in the region became considerable. Most of his tunes swung like mad, and his playing even rubbed off on white musicians who heard him (his song "Step It Up and Go" is still in the repertoire of some bluegrass groups).

Fuller might have had a long career, but kidney problems developed in 1940. He managed one final trip to Chicago to record, returning to Durham, North Carolina where he had an operation. It seemed he would recover, but blood poisoning set in. He died on February 13, 1941.

DISCOGRAPHY
Blind Boy Fuller recorded so prolifically that there are numerous reissues available, including *Blind Boy Fuller: 1935-1940)* (Blues Classics), *Death Valley Blues* (Oldie Blues), *Truckin' My Blues Away* (Yazoo), *Shake Your Shimmy* and *Blind Boy Fuller on Down* (Magpie).

Mississippi John Hurt

Mississippi John Hurt was a unique blues artist for a number of reasons. He was not a delta-based stylist and his music was far more complex and gentle than that of delta legends like Charley Patton. Indeed, his music had little to do with the formalized blues, but was rooted in the pre-blues traditions of the nineteenth century. He played guitar in a complex, fingerpicking style rich in its sound and very likely a predecessor of what later came to be known as "Travis picking." He also cited Jimmie Rodgers as an influence.

Ironically, unlike many of the delta bluesmen, Hurt's greatest impact was made after he was rediscovered in 1963. Where some rediscovered bluesmen were in poor health or otherwise unable to effectively recreate their earlier music, Hurt played as well as he had when he first recorded in the 1920's. His fingerpicking style was heard by many people, as he toured the country's folk music venues in the early to mid '60s, and had an impact on a number of folk artists, including John Sebastian of the Lovin' Spoonful.

John Smith Hurt was born July 3, 1893 in Teoc, Mississippi and moved with his family to Avalon, Mississippi in 1895. He taught himself guitar when he was about ten, and became popular in the area near Jackson, southeast of the delta. He was not a fulltime performer, and had settled into a farming life, playing music on the side, when he was discovered by representatives of the OKeh label in 1928. He recorded a number of pleasant traditional ballads, such as "Stack-O-Lee" for the label, then faded back into farming until his rediscovery. The excellence of his music and his playing were virtually untouched despite his age (70 at the time he resumed performing), and he recorded extensively, first for the Virginia-based Piedmont label, then several outstanding albums for Vanguard, and for the Library of Congress. He continued to perform until November, 1966 when he died of a heart attack.

DISCOGRAPHY
Mississippi John Hurt's original 1928 recordings have been reissued on *1928 Sessions* (Yazoo). His later sides, done after his rediscovery in the early '60s, can be heard on *Monday Morning Blues* (Flyright), *Today, The Immortal Mississippi John Hurt, The Best of Mississippi John Hurt* and *Last Sessions* (all on Vanguard).

Willie Lee Johnson

Distortion in electric guitar playing has a heritage that goes back far before James Burton's playing on "Susie Q" or Paul Burlison's work with Johnny Burnette and the Rock and Roll Trio in the '50s. Junior Barnard had been using it in the '40s with Johnnie Lee Wills and Bob Wills' Texas Playboys. And in the blues, Willie Lee Johnson pioneered distortion as a member of Howlin' Wolf's Memphis band.

The ferocity and power of Willie Johnson's playing came through most clearly on the recordings he did in the early '50s with Howlin' Wolf at Sam Phillips' Sun studio, in Memphis, Tennessee. Wolf was just beginning his recording career at the time and Johnson's rasping guitar, made so by an amp that sounded like it had a blown speaker, was the perfect foil for Wolf's raw, gravelly voice. As a guitarist, Johnson had his share of technical limitations, but was nonetheless capable of harsh, swooping solo lines, the primal fury of his sound more than compensating for his weak points.

Willie Lee Johnson was born March 4, 1923 in Senatobia, Mississippi, and began playing guitar at local parties in the area before joining Wolf's band in 1941. He worked around Memphis in combos through the '40s and from 1949 on was a regular part of the Wolf gang. His guitar, obviously distorted, came through loud and clear on such early Wolf favorites as "Moanin' at Midnight" (1950) and "House Rockin' Boogie" (on which Wolf exhorts *"Play that git-tar, Willie Johnson, 'til it smoke!"*) which features extended Johnson solo breaks alternated with raw power chords. In fact, Robert Palmer's superb book *Deep Blues* points out that Burlison was working at KWEM in West Memphis, Arkansas at the same time Wolf was leading his combos, and though he has always insisted that a bad tube in his amp created his sound, it's difficult to imagine that the guitar work of Willie Johnson was not also on his mind.

Johnson remained in Memphis when Wolf went north to Chicago, and for a time led his own combo in Memphis. He cut one session for Sam Phillips in 1952 as a sideman with pianist-singer Albert Williams, that includes his guitar so distorted it's almost saxophone-like on four numbers, including a remake of Robert Johnson's (no relation) "Sweet Home Chicago," with a mouthwatering solo. In 1955 Willie Lee and harp player Sammy Lewis recorded their own session for Sun that showed Johnson to be a respectable vocalist and as formidable a guitarist as ever. Shortly after that, he followed Wolf to Chicago. They renewed their musical relationship there for a time, and Johnson worked professionally until the early '70s. Since then he has apparently been inactive in music.

DISCOGRAPHY

The essential Willie Johnson recordings with Howlin' Wolf are available on *Ridin' in the Moonlight* (Ace) and *Legendary Sun Performers* (Charly). Johnson's "So Long Baby, Goodbye" with Sammy Lewis and "Sweet Home Chicago" with Albert Williams are both on *The Sun Box* (Charly), an anthology on Sun Records' country, blues, and rockabilly recordings.

Muddy Waters

In addition to being among the greatest—if not the greatest—force in the post-war Chicago blues scene, Muddy Waters was always known both for his awesome, powerful voice and for his clear, delta-based electric slide guitar. The majesty of his music made him the most honored name in Chicago blues, a major figure in the development of rock and roll, and a legend long before his death of heart failure in 1983.

More than any other individual, Muddy successfully brought the delta guitar style into the urban world, switching from acoustic to electric guitar in 1944, the year after he'd arrived in Chicago. Still more importantly, he was the catalyst for the entire "band" sound of the post-war Chicago blues, evolving from mere solo guitar to guitar with bass, then to guitar with bass, harmonica, second guitar, piano and drums. In the process Muddy set the style for the entire south side scene. His early bands boasted the finest bluesmen of the day, including guitarist Jimmy Rogers, harp player Little Walter Jacobs and drummer/vocalist Baby Face Leroy Foster. Later on such legends as pianist Otis Spann, harp players Jimmy Cotton and Walter Horton, and guitarist Pat Hare were key members.

McKinley Morganfield was born in Rolling Fork, Mississippi April 4, 1915. He obtained his famous nickname early in life, a reference to his habit of playing at a creek near the house. He became interested in music early, too, and in the time-honored delta tradition, built himself a guitar when he was 17, entranced by such delta guitar legends as Son House and Robert Johnson.

As Muddy matured he alternated between driving a tractor and running a "juke house," selling moonshine, running gambling games, and selling food. He did his first recordings in 1941 for the Library of Congress, and made more in 1942. In 1943 he moved north to Chicago, and, under the sponsorship of the great bluesman Big Bill Broonzy, began working clubs. After some abortive sessions for Columbia, he attracted the interest of the Chess brothers, who owned the local Aristocrat label. Though they were initially skeptical of him, when they issued "I Can't Be Satisfied" in 1948 they had a hit, and Muddy's musical career was formally launched.

Over the next decade came an awesome collection of material, from the apocalyptic "Rolling Stone," to "Rollin' and Tumblin'," including his voice-like, cutting slide solo on "Screamin' and Cryin'," "Louisiana Blues," "Long Distance Ca," a tension-filled, dramatic "Honey Bee," "Hoochie Koochie Man," "I Just Want to Make Love to You" and countless others. All of these songs became associated with Muddy, and his guitar pierced, teased and directed most of his greatest hits. There were periods when he played less than he sang, and his electric sound initially caused consternation when he played England in 1958 (the British expected acoustic "folk blues"). But when the blues revival arrived in both England and America in the '60s, and young rock artists freely credited Waters, his stature increased. He was not always well served by record producers during that time, however.

It was a disciple, Texas blues-rock guitar virtuoso Johnny Winter, who revived Muddy's musical career, taking him back to his roots on four superb albums for the Blue Sky label that proved him as dynamic as ever. Muddy Waters died of heart failure on April 30, 1983.

DISCOGRAPHY
A variety of Muddy Waters material has been available for many years, particularly after the blues revival of the '60s created a sustaining audience for his music. His earliest material for the Library of Congress had been issued on *Down on Stovall's Plantation* (Testament). The most essential Chess recordings are on *Rolling Stone* (Chess). Some obscure and previously unreleased material emerged on the 1985 Chess LP *Rare Unissued*. But there are far more Waters recordings available on American and European labels. Among them are *Back in the Early Days* and *Good News* (Syndicate Chapter), and *The Real Folk Blues, More Real Folk Blues* and *Fathers and Sons* (the latter with backing by Mike Bloomfield, among others), all French Chess. Of his later recordings, *I'm Ready, Muddy "Mississippi" Waters Live* and *Hard Again* (Columbia/Blue Sky), feature excellent music, produced by longtime Waters fan Johnny Winter.

COUNTRY MUSIC

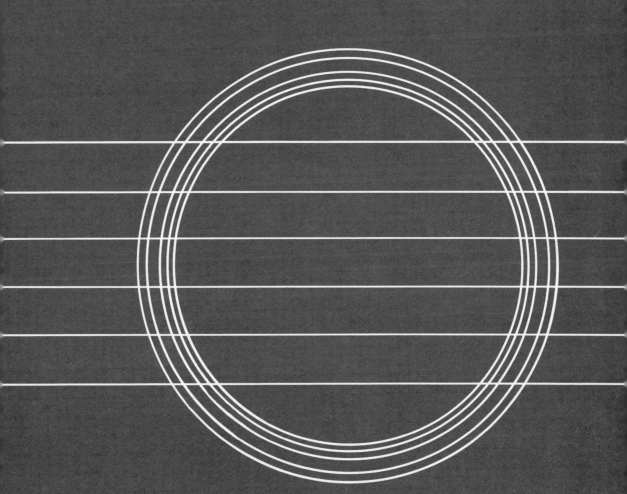

EARLY COUNTRY GUITARISTS

As late as the first decade of this century guitars were a rarity among country musicians, most of whom preferred banjos, fiddles and mandolins. That began changing for a number of reasons. The advent of mail order catalogues made inexpensive, mass-produced guitars more readily available than before. And despite the racism and segregation of that period, many white musicians—even in the rural south—listened to black rural musicians and picked up their ideas (and vice versa; there were many excellent black fiddlers who played square dances and other "white" music). As blacks began embracing the guitar in the early 1900s, its value wasn't lost on whites, who began copying black guitar styles. But in its earliest incarnation as a country music instrument, the guitar was primarily used to provide rhythm accompaniment to other stringed instruments or to the voice.

However, a number of players chose their own approaches. The black influence on some was particularly profound in some cases, less so in others. This group of guitarists was not satisfied to simply strum chords, but experimented with solos, picking styles, or at the very least, accompaniment techniques that reflected individuality. Some of these musicians became legends; others recorded very little and remain obscure. Some abandoned music after a few years, while others continued performing until they died.

Three guitarists in particular left their imprint on the guitar in the early days of commercial country music, inspiring other musicians and spawning playing styles that, despite decades of change, have never fallen out of favor and probably never will. The three are Sam McGee, Jimmie Rodgers and Maybelle Carter.

SAM McGEE

McGee, who achieved most of his exposure as a veteran member of the Grand Ole Opry, was one of the first major fingerpicking guitarists to emerge in the 1920s. Though his impact was never on a scale of that of Merle Travis, McGee created a complex and entertaining ragtime-derived guitar style, drawing heavily on black guitarists for inspiration.

Born south of Nashville in Williamson County, Tennessee on May 1, 1894, McGee came from a musical family; his father was an old-time fiddler. A number of his uncles also fiddled, and impromptu jam sessions were common-place. Sam began picking a banjo around 1904, at a time his brother Kirk was beginning to show an interest in music as well. By 1910 Sam was interested in the guitar, and as he told his biographer Charles Wolfe, "The guitar was not a common instrument when I first started playing it...Really, it seemed like more Negroes [were] playing it than whites."

So it was from black musicians that he got his inspiration. Among them were the Stewart brothers, two black laborers, and another excellent black guitarist named Jam Sapp. One

white man, Tom Hood, taught Sam both chords and songs.

McGee learned other techniques from blacks, including the use of a slide, or bottleneck. The picking technique most associated with McGee, however, is a ragtimey fingerpicking style utilizing the index and middle finger and a single thumbpick as well. It permitted him to create music that flowed from the guitar in a spritely, relaxed manner. But playing remained for him a sideline. In 1922 McGee began working as a blacksmith, a profession he continued until he met the legendary country entertainer, banjoist/vocalist Uncle Dave Macon, in 1925.

He abandoned blacksmithing to tour with Macon, working vaudeville shows throughout the South. Macon, an ebullient, effervescent entertainer, featured Sam prominently in his act. In 1926 Macon and McGee began performing on the WSM Barn Dance. That same year he began recording with Macon, recording three instrumentals and two vocals. Among the instrumentals was his classic "Buckdancer's Choice." In 1927 Kirk

McGee, now an accomplished fiddler, began working with Sam and Uncle Dave. Sam and Kirk recorded together. In 1931 Sam and Uncle Dave split, and, still a part of the Opry, the McGees formed the Dixieliners with fiddler Arthur Smith. The Dixieliners were enormously popular on the Opry until they broke up in 1938, after which Sam and Kirk continued as a team.

The pair did numerous recordings with the Dixieliners, though Sam recorded his final solo session in 1934. He and Kirk continued on the Opry more or less regularly for the next 37 years. During the late '50s, the folk music revival brought renewed interest to their music, and in 1957 Arthur Smith reunited with Sam and Kirk as the Dixieliners, recorded for the New York-based Folkways label and toured northern cities, playing for folk music fans. In 1961 Sam and Kirk recorded some sides for Starday, the Nashville record label specializing in hard country and blue

grass, and Sam recorded with another veteran Opry group, the Crook Brothers. The Dixieliners reunited to record for Folkways again in 1965, but it wasn't until 1969 that Sam did sessions once more under his own name, recording a superb album, *Grandad of the Country Guitar Pickers*, for the Berkeley, California based Arhoolie label.

Unlike many veteran performers, Sam's abilities and vitality were relatively unimpaired after more than forty years. He continued to be a revered member of the Opry, one of the few remaining links to the show's earliest days. He was one of the first musicians to perform in the show's new home at Opryland in 1974, and did three more LPs worth of material between 1972 and 1975. Finally, still healthy and vigorous at the age of 81, Sam McGee was fatally injured in a 1975 tractor accident at his farm. His brother Kirk continued playing the Opry until his death in 1983.

JIMMIE RODGERS

It may seem odd that Jimmie Rodgers, never a guitar soloist, is listed among a group of great guitarists. He was primarily a guitarist who accompanied his own vocals. Nonetheless, Rodgers' austere guitar style and the way he used it on his recordings played a major role in the guitar's acceptance among country musicians. He inspired an entire school of solo performers, in part because his guitar style, though simple, had amazing durability and appeal.

Rogers influenced scores of performers, among them stars like Gene Autry, Jimmie Davis, Hank Snow, Ernest Tubb and Lefty Frizzell. Using strongly articulated but basic chords, with patterns of ascending and descending bass runs, Jimmie's playing was the perfect complement to his singing; his trademark licks have become classics that still show on records. Listen, for example, to Waylon Jennings' first recording of "Honky Tonk Heroes"; the guitar intro is straight out of Rodgers. Rodgers' biographer, Nolan Porterfield, has written of his playing that "[It] was no more polished than his banjo picking, but

somehow he used the instrument effectively, almost as a natural extension of the lyrics and of the yodel, at once mournful and spritely, that punctuated each verse."

Rodgers, born in Meridian, Mississippi in 1897, was influenced early on by the blues music he heard in the region, much of it played and sung by black railroad workers. By the time he was a teenager he was trying his hand performing in medicine shows, but like his father, he began to work on the railroad, becoming a brakeman. However, Jimmie continued playing music and left the railroad, partly due to his interest in good times, but largely due to the development of the tuberculosis that killed him.

Having suffered one failed marriage, he married again in 1920, and spent a number of years scuffling, occasionally returning to the railroad or taking other work. By 1927 he was performing with a group on an Asheville, North Carolina radio station, and had heard of a recording session to be held in Bristol, on the Tennessee/Virginia border, for which Ralph Peer of the Victor Recording Company was seeking local talent. Rodgers traveled to Bristol. Peer liked Jimmie's playing enough to record him alone, without his backup band. The first recording did modestly well, and a second session in November of 1927 yielded the classic "Blue Yodel #1 (T for Texas)," which became an enormous success and firmly established Rodgers. The song's guitar accompaniment contained many of his elements most imitated, including emphatic bass notes and hard-edged chords.

It may have been the simplicity of Rodgers' guitar work that made it so attractive and influential. It was certainly easy enough, in most cases, to emulate. In fact, many of his famous "Blue Yodels" were similar in their musical structure. It mattered not. Soon there were Jimmie Rodgers clones playing guitar as he did and attempting, with varying degrees of success, to emulate his singing.

For the next five years, through bouts of sickness, wealth and—towards the end of his life—relative poverty resulting from overspending, Rodgers continued performing and recording, often using fine guitarists like Slim Bryant or Billy Burkes on his sessions. He was well aware of the inevitable outcome of his illness; by the time of his final sessions in New York in May 1933, TB had so severely sapped Jimmie's strength that he could only sing, and studio guitarists were employed. Jimmie Rodgers died in the Taft Hotel in New York City on May 26, 1933.

MAYBELLE CARTER

Maybelle Carter, like Jimmie Rodgers, largely played guitar as accompaniment to vocals. However, her style has always attracted far more attention than Rodgers', in part because it became an integral part of folk music. The folk music boom of the late '50s and early '60s, along with her appearances at the Newport Folk festivals, brought her an urban audience who clearly understood her contributions. And she picked her old Gibson L-5, until arthritis forced her to lay it down.

Maybelle Addington was born in Nickelsville, in the mountains of rural western Virginia, on May 10, 1909. She began playing and singing at an early age, and was recognized as a sort of prodigy by her family and friends. In 1926, she married Ezra J. Carter, brother of A.P. Carter and husband of Sara Carter. Though A.P. and Sara had been offered a recording contract some time before the wedding, Maybelle's addition to the duo seemed to catalyze their sound. Though she started out with a round-hole Gibson guitar, she later paid $125 for one of Gibson's finest archtop guitars, the L-5 (the same instrument

being played by jazz legend Eddie Lang). It was an anomaly among rural performers to use such a high-quality instrument. Aside from those who had Martins, few rural performers employed such expensive and elaborate instruments. Maybelle's purchase was indicative of her serious approach to music.

Few other acts had anything as distinctive as Maybelle's guitar playing, either. In some ways it was like the Merle Travis style turned inside out. The melody was played on the bass strings while the index finger brushed the treble strings to create a strong, steady rhythm and partial chords. She used a thumbpick and two steel finger picks, according to her son-in-law Johnny Cash.

Remarkably, the Carters adapted their songs to fit Maybelle's playing, which became the keystone of their style, determining the arrangements of songs, and always at the center holding songs together during their vocals. Their tempos were rock-steady because of her playing. Their classic 1928 recording of "Wildwood Flower" is the single song that best defines Maybelle's playing.

Among the major performers who drew upon Maybelle's influence throughout the years were Hank Garland, Joe Maphis, Doc Watson and Woody Guthrie, who even appropriated melodies of Carter Family numbers such as "John Hardy," which he used for his classic Dust Bowl ballad "Tom Joad." Guthrie also lifted plenty of licks from Maybelle, as did other folk performers.

The Carters continued to perform together, despite A.P. and Sara's 1939 divorce, into the early 1940s. They recorded for Decca with superb guitar from Maybelle, and worked throughout the south, moving to Del Rio, Texas where they broadcast over the megawatt "X" stations, which used high-powered transmitters that far exceeded the U.S. power limits (the transmitters themselves were located across the border in Mexico).

Maybelle's daughters Helen, Anita and June had joined the act in 1939, but after 1943 the original Carter Family split up. A.P. returned to the Carter's ancestral home in Maces Spring, Virginia, and Sara moved to California with her second husband. Maybelle, however, continued the act with her daughters into the '70s, though Anita and June Carter also pursued solo recording careers, and Maybelle herself occasionally worked solo and sporadically retired to be with her husband and work as a practical nurse. The folk boom revitalized her career. She appeared at the Newport Folk Festival in 1963 and reunited with Sara at the 1967 Newport festival; that same year they recorded for Columbia, and Maybelle worked on the Opry. By 1969, Maybelle, Anita and Helen were working closely with Johnny Cash, who had married June in 1967. They performed on the road with him, and they worked on his ABC variety show, as well.

Maybelle's renewed exposure was further enhanced when the original Carter Family was voted into the Country Music Hall of Fame in 1970. Maybelle continued working on Cash's show, and involved herself in the Nitty Gritty Dirt Band's *Will the Circle Be Unbroken* project in the summer of 1971. She remained prominent, though arthritis in her hands eventually confined her to playing autoharp.

Maybelle Carter died on October 23, 1978; her brother-in-law, A.P. had died in 1960 and Sara died a year after Maybelle. Though it sounds horribly cliched, the Carter Family's—and Maybelle's—legacy remains strong. Its impact on folk music, bluegrass and even mainstream country music has never ended. It is doubtful it ever will.

Other guitarists made lesser contributions to the development of early country guitar styles. Riley Puckett has been described extensively in a variety of publications as a bluegrass guitar innovator. Born in 1894 in Georgia, he was accidently blinded at the age of three months and after learning banjo went on to learn guitar, working with Clayton McMichen's Hometown Boys and Gid Tanner's Skillet Lickers. Puckett was known for a technique that was nothing if not idiosyncratic, often involving bass runs played in double or quadruple time. But just how valuable Puckett's contributions were is debatable. Interviews with musicians who worked with him reflect a variety of opinions on just how good a guitarist he was, and at times on records he played sloppily. So vague is the information, even on his picking technique (there are differing accounts of just how he played), that it is difficult to assess his overall contributions. Puckett died in 1946.

Many guitarists had impact on the development of country guitar playing during the '20s and '30s, among them some about whom little is known: players like Dick Justice, and Roy Harvey, guitarist with Charlie Poole's North Carolina Ramblers, who used an early version of fingerpicking to record excellent discs with both Leonard Copeland and Jess Johnson. But by and large, it was McGee, Rodgers and Carter who paved the way for every one of the players discussed in subsequent essays.

DISCOGRAPHY

Sam McGee

Three Sam McGee albums, all modern recordings, are available, but regrettably, the great McGee Brothers sides and Sam's solo recordings are largely out of print. *Look Who's Here* (Folkways) features Sam and Kirk with Arthur Smith in a reunion of the Dixieliners. *Milk 'Em in the Morning Blues* (Folkways) is equally fine, and *Grandad of the Country Guitar Pickers* (Arhoolie) includes good solo material, including a remake of his classic "Buckdancer's Choice."

Jimmie Rodgers

Despite his unimpeachable status as the father of country music, surprisingly little of Rodgers' material remains in print (a huge Japanese boxed set of all his recordings was available as an import some years ago). However, all his most essential Victor recordings are available on the following album: *Jimmie Rodgers: A Legendary Performer, Vol. 1,* (RCA).

Maybelle Carter

A variety of Carter Family recordings featuring Maybelle Carter can be found. Along with *The Carter Family: A Legendary Performer, Vol. 1,* featuring their earliest and best-known Victor sides, are *Look!* (Old Time Classics), offering other Victor recordings, and the outstanding *Carter Family on Border Radio* (JEMF), comprising tunes from the band's later years. One notable solo effort is *Mother Maybelle Carter* (Columbia), which concentrates on her singing and playing.

CHET ATKINS

Aside from Les Paul and Jimi Hendrix, no single guitarist had a more profound effect on American culture in the '50s and '60s than Chet Atkins. His appeal transcended categories. Country fans admired his fleet, creative instrumental approach to traditional songs; fans appreciated his smooth, languid versions of hits; jazz fans respected the overtones of Django Reinhardt that he managed to incorporate regardless of the type of tune he played, and classical fans admired his precision and finesse.

More tellingly, Chet was the most visible country guitarist of that period. Record store bins were filled with his albums; the records themselves featured something of quality for everybody regardless of their musical taste. Since he recorded for RCA Victor, one of America's top record companies, and was an acknowledged asset to the company as a producer (and later an executive), Atkins' records got more exposure than those of any other country instrumentalist of the period. Certainly other country guitarists were issuing albums: Merle Travis, Jimmy Bryant, Arthur

"Guitar Boogie" Smith and Grady Martin among them. But most of those sold only to a hardcore country audience.

Atkins' influence, particularly on younger guitarists, was immense, both before and after rock became prominent. Chet, after all, worked on some of Elvis Presley's first RCA hits and produced (and played on) a number of other rockabilly discs for RCA and other labels. Early rock stars like Duane Eddy, Scotty Moore and Eddie Cochran all tried to emulate Chet at one time or another (both Cochran and Eddy played Gretsch Chet Atkins model electrics on many of their hit recordings). Even the Beatles' George Harrison was an Atkins fan. A cursory listen to such Beatles recordings like "She's a Woman" and "I'm a Loser" reveal Atkins' flavor in Harrison's breaks.

Even more importantly, Chet Atkins established true credibility for all country music instrumentalists, making the "hayseed" stereotype obsolete. Certainly he was not the only great country guitarist around, nor the only versatile one. Hank Garland, Jimmy

Bryant, Joe Maphis and Grady Martin all played in a range of contexts, including jazz, pop and rockabilly. But none concentrated their own instrumental recording careers as Chet did, though they often played with equal brilliance. So Chet's recognition factor was the highest. The "Mr. Guitar" moniker that was hung on him sometime in the '50s may have seemed so much public relations hype, but only Les Paul was as celebrated during that time. Even the greatest jazz guitarists—Barney Kessel, Tal Farlow, Johnny Smith and Oscar Moore—were little known to the general public then.

This is not to say that Atkins was consistently brilliant. Indeed, beginning in the '60s his approach became wildly inconsistent: adventurous one moment, bland and safe the next. At his worst Chet can be dull, sometimes infuriatingly so. The controversy about his "Nashville sound" production techniques, adding elements such as strings and vocal choruses borrowed from pop arrangements to country recordings, hasn't yet died down. Atkins, for his part, admitted nearly a decade ago that the trend had gone too far, and apologized for his role in it (something none of the other responsible parties ever had the nerve to do).

Soppy sweetning aside, Atkins' accolades and awards never stopped coming. He's won, at last count, four Grammy awards from the National Academy of Recording Arts and Sciences; for a number of years he won *Cash Box's* award for Outstanding Instrumentalist. He's been nominated for the Country Music Association's Instrumentalist of the Year Award annually since it was instituted in 1967, winning in 1967, '68, '69 and '83; six times he's been nominated for CMA awards for instrumental groups he'd organized and/or participated in between 1967 and '80. Though he doesn't play (and admittedly doesn't understand) modern jazz, he's won the guitar category in *Playboy's* jazz and pop polls four times.

All of these honors belie his beginnings. Chester Burton Atkins was born June 20, 1924 in Luttrell, a tiny whistlestop town in the Clinch Mountains of eastern Tennessee,

twenty miles from Knoxville. His father, James Arley Atkins, was a trained musician who taught piano and voice. His older brother Jimmy left home at 16 to become a professional guitarist.

The Atkins family's existence was hardscrabble at best. They had a small farm, but wanted for many things. However, Chet was able to indulge his interest in music early on, first with a ukelele. The family's fortunes weren't helped when his parents divorced in 1933. Chet remained with his mother, brothers and sisters, and learned to play fiddle. His mother remarried, and her new husband, Willie Strevel, was a blues fan who played a bit of slide guitar and listened to Blind Lemon Jefferson records. Chet traded Strevel two guns for one of his guitars and began learning to play.

His adolescence became even more difficult; by 1935 Chet's problematic asthma had worsened so that he was sent to Columbus, Georgia to live with his father, who also had remarried. The transition was difficult for Chet, but he adapted, and he continued to teach himself guitar, adding a primitive two-tube radio to his learning aids. He took his guitar everywhere he went, having become obsessed with mastering it.

He had some tangible heroes on the instrument by the late '30s. His brother Jim had become a part of the Les Paul Trio, and regularly broadcast as part of Fred Waring's entertainment troupe over NBC from New York. Chet was influenced by Jim and also by Les, who then was beginning experiments that would change the very nature of the electric guitar. Yet he remained undecided about his musical direction until he tuned in his crystal set one night to 50,000 watt WLW radio in Cincinnati and heard the thumb-and-finger guitar picking of Merle Travis, which came as a revelation.

"His guitar style was closer to that sound I had been searching for than anything I had ever heard," wrote Chet in his autobiography. "The clever way he played melody and rhythm at the time knocked me over. I knew he was fingerpicking but I didn't know how he was doing it."

The WLW signal being intermittent in Atkins' area made it tough for him to catch Travis regularly, so he relied on his own devices. Hearing Les Paul and Travis led Chet to amplify his acoustic guitar; after building a crude amplification system, he found he had to drag his setup to wherever there was electricity (often in a school or church). He got his first work from local radio stations in Georgia, and was improving noticeably in his technique.

World War II broke up the Georgia Atkinses and by 1942 Chet, who was rejected from the Army for his asthma, found there was nothing to prevent him from taking a stab at playing professionally. His first job was at WNOX in Knoxville, ironically, playing fiddle behind comedian/vocalists Archie Campbell (later of Hee-Haw fame) and Bill Carlisle. Atkins' guitar abilities were quickly noticed, and he became a fixture at the station. Being around the music library afforded him the opportunity to study other genres, and it was here that the roots of his later eclecticism were sown. He listened to every type of music and instrument he could find, searching for ideas he could apply to the guitar.

His adaptability was the great irony of Atkins' early career. When he worked with a pop band at WNOX some of the musicians denigrated him as a "hillbilly." Conversely, at various times during his radio career he lost jobs for playing music that was "too modern" or "too sophisticated" for the tastes of the hillbilly performers who employed him. In 1945 he moved to WLW, the former stomping ground of his idol Travis (who'd left for California by that time). Here Chet ran into his first rejection, being fired late that year. After a brief interlude in North Carolina, he moved to Chicago in early 1946 and was hired as Red Foley's guitarist, a job which took him to Nashville for the first time. There he made his debut recording under his own name for Bullet Records. "Guitar Blues," a mellow, after-hours number, featured a sophisticated arrangement by pianist Owen Bradley. The influence of Travis was present, but echoes of both Les Paul and George Barnes can be heard as well. The use of a bluesy clarinet anti-cipated Chet's later willingness to work with horns.

He remained with Foley only briefly, then began several years of hopping from radio station to radio station, often losing his job for the reasons described above. It was a frustrating period for Atkins, exacerbated by his knowledge that his musical skills were steadily improving. But a series of transcriptions he did while at KWTO in Springfield, Missouri caught the attention of RCA Victor's Steve Sholes, and on August 11, 1947, Chet had his first Victor recording date in Chicago.

Sholes clearly thought of Chet as a potential competitor for Merle Travis, who was then solidly established as a hit vocalist and increasingly influential guitarist. Chet gamely tried to sing, but never did as well as Travis vocally. His playing, however, was another matter. "Canned Heat," an instrumental solidly in the Travis mold, revealed Chet's intensity equal to Merle's, and his rhythmic drive obviously modeled on Django Reinhardt's.

Atkins' "I've Been Working on the Guitar," recorded in November 1947, was also rooted in the Travis style (it was an adaptation of "I've Been Working on the Railroad") and contained some vigorous interplay between Chet and other players, including his brother Jim on rhythm guitar.

Yet Chet's most exciting early recordings were done with the comedy team of Homer and Jethro; after signing with RCA, he'd returned to WNOX, where the duo was also working. Best known as country song parodists, Henry "Homer" Haynes was also a driving jazz rhythm guitarist and Kenneth "Jethro" Burns an exciting jazz mandolin soloist. When teamed with Atkins their hard-driving, swinging sound was born, blessed by the influence of Django Reinhardt's 1930s recordings.

The Reinhardt flavor was particularly apparent on Chet's 1949 "Galloping on the Guitar," a recording that exhibited his increasing originality, still based on Travis but also bearing the harmonic ideas of Les Paul and Django. No longer dependent upon thumb-and-finger picking alone, Chet now alternated it with skillfully picked single-string leads and slurs, and incorporated Travis' finger rolls into the melody line. Similarly exciting were "Barber Shop Rag" and the furious "Main Street Breakdown," a number of dazzling instrumental interplay between Atkins and Burns, their lightning-fast licks supported by Haynes' unrelenting rhythm.

The popularity of these discs was such that disc jockeys across the country used them as theme songs.

During this period Atkins was working, too, as a featured sideman with Maybelle and the Carter Sisters, the recent incarnation of the venerable Carter Family. He left WNOX with them and moved back to KWTO in Springfield, where they were billed as The Carter Family and Chet Atkins. Their popularity impressed the Grand Ole Opry, which invited them to join the show in spring of 1950. In June Chet moved to Nashville. He'd become Steve Sholes' protege, often supervising or setting up RCA sessions when Sholes himself couldn't do so. Chet was performing on the Opry again, which increased his fame nationwide. He also began working on records by other artists, among them Hank Williams' "I'll Never Get Out of This World Alive."

Meanwhile his own sessions continued, often in New York, where he recorded a fluid version of "Chinatown, My Chinatown" in July 1952 that made incredibly creative use of harmonics, a technique previously employed only by steel guitarists, that involved lightly touching the strings at a given spot to create a "pinging" sound (also known as "chiming"). Still more important was Atkins' 1953 recording of the strutting, antebellum "Country Gentleman," a simple melody that showed his harmonic ideas and string-muting skills off to good effect and became the song most often associated with him. A lesser-known, but equally impressive recording from that same period was his low-keyed, good natured "Downhill Drag."

By this time Chet was working independently, doing his own recordings and constant sessionwork as Nashville's music industry began its transformation into the multimillion dollar operation it is today. In 1955 RCA opened its own studio in town, and Chet became manager of the facility. Late that year Sholes signed Elvis Presley to RCA, and Chet was on Preeley's earliest RCA session in January 1956, playing rhythm guitar behind Scotty Moore, Elvis' regular lead guitarist.

What happened in the wake of Presley's success involved Atkins and his playing style. Chet continued his own recording, cutting the excellent "Trambone," which again combined his own creative ideas within basic Travis syncopation. By 1955, Chet was popular enough to help design his own guitar models. Gretsch had begun building its hollowbody 6120 model, named for Chet, and a solid body model as well. Since his record sales and profile were high, the guitar sold well. In 1957 he recorded a syncopated version of "Walk, Don't Run," written and previously recorded by jazz guitar great Johnny Smith. Chet's rendition inspired the Ventures' 1960 rock hit.

But more directly, Presley and the rise of rock temporarily set Nashville on its ear; country radio stations changed to rock formats, and the entire industry was hurt. However, many rockers, including some that RCA themselves had signed, came to Nashville to record. As a result Chet found himself playing rock licks that in most cases differed little from the country things he was playing (Moore, after all, appropriated licks from Atkins and Travis on Presley's Sun sides). Some of his finest rock work came on RCA records by female rockabilly Janis Martin, as well as the classic Cadence recordings by the Everly Brothers (sons of Ike Everly, one of Travis' guitar mentors, coincidentally).

Rock music has also influenced Chet Atkins. His 1958 "Slinky," for example, opens with a (probably unintentional) quote from James Burton's hypnotic riff that dominated Dale Hawkins' 1957 "Suzie Q," and was combined with a slow electronic vibrato, a measure of Atkins' increasing experimentation with tone-alternating devices like tape echo and wah-wahs. This had an enormous impact on many young guitarists, including some who later became rock players.

However, it must be said that through the

late '50s and '60s, though Chet could make excellent music, he was also making a lot of boring and bland albums, loading them up with pop hits of the day, playing them perfectly but without much fire. Two of his best efforts from this period were the 1958 *Session with Chet Atkins*, a relaxed, easygoing LP, and *String Dustin'* by the Country All-Stars, a hot, driving studio band comprising Chet, Homer and Jethro, steel guitarist Bud Isaacs and fiddler Dale Potter. It seemed that as Chet became increasingly involved in the corporate operations of RCA (particularly after he assumed Steve Sholes's position in the '60s, recording took a back seat to his production and administrative work. Throughout the '60s he made albums with the Boston Pops and a variety of other bland collaborators, often using the "Nashville sound" format (strings, voices and minimal country characteristics) to make hits for Jim Reeves, Skeeter Davis and Eddy Arnold.

Indeed, in the late '60s, Atkins' strongest music came when he paired himself with another, equally creative musician who could challenge and inspire him. His collaborative effort with Jerry Reed, *Me and Jerry*, offered excellent work from both men. Likewise, 1973's *Atkins-Travis Travelling Show*, which brought Chet and Merle together on disc for the first time, was an excellent teacher-meets-pupil display with some fine music, despite the affected dialogue on some tracks. But it was the 1976 *Chester & Lester* album, pairing Chet with his longtime friend and mentor Les Paul, that unveiled both guitarists' best picking in years. Unrehearsed, the two men played off each other on pop standards that reminded everyone of their cumulative greatness. Their 1978 followup, *Guitar Monsters*, continued in the same mold. *Reflections*, Chet's 1980 duet with Doc Watson, returned him to an austere country context that flattered both men. *Standard Brands*, which paired Atkins with his friend and disciple Lenny Breau playing pop standards, proved that in the right situation Chet was as vital as ever.

In 1981 Atkins severed the last of his ties with RCA Victor, having stepped down several years earlier from the administrative posi-

tion he'd held. He switched to CBS Records. It appeared, sadly enough, that in a period where the pop-oriented country music that Atkins had pioneered in the late '50s was selling stronger than ever, his adventurousness had further atrophied. Chet's debut for CBS was *Work It Out*, an album inexplicably built around his interest in having appropriate music to listen to on a Walkman cassette player while jogging. The music was pure dentist's office Muzak—like too many of his earlier albums, played without mistakes or any fire.

Perhaps Chet Atkins' most creative days are over, but surely he can still play with unparalleled virtuosity. Whether or not he ever again reveals the spirit of adventure he once had doesn't matter. Chet Atkins helped bring the guitar into the mainstream of American commercial music, and (with Merle Travis, of course) gave finger-style picking, a technique that might have remained as obscure as, say, clawhammer banjo, to the world. For those achievements—and his superb recordings—we should be eternally grateful.

DISCOGRAPHY

From the early '50s on, Chet Atkins recorded dozens of albums for RCA Victor. However most of them, including many considered to be among his best, are out of print. That he's no longer with RCA hasn't helped matters much. But his most essential recordings are still available.

One album that goes in and out of print is *Boogie with a Bullet* (Redita), a Dutch album with material from the Bullet label, including Chet's original 1946 recording of "Guitar Blues." *A Legendary Performer Vol. 1* (RCA) features his first session for RCA as well as tunes like "Chinatown, My Chinatown," with a superb book loaded with documentation of his career (reproduced session sheets show discographical data). *Now and...Then* is an outstanding two-record set issued by RCA to commemorate Chet's twenty-fifth anniversary recording for the label, and includes "Canned Heat," "Galloping on the Guitar," "Main Street Breakdown," "Country Gentleman," "Walk, Don't Run," "Trambone," "Blue Ocean Echo" and Yakety Axe."

Of his later material, *Chester & Lester*, his delightful collaboration with Les Paul, is still available. The *Reflections* album with Doc Watson is apparently out of print, but still available, as is *Country—After All These Years*, one of his better late RCA sets. *Stand-ard Brands* with Lenny Breau and *The Best of Chet Atkins and Friends*, featuring Chet working with other performers and instrumentalists, are also worthwhile.

His Columbia efforts have so far been eminently forgettable, though that may change as time goes by.

JIMMY BRYANT

immy Bryant was only 55 when lung cancer ended his life in 1980. Though Bryant was a legend among many country and jazz guitarists, among them Barney Kessel and Albert Lee (who was directly influenced by Bryant), most country and rock fans never heard of him. Like most other studio guitarists, Bryant was saddled with anonymity most of the time, though he made a good living at his craft.

But he wasn't always an obscure studio player; from the late '40s to the middle '50s Bryant was one of the hottest, best-known country guitarists of the southern California country music scene. He was a sideman on countless sessions, and he played with the fabled steel guitarist Speedy West, recording some of the most adventurous and electrifying guitar/steel duets ever conceived. Neither man feared risks, and the results of their risks were often stunning. Playing together in tight harmony, Bryant would suddenly pull away to create shimmering cascades of notes, tastefully and without the wretched excess that

often undermines the music played by "fast" guitarists.

Why Bryant never gained the stature of a Chet Atkins is anyone's guess. Perhaps it was that his recording career wasn't that extensive and lasted only a few years; certainly some of his tracks were a bit sophisticated, though they were admired by other musicians around the world. Maybe Bryant and West were so busy, so preoccupied with studio work, that they simply didn't take their own opportunities too seriously. It's not clear, and probably never will be.

What Bryant brought to country guitar was less a new technique than a new melodic awareness, an advanced technique and spirit of adventure that few others could match. Joe Maphis, for example, could play as fast as Bryant, but his strength was playing straight melodies, not far flung improvisation. Bryant, on the other hand, could excel on both rich melody lines and on creative, breathtaking improvisations.

Bryant was born in Moultrie, Georgia in

1925. (His father was a fiddle player, and after Jimmy learned to play fiddle and guitar, he began traveling around the country with his dad, playing rhythm guitar behind the fiddle. They remained on the road for seven years, after which Jimmy became an itinerant musician on his own. Once, in Panama City, Florida, he fiddled behind a young Hank Williams, then trying to get started in music.

At the age of 16, in 1941, he was inducted into the United States Army, serving in the infantry and, after being wounded, with Special Services, among other soldier/performers. A country fiddler was not needed, so Bryant spent much time listening to the well-known jazz guitarist Tony Mottola, assigned to the same barracks.

Hearing Mottola caused Jimmy to take guitar playing more seriously than he had in the past, when he'd done little more than play basic chords behind others. He practiced, and after being discharged sunk all his severance pay into an electric guitar and amp, then went back to Georgia. He joined a small group in Moultrie and moved with them to Los Angeles around 1948, where they worked on radio.

At some point Tex Williams, one of the areas' biggest stars following his 1947 million-selling hit "Smoke! Smoke! Smoke! (That Cigarette)," invited Bryant to record with his band the Western Caravan. Exactly what Bryant recorded with Williams is unclear; however, he's almost certainly the fluent guitarist on Williams' 1950 recording of "Wild Card." He also is very likely present on a number of Tennessee Ernie Ford's early country numbers, including "Smoky Mountain Boogie," "Shotgun Boogie" and "Catfish Boogie."

Bryant developed a working relationship with Capitol which led to better things for him. He signed to a Capitol recording contract of his own, and also joined Capitol producer Cliffie Stone's Hometown Jamboree radio and TV program, as the lead guitarist for the show's band. He also recorded with numerous Capitol artists as a sideman.

Also in that band was a Missouri steel guitarist named Wesley "Speedy" West, formerly of the Spade Cooley and Hank Penny western swing bands. West was developing a reputation in southern California for his musically flamboyant approach to the steel, an approach that included effects no other steel guitarist of the period could equal. West's style was both exciting and futuristic, having much the same effect in the '50s that Jimi Hendrix had on '60s guitarists. His crazy, swooping, skittering runs up the neck, his crashing, metallic chords that exploded like a volcanic bubble were sounds unheard of at the time. Though criticized as overly dependent on gimmicks, West was, in fact, a thoroughly musical player who became a top L.A. session musician, able to work well in any context. He was the ideal musical partner for Bryant.

Though one of Jimmy's first recordings under his own name was "Bryant's Boogie," a fluid, medium tempo boogie woogie with single line improvisations and chord choruses that took it far beyond the one-dimensional characteristics of so many other guitar boogies, it was with West that he truly flourished. Cliffie Stone quickly noted their synergy and dubbed them the "Flaming Guitars." They created a musical partnership that produced some of the most exciting steel electric guitar music ever. Often moving from country into freely improvised jazz, they rarely covered known tunes, preferring to create their own. West recalled how they worked years afterward: "One of us might hum a lick and the other would start working out the twin guitar harmony to it. If the lick didn't prove successful we'd either put it out of our minds, play it backwards or hum another one."

With Bryant's—and Cliffie Stone's—strong ties to Capitol, the Bryant-West team was free to record their instrumentals, West using his superb custom-built Bigsby steel and Bryant playing the then-revolutionary Fender Broadcaster. Many of their best-known numbers were worked out, beginning with a close-harmony introduction, after which one musician would take off on a breathtaking improvisational break before handing it off to the other. They would support each other during these breaks, playing little fills or slipping in chords where appropriate. Tunes like "Serenade to a Frog," "Midnight Ramble," "Bryant's Bounce" and their 1954 hit of "Stratosphere Boogie," among the single most exciting guitar recordings ever made, established their reputation. When they did tackle someone else's song, for instanceethe old Bob Wills/Les Anderson steel instrumental "This Is the Southland," or "Arkansas Traveler," they quickly made it their own. The latter tune became an awesome country/jazz performance, which left its impression on Albert Lee, among many others.

Bryant's abilities made him a necessity on many of Capitol's country recording sessions of the '50s. He also recorded with Bing Crosby, Kay Starr, Billy May's orchestra and, most intriguingly, Stan Kenton's orchestra. This was ironic, considering the simplistic, negative comments Kenton made about country music towards the end of his life. But Kenton respected Bryant enough to let him improvise his solo breaks without sheet music. Bryant's talent earned him the respect of other L.A. jazz guitarists who worked the studios, among them Howard Roberts and Barney Kessel.

By the mid-'50s the Bryant/West team was still a fixture in sessions; Bryant's own estimation was that he recorded with 124 different artists from 1955 to '56. But after rock music swept the country in 1956, country sessions fell off drastically in California. Many younger country performers opted for rock, and Speedy West became a producer before moving to Oklahoma in the 1960's to manage Fender's regional warehouse in Tulsa. Bryant's studio career, however, continued to flourish, though he did have to learn to read music as more producers insisted on set arrangements.

In the mid-'60s, he began recording again under his own name for Liberty dates produced by his friend and admirer Scott Turner. Jimmy recorded several albums for the label, among them *Bryant's Back in Town, Laughing Guitar, Crying Guitar* (one side of upbeat songs and one side of ballads), the schlocky, over-arranged *We Are Young* (recorded in Nashville) and the superb *Fastest*

Guitar in the Country. The latter album combined excellent arrangements of pop and jazz tunes including "Stumbling," "Little Rock Getaway" and "Caravan" with Bryant originals like the rocking "Georgia Boogie" and the cool, west coast jazz arrangement "Voxwagon." Bryant's playing was consistent, though at times he fell back too much on his rapid-fire technique and stock licks. The smoothness of his playing had a slightly more biting tone on country tunes such as "Sugarfoot Rag," which was not totally desired, as it made him sound much like Joe Maphis. One of the unheralded highlights of the album, however, was Bryant's swinging fiddle playing, overdubbed on the record.

He retained considerable respect among guitarists, particularly those around Los Angeles. The Academy of Country Music, the L.A.-based music industry group, honored him as its Best Guitarist in 1966, '67 and '68. Through the early '70s he lived in L.A., recording with, among others, the legendary steel guitarist Noel Boggs. Their 1973 waxing of "Boodle Dee Beep," an instrumental in the style of western swing instrumentals of the '40s, featured Boggs, Bryant and fiddler Harold Hensley in excellent form (despite a mediocre rhythm section), though Bryant rushed the tempo in places.

In the mid-'70s Jimmy went to Nashville and became an endorser of Hohner guitars (his choice of products to endorse was fairly weak—in the '60s he endorsed Vox guitars, almost universally panned by professional guitarists). Bryant and Speedy West reunited for occasional performances, and around 1976 steel guitarist/producer Pete Drake reunited them in Nashville, though the tapes have inexplicably remained unissued.

Bryant, a heavy smoker, was discovered to have terminal lung cancer in 1979, but this was not enough to retire him. He was determined to continue playing as long as he could. And so he returned to L.A., where Local 47 of the American Federation of Musicians organized a benefit concert for him (at which he performed). Finally he returned home to Moultrie, where he died in September 1980.

Today, it appears that aside from Albert

Lee (who jammed with Bryant at the Palomino Club not long before Bryant died), many players and fans have forgotten Jimmy Bryant's contributions. That's not totally surprising, given the modest success of his solo recording career. However, his musicianship made him one of the pioneers of the "country jazz" idiom, and it's indeed sad that so few are interested in his pioneering work.

DISCOGRAPHY

Regrettably, none—literally none—of Jimmy Bryant's work under his own name is available. None of the Capitol recordings including his classic Country Cabin Jazz, are anywhere to be found, and all of his material for Imperial including *Fastest Guitar, Bryant's Back in Town* and *We Are Young* is long out of print as well. However, *Two Guitars Country Style,* recorded with Speedy West, is now available as an import from French EMI records, reissued in its original cover. And as with Merle Travis, the original Capitol 78s and albums (including those with Speedy West) go for phenomenal prices in record auctions.

HANK GARLAND

Hank Garland epitomized the image of the Nashville studio musician: able to walk into a session, set up the instrument, hear a song just once and in a matter of minutes, after huddling with the rest of the pickers on the date, come up with the perfect arrangement of the tune. He was one for whom music was as essential as food, water or sleep. The hours of daily sessions didn't sate his appetite; he regularly haunted the Nashville jam session circuit, playing jazz and swing numbers with his peers and amazing everyone with his prodigious abilities.

Studio musicians tend to be well-paid, but there is a tangible price; only a handful are known outside their milieu. In essence, they are well-compensated for remaining anonymous to the buying public. Some have transcended that anonymity through the strength of their ability or particular personality, and Hank Garland was, along with Chet Atkins, one of the first to do so.

Garland's professional career spanned but 15 years, but the impact he left was considerable and long-lasting. *Jazz Winds from a New*

Direction, the Columbia album he recorded over twenty years ago, remains in print through the graces of Columbia Special Products. His influence on well-known guitarists like George Benson, Willie Nelson, Bucky Barrett and Albert Lee have been formally established through various published interviews. The tragedy is that a violent auto accident in 1961 ended Garland's musical career—and nearly ended his life. Hank was never able to regain much of the technical finesse he'd worked so long to develop. There have been a number of tragic figures among Nashville musicians—people brought down by alcoholism, drug abuse or simply flaws of personality, but few are so tragic as Garland.

He was born Walter Louis Garland in the small town of Cowpens, South Carolina in 1930, and as a child fell in love with the drop-thumb guitar style of Maybelle Carter. He took his first lessons from a man named Fowler, who taught him basic chords and positions. Through his teens, Hank listened to WSPA radio in Spartanburg, the city that lay to the southwest. Arthur "Guitar Boogie"

Smith, one of the early country guitarists to play single-string solos, had a radio show on the station, and left a strong impression on Garland.

By the 1940's he'd become obsessed with his instrument, spending every waking moment when not in school practicing, or playing as a sideman in a local country group led by Shorty Painter using his first electric guitar. Hank was at Alexander's Music Store in Spartanburg one day in 1945 when he was introduced to Grand Ole Opry bandleader Paul Howard, whose western swing group was known as the Arkansas Cotton Pickers. Howard listened to Garland play and immediately invited the adolescent wonder to Nashville. Hank's somewhat skeptical parents took him there, and after some confusion (Howard didn't recall the invitation), he was introduced on the Opry stage and, with the Cotton Pickers backing him, proceeded to tear the place apart with a hot boogie woogie. Howard immediately hired him, but because of child labor laws requiring a person to be 16 to work full time, Hank wound up back in Spartanburg after just a few weeks.

Howard brought him back to Nashville when Hank turned 16, in November 1946. There are no known recorded examples of his playing with the Cotton Pickers, but for a budding guitar soloist it was probably the best place to be, for Howard's music took its cues from the jazz-influenced sound of Bob Wills and His Texas Playboys, who regularly featured fiddle, piano, steel guitar and electric lead guitar soloists. Chet Atkins, then new to the Opry himself, recalled Garland's playing in that period was modeled somewhat after Wills' guitarist Jimmy Wyble.

But he also, according to Atkins, had his drawbacks. "(Hank) rushed an awful lot; he'd pick up tempo," Atkins remembers. This is not an uncommon trait in teenaged guitarists, who often achieve technical prowess before they gain musical maturity. What Hank needed—and got—were musical father figures in the persons of guitarists Harold Bradley and Billy Byrd. Bradley, younger brother of legendary Nashville arranger/producer Owen Bradley, was himself just beginning a career

as a Nashville studio guitarist that continues to this day. Byrd was to gain fame for his spare, economical leads behind singer Ernest Tubb.

Both Bradley and Byrd were disciples of the late Charlie Christian, and also listened to Django Reinhardt and other jazz guitarists. Hank moved into an apartment in Byrd's home, and the older guitarists spent hours introducing him to music he'd never heard back in Cowpens, giving him technical tips and offering insights into jazz improvisation. In the process, Hank developed the ideas and direction that would permit him to carve his own niche in Nashville, and fostered a love of jazz that never left him. Soon Garland was obsessed with the music of both Christian and Reinhardt.

But from a strictly pragmatic standpoint, his enthusiasm didn't pay the rent. Garland joined the backup band of singer Cowboy Copas. Copas, best known for such songs as "Filipino Baby" and "The Tragic Romance," was a more conservative leader than Howard, and Hank wasn't given the solo space he had with Howard's band. Yet it appears he did his first recording with Copas. The fleet-fingered guitarist on Copas' King recordings of "Don't Let Your Deal Go Down," and "Down in Nashville, Tennessee" shows a formidable technique, unlike any other Nashville-based guitarist of the period.

Even more telling was his solo on Autry Inman's 1949 Bullet recording "You Better Leave Them Other Guys Alone." Still with the Copas band (who backed Inman on the session), Hank contributed a bright, sprinting solo line, laden with the cascades of notes that Reinhardt was famous for. Garland's playing is intense, his technique dazzlingly fast, and there are clear improvements in his improvisational abilities and tone, undoubtedly influenced by Bradley's and Byrd's tutelage.

Garland's record collection contained plenty of Django Reinhardt's work. Studio bassist Bob Moore, who roomed with Hank for a time, recalls him listening to Django's recordings nonstop when he wasn't touring with Copas.

During the late '40s, Nashville made its first significant strides toward becoming a major recording industry center. The Castle Recording Studio, which opened in the Tulane Hotel in 1947, brought state-of-the-art recording equipment to town for the first time, which gave artists who worked the Opry a chance to record without having to travel to Cincinnati, New York, Dallas or Chicago studios. A need for good backup musicians existed in town, so much so that even local pop instrumentalists wound up working on country sessions.

By 1949 Hank's abilities had become common knowledge in Nashville. Decca Records producer Paul Cohen and his assistant, Owen Bradley, began using Hank on sessions, then signed him as a solo vocalist. His first session, on August 25, 1949, featured three covers of Floyd Tillman songs, sung in a lackluster voice, and one instrumental, "Sugarfoot Rag," which Hank had originally written as a fingering practice exercise.

Someone saw some potential in the melody, for lyrics were written by Vaughan Horton (under the pseudonym George Vaughan) and the song was given to Red Foley, who recorded it—with Hank on lead guitar—on November 10, 1949. Since the flipside of the record was Foley's hit "Chattanoogie Shoe Shine Boy," "Sugarfoot Rag" got to number five on the country sales charts. Label credit for the guitar soloist was given to "Sugarfoot" Garland, a nickname that stuck to Hank throughout his career. His solos make it clear that he has grown; he showed a well-defined, distinctive approach. His attack is marked by a precision only a few other Nashville guitarists could even approach. Though his line adheres closely to the melody with little improvisation, its flow is so effortless that in the end Foley's vocals seem almost secondary.

Garland continued recording under his own name for Decca through 1951, creating songs that, despite minimal sales, underscored his growing abilities. "E-String Rag," despite inane lyrics, features phenomenal solo passages, as does his boggie-woogie influenced "Guitar Shuffle." His instrumentals were even better than Hank's vocal numbers. "Hillbilly Express" and "Seventh and Union" were both strong tunes that permitted him to

stretch out and improvise. There was little overt jazz flavor, but the easygoing, swinging tempos revealed a soloist of the first order and Hank's stinging (though not distorted) tone complemented his wonderfully lyrical technique.

By the early '50s, Garland was a fixture in the Nashville studios. On Eddie Hill's 1951 recording of "The Hot Guitar," Hank and Chet Atkins took turns imitating each other's styles, as well as those of other top guitarists like Les Paul. Hank also recorded for Dot, but the Dot sides did him little justice as most were bland restatements of tired pop numbers like "Tea for Two." Only his considerable instrumental prowess permitted him to transcend the hokey arrangements.

In 1954, at Gibson's behest, Hank and his mentor Billy Byrd designed a guitar for the company. Gibson dubbed the instrument the "Byrdland," and began marketing it in 1955. It remains one of Gibson's strongest selling models today, popular with rock and jazz players (ironically, few country performers use it).

Garland's session work increased as the Nashville recording studios proliferated in town. He played a pulsating, bluesy figure on pianist Roy Hall's 1955 original recording of "Whole Lotta Shakin' Goin' On," which Jerry Lee Lewis would turn into a rock and roll classic just two years later. So intent was Garland at getting the correct feel for the song that, as he later told Harold Bradley, he listened to WLAC, Nashville's black rhythm and blues station, to pick up guitar ideas from the blues records the station played.

By 1956, as Elvis Presley's shadow loomed large over America, more rockabilly recordings were being done in Nashville. By 1957 country record sales were beginning to fall off, and some of Nashville's best fiddlers and steel guitarists were finding themselves with less work as artists tried to jump on the Presley bandwagon. Hank, however, had an edge due to his versatility, and both he and Grady Martin began working the numerous Nashville rockabilly sessions, with both rock artists like the Everly Brothers and Ronnie Self, and with country artists trying to rock, Webb Pierce and Red Foley among them.

Garland seemingly had no trouble mimicking rock licks, considering his intense, often blazing riffs on records like Foley's "Crazy Little Guitar Man." As pop artists began to use Nashville studios for sessions he got calls from them as well. One of his most impressive—and memorable—moments came with Patti Page's 1958 Mercury recording of "Just Because," where Garland takes a corny arrangement and improvises a country/jazz accompaniment that lifts it out of mediocrity.

When Nashville producers began to inject pop music elements into country recordings to create the successful (and controversial) "Nashville sound" in hopes of expanding the country audience, Garland was one of the musicians they depended upon. Even more important was his association with Elvis Presley. In 1957 Scotty Moore, Elvis' guitarist since '54, left in a pay dispute, and in June '58, when Presley was recording on leave from the Army, Hank was featured playing screaming, electrifying leads on "I Need Your Love Tonight," "I Got Stung," "(Now and Then There's) A Fool Such as I" and "A Big Hunk of Love." His leads here were taut and intense, a measure of his ability to play rock as if he'd never played anything else.

In 1959 Hank played the stately lead guitar on Jim Reeves' hit recording of "He'll Have to Go." Still more significantly, he began recording on his own in an entirely different context. During the time Hank was building his reputation in the studios, he was nurturing his love for and understanding of modern jazz. When he'd toured with Eddy Arnold in the early '50s, Hank found much to enjoy during Arnold's stops for radio and TV appearances in New York City, for during his off-hours he could catch top jazz guitarists like Barry Galbraith and Tal Farlow at Manhattan nightclubs. For a time in New York Garland took lessons in jazz rhythm guitar from Galbraith, and later introduced Harold Bradley to the brilliance of Farlow and Wes Montgomery.

Granted, there wasn't room for modern jazz in Nashville's studios, but Hank found an outlet, along with Chet Atkins, drummer Buddy Harman, bassist Bob Moore, pianist Floyd Cramer, saxophonist Boots Randolph

and eighteen-year-old vibraphonist Gary Burton at Jimmy Hyde's Carousel Club in Printer's Alley in downtown Nashville. Their jam sessions there were legendary; one night Garland blew away members of Stan Kenton's orchestra who stopped by the club.

Garland's first real jazz recordings were done in 1959, issued as an instrumental LP by the SESAC song licensing firm. Backing him were Moore, Burton, pianist Bill Pursell and drummers Harman and Doug Kirkham. The overall feel of the LP is light and airy, and the interplay between Burton and Garland is highly reminiscent of the interplay between a Garland hero, Tal Farlow, and Red Norvo in the trio led by the vibist (and completed by bassist Charles Mingus). Indeed, Garland's jazz technique is clearly rooted in that of Farlow, with overtones of Jimmy Raney as well.

Garland and most of the Nashville jam session group were invited to the 1960 Newport Jazz Festival. Riots closed the festival, but the band album *After the Riot at Newport* (on RCA) was recorded live on the porch of a nearby house, and it features some strong soloing, particularly on the original version of "Relaxin'," which became one of Hank's jazz trademarks.

Meanwhile, there were ample sessions to pay the rent with in Nashville. Hank continued to record with Elvis Presley and countless other Nashville performers, but his jazz talents resulted in a Columbia recording contract. On August 25, 1960 he entered the studio with Burton, New York bassist Joe Benjamin and Joe Morello, Dave Brubeck's drummer, with whom he'd worked in Paul Howard's band, to record *Jazz Winds from a New Direction*, Garland's auspicious entrance to the jazz world. His close friend, guitarist Grady Martin, supervised the session.

There was no question by now of Hank's potential. He still adhered to Farlow's influence, but was not bound by it. His counterpoint to Burton's vibraphone on "All the Things You Are" is one example of his thorough self-confidence. His rhythm comping is equally sensitive. "Three-Four the Blues" has strong overtones of Wes Montgomery's "West Coast Blues," recorded earlier that year, and the version of "Move," the cool classic Farlow recorded with Norvo in 1950, is clearly modeled on their precedent, and appears to be as much a tribute as a reinterpretation. "Always" is a harmonically rich, understated performance featuring Hank on acoustic guitar.

Jazz Winds achieved considerable critical acclaim, and set a standard that only a handful of country-based guitarists ever reached. It solidly established Garland as a promising newcomer to the jazz field. But sessions were still his lifeblood and he did some great sessions during this period. He teamed with Chet Atkins to play twin acoustic guitars on Don Gibson's hit "Sea of Heartbreak" in 1961. On April 25, 1961 he was on hand with Elvis in Honolulu for his famous "farewell concert" which featured alternating leads by Hank and Scotty Moore. Garland, Harold Bradley and jazz guitar legend Johnny Smith were brought in by Atkins to play triple classical guitars on Don Gibson's Girls, Guitars and Gibson album for RCA, and Hank's echoplexed electric lead introduced Patsy Cline's hit "I Fall to Pieces."

Unfortunately, things weren't going well for Hank in his personal life. By September of 1961 he and his wife Evelyn were having serious marital problems, and on the afternoon of September 8 he drove north out of Nashville at a high rate of speed looking for his wife, whom he thought had left for her parents' home in Milwaukee. Near the town of Springfield, Tennessee, he was involved in a violent, near-fatal automobile accident that left him comatose for a time.

When Garland regained consciousness, it became clear his brain had been affected. His bold, driving personality was passive, and much of his coordination was gone; he had memory problems. Though he made a valiant effort to return to the Nashville studios, he was unable to consistently coordinate himself, and he left Nashville a couple years later. His tragedy didn't end there—his wife later died in an auto accident. His brother Bill worked with Hank to help him regain much of his coordination, though he was clearly unable to return to Nashville. Times had changed since the early '60s; producers who formerly let musicians create their own arrangements on record dates took back that latitude, insisting musicians play arrangements precisely as specified.

It was regrettable that Hank Garland's career ended so early. At the time he was injured he was clearly at a turning point. Having developed a formidable reputation as a country and jazz guitarist, he could have gone in either direction. Despite the anonymity which so many of his peers routinely, even happily, accepted, Hank had developed his own ideas, and had not had to compromise his love of jazz. Considering that such esteemed jazzmen as Barney Kessel and Herb Ellis alternated jazz recordings and performances with lucrative studio work for years, Garland might have used his studio work to subsidize his jazz career.

But we will never know what might have been for Hank Garland. All that's left are his varied recordings, comprising a legacy many equally talented guitarists would be proud to call their own.

DISCOGRAPHY

Regrettably, almost none of Hank Garland's own recorded material remains in print or easily available today. His recordings as a leader for Decca were never issued together on an LP (though they certainly should be); of his excellent jazz-oriented material, only one album, the classic Jazz Winds from a New Direction, is available as a reissue (with the original cover and notes) from Columbia Special Products. None of the others—Velvet Guitar (Columbia), After the Riot at Newport (RCA) or The Unforgettable Hank Garland are in print today. The likely place to find these—if you're extremely fortunate—is in the "record auctions" held by mail for collectors. One individual who turns up a respectable number of Garland 78s, 45s and LPs is Keith Kolby (6604 Chapel Lane, Fort Worth, Texas 76135), who runs regular record auctions.

ALBERT LEE

Albert Lee, like his idols Jimmy Bryant, Hank Garland and James Burton, is one of the handful of country guitarists able to function outside of country contexts. Just as Burton has moved between rock and country, Garland in rock, pop, country and jazz, and Bryant in those idioms, too, Lee, who steeped himself in country and rockabilly as a youth, has enjoyed similar widespread success. He first gained notice as a rock player, and established himself in that before going country. And hardly anyone has noticed that Lee, one of America's top modern country guitarists, is British.

Lee has managed to work with a number of prominent musicians, including British rocker Chris Farlowe, Emmylou Harris, Jerry Lee Lewis, Dave Edmunds, Eric Clapton and Ricky Skaggs. It is a tribute to his remarkably durable style that he hasn't had to radically change his playing to fit each artist's needs. In general, what has worked with one has worked with all—basically because Lee's eclecticism draws on blues, rock and country.

But Lee is most solidly rooted in the coun-try and blues traditions; one hears echoes of not only Burton, Bryant and Garland, but also of Joe Maphis, Cliff Gallup, Scotty Moore and Phil Baugh in his playing.

The basic elements of Lee's playing include a piercing sound (he favors the Fender Tele caster) and a smooth fluency that at its wildest sounds overdubbed and isn't. Despite the cascades of notes he can play, Albert, even at his wildest, is never self-indulgent. He does not pursue flash for its own sake, but only for its enhancement value. Lee can play lines taut with tension, or create sensitive, delicate passages, all with clean, clear precision. His embellishments seldom challenge the melody; he's decorative without being intrusive. Lee is also a rhythmic virtuoso; he can syncopate an uptempo tune to make it swing like crazy.

Lee's choice of guitar is crucial. Like Burton and Baugh, he has spent most of his time with a Fender Telecaster, which Bryant and Gallup used during the high points of their careers, and Lee has been creative in harnessing the Tele's unique qualities—its cutting highs, its solid, twanging lows—to make them as much a part of his style as anything he does with his fingers. Telecasters do not work well in every musical context (Canadian guitarist Ed Bickert, for example, is one of the few jazzmen to use one), but some players able to master its peculiarities have created lasting music, and they include Albert Lee.

Lee was born December 21, 1943 in Herefordshire, England. He began his musical career by studying piano, which he still plays. His earliest interest was in rockabilly, specifically that of Buddy Holly and later Gene Vincent, Ricky Nelson (with Joe Maphis and James Burton playing the guitar leads), a number of r&b performers and Hank Garland. Lee first recorded in 1961, backing an obscure British singer named Jackie Lynton. Then, around 1962, he heard Jimmy Bryant.

"I heard a record on British radio," he told me in 1981, "and it was called 'Arkansas Traveler' by [steel guitarist] Speedy West and Jimmy Bryant, off an album called *Two Guitars Country Style*. A friend of mine gave the album to me and it just blew me away."

Two years later Albert became part of Chris Farlowe's band the Thunderbirds, which was popular in Britain but practically ignored in America. British hits included "Out of Time," a Mick Jagger/Keith Richard tune that hit number one. The band members eventually went their separate ways, though Lee continued working with Farlowe until '68. Then for two years he freelanced with bands including Country Fever, a group respected for the excellent backup it provided American country performers touring England. In 1970 Albert helped found Heads, Hands and Feet, a superb and grossly underrated band with a straightforward sound that was overlooked amid the psychedelia of the period. By '72 they were defunct, and Albert returned to freelancing.

Lee managed to keep going by working with several former Heads, Hands and Feet members on the 1973 two-record Jerry Lee Lewis album *The Session* (Mercury), which also featured such British rock luminaries as Alvin Lee, Peter Frampton and Rory Gallagher. It was Albert, however, who stood out among the heavy guitarists. He played on the

bulk of the tracks, and contributed some outstanding solos in the rockabilly/country r&b context. His solo work on "Music to the Man," for example, shows a firm command of the Burton/Baugh Telecaster style and a muscular, rhythmic attack. The version of "Sea Cruise" features Albert's searing and effective break. His spare solo on "Trouble in Mind," played with a harsh pick action, cuts through an otherwise bloated non-arrangement.

Lee recorded and toured with the late Buddy Holly's revived Crickets when they worked in England, and in 1974 came to America where he made contact with such individuals as Don Everly of the then-defunct Everly Brothers. He began to establish himself in Los Angeles before leaving on a tour with Joe Cocker. His connection with Cocker led Lee to a contract with A&M Records that yielded part of a solo LP before he was brought into Emmylou Harris' Hot Band to replace James Burton in 1976. He joined just in time to work on her excellent album *Luxury Liner* (released in '77).

Without a doubt, some of Lee's best work is heard on this album. From the title track which opens side one, he seems almost as much the driving force as Emmylou herself. His closing solo on "Luxury Liner," though overdubbed, features awesome, smooth runs, played with a fire comparable to that of Joe Maphis, laden with slapback echo that makes each note bounce off the one before it. His languid contribution to "Pancho and Lefty" is in total contrast to his earlier wildness. His embellishments are slight but valuable on Chuck Berry's "You Never Can Tell," and his solo, though true to Berry's spirit, has an upper-register sparkle all its own.

Lee's work with Emmylou was still underway when he completed the A&M album he'd begun before joining her. Emmylou's producer/husband Brian Ahern and most of the Hot Band assisted him on his record. *Hiding*, released in '79, was an excellent if unheralded country-rock set that combined the best of both idioms. Lee's nasal vocals are, however, an acquired taste. "Country Boy," an old song, gets a revitalizing treatment with some excellent Lee Telecaster work and his equally fine picking on an amplified gut-string guitar. He also plays some beautifully understated mandolin on his version of the Louvin Brothers' "Are You Wasting My Time?"

Lee continued recording with Emmylou, even after he left her Hot Band in 1978. He was featured on *Quarter Moon in a Ten Cent Town,* and did some particularly outstanding playing on her 1979 *Blue Kentucky Girl,* providing a solo on Willie Nelson's "Sister's Coming Home" that is virtually indistinguishable from a pedal steel. On Harris' 1981 album *Evangeline* he brilliantly interprets Les Paul's style on Emmylou's revival of the 1951 Les Paul/Mary Ford classic "How High the Moon." Lee retains his characteristic approach but evokes that same sense of playfulness and humor that has always marked Paul's best work. Lee plays an ill-defined (probably badly mixed) solo on "Oh, Atlanta," but he shines again on a remake of the Chordettes' 1950s hit "Mister Sandman," conjuring up light but important embellishments to give the song both pop and country flavorings.

All the while Lee was doing sessions with other artists, including Ricky Skaggs, who was beginning to perfect the fusion of bluegrass, honky tonk, western swing and rockabilly that brought him popular success in 1981. Skaggs had worked alongside Albert in Harris' Hot Band and had considerable feeling for his work.

Albert joined Eric Clapton's band early in 1979. Despite his own efforts, he seemed more comfortable backing a top performer playing to massive crowds, and not having to work up from the smaller clubs as he would have were he a solo artist. Joining Clapton's band nonetheless seemed an odd choice for Lee. Clapton, a blues-rooted rock guitar legend in *every* sense of the word, might have caused a clash of egos, if not of styles.

Yet in another way it was not so illogical a match, considering Clapton's success with country songs like Don Williams' "Lay Down Sally" and "Tulsa Time" as well as with tunes like J.J. Cale's "Cocaine," which fit a similar mold. Nor did Albert see his playing with Clap-

ton to be so unusual.

"We both started out listening to the same records in the late '50s and early '60s," Albert said in 1981. "We were both listening to Buddy Holly and Jerry Lee Lewis. He discovered blues and I did, too, but not to the extent Eric did."

Lee had a supporting role in Clapton's band, playing rhythm guitar, occasional keyboards and doing harmony vocals—extremely well. He was involved with the 1979 live concert at the Budokan in Tokyo released as *Just One Night* (RSO), a double album and performed "Setting Me Up," a song he'd recorded on *Hiding* (A&M). Lee was also a part of the band on Clapton's *Another Ticket* (RSO), though again he had a secondary role; likewise on Clapton's 1983 *Money and Cigarettes* (Warner Bros.).

By 1981, still working with Clapton, Albert also continued to take studio work, while living both in England and L.A. Some of his finest supporting work ever was done on song writer/signer Rodney Crowell's 1981 LP *Rodney Crowell,* where Lee was reunited with several former members of the Hot Band. His playing was particularly lucid on "Stars on the Water," lyrical and lovely on "She Ain't Going Nowhere" and screaming on "Don't Need No Other Now," a song heavy with '60s r&b feel. His break on the ethereal "Shame on The Moon," though fragmented, was beautifully understated, and his melodic passages on "Til I Gain Control Again" are among the high points of the recording. "Old Pipeliner," a Moon Mullican number originally recorded for King as "Pipeliner Blues," is flatout rockabilly featuring Albert at his wildest.

Meantime, he was in the studio again for himself, recording *Albert Lee* for Polydor, which he conceived as a rocker. "I think my last one got to be too laid back," he said in 1981. "I enjoy listening to it, but it wasn't as commercial as I could have made it."

Albert Lee (1982), produced by Rodney Crowell, saw Lee's wish fully realized. Hot Band alumni like bassist Emory Gordy, former Elvis drummer Larry Londin and former Little Feat pianist Bill Payne, among others, collaborated with Albert to create a hard-driving rock 'n' roll and rockabilly album that paid homage to the past without being stranded there. Lee's guitar has a pungency, a verve about it that never lets up. Even his vocals, which had been shaky and tentative early on, reflect far more confidence. The country edge is less pronounced in his playing, but the brilliant rock potential heard on his earlier work (like the Jerry Lee Lewis sessions) has been realized with polish and finesse. Perhaps due to his time with Clapton, or just his personal growth, Albert Lee has become a formidable influence on both country and rock guitarists in the last few years. Today, Albert is working with the reunited Everly Brothers in addition to touring with Clapton.

One hopes that Albert continues to maintain the strains of tradition that have always pervaded his playing, and that he will achieve enough success to be able to remind guitarists of forgotten legends like Jimmy Bryant, with whom he jammed in L.A. not long before Bryant died of cancer in 1980. But ultimately, Albert Lee will be judged by his own work, which so far has been nothing less than consistently brilliant.

DISCOGRAPHY

Alas, none of Albert Lee's hard-driving work with Heads, Hands and Feet is in print. The band did three albums, *Heads, Hands and Feet, Tracks,* and *Old Soldiers Never Die* and all were deleted shortly after being issued. Regrettably, Albert's exciting work as part of Jerry Lee Lewis' backup band on *The Session* (Mercury) is also gone from the label's catalog.

On the other hand, all of his work with Emmylou Harris' Hot Band can be easily found, including *Luxury Liner, Quarter Moon in a Ten Cent Town, Blue Kentucky Girl,* and *Evangeline. As a sideman with Ricky Skaggs he can be heard on Sweet Temptation* (Sugar Hill) and *Don't Cheat in Our Hometown (Sugar Hill/Epic),* the latter album made up largely of recordings Skaggs did before achieving success in 1981.

Lee can also be heard on the excellent *Rodney Crowell* (Warner Brothers), as well as Crowell's earlier albums, *Ain't Livin' Long Like This* and *Saturate Before Using* (Warner Brothers), Rosanne Cash's *Right or Wrong* (Columbia), fiddler Byron Berline's *Outrageous* (Flying Fish) and Joe Cocker's *Stringray* album (A&M). Albert's work with Eric Clapton is heard on *Just One Night* (RSO), *Another Ticket* (RSO) and *Money and Cigarettes* (RSO). In addition, he appears on the Everly Brothers' 1983 *Reunion Concert (Passport Records).*

Lee's two solo efforts, Hiding (A&M) and Albert Lee (A&M), are both still available, the latter being easy to find since it was issued in 1983. Hiding, released in 1979, may be ordered or found in many larger stores.

JOE MAPHIS

Joe Maphis was country music's first "flash" guitarist. His lightning-fast flatpicking technique had nary a hint of subtlety about it; just a few bars were sufficient to electrify even the most cynical listener. The notes fly from his electric guitar at the pace of a machine gun, one after the other at a velocity almost too high to measure. Maphis is one of those guitarists you only need to hear once to recognize him everytime thereafter.

Few people realize that Maphis was, in fact, a flatpicking pioneer in the country field. At the time he taught himself the admittedly difficult technique of rapid, clean flatpicking, few country guitarists were doing anything more than strumming fingerpicking. By and large, the guitar was used as an instrument of accompaniment in country music, a ringing rhythmic backing for a fiddle, banjo, voice or mandolin. Aside from another early flatpicker, Arthur "Guitar Boogie" Smith, a contemporary of Maphis', nobody else of consequence was doing it.

Maphis never set out to be an innovator. In-

deed, his interest in the idea was more a product of youthful curiosity than any calculated effort to distinguish himself from his peers. That, more than anything else, most likely explains the man's humility despite the decades during which many have held him in awe, including some of Hollywood's top musical arrangers and more schooled guitarists like classically trained, nylon-string jazz virtuoso Charlie Byrd.

At least part of Maphis' gift can be directly traced to his environment. Born in Suffolk, Virginia in 1921, he spent his formative years in Cumberland, Maryland, in the state's narrow panhandle that separates Pennsylvania from West Virginia. He grew up in a family of musicians; his father played rhythm guitar in a local square dance band called the Railsplitters; Joe joined his father—playing a mail-order guitar—at the age of eleven. He'd listened to other guitarists for inspiration, most notably Maybelle Carter and Riley Puckett, whose 1927 recording of "Fuzzy Rag" left a lasting impression on him.

Yet Joe had ideas of his own as he listened to the Railsplitters' fiddler, Ivan Kearns. If Kearns could play leads on his fiddle, why should the guitar be relegated to simply rhythm chords? Why couldn't the guitarist also play melody lines? Undoubtedly Joe's idea was hardly original. By the time he was working with the Railsplitters, Eddie Lang, Lonnie Johnson and numerous others had similar ideas. But for country music this concept was fairly sophisticated. And to compete with a fiddle, Joe's technique would have to be clean and rapidfire, for square dance music in western Maryland was largely uptempo.

What Maphis set out to do took no small amount of time. To effectively gain the technique required to flatpick means hours of practice, to learn how to pick the notes so they ring out clearly while maintaining a steady, unfaltering tempo. It usually has to be learned in gradual steps, starting slowly and steadily picking up tempo until the notes flow freely, almost casually, from the instrument.

Maphis developed such a style after much practice and began using it with the Railsplitters. He also expanded his picking technique so that he could play similar flatpicking solos on four-string tenor banjo and mandolin (he learned fiddle and standup bass as well, giving him considerable versatility for an amateur musician). Wondrously as he regularly soloed with the Railsplitters, he never garnered much attention. "If people did pay attention, they'd say, 'What's that kid doing? He should be playing rhythm for the fiddle,'" Maphis recalled in 1981 in an interview with the author.

By 1938 he'd made up his mind to concentrate on a full-time musical career. He traveled south to Fredericksburg, Virginia, where he hoped to land a job with Blackie Skiles and his Lazy K Ranch Boys. They had no need for another musician, but after hearing Joe pick up and play every one of their instruments they decided that hiring him was smarter than letting any rival band recruit him. If Joe had attracted little notice for his playing with the Railsplitters, the Lazy K bunch found his versatility such an asset that in the midst of a

show each member would hand Joe his instrument, which he proceeded to play with ease. It was that versatility that later earned him the title "King of the Strings."

At the time he was doing his guitar work on a Martin D-28, impressing everyone who heard his guitar leads. The band went south to Richmond, Virginia, and joined the staff of 50,000 watt WRVA radio, but they soon disbanded. Joe was picked up by Sunshine Sue Workman and Her Rangers, a traditional country group that featured Maphis both as a master instrumentalist and hillbilly comedian. In 1942 when the entire act moved from WRVA to Cincinnati's WLW, then one of the top radio stations in the midwest, it boasted a roster of talent that included Merle Travis, Grandpa Jones, Hank Penny, Bradley Kincaid and other future stars of country music. Drafted in 1944, Joe spent two years in the Pacific as an Army Special Services entertainer before returning home.

After a brief stint on WLS in Chicago he rejoined the Sunshine Sue aggregation at WRVA, this time forming his own group as well. He also began using an electric guitar for the first time, and in December 1947 did his first recordings with harmonica player/vocalist Floyd "Salty" Holmes. Joe's playing on these recordings displays less flatpicking and more the influence of Merle Travis, with whom he'd become close while at WLW. He approached Travis' style in his own way, however, using a flatpick held between his right hand's thumb and index finger to play the bass accompaniment while picking out lead on the treble strings with his middle finger. His pulsating solo on "Lonesome Railroad Blues" with Holmes adds excitement to an otherwise mundane performance. On another number, "Nine Times out of Ten," Maphis contributes strong single-string improvisations around the melody and a biting, articulate flatpicked solo, moving then into Travis-styled accompaniment for the song's fiddle break.

He stayed on the WRVA Barn Dance until 1951, when he married one of the show's vocalists, Rose Lee, and they created an act of their own featuring vocals and Joe's instrumental pyrotechnics. When they were invited to move to Los Angeles that year to work on a daily country music television program, the Maphises accepted, and within days after leaving Richmond were working with Travis, singer Johnny Bond and others on a live show that lasted several hours each day. Within weeks they were local celebrities.

A year later they made what was perhaps their most fortuitous move—to *Town Hall Party*, a barn dance-styled TV show broadcast from nearby Compton, California. The Maphises also began working clubs in southern California, and Joe's instrumental abilities got him on a number of recording sessions, backing such other *Town Hall Party* performers as Bond, picking out inventive, tasteful solos on his Gibson Super 400.

The Gibson, however, was about to be replaced by a highly unconventional instrument built by a budding guitar maker: 18-year-old Semie Moseley. Eager to build a guitar for Maphis, Moseley was introduced to Joe by a local minister. Maphis was clear about the type of sound he wanted: it had to have the full, rounded tone of his Super 400. Moseley suggested a doublenecked instrument, and at Maphis' suggestion added a second neck that carried a six-string octave guitar (tuned in standard guitar tuning, but an octave higher). The guitar was a solid-bodied instrument, with the body hollowed out to cut down its weight. In 1954 Moseley presented his elaborately inlaid instrument to Maphis during a *Town Hall Party* broadcast, and Joe's first number on his new guitar was "Fire n the Strings," his signature tune.

The song was his own interpretation of the old fiddle tune "Fire on the Mountain," which he recorded a year later for Columbia Records. This version of "Fire on the Strings," done in 1955 in Hollywood with the *Town Hall Party* staff band, became Joe Maphis' instrumental showcase, albeit one geared more to flash than musical value. His tone is stinging, his attack precise and confident. After a fiddle break by Margie Warren, Joe proceeds to flatpick the same melody on tenor banjo; after a second fiddle break, he plays the same break (all of them restatements of the melody)

on mandolin. Following the third and final fiddle break, he returns to electric guitar to again state the melody. Certainly such a song is not as effective on record as it would be onstage, but it does give some insight into Maphis' instrumental prowess.

Other numbers, however, provide far better examples of his work. His February 1956 recording of "Guitar Rock and Roll," backed again by the *Town Hall Party* band features some superb, fluid playing, but with a far bluesier edge (though with minimal stringbending). Some of his figures are clearly based on those played by Scotty Moore on some of Elvis Presley's early RCA recordings; one lick almost certainly comes from Moore's solo on Presley's recording of "Rip It Up." The performance, however, is anything but derivative—indeed, it shows the sort of adaptability that made Maphis a fixture in Hollywood's studios. Somewhat more derivative is "Tennessee Two Step," recorded at the same session. The song has clear echoes of Chet Atkins' 1953 recording of "Country Gentleman." Joe's string-muting, not unlike the muting Atkins used, makes the connection even stronger.

By 1956 Joe's reputation had begun to mushroom in Los Angeles. Many in the area who had little truck with country music watched *Town Hall Party*, and his virtuosity soon reached the ears of professional arrangers including guitarist Jack Marshall and Elmer Bernstein. They began using Maphis on soundtracks for such films as *Thunder Road* and *God's Little Acre*. That he could handle such dates without reading a note of music amazed many studio musicians. Merle Travis once told of Joe asking for a music stand during one soundtrack session, turning it flat, and laying his coffee cup and an ashtray on it. Neither Marshall nor Bernstein was fazed by this, and soon the reading musicians on the dates were complimenting Joe on his abilities, accepting him as if he'd been conservatory-trained.

In 1957, Maphis got another call—this time from Ozzie Nelson, who needed a lead guitarist to back his son Ricky, who was starting to sing rock and roll on *The Adventures of*

Ozzie and Harriet TV show. Nelson, a former orchestra leader, was impressed enough to recruit Joe to work on both the TV soundtracks and on Ricky's first Imperial Records sessions. Maphis, playing as hot and funky as any rock guitarist, contributed the solos for such early Nelson hits as "Be Bop Baby," "Waitin' in School" and "Stood Up." Though at times he clearly attempts to add stock rock licks, on most tracks he simply plays in his own style. On "Be Bop Baby," for example, he plays Merle Travis-styled licks behind Ricky's vocal.

All of this brought Joe more pop sessions, to which he contributed equally intense leads behind singer Wanda Jackson's rockabilly recordings of "Let's Have a Party," "Silver Threads and Golden Needles" and Four Preps' hits like "26 Miles." But some of his best and most influential work in that period was with his own protégé, teenage guitarist Larry Collins of the Collins Kids. Larry and his older sister Lorrie had joined *Town Hall Party* as a youthful country duo in 1953, when Larry was nine years old. Joe took him under his wing, teaching him much of what he knew. So closely did Collins identify with Joe that Semie Moseley made him a doublenecked guitar similar to Joe's. When the Collinses began recording for Columbia Maphis participated in most of their sessions, both country and (after 1956) rockabilly.

As Larry's instrumental prowess grew he and Joe began working out guitar duets of their own; they recorded four of them in September 1957. With two compositions by each guitarist, the four songs display some of the most awesome country/rock guitar synergy on record. All four songs were later released as a Columbia EP recording titled *Joe Maphis and Larry Collins*. Not surprisingly, Maphis' tune "Early American" depends on stock country licks, as he and Collins state the melody in two-part harmony so precisely, and in such tight ensemble as to resemble one of Les Paul's overdubbed masterpieces. "The Rockin' Gypsy" is a bizarre minor-key rhumba, played in quasi-flamenco style with Maphis sliding into Latin-flavored Travis licks while Collins complements him harmonically.

It's certainly one of Joe's more unusual solo performances. "Bye, Bye," a Collins number, is a loping blues which features him in high-register as Maphis plays rhythm on his bass strings. But it is the last song recorded at the session, "Hurricane," that defines both players' sense of adventure. Here they come together as one, indistinguishable, in a churning, pulsing maelstrom of dizzying licks and power chords. It is without question one of the most galvanizing guitar duets ever recorded.

Maphis worked on and off when he could with Ricky Nelson, but gladly stepped aside for James Burton, the guitarist most associated with Nelson's recordings. From the '60s on Joe recorded for labels like Capitol, Starday, Chart and Sacred. There was not any great change or development in his style, even when he joined the tradition-oriented CMH label in 1978. Joe and Rose Lee Maphis have remained on the road over the years, performing in a variety of shows.

Maphis hasn't always gotten the credit he deserves for his contributions. His enormous influence on Larry Collins actually went far beyond Collins, who himself exerted an enormous influence on surf guitar master Dick Dale, who copied his clean picking and use of the bass strings to provide hard hitting, rhythmic excitement—a technique Collins got directly from Maphis. Some guitar fans know Joe only as the man who gave singer Barbara Mandrell her start as a performer when she was just 12.

But Joe Maphis, one of country music's first flatpickers, has left behind a legacy of considerable substance. Playing with few special effects aside from a hint of reverb, he manages to astound almost everyone who hears him, and that, as much as anything, is the mark of a truly great guitarist.

DISCOGRAPHY

Joe Maphis' recorded legacy is, like that of so many players of his generation, largely but not totally unavailable today. Several of his showcase recordings for Columbia, including the legendary "Fire on the Strings," and his collaborations with Larry Collins, are available on *Rockin' Rollin' Larry Rollins and Joe*

Maphis (Bear Family). His playing is also heard on *Rockin' Rollin' Collins Kids*, Vols. One and Two (Bear Family), though he functions strictly as a backup musician. Also an American issue, *The Collins Kids* (Epic), features some of Maphis' finest work. Liberty's Legendary Masters series includes a Ricky Nelson double album of his best Imperial recordings featuring Joe on tracks including "Be Bop Baby," "Waitin' in School" and "Stood Up," before James Burton took over the lead guitar slot in Rick's band.

Though Maphis also recorded for a variety of other labels, among them Capitol, Starday, Chart, and Canaan, none of that material is available in any form. And though he recorded for CMH in the late '70s and early '80s, the label deleted most of his work for them, though it's still possible to find *Grass & Jazz, Dim Lights, Thick Smoke,* and *Honky-Tonk Cowboy* and *Country Guitar Greats* with Merle Travis in some larger record stores. The only Maphis material currently in print on CMH seems to be *The Joe Maphis Flatpicking Spectacular*, a double album largely of acoustic guitar instrumentals.

GRADY MARTIN

For every Chet Atkins, Jerry Reed or Charlie Daniels who leaves the Nashville studios to concentrate on his own performing career, at least three or four Nashville studio guitarists have opted to remain in the financially secure, albeit anonymous world of the studios, where depending on their popularity with producers (and to some extent, their diplomacy) they can do several three-hour sessions a day and not only afford a condo, but also a house in the country and a speedboat to run on Old Hickory Lake, northeast of the city.

A number of brilliant guitarists like Jack Shook, Ray Edenton, Harold Bradley, Velma Williams and Kelso Herston have suffered from this anonymity. Nor is the name Thomas Grady Martin a household word. But for thirty years, Martin's virtuosity and inventiveness have graced thousands of country, pop and rock recordings, and played a direct role in making some of them hits.

To a great extent, Martin's generation (he is a contemporary of Chet Atkins and Hank Garland) has passed out of the active Nashville studio scene. Like his surviving peers—particularly Harold Bradley and pianist Floyd Cramer—he has returned to club and concert performing. A newer, younger group of pickers has replaced them in the studios.

One reason for this is that in the '40s, '50s and '60s, most Nashville producers were themselves musicians. Some would leave the producer's chair to work out an arrangement with the band; Chet Atkins and Owen Bradley (a former dance band pianist) worked in that manner for years. They had, it seemed, an unending flow of new ideas that not only benefitted individual artists, but enhanced—and may have established—Nashville's reputation as a recording center. Few of these producer/musicians read—or wanted to read—music.

But things have changed. Today producers and arrangers call the shots. The musicians may still not read, but they damn well better play what they are told when they're told. Individual initiative and input seem to have been replaced by a corporate mentality that dictates Nashville recordings should sound alike with regard to the use of elaborate symphonic arrangements.

Martin was one of those rare guitarists who had a distinctive style of his own, but made his reputation on his stunning versatility. He could play literally anything in any style required. He was one of the first in Nashville to use a nylon-stringed guitar regularly (though his friend Harold Bradley used one earlier); he was one of the first to play funky, bluesy licks on Nashville records and (accidentally) to use a "fuzztone" on a record. He did this in 1960, when Jimi Hendrix was still playing in Seattle rhythm and blues bands. Indeed, Martin's versatility was his greatest contribution. Regardless of what sound a record required, Grady Martin could do it, and in the process he created music that may have helped make great country records true classics.

Martin's own playing style, exclusive of what he had to play on some records, combined consummate discipline with a funky, razor-edge, made ample use of string-bending and featured a strong attack. Despite its brash overtones, however, he had a gift for integrating it into nearly any context in which he was working.

Guitar-mad kids may not have idolized Grady the way they did Chet, but he was nonetheless a guitarist obsessed with getting more out of his instrument. Like almost all of the first generation Nashville studio guitarists, music was an end in itself, not just a meal ticket.

He was born in Chapel Hill, Tennessee about thirty miles due south of Nashville on January 17, 1929. Growing up on the family farm, he found pleasure in listening to the Grand Ole Opry on the family's battery radio, and learned the fiddle. He drank in fiddle music wherever he could hear it, attending the country music shows that toured his area.

In 1944 Nashville radio personality Big Jeff Bess (husband of the late Tootsie Bess, founder of Nashville's famous Orchid Lounge) heard Martin's fiddling and, as Paul Howard had with Hank Garland, asked the Martins to let Grady come to Nashville to work on his show. With some reluctance, the Martins agreed. After gigging with Bess for a time,

Grady joined the backing group of the Bailes Brothers, with whom he went on the Grand Ole Opry.

Martin was alternating between fiddle and guitar by that time, and came up with a guitar style that was hard-edged without being abrasive. Exactly how he arrived at it isn't clear, but not long after he got to town he became friendly with a brilliant young guitarist, the diminutive, thoroughly underrated Jabbo Arrington. Jabbo had begun to develop a twin guitar style with Grady, similar to the one Jimmy Wyble and Cameron Hill were playing with Bob Wills and his Texas Playboys on hits like "Roly Poly" and "Smoke on the Water."

The first of Martin's thousands of recording sessions came in September 1946, when he, Arrington and a small group of Nashville-based musicians went to Chicago to record with Opry performers Curly Fox and his wife, Texas Ruby Owens. The duo was trying to move into an amplified, western swing-oriented context. The music remained relatively country on the first session. But the eight songs recorded at that session contained a driving electric guitar ensemble. Both Grady and Jabbo played heavily amplified, precisely arranged harmonized breaks that were in some ways the best things on the records. Few guitarists at the time (excepting those in the southwest) were doing anything similar. "Traveling Blues" and the stop-time intro to "Nobody Else But You" sound incredible even today.

Grady worked around Nashville through the late '40s, recording sessions and playing the Opry with Paul Howard's band. When Howard left Nashville in 1949 the Martin/Arrington team became the nucleus of Little Jimmy Dickens' new backup band the Country Boys. Here their twin guitars were honed to an even finer degree of precision. The twin guitar sound which hadn't had much effect earlier now became (and remains) a Dickens trademark, and was particularly outstanding on his early hits like "A-Sleepin' at the Foot of the Bed" and "Hillbilly Fever," sparkling to complement Dickens' sassy musical persona. It also made the Country Boys one of the finest touring bands in country music at the time.

When Arrington died of heart trouble in the mid-'50s, Grady continued with Dickens and Thumbs Carlille joined the team.

Meanwhile the Nashville recording business had grown; RCA, Columbia and Decca all increased their local activity, partly due to the 1947 opening of the Castle Studio, a state-of-the-art facility. Grady entered that early studio scene, and in 1949 played a raunchy, bluesy solo with string-choking that anticipated later rock solos on Red Foley's "Chattanoogie Shoe Shine Boy," one of 1950's top country hits. Grady became closely allied with Foley in the early '50s, accompanying him to Springfield, Missouri where he worked on Foley's Ozark Jubilee TV show, the first network country music show (ABC). He also did some impressive solo work on other Foley records, adding a biting lead to the 1950 "Birmingham Bounce," a haunting solo on 1952's "Midnight" and a screaming break on "Plantation Boogie" which sounds almost 20 years ahead of its time.

By the early '50s Grady had become one of the major studio guitarists in town, still playing fiddle occasionally (one of his final public appearances with the instrument was when he backed Hank Williams on Kate Smith's TV show in '52). As recording activity in town increased he got busier, doing sessions for Decca, Columbia and RCA. He led pop sessions of his own for Decca, with studio musicians known as the Slew Foot Five. These recordings aren't among his best, and were geared primarily for the pop market.

One of Martin's least-known—and finest—solo efforts came in 1955, when he assembled a topnotch group of studio players—including fiddler Tommy Jackson, steel guitarist Bud Isaacs, Hank Garland and bassist Bob Moore—at the Ryman Auditorium to record a set of instrumentals later released as part of Decca's *Country and Western Dance-O-Rama* series of western swing LPs. The recordings featured some of the most freewheeling guitar music to come out of Nashville at the time. Grady played twin fiddles with Jackson on several tracks, and Garland, Isaacs and Martin traded scintillating choruses on "Pork Chop Stomp" and "Wooly Boogie." The album captured Grady's jazzier side, which wasn't often apparent on the country records he made for other artists.

The rockabilly revolution following Elvis Presley that sent shudders through Nashville may have hurt other, more country-oriented sidemen (fiddlers and steel players in particular), but Grady, like Hank Garland, was versatile enough to adapt. Some of his most intense playing was done on such recordings as Ronnie Self's 1956 "Big Fool," where he played a searing, Merle Travis-inspired solo, and Johnny Horton's excellent rockabilly versions of "I'm Coming Home," "Honky Tonk Man" and "Honky Tonk Hardwood Floor." Martin's rhythm guitar graced Buddy Holly's first recording session in Nashville in January of 1956.

His commercial intuition aided other country recordings during this time. His brief but effective lead guitar introduction to Johnny Horton's 1959 hit "Battle of New Orleans," for example, was simple but memorable.

More significant was his use of nylon-string classical guitar on records. It's most likely him playing on Horton's version of "They'll Never Take Her Love from Me." But it was on Marty Robbins' classic 1959 "El Paso" that Martin's undulating, flamenco-flavored accompaniment was crucial, establishing the song's Mexican flavor. Granted, the song may have been equally successful without him, but the motif he created around Robbins' vocals has, over the years, remained part of the song (Grady's riffs were copied by Jack Pruett, Robbin's regular guitarist, each time the song was performed on stage).

In the summer of 1960 Martin unwittingly was involved in another innovation when he played 6-string bass on Marty Robbins' bluesy number "Don't Worry." In the midst of Grady's solo, a preamp in the studio's mixing board on the channel carrying Grady's microphone malfunctioned. The result was one of those happy twists of fate. A playback of the take revealed a roaring, distorted sound that producer Don Law liked enough to leave on the record (though he was talked out of calling the backup band the "Bumblebees" on the label). This was one of the earliest examples of what became known as "fuzztone" on records. The errant preamp was removed from the console, but was used to produce similar sounds whenever a producer or artist wanted them.

Grady's playing became even more valuable through the early '60s, partly because Hank Garland's auto accident left him unable to work in the studios. Previously, Garland, Grady and Harold Bradley often worked as a guitar triumverate on sessions. Grady specialized in commercial playing, Garland in more jazzy licks and Bradley in rhythm guitar and pop sounds. With Garland gone, Grady continued, but Bradley became the jazz specialist and rhythm guitarist Ray Edenton took Bradley's place.

By the early '60s, Nashville was solidly established as a major American recording center. In 1964 Grady's playing superbly complemented two of the year's biggest hits. His delicate nylon-string obligattos on Lefty Frizzel's "Saginaw, Michigan" were nearly as effective as they were on "El Paso." And on Roy Orbison's "Oh, Pretty Woman," a number one pop hit (and Orbison's biggest seller), Martin's insistent opening riff, created mostly on the bass strings, became the song's musical hook and a classic among rock guitar licks. Grady returned to his old boss Little Jimmy Dickens for his 1965 crossover hit "May the Bird of Paradise Fly Up Your Nose," where his stinging electric figures sound much as they did when he toured with Dickens.

Over the next few years he was featured on numerous tunes, and led some sessions of his own as well. Among the hits that featured him were Ray Price's "For the Good Times," in 1969, Kris Kristofferson's "Why Me, Lord" in 1973 and Jeanne Pruett's "Satin Sheets," on which Grady played the slow, bluesy line that underpins the melody. He also played on most of Conway Twitty's hit records and most of Loretta Lynn's, too.

However, by the late '70s recording technology was changing, and so—again—was country music. A new generation was taking over. They were not the controversial "Outlaws" like Willie Nelson, Tompall Glaser or Waylon Jennings, but a new generation of producers and artists, many of whom had little background in country music. Suddenly the creative spontaneity that had nurtured Grady and his peers began to evaporate. Arrangers who insisted their music be played without variation began to proliferate. Younger musicians came in, and even though studio musicians now routinely were credited on albums, the name Grady Martin was seen less often. He was not the only veteran in this situation; bassist Bob Moore and drummer Buddy Harman were also less ubiquitous than they once were. Martin turned to producing albums with the bluegrass/pop band Brush Arbor. He also joined Jerry Reed's backup band, returning to live-on-stage performing. Though he'd appeared on TV through the years, he now spent some of the time he'd once spent in studios playing in public.

In 1979, Martin and Reed were hanging out with Willie Nelson; Grady and Nelson had been close for some time. Listening to the records Willie made for RCA from 1965 to 1971, it is clear that the nylon-string guitar on those records—much of it played by Grady himself—probably had influenced both Willie's more recent use of nylon-stringed guitar and his technique in playing it. Grady joined Willie's band for the film *Honeysuckle Rose*, and became a permanent member of the Nelson "family" after that. He remains there today, an honored presence who can be seen, heard and appreciated wherever Nelson performs.

Through the years there's been little written about Grady Martin, it seems. Many younger country fans know nothing of him, or know of him only through Willie Nelson. For his part, Grady has not been the most forthcoming of veteran Nashville musicians; he shuns interviews, even ones that would clarify once and for all his vast contributions to the Nashville studio industry and country music over his nearly forty years in the business. Considering the extensive documentation of the careers of Chet Atkins, Jerry Reed, Charlie Daniels and Hank Garland, there is not much on Grady (he himself admits he has forgotten many songs and dates). However, in December 1983 the Nashville Music Association hosted a gala tribute to Martin, giving him its first Master Award in recognition of his achievements. With Owen and Harold Bradley, Buddy Harman, Little Jimmy Dickens, Jerry Reed, Brenda Lee and Floyd Cramer on hand, the presentation, hosted by Willie Nelson, was a long-overdue bow of appreciation to guitarist Grady Martin, whose music has delighted millions of listeners who never even knew who he was.

DISCOGRAPHY

As in the case of Hank Garland, none of Grady's own records are currently available. And it would be impossible to list—even partially—all the records he played on during his years in the Nashville studios. One regrettably hard to get collection that featured Martin was Bud Isaacs' *Steel Guitar in the Mid-'50's* on the German Danny label. This limited edition set, though it featured Isaacs' steel, was taken from Red Foley transcriptions recorded in Springfield, Missouri, and featured Grady as lead guitarist. Though he's not credited on the albums, his playing is un-

mistakable, and at best, he evokes the spirit of the 1955 Dance-O-Rama album, also out of print, except possibly as an import. If you can find a copy of it at a collector-oriented record shop, you've got some of Grady's best work on record.

But a few of his efforts as a sideman are worth seeking out—if only for his outstanding work. Among them are Johnny Horton's *Honky Tonk Man* (Columbia, available as a budget album) and featuring Grady's super, spare leads on the title track, "I Got A Hole In My Pierogue," "I'm Comin' Home" and "Honky Tonk Hardwood Floor." The same tracks are available on *Rockin's Rollin' Johnny Horton*, a reissue of the Columbia material on the German Bear Family label. Martin's work with Marty Robbins is available on *Marty's Greatest Hits* (Columbia), a budget release, or the more recent *A Lifetime of Song: 1951-1982,* (Columbia) issued in the wake of Robbins' death.

Grady can also be heard on just about any of Willie Nelson's recent Columbia albums. With Willie's studio accessible to him, Grady Martin will have a chance to record another solo album soon.

ELDON SHAMBLIN

There have been many great rhythm players in bluegrass (one is Lester Flatt) and in the Nashville studios (Jack Shook, Velma Williams and Ray Edenton among them). But only Eldon Shamblin, the man who single-handedly made Bob Wills' Texas Playboys into a truly cohesive unit, resembles a true virtuoso in the western swing idiom.

Shamblin's rhythm guitar, from 1937 to 1942 and from 1947 on and off into the mid-'50s, was the musical glue that held the Playboys together. His harmonically sophisticated chords and runs gave their sound a depth and smoothness that it did not have without him. Eldon's few solos were models of precision and melodic sophistication, and his pioneering ensemble work with steel guitarist Leon McAuliffe left a legacy that extends not only into country music of the '40s and '50s, but into rockabilly and even into the twin-guitar ensembles of the Allman Brothers and other southern rock bands of more recent times.

Though Shamblin started out owing much to Eddie Lang and then Django Reinhardt, he later became a solid soloist in the Charlie

Christian mode and later still was influenced by the raw, explosive playing of Junior Barnard with the Playboys. Shamblin's playing did not change drastically as it grew; he simply added the new influences to his repertoire, choosing whichever one he felt worked best for a song. A self-taught arranger who learned music by the seat of his pants, Shamblin had likewise developed an impeccable sense of musical taste.

Eldon's own style of playing is relatively complex, combining passing and substitute chords with smooth bass runs, a concept he devised to compensate for the weak bass players that Bob Wills had a tendency to hire in the '30s. However, the nature of some of these runs is not original; Eddie Lang had been doing similar things on records long before. The sophistication of Shamblin's style has held up well over the years, sounding as modern today as it did when he first joined the Playboys.

Eldon Shamblin was born April 24, 1916 in Weatherford, Oklahoma and began playing guitar in his teens. He had relatively few influences when starting out, though he listened to the records of Django Reinhardt when they became available, and also appreciated the jazz guitar duets of Frank Victor and Harry Volpe, who recorded for Decca in the '30s. From the beginning, Eldon's frame of reference was pop music and jazz.

He started his career at age seventeen playing Oklahoma City honky-tonks and beer joints for whatever money he could get. In 1935 he joined Dave Edwards' Alabama Boys, one of the early Oklahoma western swing units (it contained numerous future Texas Playboys) and moved with them to Tulsa, where he left the band to join KTUL in Tulsa as a staff guitarist playing swing music. Wills heard him there, and on November 8, 1937, Shamblin moved from KTUL to KVOO, the 50,000 watt home of the Texas Playboys, the top attraction in the region.

Among the reasons Shamblin was brought into the band was the fact that the sophisticated big band swing Wills was trying to play was beyond his reach at that time. His band lacked skilled arrangers and musicians capable of creating a sophisticated, cohesive sound for the Playboys. All too often his rhythm sections were ponderous and mediocre; the horns, though often lively, were sometimes colorless and dull. For all intents and purposes the band's success came from its spirit and depended upon Wills' magnetic personality. But strictly from a musical standpoint, and despite several successful recordings, the Texas Playboys often sounded downright hokey.

Eldon saw that right away, and set to making changes. His guitar playing was the most notable one. Herman Arnspiger, who'd worked as guitarist in the Wills fiddle band of 1929 (he and Wills were the whole band), with the Light Crust Doughboys until Wills left in 1933 and with the Texas Playboys from 1934 on, played excellent accompaniment on old-time fiddle tunes. But as horns were added, Arnspiger was getting out of his league, for he lacked both the musical sophistication and the feel for the swing music Bob wished to play. Eldon, who'd listened to and played in swing groups, could fill that void.

Eldon's first recording session with the Playboys was held in Dallas on May 16, 1938 according to western swing discographer Bob Pinson's comprehensive Wills discography. Shamblin's influence was just beginning to be felt, and many of the band's ragged edges, particularly with the horns, were still much in evidence. But one noticeable change came in the opening of their version of Bessie Smith's hit "Down Hearted Blues," where Eldon played a delicately phrased single-string introduction in the Eddie Lang style that led into Wills' vocal. This marked a new era for the Spanish guitar in the Texas Playboys. Throughout the performance Eldon played rhythm phrases that echoed ideas similar to Lang's, and gave the Playboys a new solidity. "Down Hearted Blues," at least partly due to Shamblin (as well as Charlie Laughton's stinging trumpet and Wills' spirited vocal), was an unqualified success that only hinted at things to come. At a November 1938 session Shamblin contributed a similarly Lang-influenced solo on "That's What I Like About the South."

By 1940, the group's arrangements were precise but retained a loose informality; Eldon's guitar became the pulse of the band, driving them as Freddie Green propelled the Count Basie Orchestra. On numbers like "Time Changes Everything," Eldon's rhythm guitar has clearly smoothed out the band's sound and tempos, which become lighter and more appealing. Even on tunes like the "Medley of Spanish Waltzes" his bass runs and arpeggios are subtly holding things together. Likewise, on "Big Beaver," an old melody Wills had heard as a young man and had first used on "Steel Guitar Stomp," Shamblin's arranging talents and guitar were crucial. He gave the song a sophistication that would have been the envy of the Dorsey Brothers or Glenn Miller, and his guitar pulsated subtly but noticeably throughout, its chords laying the groundwork for some fine horn solos.

Early in 1940 Eldon took Wills' band into a new dimension. Having spent much time on rhythm guitar, he moved into the electric lead guitar sound being pioneered by jazz innovator Charlie Christian. During a rehearsal Shamblin and steel guitarist Leon McAuliffe were noodling around when McAuliffe began playing "Joe Turner Blues" on his steel; Shamblin began to harmonize, and in an instant they'd created the twin-guitar concept: electric lead and electric steel playing in tight ensemble. They first used the idea on their duet break in the 1940 instrumental "Bob Wills Special," then created the instrumental "Twin Guitar Special," recorded in February 1941. These were the first stirrings of a sound that would dominate the Texas Playboys on and off through the remainder of its existence.

Bass runs were also important to Shamblin's sound, creating a rhythmic momentum that in part compensated for the weaker bassists Wills hired. On "Take Me Back to Tulsa," one of the band's most enduring numbers, Wills specifically asked Shamblin to add extensive—and effective—runs. Though he lacked formal musical training, Wills had an uncanny sense about what worked musically, and the runs certainly added color to "Tulsa."

During these years Shamblin may have—unknowingly—been the first country guitarist to use a solidbody. He obtained a Rickennacker Electro model—the first commercially manufactured solidbody electric Spanish guitar introduced around 1935. It looked identical to a lap steel guitar, and though Eldon was breaking ground, Wills disapproved. As Shamblin recalled in a 1975 *Guitar Player* article, "(Bob) said 'I like the sound of that thing, but there ain't nobody in the world going to know you're playing a guitar.' So he wouldn't let me play it."

World War II ended Shamblin's first stint with the Playboys as he entered the Army, attaining the rank of captain. Around 1947 he returned to a radically different Texas Playboys band. The large horn section was gone, replaced by fiddles, an occasional sax or trumpet, and an electric string ensemble similar to, but more sophisticated than, what he and McAuliffe were doing in 1940. Steel guitarist Herb Remington, Shamblin, guitarist Junior Barnard and electric mandolin virtuoso Tiny Moore constituted a formidable replacement for the brass and reeds and the standards of excellence that had begun with Eldon's joining the band in the pre-war years continued.

Shamblin's abilities merged with Moore's to give the band sophisticated, daring arrangements, particularly on numbers like their exhilarating adaptation of Benny Goodman's "Mission to Moscow," which they recorded for Wills' Tiffany Transcriptions series in August 1947. Though the 1942 original had an advanced arrangement by Goodman's pianist Mel Powell, Shamblin and Moore managed to remain true to Powell while recasting the song within the Wills context—no mean feat.

Eldon also had an important role as the band's manager, as the Playboys settled at Wills Point near Sacramento in 1947, handling most of the financial affairs in addition to playing. It was not always pleasant; it was Eldon to whom Wills entrusted the firing of Tommy Duncan, the Playboys' main vocalist since 1933. Eldon continued working with Wills, playing peerless rhythm and occasional leads, into the mid-'50s. Around 1954, while working at KXLA radio in Los Angeles with Wills, Eldon managed to create fireworks on a par with the late Playboys guitarist Junior Barnard's, playing freewheeling, raw solos unlike anything he'd done previously.

In 1954 Shamblin left the Playboys to join Wills' soundalike Hoyle Nix, who led a western swing band around Big Spring, Texas, then returned to Wills in 1956. Through the years Eldon had raised a family, and in 1957 he decided to return to Tulsa. After more than twenty years of professional music (minus his Army stint) he went into the business of tuning pianos and repairing electric organs. He continued to play locally (using an early Fender Stratocaster given to him by Leo Fender while he was still with the Playboys), but he didn't believe he would do anything more than play around the Tulsa area.

Then, in 1970 Merle Haggard, a longtime Wills fanatic, decided to recreate the music that had inspired him as a boy. As one of America's top country performers, Haggard was in a position to record what he wanted.

Gathering a group of former Playboys, including Eldon (and excluding Wills, then recovering from a massive stroke), he went into a studio with them and his own band, the Strangers. Haggard created *A Tribute to the Best Damn Fiddle Player in the World,* the album that helped create the western swing revival of the mid-'70s. Suddenly there was renewed interest in western swing, and Eldon, whose work on the Haggard album proved that his instrumental abilities were as fluent as in 1940, suddenly became a topic of interest. In November 1971 Haggard brought Wills, then sufficiently recovered, together with Shamblin and nine other ex-Playboys for a reunion at Haggard's Bakersfield home, where they recorded some fine music that was never issued.

By 1976, with the revival in full swing, Eldon was attracting more notice. Working with Speedy West's western swing band, and a variety of western and swing-oriented acts, Eldon gained admiration from critics and fans alike with his delicate, complex rhythm guitar style. He played surprisingly modern leads with mandolinist Jethro Burns, Eddie Lang's former partner violinist Joe Venuti and jazz steel guitarist Curly Chalker for a fine album, *'S Wonderful,* that concentrated on jazz standards. He was working in a variety of contexts by this time, and becoming increasingly close to Merle Haggard. In 1975 he became a member of Haggard's band the Strangers along with Tiny Moore, to help Haggard recreate the Wills sound and add his superlative musicianship. He left Haggard to return to Tulsa around 1981.

Several years ago he recorded *Guitar Genius,* an album demonstrating his solo abilities were credible, if less effective than his rhythm work. Ultimately, Eldon Shamblin will be remembered not for the sort of wild solos that characterized Wills' guitarist Junior Barnard, but for his flawless rhythm guitar, a style never documented in a method book, and never surpassed.

DISCOGRAPHY

There are plenty of examples of Eldon Shamblin's finest recorded work with both Bob Wills and others in just about any large record store. Among these are the superb two-LP *Bob Wills Anthology* (Columbia), which has "Twin Guitar Special," "Take Me Back to Tulsa," "Time Changes Everything," "New San Antonio Rose" and others from the Playboys' finest period. Also available, with Wills tracks featuring excellent Shamblin arranging and guitar, are *Lone Star Rag* (Columbia Special Products) and *Bob Wills* (Columbia Historical series). The Time-Life Country Classics Series has a three-LP retrospective overlapping with the Columbia discs, but also including some unissued material. *Okeh Western Swing* (Epic), offers an entire LP side of Wills material, much of it unissued.

For some of the first material Eldon did upon rejoining the Playboys after World War II, *The Tiffany Transcriptions* Volumes 1, 2 and 3 (Kaleidoscope) features some fine examples, including some excellent electric string arrangements with Tiny Moore's electric mandolin and Herb Remington's steel guitar. MGM's *24 Great Hits,* despite an inaccurate title, has more wonderful work by Eldon.

Shamblin's western swing revival work can be heard on Merle Haggard's *A Tribute to the Best Damn Fiddle Player in the World* (Capitol), as well as *For the Last Time,* the 1973 session that reunited an ailing Bob Wills with Shamblin, Leon McAuliffe and other key members of the prewar and postwar bands and gives some outstanding examples of Shamblin's rhythm playing. He also is priceless on *'S Wonderful* (Flying Fish) with Joe Venuti, Curly Chalker and Jethro Burns, and *Reunion,* with a reconstituted western swing band led by Johnnie Lee Wills (Fine Catch). His single album as a leader, *Guitar Genius* (Delta), comprises a variety of western swing and pop material, but is almost too laid back to hold one's interest for long. Happily, Eldon Shamblin has continued to play, though he no longer tours with Merle Haggard as he once did, and one hopes more recordings—both reissued and new—will be coming from him in the future.

MERLE TRAVIS

erle Travis gave much to guitarists over the years, and his contributions go far beyond the fingerpicking style he helped to popularize. To consider Travis as a guitarist alone is inadequate, for he excelled in so many areas—songwriting, journalism, country music history, and performing—that the title of country music renaissance man is the only one that really applies.

Travis' guitar playing, whether electric or acoustic, changed little over his career. He took the thumb and index finger style he'd learned in rural Kentucky, a style that had been refined by numerous players who preceded him, and brought it to the world, inspiring scores of guitarists. Among those Merle directly inspired were Chet Atkins, who once suggested that he would probably be "looking at the rear end of a mule if it weren't for (Travis)." Hank Thompson, Doc Watson, Roy Lanham, Scotty Moore, Duane Eddy and Jackie Phelps were others who drank from the Travis chalice. Because of Scotty Moore's Travis-styled leads on such of Elvis

Presley's early Sun recordings as "That's All Right (Mama)," that technique became an integral part of the rockabilly sound, and remains so today.

Describing the Travis style itself is relatively simple; detailing its origins are another matter altogether. The rudiments of the style involve the thumb, equipped with a plastic thumbpick, picking out a syncopated bass accompaniment while the heel of the right hand mutes the bass strings to make them more percussive. Simultaneously, the index finger of the right hand is picking out melody or accompaniment on the treble strings. The thumb occasionally brushes the third and fourth strings to give the impression of a bass-chord accompaniment. To add a further flourish, the right-hand index, middle and ring fingers play a "roll" across the strings similar to a banjo roll, which provides both contrast and embellishment.

It sounds to the casual listener, particularly upon first hearing, like the music is coming from more than one guitar. It is a style totally self-contained, a one-man band without percussion, and works well unaccompanied or with a rhythm section.

The style actually originated, it appears, among black southern guitarists, who were fingerpicking guitars before white musicians ever began to take guitars seriously. Among those who may well have influenced the development of what became known as the "Travis style" were Sylvester Weaver and Arnold Shultz. Weaver occasionally used a similar style on numbers like "Smoketown Strut" (he was also the first blues guitarist ever to record, in 1923). Shultz, who was well-known around the western Kentucky area where Travis grew up, often played fiddle and guitar at white square dances (he had considerable inspirational effect on bluegrass founder Bill Monroe, who occasionally played a dance with him). Shultz influenced a Muhlenberg County fingerpicker named Kennedy Jones.

According to Mose Rager, one of the men responsible for teaching Travis to fingerpick, Jones took what he learned by listening to Schultz and added his own ideas, among them the use of a thumbpick and the three-finger roll. Jones also played numbers like "Buck and Wing" that later found their way into Travis' repertoire. Lester "Plucker" English, another local guitarist, was not so much a fingerpicker as a fine guitarist with an incredible knowledge of chords and the blues. By the time Mose Rager and his friend, Ike Everly, had assimilated all of this, they had their own interpretations of the style that Travis would take far beyond Muhlenberg County.

Merle Robert Travis was born November 17, 1918 in Rosewood, Muhlenberg County, Kentucky. His father, originally a tobacco farmer, quit farming for the coal mines that dotted the area, and Merle, after initially trying to play a banjo, became attracted to the various fingerpickers in the region. He took to Everly and Rager right away, listening to them pick out their versions of pop songs of the day (contrary to what many think, most of the Muhlenberg County guitarists' repertoires consisted largely of pop—not coun-

try—numbers). It got to the point that almost everywhere Rager and Everly showed up to play, Travis was standing by, watching and learning.

Everly and Rager were more than happy to teach him the rudiments of their style, and by the mid-'30s Travis had a solid grasp of it. After a hitch in the Depression-era Civilian Conservation Corps he moved to Evansville, Indiana, not far north of Muhlenberg County across the Ohio River, where he stunned an audience at a local dance marathon with his fingerpicked rendition of "Tiger Rag." The dance was broadcast on local radio, and Merle soon caught on with a local group known as the Tennessee Tomcats. From there he joined the more prestigious Clayton McMichen and his Georgia Wildcats, where he performed under the nickname of "Ridgerunner" Travis.

In 1939, Merle was working with a group known as the Drifting Pioneers, who were hired as staff musicians at 50,000 watt WLW radio in Cincinnati. Merle was soon playing guitar solos on the station (and taking flak from management for his use of an electric guitar—then a controversial new idea in country music). WLW's wide broadcast range introduced Merle's playing to thousands, particularly in the south and midwest. Sometime around 1940, the WLW signal beamed into rural Georgia, where Chet Atkins first heard the style that changed his life.

Merle stayed at WLW through 1943 and did his first recordings (and the label's) for the newly-formed King Records of Cincinnati with Grandpa Jones. He also recorded for King alone, as "Bob McCarthy," to circumvent WLW's policy against staffers making records. In February 1944, Travis and Jones did a second session for King; Travis recorded "What Will I Do," a ballad written by the Delmore Brothers' Alton Delmore, and provided a confident, relaxed fingerpicked solo, perhaps his first solo break on record.

Travis left WLW in March 1944 for the west coast, where opportunities for entertainers were enhanced by the huge influx of servicemen and factory workers (many from the south and the Dust Bowl) working in war production. He was correct in his judgment. Not only was he soon working as an extra in western films, he also became a popular sideman in Texas Jim Lewis', Porky Freeman's and particularly Ray Whitley's western swing bands, as a featured guitar soloist.

By 1945 Travis had made his first records under his own name: one as a singer with Porky Freeman's trio (playing no lead guitar—Freeman himself was a good single-string guitarist and one of the pioneers of boogie woogie guitar playing), the other for the Atlas label. The latter recording, "That's All," was a bluesy, gospel-oriented recording that offered no fingerpicking, but did spotlight a stinging single-string blues solo that revealed another, albeit obscure side of Merle's style.

He was also becoming a popular session guitarist, playing some of the most blistering fingerpicked solos ever committed to record. In the fall of '45 he recorded with Hank Penny, an old friend from WLW who became an L.A. western swing bandleader. The session included a dozen songs, virtually all of them rhythmically propelled by Merle's syncopated, piledriving thumbpicking. One number was a Travis tour-de-force. "Merle's Buck Dance," a variation on the old "Buck and Wing" number Mose Rager had learned from Kennedy Jones, had a ringing, progressive sound, in part because of Merle's shimmering electric guitar tone. And on "Steel Guitar Stomp," an instrumental featuring the legendary swing steel player Noel Boggs, Merle contributed a wild, forceful break that overflowed with screaming crescendoes, richly textured rolls and unprecedented tonal colors, all packed into just 30 seconds. If that sounds awesome and definitive, he managed to top it not long afterward, when he played a similarly, blistering lead guitar break on Shug Fisher and the Ranchmen Trio's Capitol recording "Riding Down To Santa Fe."

Except from admiring and awed guitarists, Travis got no credit for these solos, but his reputation grew nonetheless. By 1945 he was leading his own western band and in March 1946 he signed with Capitol Records as a vocalist. His first release, "No Vacancy" b/w "Cincinnati Lou," was a country hit. Though he took no guitar breaks, Merle's guitar playing was a part of the record. Both songs were original compositions, and the Travis guitar style provided a rhythmic foundation for nearly every song he wrote, as well as the vast majority of those he recorded.

From then on Travis' honky tonk hits—"Divorce Me C.O.D.," "Sweet Temptation," "So Round! So Firm! So Fully Packed" and all the others, featured at least one brief guitar break. He also recorded a series of radio transcriptions for Capitol: some were vocals with acoustic guitar and others solo guitar instrumentals of varying lengths. On the latter songs, Merle often reached back to songs he'd absorbed in Muhlenberg County, songs with titles like "Everly Rag" and, of course, pop tunes like "Bicycle Built for Two" and "Tuck Me to Sleep in My Old 'Tucky Home." The transcriptions, played on radio stations across the country, helped to further spread the influence of his guitar playing. In 1946 he also recorded an album for Capitol titled *Folk Songs of the Hills*, an album of old and newly composed original tunes that included future country classics like "16 Tons," "Dark as a Dungeon" and "Nine Pound Hammer."

It's important to discuss another, more controversial aspect of Merle's guitar experience here. Around 1947 he met craftsman/inventor Paul Bigsby. Merle wanted to build a guitar that had the kind of sustain a solidbody electric steel guitar had, and Bigsby insisted he could build such an instrument. Merle sketched what he wanted on a piece of KXLA radio stationery, and Bigsby built him a beautiful, cutaway solidbody guitar of bird's-eye maple with a headstock designed with the keys all on one side and a single pickup. It was a thing of singular beauty, and resides today in the Country Music Hall of Fame in Nashville.

But in later years, Merle insisted that he, in effect, "invented" the Fender guitar—a claim Leo Fender disputed. The facts favor Fender. In truth, the Bigsby Travis played wasn't the first solidbody electric Spanish guitar;

Rickenbacker introduced its Electro model in 1935. Also, Leo Fender himself was experimenting with a solidbody electric as early as 1944. Travis' guitar is smaller than the boxier Broadcaster (later Telecaster) Fender introduced in 1949, and if anything the Bigsby resembles a Les Paul prototype rather than a Fender (though it didn't influence Les' design). However, the headstock for Fender's Stratocaster, introduced in 1954, is identical to Travis' Bigsby.

Travis' earliest solo instrumental LP came in the mid-'50s. *The Merle Travis Guitar* featured solo electric fingerpicked versions of a number of Muhlenberg County favorites like "Bicycle Built for Two," "Goodbye My Blue Bell" and "Bugle Call Rag" as well as local favorites like "Saturday Night Shuffle," another variation on the old "Buck and Wing" number. His attack and phrasing were flawless and shimmering, his tone diamond-hard. Another Muhlenberg favorite not on the album, but later released as a single, was "Cannonball Rag," a Kennedy Jones tune that is perhaps Travis' best-known instrumental.

By the '50s his influence and impact were clear, even though Chet Atkins was doing far more instrumental recording. Hank Thompson, vocalist and western bandleader, so admired Merle that not only did he learn his style, he had Gibson build him a custom-inlaid Super 400 electric identical to the one Travis used.

Merle's instrumental style changed little, and he still did outstanding vocal recordings, among them an awe-inspiring version of Rusty Draper's "Gambler's Guitar," featuring some of his most furious playing in years. Other recordings were bluesy vocals done with guitarist Roy Lanham and his vocal/instrumental group, the Whippoorwills. Tennessee Ernie Ford's 1955 million-selling version of "Sixteen Tons" brought Merle into prominence, and *Folk Songs of the Hills*, the 1947 78-rpm album that originally included "Sixteen Tons," was issued as an LP titled *Back Home*.

But Travis didn't take to his sudden celebrity well. His view of himself and his accomplishments often seemed to degenerate into brutal self-deprecation. He was often dependent on alcohol and pills (he was incarcerated for drug abuse at California's Carmarillo State Hospital for a time). His longtime friend Hank Penny, who'd known him since the WLW days, said that every time Merle's career took an upswing, "a near-tragedy occurred." Though Travis became a legend, elected to the Country Music Hall of Fame in 1977, he seemed to enjoy adulation as much as the average citizen would enjoy an IRS audit.

He did continue performing, however. The Capitol transcriptions he did in the late '40s, all his instrumentals and a few vocals were issued as *Walkin' the Strings* around 1960. Around 1962 *Travis!* was released, featuring jazzy recreations of his '40s hits, with the superb steel guitar of Curly Chalker. In 1964 he created a brilliant sequel to *Back Home* with *Songs of the Coal Mines,* containing more outstanding evocations of life in Muhlenberg County. A year later came *Merle Travis and Joe Maphis,* an album of fiery duets between the two old friends. *Strictly Guitar,* issued around 1968, featured more pop instrumentals, which Travis played on electric guitar with a rhythm section, including "Heart of My Heart," his outstanding version of Fats Waller's "Dance of the Goldenrod," and the brilliant "Cannonball Rag," long a staple of his repertoire. His final Capitol album with Johnny Bond—issued in the early '60s—was the horrendously overproduced *Songs of the Delmore Brothers,* an album that did neither Bond, Travis nor the Delmores justice.

Merle recorded very little in the early '70s. He played some fine guitar on the Nitty Gritty Dirt Band's 1973 album *Will the Circle Be Unbroken,* which featured Doc Watson, Earl Scruggs, Roy Acuff and Maybelle Carter (it was Merle's first meeting with Watson captured on record). He also managed to record a rockabilly EP with Texas rocker Ray Campi in the mid-'70s. Finally, in 1980, after leaving California for the Cherokee Nation of eastern Oklahoma, he returned to recording with the tradition-oriented CMH label of Los Angeles. After a second two-LP set of instrumentals with Joe Maphis came the fine 1980 double

LP retrospective *The Merle Travis Story* (CMH), featuring recreations of all his major coal mine, honky tonk and instrumental classics. The follow-up, *Light Singin' and Heavy Pickin'*, was listless and dull while *Guitar Standards*, another double set, featured more pop instrumentals recorded with a small, sympathetic group of Nashville sessionmen in an Albuquerque, New Mexico studio. The 1981 *Travis Pickin'*, nominated for a Grammy, contained more solo acoustic instrumentals, a throwback to the Capitol transcriptions contained on *Walkin' the Strings*. It was his last solo LP.

He continued working and recording, doing another CMH double set that paid tribute to his old employer Clayton McMichen, but Merle's voice was horribly worn out, and he looked ancient on the album cover. The toll of his years of self-abuse was showing. His coordination was not what it had been. He turned to writing warm and witty reminiscences of his early career, his perceptive historical perspective combining with a raconteur's skill. These reminiscences were published in the *JEMF Quarterly, Guitar World,* and *Country Music.*

It was clear Merle was still going downhill physically. On October 19, 1983 he collapsed of a heart attack at his home near Tahlequah, Oklahoma. Rushed to a nearby hospital, Travis died the next morning. Funeral services were held in Oklahoma, and featured a special program by his protégé, vocalist/guitarist Tom Bresh, who learned to play in the Travis style from Merle himself.

Merle Travis may have been uncomfortable with his fame, but his efforts helped make the guitar—particularly the electric guitar—a viable solo instrument in country music. For that, for the inspiration he gave to others, as well as his marvelous playing, singing, songwriting and journalism, we can all be grateful.

DISCOGRAPHY

It is unfortunate that of all Travis' classic Capitol albums released in the '50s and '60s, only *The Best of Merle Travis* and *Walkin' the Strings* are currently available (the former as a budget album, the latter as a French import). The rest of the other Capitol albums are out of print (though *The Merle Travis Guitar* was reissued in the mid-'70s as a budget package), and the originals bring anywhere from $30 to $50 in collector's auctions. Likewise, none of Travis' early recordings on King, ARA or Atlas are available (and the original 78s go for fantastic prices in auctions, too).

However, one recent reissue series makes available a number of Travis' classic 1940s honky tonk sides is the two-volume *Country Music Is Here to Stay: 20 Golden Greats Volumes One and Two.* This excellent collection doesn't come from Capitol's American operation, but from its Australian division. Generously programmed with 20 songs per album, it includes, along with most of Capitol's country hits of the period, Travis' original versions of "No Vacancy," "Information, Please," "So Round! So Firm! So Fully Packed" and "Fat Gal." It also includes three of the 1946 solo acoustic recordings from *Folk Songs of the Hills.* It's never certain how long these foreign collections stay in print, but like all the imports noted in this book, Down Home Music is the most likely source for them.

There is other Travis material available, though its future, too, is uncertain. The later recordings he made for CMH are generally available, though the label's recent financial problems have caused it to delete a number of its earlier LPs. The strongest sets are definitely the two-LP *Merle Travis Story* and *Guitar Standards*, a second two-album set dedicated to Tin Pan Alley instrumentals. *Travis Pickin'* is also still available. Less easy to find are *Light Singin' and Heavy Pickin'* and *Country Guitar Greats* with Joe Maphis. *The Guitar Player,* on Shasta Records, is a compendium of Travis' appearances on Jimmy Wakely's CBS radio show of the mid-'50's and features some excellent guitar work (check out "Gambler's Guitar" in particular). The Nitty Gritty Dirt Band's *Will the Circle Be Unbroken,* (United Artists), though not among Merle Travis' most distinguished work, is still available.

DOC WATSON

Doc Watson represents a vital link to traditional country music. The great hillbilly string bands of the 1920s and '30s are long gone, their few surviving members well into their seventies or eighties. The pioneers of bluegrass are in their sixties and seventies, and many of the traditional folk balladeers such as John Jacob Niles are also part of history. Watson has managed to preserve these styles in his own repertoire.

Watson demonstrates continued vitality of these styles to thousands in a way that old 78s just can't do. He offers them up not as museum pieces, but as valid, vital music. Nor does he confine himself to those styles, having a solid command of mainstream country music of the '40s and '50s and a clear understanding of the blues that enhance his repertoire.

Watson's playing has had considerable impact on today's school of younger acoustic-flatpicking guitarists like Jon Sholle, Dan Crary, Norman Blake and Tony Rice, all brilliant exponents with their own distinctive approaches. Certainly Watson contributed to flatpicking, though he had antecedents in Joe

Maphis, Arthur "Guitar Boogie" Smith and Riley Puckett. What Doc did was synthesize their styles into a lucid, confident technique of his own—the precision and purity of his playing makes him instantly recognizable. He took Maphis' dizzying flatpicking, Arthur Smith's clean, clear phrasing and Puckett's old-timey, more primitive techniques and melded them into his own sound. One can hear them along with Merle Travis and Chet Atkins, all pillars of the Doc Watson sound.

As a fingerpicker, Watson is clearly influenced by the late Merle Travis (who also provided a first name for Watson's son and performing partner). Doc's fingerpicking has all the syncopation and swing of the Travis style at its finest, and Doc, playing along with his son Merle, can create lush textures which, with the occasional juxtaposition of blues riffs, can give his music a stark, foreboding eeriness.

Doc and Merle have been performing together for nearly two decades now, after emerging from relative obscurity in their native North Carolina. But Doc has also been surprisingly effective with other artists; he began his career as a sideman, which made him more than capable of functioning within a group. Recording with everyone from Jean Ritchie to Flatt and Scruggs, Bill Monroe to the Nitty Gritty Dirt Band, he has shown an admirable consistency. Working with his son, with other pickers, or alone, Doc Watson creates music of rare beauty.

Born Arthel Watson on March 3, 1923 in Deep Gap in western North Carolina, blind since birth, he grew up surrounded by music. His father, a farmer, sang in a nearby Baptist church; he matured hearing the old-time string bands in their heyday. People like Gid Tanner, Charlie Poole and Riley Puckett, all primary exponents of the string band style, left a lasting influence, for Doc still records and performs their music. Traditional folksongs, handed down generation to generation, were routinely sung in the area. But Doc's influences were not as purely rural as one would think; the phonograph was popular, and he drank in the music of the Allen Brothers, the Delmore Brothers (a particularly powerful influence), Jimmie Rodgers and the Carter Family.

Doc's first instrument was harmonica, then five-string fretless banjo (he still plays five-string in a clawhammer style). When he was thirteen, about the time he started attending the Raleigh School for the Blind, he got a guitar. Back in Deep Gap, he and his brother Linny began playing the songs they heard on WCYB of Bristol, Tennessee and on records together.

Watson made his first public appearance around 1940, playing Rodgers' "Muleskinner Blues" at a Boone, North Carolina, fiddlers' convention. His performance earned him a modest local reputation, and offers to perform followed. Around 1942 he was playing at an amateur show at a furniture store; his friend Paul Greer, emceeing the show, was trying to come up with a simple nickname, easier to pronounce, for Arthel. A woman heard the discussion. "Call him 'Doc,'!" she suggested, probably thinking of Sherlock Holmes' sidekick. "Doc" was quickly adopted.

Music remained a sideline for Watson through World War II and into the early '50s. In 1954 he met Tennessee pianist Jack Williams, who was sufficiently impressed with Doc's playing to suggest they form a country dance band to work in east Tennessee and western North Carolina. Jack Williams and the Country Gentlemen was born, and its very nature throws a monkey wrench into the public perception of Doc Watson as an obscure virtuoso picking his acoustic guitar in the idyllic setting of rural North Carolina.

Jack Williams and the Country Gentlemen were a hard-core honky-tonk band—complete with electric instruments—that gigged in bars, VFW posts and similar venues. And Doc was not then picking a Martin; he used an original 1953 Gibson Les Paul. The band fluctuated between four and five pieces, and as rockabilly became popular, thought it appropriate to add "Blue Suede Shoes" and other rock tunes to its repertoire. The idea of Doc Watson ripping off a screaming rockabilly guitar solo might be hard to buy, but he did it—for several years. This experience helped expand his repertoire to country hits of the day, some of which have remained with him since.

Whether Doc was flatpicking exactly the same way he does now is somewhat in doubt. In speaking with Watson's long-time associate Clint Howard, bluegrass/old-time music authority Charles Wolfe got an unusual account of the origins of the fiddle tunes Watson flatpicks. According to Howard, Williams' band had no fiddler, and after 11:30 p.m. on many of its dance jobs, patrons started requesting square dance music. Since the band lacked a fiddler, Doc would crank up his Les Paul and pick out fiddle tunes much as he does now.

This story may be apocryphal, but Joe Maphis was doing the same thing back in the mid-'30s. And while Doc did gain increasing skill with flatpicking, never during this period did he abandon traditional music in any way. He worked as an accompanist with veteran musician Clarence "Tom" Ashley, a fountainhead of traditional music who'd spent years working in medicine shows, performing both as a solo artist and with old-timey string bands in the early days of recording. Ashley appeared with other country acts, including Charlie Monroe and the Kentucky Pardners, before returning to farming in North Carolina.

Doc was among the few accompanists able to follow Ashley's individualistic style, and by 1960 Ashley had attracted the attention of folk music collectors and researchers, among them pioneering Appalachian music authority Ralph Rinzler. That year Rinzler traveled to North Carolina to record Ashley and met Watson in the process. Doc participated in the subsequent recording, *Old Time Music at Clarence Ashley's* (on Folkways). Ashley, with Doc and the rest of his small group, traveled to New York City in 1961 for concerts at Town Hall, and in 1962 Watson, who'd been impressive with Ashley, returned to perform solo. He devastated an audience at the 1963 Newport Folk Festival, and later that year performed with Flatt and Scruggs at Manhattan's Town Hall.

In the meantime other Folkways recordings were produced, including *The Watson Family, Volumes 1 and 2* that featured Doc, his mother, brother Arnold and Gaither Carlton, Arnold Watson's father-in-law. These albums provide valuable insights into the family's understanding of traditional music and its importance to them. In 1964 Doc signed to Vanguard Records as a solo performing artist, and it was with Vanguard that he began to record a series of classic guitar and vocal albums that have had an immense influence on budding flatpickers and fingerpickers worldwide.

As vital as was his first album, *Doc Watson*, the addition to Doc's act in 1965 of his fifteen-year-old son Merle seemed to give Doc an added spark. A superb guitarist in his own right, Merle brought a complementary technique and youthfulness to the stage that kept the act fresh and exciting. The guitar interaction between the two was of a consistently high quality.

During the late '60s he cut a number of albums, including some live performances from Newport. *Doc Watson in Nashville* featured him backed by the best session musicians

in town, including guitarist Grady Martin, pianist Floyd Cramer and Buddy Spicher on fiddle. But if one single album defines and exemplifies Watson's repertoire and guitar virtuosity it's *On Stage*, a compilation of live performances from Manhattan's Town Hall and Cornell University released in 1970. On this double album, Doc and Merle are in near-perfect form.

The selection of songs comprises all of the musical forms that interest Doc. The Delmore Brothers' "Brown's Ferry Blues" and their version of "Deep River Blues," a traditional tune, arranged with a pulsating Merle Travis-like accompaniment, were highly effective. Other traditional tunes such as "The Wreck of the 1262," "Lost John", "Banks of the Ohio" and "Little Sadie" were also included. Representing more modern genres were Jimmie Rodgers' "Jimmie's Texas Blues," "When the Work's All Done This Fall" and "The Clouds Are Gwine to Roll Away" by country songwriter Carson Robison, and more modern material like Hank Snow's "I'm Movin' On" and John D. Loudermilk's exquisite minor-key instrumental "Windy and Warm," also picked in Merle Travis' style.

Though Doc introduces most of his numbers in the standard folk manner, expounding verbally on the song's heritage, his approach is anything but academic. These songs come alive. The tragedy of "Banks of the Ohio" is effectively conveyed as the combbned guitars of Doc and his son create a rolling accompaniment to the lyrics. "Jimmie's Texas Blues" gets an excellent treatment with Doc playing in Rodgers' style, but with far more verve. "Southbound," a song largely written by Merle Watson, features intricate fingerpicked guitar accommaniment at a furious clip, as does "Doc's Guitar." The Watsons' version of "Nine Pound Hammer," entitled "Roll On Buddy," is almost as good as Merle Travis' 1947 version.

Doc's flatpicking is awe-inspiring, particularly on the fiddle tunes. On the medley of "Salt River" and "Bill Cheatham" he plays with remarkable clarity, articulating every note that a fiddler would have played while Merle picks out punchy rhythm guitar behind him. The adaptation of "Billy in the Low Ground," a tune normally associated with Texas fiddlers, is played with the same finesse and evenness of touch and tone.

An equally fine collection released in 1971, *Ballads from Deep Gap*, is a studio recording featuring Doc, Merle and bassist Eric Weissberg (whose version of "Dueling Banjos" was a 1973 hit). Again the material comes from several sources, including Jimmie Rodgers ("My Rough and Rowdy Ways") and Mississippi John Hurt (a version of "Stack O'Lee"—Doc learned Hurt's gentle, ragtime fingerpicking style from the master himself). A tense, pulsing rendition of "The Cuckoo" features Merle's clawhammer banjo. Doc flat-picks an outstanding instrumental called "Texas Gales," taken from a vintage recording by Charlie Bowman.

Around the time *Deep Gap* was issued, Doc had left Vanguard for the small Poppy label. Poppy seemed interested in moving Doc out of a strictly acoustic duet context, placing Doc and his son with small but generally tasteful rhythm sections. The problem was that Doc's guitar work was generally dee-mphasized in favor of vocals. *Elementary Doctor Watson*, his first Poppy album, featured everything from Gershwin's "Summertime" to Eddy Arnold's "I Couldn't Believe It Was True," yet Watson played some excellent guitar nonetheless. His version of the Delmore Brothers' late 1945 release of "Freight Train Boogie" showed his mastery of hot boogie guitar and retained the spirit of the original. His version of Merle Travis' honky tonk hit "Three Times Seven" was equally faithful.

Two other Poppy albums followed: *Then and Now* (in 1973) and *Two Days in November* (in '74), both emphasizing vocals and occasional misguided attempts at string arrangements. Ironically, both albums won Grammy awards for Best Ethnic Recording in their respective years. Doc's United Artists period was his weakest. He issued a number of albums that, though competent and well-played, lacked the fire and passion of his earlier work. Among them were *Lonesome Road, Doc and the Boys* and *Look Away!*. *Live 'n' Pickin'*, recorded in San Francisco in 1978, was somewhat more spirited.

One of Doc's finest achievements in recent years is his 1980 set *Reflections*. Recorded with Chet Atkins, this LP shows two virtuoso musicians having great empathy for each other's work, with the common inspiration of rural backgrounds and the profound influence of Merle Travis. The contrast of Chet's nylon-string playing with Doc's steel string was refreshing. One particularly appealing piece, "Flatt Did It," strings together variations on famous Lester Flatt guitar runs (including the famous "G-run" Flatt developed). The traditional material stimulated some of the most fervent playing either man had recorded for some time.

Flying Fish, the Chicago-based ethnic music record company, was Doc's next label. Joining them in the early '80s, he recorded the outstanding *Doc and Merle Watson's Guitar Album,* (1983) the first album ever to concentrate on the father-son guitar interaction with such stunning results. "Black Mountain Rag," one of the fiddle tunes Doc had flatpicked for years is rerecorded with all its fire intact. "Goin' To Chicago Blues" features some surprising and articulate T-Bone Walker-styled single-string playing, and "Cotton Row" is a study in Doc's smooth, fluent fingerpicking, balanced by Merle's slide guitar. Only on "Liza," recorded as a swing number, does Doc falter. Despite his respect for jazz, he is unable to swing on such material, often fighting to keep away from bluegrass rhythms and losing the battle. Nonetheless, the album is clearly one of his finest, and was nominated for another Grammy in early 1984 as Best Ethnic Recording.

Sometime ago folklorist A.L. Lloyd wrote a brief but lucid essay on Watson for one of his Vanguard albums, wherein Lloyd details the "three musics (that) come together harmoniously in Doc Watson"—folk, rural string band and more modern country. Of that synthesis, he says, "From all of these musics, Doc has taken into his head whatever he found good." It's hard to quarrel with that.

DISCOGRAPHY

Virtually all of Doc Watson's recordings are still available. The earliest album he made, *Old Time Music at Clarence Ashley's* (Folkways, 1960) is in print. So is *The Watson Family Album* (Rounder), featuring various members of his clan performing the music they grew up with.

His Vanguard albums also remain largely available, including his first self-billed LP *Doc Watson: Southbound*, which features his most outstanding guitar work; *Doc Watson & Son*, the album that introduced Merle's superb playing. *Home Again!* and *Doc Watson in Nashville* are still in print, as are *Doc Watson on Stage, The Essential Doc Watson* (both double albums), and the equally essential *Ballads from Deep Gap*.

Some of the Poppy and United Artists material is also still in print, though not all those LPs have been retained in their catalogues. *Look Away!* and *Lonesome Road* (Liberty), the latter one of his weaker sets, can be found. *Doc Watson Favorites* (Liberty) anthologizes several of the other Poppy and United Artists albums, as does *Memories*, a United Artists two-disc compilation (which some mail order houses still list in their catalogues).

The Flying Fish albums, *Red Rocking Chair* and *Doc and Merle Watson's Guitar Album* are, of course, readily available in record stores.

SECONDARY ESSAYS

Junior Barnard

Les Paul and others may have been experimenting with distortion in the '30s and '40s, but no guitarist was using it as effectively or as regularly as Lester Barnard, Jr., one of the most outstanding guitarists ever to work as one of Bob Wills's Texas Playboys. Unlike the delicate Eddie Lang-derived jazz of Eldon Shamblin or the Charlie Christian-influenced Jimmy Wyble, Junior's playing was laden with raw, unsubtle blues-based riffs that hit one in the stomach. He was playing raunchy blues licks that anticipated guitarists like Willie Lee Johnson, Freddy King, James Burton and Eric Clapton. His tone was thick and raspy, nudging his speakers one step closer to premature demise.

Born in Tulsa in 1920, Barnard grew up in the city when it was a veritable jazz hotbed. His brother Gene recalls his feel for the blues, and indeed, some of his later string-bending may have been the result of the influence of Lonnie Johnson or Scrapper Blackwell (though this cannot be determined for sure). After working at KTUL radio in Tulsa until 1941, he wound up with Johnnie Lee Wills

and his Boys, a band led by Bob Wills's younger brother. He played an outstanding—if somewhat restrained—solo on their 1941 Decca recording of "Milk Cow Blues," and joined the Texas Playboys in 1942. Playing on and off with the band for the next three years, he was with it by late 1945 when the Playboys were based near Fresno. His tight, raw solos graced Wills's Columbia recordings, among them "Punkin' Stomp," "Brain Cloudy Blues," "Bob Wills Boogie" and—Junior's greatest recorded instrumental moment—"Fat Boy Rag." The song had begun as a jam session in the midst of the Playboys' San Francisco sessions for the Tiffany Transcriptions series they recorded during 1946 and 1947. Later, it was combined with another Barnard number titled "Soppin' Syrup" for a Columbia recording.

Using an Epiphone Emperor with two pickups and each pickup run through a separate amplifier, Barnard's thick, sustained tone was matchless. He did other recordings, including a gutty (if flawed) solo on Luke Wills's recording of "Bring It On Down to My House,

Honey," but by 1949, after several periods in and out of the Playboys, he left for good. He organized his own band, the Radio Gang, and worked dances in the Fresno area until 1951, when he died of injuries sustained in an auto accident.

DISCOGRAPHY

Junior Barnard's playing can be well-traced today due to a number of interesting reissues. The Johnnie Lee Wills version of "Milk Cow Blues" can be heard on the western swing anthology *Operators' Specials* on the British String label. The original jam session version of "Fat Boy Rag" is not currently available, but the Columbia version is including the Time-Life Country Classics volume on Wills. Numerous examples of Barnard's work with Wills can be heard on *31st Street Blues* (Longhorn), as well as *The Tiffany Transcriptions, Volumes 1, 2 and 3* (Kaleidoscope).

Phil Baugh

Most people never heard of Phil Baugh, but that's not surprising; many country guitar innovators have suffered similar fates. Yet every country guitarist who has ever picked up a Fender Telecaster owes him a debt, for Baugh was one of the pioneers, along with James Burton, of the high-pitched "chicken-pickin'" idiom that defined the "Bakersfield Sound" of the mid '60s as played by Wynn Stewart, Buck Owens and Merle Haggard.

If that seems like dry historical pap, consider that the Bakersfield sound so influenced Waylon Jennings that for over a decade now its premiere steel guitarist, Ralph Mooney, has been an integral part of Waylon's band the Waylors. Baugh, particularly on the records of Stewart and possibly on Haggard's earliest hits, was prominently featured, taking advantage of the Telecaster's naturally treble timbre to create harsh, screaming leads. Baugh, born in 1937, had a single hit of his own in 1965 with "Country Guitar" on the Longhorn Label, which featured his imitations of various guitarists (among them Les Paul, Billy Byrd and Duane Eddy). The song hit the Billboard charts at number 15, and he was later billed as an outstanding country instrumentalist. Baugh used only a volume pedal as an effect to create pedal steel sounds, but in the '70s, after moving to Nashville, he began using a pedal steel-like mechanism attached to his guitar's bridge. Today he remains in Nashville, often working with his band Sound Factory, which also features steel virtuoso Buddy Emmons.

DISCOGRAPHY

Phil Baugh's excellent *Country Guitar* album on Longhorn is again available, and shows off his versatile, creative playing extremely well. The reissue includes "One Man Band," not on the original album, which spotlights Baugh imitating various instruments with his Telecaster, and doing so quite effectively.

Jerry Reed

Today Jerry Reed is ingrained in the American consciousness through his movie redneck image and his raucous, sound-alike hit records. His achievements as a guitarist have been softpedaled to say the least. Nonetheless, Reed has been responsible for some outstanding country guitar playing over the years, both on his own recordings and as a veteran Nashville studio musician, all of which took place before listeners outside Nashville knew who he was.

Jerry Reed Hubbard was born in Atlanta in 1937 and began playing guitar while still in grade school. After a brief interlude working in local cotton mills, during which time he continued playing, Reed came to the attention of local promoter Bill Lowery, who helped him get a Capitol recording contract in 1955, at the dawn of the rockabilly era. His early releases were respectable, though sold minimally, though his rockabilly consciousness showed through in his songwriting. After a military stint, Reed moved to Nashville, where his abilities as a guitarist, fingerpicking his own version of the Chet Atkins/Merle Travis style, gradually raised him to the A-team of local session musicians. Among the hit recordings he worked on were Bobby Bare's "Detroit City."

Even more significantly, Reed's rockabilly abilities brought him into contact with Elvis Presley, who recorded his songs "Guitar Man" and "U.S. Male" in 1966 and 1967 respectively, with Reed playing lead guitar on the sessions. Chet Atkins took Reed under his wing and created the raucous persona that served him on records like the Presley-inspired "The Tupelo Mississippi Flash" and "Amos Moses."

Reed as guitarist has two distinctive techniques, his best-known being the "claw" style of fingerpicking in which he attacks the strings aggressively, using them both melodically and rhythmically. Where Travis played with thumb and index finger and Atkins played with thumb and two fingers, Reed uses them all, and is particularly outstanding on several instrumental albums, both alone and with Atkins. However, in recent years he has laid fingerpicking aside in the interest of developing his flatpicking electric guitar capability, and on recent albums like *Half and Half* (RCA) he's shown that his touch and talents are intact, despite the fact he is less distinctive as a flatpicker. It will most likely be in the latter category that his contributions to the guitar will be remembered.

DISCOGRAPHY

Unfortunately, not much of Jerry Reed's work is in print today. Easiest to find are his *Greatest Hits* on RCA. Little, if any, of his instrumental work is available in any form.

Zeke Turner

Grady Martin, Hank Garland and Chet Atkins were easily among the most-recorded studio guitarists in country music. Before them came Zeke Turner. Born James C. Grishaw in Lynchburg, Virginia in 1923, his earliest influences were the unheralded tenor guitarist Otto "Coco" Heimal of the team of Candy and Coco, as well as jazzman George Barnes and Light Crust Doughboys electric guitarist Muryel "Zeke" Campbell. Heimal's snappy, bright attack and fleet improvisational lines both amply influenced Turner's later style.

His older brother, guitarist Eddie Grishaw (aka Zeb Turner), was equally talented, but Zeke's first excursion to Nashville, in 1945, put him in an excellent position. After recording with the Nashville-based Bullet Records, he connected with Red Foley around 1946, replacing Chet Atkins in Foley's backup band and working the Opry and Foley's early morning WSM radio show. In between, Turner and the remainder of Foley's excellent band (Zeb, fiddler Tommy Jackson, bassist Louis Innis and steel guitarist Jerry Byrd) began to get regular employment in the studios.

Turner's abilities as a lead guitarist, playing twin leads with Zeb and even three-way harmonies with Byrd (as on Red Foley's "Blues in My Heart"), became apparent quickly. He could not only create tight, economical leads, but had an unique "dead-string" approach to rhythm guitar, playing figures which he muted with his right hand. This technique, which enhanced the rhythmic base of numerous records in the days before drums, was particularly effective on such early Hank Williams recordings as "My Bucket's Got a Hole in It," "Move It on Over" (his solo break here influenced scores of early rock guitarists) and "Lovesick Blues." Equally influential among rockabillies was Turner's low-register solo (he favored the bass strings) on Foley's 1948 hit "Tennessee Saturday Night." But perhaps his best-known break was the unrelenting rhythm on the Delmore Brothers' 1949 "Blues Stay Away from Me," one of the biggest country smashes of 1949, with one of the most frequently copied riffs in country music. Another less famous riff was one Turner created for the Delmores' "Good Time Saturday Night," which was later appropriated by Carl Perkins for his 1958 recording "Perkins Wiggle" on Sun (not issued until the late '70s).

Turner no longer plays professionally, but his tight, economical and much-imitated style in many ways helped set the standards for solo breaks on country music recordings.

DISCOGRAPHY

Most of the recordings Zeke Turner worked on are, regrettably, unavailable today. However, his most important work with Hank Williams can be heard on *Hank Williams' 40 Greatest Hits* (Polygram) and *Hank Williams* (Time-Life Country Classics Series). His legendary guitar work with the Delmores can be heard on *Songs by the Delmore Brothers* (Gusto). Zeke can also be heard on *The Delmore Brothers' When They Let The Hammer Down* (Bear Family). Some of Zeb's best 1949-1953 King material has been reissued on *Jersey Rock* (Bear Family).

Clarence White

Clarence White's tragic death in 1973—he was struck by a drunken driver while unloading instruments on a Palmdale, California street—came at the dawn of new stature for the brilliant bluegrass and country-rock guitarist. At the time his old friends like mandolinist David Grisman and guitarist Tony Rice were pioneering a critically acclaimed new form of acoustic music that drew upon jazz, ethnic music and rock as well as bluegrass—something White had pioneered long before. Had he lived, his place as a founder of this music would have become fully clear.

Born in Maine in 1944, Clarence moved to California with his family in 1954 and began working with his brothers in a bluegrass trio known as the Country Boys. By 1961 he was already trying out his concepts of flatpicked bluegrass guitar solos—this at a time when few guitarists in bluegrass were doing anything similar (one exception the Stanley Brothers' George Shuffler). Doc Watson, remember, was just about to be discovered by Ralph Rinzler.

When the Country Boys evolved into the Kentucky Colonels in 1962, Clarence continued to explore new ideas. His rhythm guitar style transcended the traditional "driving" rhythms. He created complex, swirling chords and choked strings, the latter technique rarely heard in a bluegrass context. He began to play jazz solos, such as a Django-inspired version of "The Sheik of Araby," with the Colonels.

By the mid '60s the Colonels were beginning to experiment with amplified instruments, and Clarence again was in the forefront. When the group disbanded, he began working with local Los Angeles country bands. He and drummer Gene Parsons also installed a unique mechanism in a Telecaster that would, through a series of springs and levers linked to the guitar's strap button, permit the pitch of the guitar's B string to be raised like a pedal steel's. Clarence used this device in his playing and was soon working sessions with the Byrds as well as his own band, Nashville West. In 1968 White and Parsons joined the Byrds, and for the next five years he gained thousands of fans who never heard of the Kentucky Colonels. Both his flatpicking and his string bender brought him attention, and on songs like "Old Blue" and "Nashville West," with the Byrds, "Comin' Into Los Angeles" with Arlo Guthrie and Linda Ronstadt's "Silver Threads and Golden Needles" he was prominently featured.

When the Byrds split in February 1973, he returned to working acoustically, bringing his rock experience and ideas to acoustic music. The Kentucky Colonels reunited, better than ever, and Clarence was in the midst of cutting his own solo LP when he died. He left one of the most varied legacies of any American guitarist, his bluegrass and rock playing both beyond criticism. Since his career has been well-documented on records, his legacy will remain a wellspring of ideas and inspiration for acoustic and electric guitarists for years to come.

DISCOGRAPHY

Clarence White's earliest work with the Kentucky Colonels can be heard on *Livin' in the Past* (Briar) and *Onstage* (Rounder). His early electric guitar work is available on the album *Nashville West* (Briar), and his stint with the Byrds spanned three albums: *Sweetheart of the Rodeo, Dr. Byrds and Mr. Hyde* and the two-record *Untitled* (all Columbia). The return to progressive acoustic bluegrass is chronicled on *Muleskinner* (Ridgerunner). Several tracks from his never-completed solo album were issued on *Silver Meteor* (Blair), an anthology of southern California country-rock.

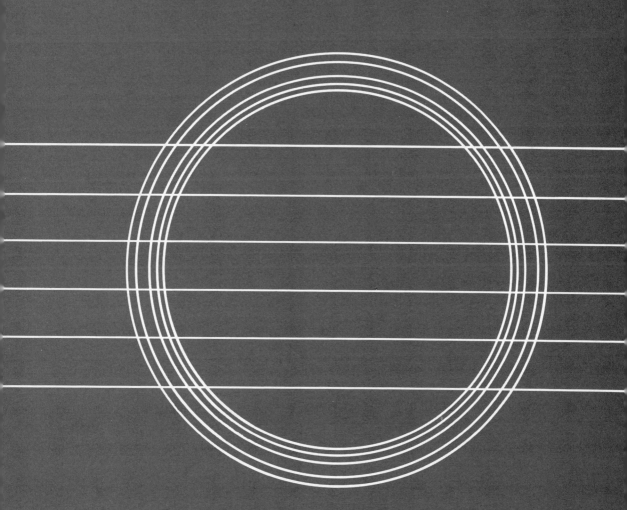

JAZZ

CHARLIE BYRD

There has always been controversy surrounding Charlie Byrd's status as a jazz guitarist. Certainly he can't be seen in the same light as Barney Kessel, Tal Farlow, Wes Montgomery or Pat Martino, all of whose roots are in the Charlie Christian school. Byrd is not completely Christian-based; his reputation is for playing jazz on the nylon string guitar, and he has deep musical roots in classical guitar, developed through years of formal study.

Yet it would be unfair to exclude him from his rightful place as a jazz guitarist for that, or for the part he played in the bossa nova craze of the early '60s. Charlie Byrd has, in fact, carved out a unique niche for himself. As the preeminent nylon-string guitarist in jazz, he has stood up to those who try to wedge him into the pigeonhole of a Brazilian-flavored mood musician. Brazilian music remains an important facet of his music, but it is precisely that—one facet.

Byrd's approach is based on his classical training, which has allowed him to play with great subtlety when a piece of music or a part-

icular passage demands it. And if anyone doubts his ability to swing, listening to him with the Great Guitars (an all-star trio consisting of himself, Herb Ellis and Barney Kessel) should convince them of his abilities, for he can play along on the old Charlie Christian favorites as if he'd been there when Christian first performed them.

Charlie Byrd was born in Chuckatuck, Virginia, on September 16, 1925. Growing up in that area near Chesapeake Bay known as the Tidewater region, he came in contact with both black and white musicians. His father, an amateur musician who played guitar and mandolin in the country tradition, was his first real musical influence. Charlie, who began playing at age nine, soaked up the blues from the black guitarists he'd heard in the region.

The radio also played a role in shaping his music. He became an early fan of Les Paul, listening avidly to Les and his trio. By the time he was in his teens, he was listening to Charlie Christian, and got hold of a Django Reinhardt 78 rpm disc that left an indelible mark on his playing. During the '40s he entered the army and worked as a musician there, playing electric guitar. He met Django Reinhardt while stationed in France, and had the opportunity to play with him. Though some critics have downgraded Reinhardt's influence on Byrd, his frequent use of octaves—a Reinhardt trademark—makes that argument somewhat specious.

Byrd worked around New York in the late '40s, and his interest in classical music continued to grow. By 1950 he'd moved to Washington, D.C. to commence classical guitar studies with the acclaimed teacher Sophocles Papas. He took this aspect of his musical career seriously enough to be accepted as a student in world famous Andres Segovia's master class in Italy. But Byrd didn't abandon jazz during this time. In fact, he was a guitarist in Woody Herman's orchestra, filling a chair that had previously been held by such prestigious players as Hy White, Billy Bauer, Chuck Wayne and Jimmy Raney.

Byrd's home base in the late '50s was Washington, and he worked extensively at the Showboat Lounge in town with a trio, but he also traveled to jazz clubs such as the Village Vanguard in New York. In December he recorded an excellent live album there with his trio. Charlie's versions of "Just Squeeze Me" and "Why Was I Born" are harmonically rich and filled with subtlety. He is already experimenting with south-of-the-border concepts, as evidenced by his version of "You Stepped Out of a Dream." But it can't be said that the album was a complete artistic success. His twenty-minute *"Fantasia" on Which Side Are You On?* (the labor protest song) has its interesting moments, but the Latin beat becomes monotonous, and his improvisations begin to sound like self-indulgent, pretentious movie music after the first few minutes.

Byrd got the chance to take his interest in exotic music to the source when the U.S. State Department booked his group on a 1961 South American tour. In Brazil, he was exposed to Latin music in its richest forms, and the notion of combining jazz improvisation and values with the music he was hearing entered his head.

He had the chance to try out his concept that next year, when he and tenor saxophonist Stan Getz recorded *Jazz Samba*. The idea in and of itself wasn't terribly new, as Laurindo Almeida had done similar work with flutist Bud Shank in the early '50s. But the Getz-Byrd collaboration, utilizing songs from Brazil's finest composers, including Antonio Carlos Jobim, made all the difference. The album became a jazz classic that had huge commercial success and was instrumental in furthering the bossa nova craze (which the media erroneously heralded as the successor to the then-popular twist craze, a measure of its inherent stupidity on musical matters).

Byrd enjoyed popularity in the early '60s with this style, but he refused to allow himself to be dominated by it. In May 1963, at the peak of his bossa nova popularity, he recorded another live album, *Byrd at the Gate*, for Riverside. The repertoire was heavily directed toward non-Brazilian, mainstream jazz, featuring such guests as trumpeter Clark Terry and saxophonist Seldon Powell augmenting his regular trio (Keter Betts, bass; Bill Reichenbach, drums).

Like so many other jazzmen, Byrd's finest work seems brought out by the presence of other great players. Perhaps it is the push or the inspiration they give him, but in any case *Byrd at the Gate* contains a number of superlative performances. "Blues for Night People," done with the trio, had much of the same drive and swing values that Wes Montgomery's music had demonstrated in previous years. If there is a fault in the entire album, it is that Charlie's classical guitar just isn't well amplified. Still, Terry in particular seemed to draw out some fine solos from Byrd, at times with the passion of his idol Reinhardt. That year Charlie Byrd won *Down Beat's* annual readers' poll in the guitar category.

Through the '60s Byrd continued to record on his own, and his records sold respectably, but most of them were in the Brazilian mold on which he based his popularity. On occasions he would record with other artists. Among these was his 1967 rendering of "The Duck" with former boss Woody Herman and his orchestra. It was not one of Byrd's better performances, seemingly hampered by a poorly amplified guitar that didn't permit the nuances and tonal colors of his playing to come through completely.

By the early '70s the bossa nova fad was largely dead; "The Girl from Ipanema"—recorded in 1964—was probably its most enduring legacy. Still, Charlie continued working around the world. In 1974 Herb Ellis and Barney Kessel and Byrd began working together as the Great Guitars. The concept was a highly favorable one, permitting three of jazz guitar's finest exponents to work together, pushing each other along, challenging and stimulating one another's creativity and most of all complementing one another.

Kessel's style, grown from his love of Charlie Christian and bebop, and Ellis' bluesy, swinging technique laden with gentle humor, both worked remarkably well with Byrd. In addition, Charlie has continued his solo performing and recording career, doing a variety of jazz and Latin material.

Today, when relatively few jazz guitarists are working in the unamplified Spanish guitar style, Charlie has continued to play superbly. In 1979 he began recording for Concord Jazz, which has been recording the Great Guitars nearly from their inception. His material has varied from straightforward mainstream jazz to exquisite Latin albums. *Bluebyrd*, his first album for Concord, featured a burning interpretation of "It Don't Mean a Thing (If It Ain't Got That Swing)" that should have put to rest those questions of the jazz values in his playing. Fats Waller's "Jitterbug Waltz" gets a light, airy treatment with some stunning phrasing. There's a dizzying version of "This Can't Be Love." An even greater surprise is a straightahead, driving version of Louis Jordan's 1949 r&b hit "Saturday Night Fish Fry" with solos so swinging and shimmering that they take on Les Paul-like characteristics.

Byrd has continued to record for Concord into the '80s in a variety of contexts. He also runs the Washington-based jazz club/ restaurant Charlie's Georgetown. He's recently recorded with Laurindo Almeida, the Brazilian who in many ways pioneered his nation's flavor in jazz before there was such a thing as bossa nova music. *Latin Odyssey* combines the talents of the two into some truly impressive renditions of South American compositions, most played in a stately manner close to their origins.

Charlie Byrd will probably—correctly—always be associated with bossa nova and Latin music, for it has constituted much of his recorded output and musical direction. Nonetheless, Byrd isn't confined to those idioms, as shown by the stylistic variety of his recordings. His understanding of all jazz styles is solid, and his ability to take on the blues or swing cannot be questioned. Likewise, his impeccable sense of taste and warmth remain beyond criticism.

DISCOGRAPHY

Some of Byrd's earliest material is no longer available. However, *First Flight* and *Midnight Guitar*, his fairly early Savoy material, are both available, as are *In Greenwich Village* and *Latin Byrd* (Milestone).

Byrd, too, has done considerable recording for Concord Jazz, including all the Great Guitars LPs previously mentioned in the Kessel discography, as well as *Bluebyrd, Brazilian Soul, Sugarloaf Suite, Brazilville* and *Latin Odyssey. The Christmas Album* is also available on Concord's classically oriented Concerto label.

CHARLIE CHRISTIAN

harlie Christian seemed out of place. Just a few days earlier he'd been playing in an Oklahoma City club for a few bucks a night. Now, on the evening of August 16, 1939 he stood in the ritzy Victor Hugo restaurant in Beverly Hills, California, clad in purple shirt, pointy-toed shoes and a string tie. He certainly did not look like a future member of the Benny Goodman organization, not next to the dapper Goodman—or Lionel Hampton, for that matter. Indeed, Christian looked every bit the Okie he was.

Goodman's producer John Hammond had been hearing things about this 23 year old guitarist who'd set everyone on their ears back in Oklahoma City. He'd arranged to bring Charlie out west. Goodman, known for his absent-mindedness, hadn't had time to listen to Christian and may well have let the cowboy getup fan his skepticism. He was certainly in no hurry to listen. But Hammond wasn't about to let the trip be wasted, so during the orchestra's intermission, just before the Goodman quintet was to go on, bassist

Artie Bernstein and Hammond set up Christian's Gibson EH-150 amplifier. Goodman saw the amplifier—and Christian—and glared over at Hammond. But it was too late, so he called for the elegant ballad "Rose Room," trying, perhaps, to throw the interloper a curve.

It took only a couple of minutes for Goodman to realize he'd missed by a mile. The incredibly sophisticated improvisations that burbled from Christian's Gibson electric guitar were permitted by Goodman to continue for over 20 choruses. The song went on 47 minutes as musicians and audience beheld the genius in their midst. By the song's end the Benny Goodman quintet had become a sextet, and Charlie Christian had become an important figure in the jazz world.

Perhaps the one thing that threw everyone about Charlie Christian when they first heard him was that his style was fully formed. There were literally no loose ends, weak spots or overextensions. He was displaying a radical new approach to guitar with every note he played, moving the electric guitar, which had been commercially produced only since 1936, into the forefront of jazz. Never again would guitarists be confined to playing rhythm accompaniment alone, or to soloing only in small groups. They could now compete with entire orchestras, horn sections or individual hornmen to create their own solo space. Because of Charlie Christian, the electric guitar rapidly transcended any suspicions that it was a mere gimmick and rapidly assumed its place as a serious instrument not only in jazz, but in American music in general.

Certainly Christian was not the first major American jazz guitarist, nor the first to give serious thought to amplification. Eddie Lang and Dick McDonough were both outstanding acoustic jazzmen who had helped establish the guitar as an important jazz instrument. Eddie Durham and Floyd Smith, among others, had played amplified instruments before Christian. But musically, none had an approach as unorthodox—or as galvanizing—as his. Within two years an entire new generation of electric jazz guitarists was born in Christian's shadow.

But by 1942 Christian himself was gone, a victim of tuberculosis aggravated by his unwillingness to follow doctor's orders. In those three brief years he had taken the electric guitar to undreamed of heights, but also had begun to veer from the swing music that nurtured him towards the newer, sophisticated jazz idiom known as bebop, a style he is credited with helping to develop. So Christian, his contributions to swing notwithstanding, formed a bridge between the swing and bop schools of jazz. Goodman, though a mentor and a colleague, was in many ways less of a contemporary than other bop pioneers like trumpeter Dizzy Gillespie and drummer Kenny Clarke.

Unlike many innovators who have to struggle through lengthy periods of obscurity and even against adverse criticism, Charlie Christian enjoyed acclaim almost from the moment he perfected his sound. Dizzy Gillespie might have had to face older jazzmen who called bebop "Chinese music" and worse.

Christian, on the other hand, had a much easier time of it. His years of dues-paying were relatively brief and his rise to fame was unencumbered.

He was born in Bonham, Texas, a dozen or so miles south of the Red River that separates Texas and Oklahoma, in 1916, into a family deeply immersed in music. His mother was a pianist; his father played guitar; his older brothers Eddie and Clarence played bass and mandolin, respectively. The Christians moved to Dallas, where the parents worked in a movie house for a time, then moved to Oklahoma City around 1921.

Charlie's interest in guitar began relatively early; he started building guitars out of cigar boxes in school, a feat that impressed the great black novelist Ralph Ellison, who grew up with Christian. The influence of his family was clear, but he clearly had his own ideas as well. "When Charlie Christian would amuse and amaze us at school with his first guitar, he would be playing his own riffs," Ellison wrote years later. "But they were based on sophisticated chords and progressions that Blind Lemon Jefferson never knew. No other cigar box made such sounds."

Some of his early music was done with a bass fiddle (possibly the influence of brother Eddie). But Charlie also played guitar with his father, who had gone blind, in a family band that worked the streets of Oklahoma City. He began gigging professionally with the Jolly Jugglers, a band led by one of his brothers, then progressed to work with the Anna Mae Winburn orchestra. At some point during these years he heard tenor saxophonist Lester Young for the first time.

Young's playing became a powerful influence on young Christian. His long solo lines and unique, linear approach (inspired, ironically, by white saxophonist Frankie Trumbauer) can clearly be heard in Christian's later work, combined with his own ideas. But by the mid '30s Charlie had signed on to play acoustic guitar and bass with Alphonso Trent's orchestra.

The idea of an amplified jazz guitar was nothing new. In May 1935 Eddie Durham had recorded a solo with Jimmie Lunceford's orchestra on "Hittin' the Bottle" using a non-electric resonator guitar. And in 1938 Durham, using an electric instrument and working as trombonist/arranger with Count Basie's band, recorded with a smaller section of the Basie band known as the Kansas City Six. He played single-string solos that in some ways anticipated Christian.

The two, Christian and Durham, met in Oklahoma City. Christian was all ears, and it's likely that he heard enough of Durham to understand the potential. Christian was still playing acoustic at the time, but wanted a horn-like sound. Durham told *Guitar Player* magazine in 1979 that he suggested Christian play only down-strokes to get the staccato sound he needed, and it's likely that Christian heeded that advice. In any case he bought himself a Gibson ES-150, then the best production model electric guitar (and the only one of substance) available and rejoined Alphonso Trent's band in 1937 or early 1938.

That band stayed together for a year, and Christian honed his ideas in two remote parts of the west: Casper, Wyoming and the Dakotas. 17 year old Mary Osborne, who would become a fine jazz guitarist in her own right, was floored when she heard the Trent band perform in Bismarck, North Dakota. All Christian's influences—Lester Young, Eddie Durham, as well as other guitarists he may have heard, such as Kansas City's Jim Daddy Walker—were beginning to coalesce.

In 1939 Christian returned to Oklahoma City and rejoined his brother Eddie at the Ritz Cafe, then left for a group led by pianist Leslie Sheffield. By the summer of 1939 the concept of electric jazz guitar was gaining ample credibility. In addition to Durham's sides with the Kansas City Six, guitarist Floyd Smith had recorded an electric steel guitar solo—"Floyd's Guitar Blues"—with Andy Kirk and his Clouds of Joy. Around that time pianist Mary Lou Williams of that group was in Oklahoma City and had the chance to hear Christian. She immediately contacted producer John Hammond, who was heading west to record Benny Goodman in Los Angeles.

Hammond arrived, met Christian, and had the same reaction Mary Osborne and Mary Lou Williams had had. He made arrangements for Charlie to take a train west, ostensibly as a guest on a Goodman radio show. Eddie Christian and some friends saw him off at the station. By August 19 Charlie was a member of the Goodman organization, featured on a "Camel Caravan" broadcast live from the Hollywood Bowl. He debuted on "Flying Home." A surviving radio dub of the performance tells the tale. After Goodman, Lionel Hampton and Christian state the theme, the guitarist emerges with a bluesy improvisation featuring complex lines and tasteful, high-register string-choking in just the correct places. He creates rhythmic comping behind Hampton's vibraphone break before returning to an ensemble riff with Hampton and the others. It is, all in all, a perfect performance.

A measure of the effect Christian had on the jazz world was that less than a month later he was recruited for an all-star recording session under Lionel Hampton's name. Suddenly the kid from Oklahoma City was comping behind saxophonists Coleman Hawkins, Ben Webster and Chuck Berry as well as trumpeter Dizzy Gillespie. On a subsequent Hampton session Charlie would swap hot choruses with trumpeter Red Allen.

But it was on Christian's first session with Goodman's sextet on September 2, 1939 that his brilliance was captured for the first time. "Rose Room" and two takes of "Flying Home" serve as permanent documents of the life he breathed into both numbers. "Stardust" reveals the essence of Christian's style. The tempo remains restrained, and he fills his solo with lush chording strongly reminiscent of Dick McDonough's. He quotes the melody of "Pretty Baby" before returning to chords, and then plays a beautifully articulated single-string solo which ends with a six note ascending figure in octaves to conclude the number.

As time went on Christian seemed to become even more comfortable within Goodman's fold. His playing on their November 22, 1939 recording of "Soft Winds" is marked by humor and self-assurance, though he largely confines himself to ensemble riffing behind Goodman's clarinet. His self-confidence as a soloist is clear on "Seven Come Eleven," a classic Goodman/Christian collaboration with a polyphonic dimension. The real test of Christian's abilities, however, comes with the full Goodman orchestra on "Honeysuckle Rose," recorded at the same session. The superb 32-bar solo he contributes shows him more than able to hold his own among the likes of Goodman and his famous trumpeter Ziggy Elman.

By the end of 1939 Christian was a success beyond his wildest fantasies. His soft-spoken personality made him immensely popular with the band, and his playing delighted audiences. Reunited with some old associates as part of the Kansas City Six at the December 24, 1939 "Spirituals to Swing" concert at Carnegie Hall, Charlie shared the spotlight with Lester Young, performing a beautiful solo on "Good Morning Blues," a break on "Way Down Yonder in New Orleans" that underscored his debt to Young, and an equally brilliant solo on "Pagin' the Devil."

The sessions continued. There were two early in 1940 with the Metronome All-Stars including Goodman, Gene Krupa, Charlie Barnet and Harry James. In March Christian was in Minneapolis jamming in a club with a trio of local musicians, including saxophonist Jerry Jerome, who seems to be inspired by the guitarist's solo lines. "I Got Rhythm," "Stardust" and "Tea for Two" give Charlie the opportunity to stretch out with exciting, spirited improvisations. The recordings of this session are of uneven sound quality, and tend to concentrate on Charlie's soloing, but his brilliance is fully realized, unconstrained by the usual one side of a 78 rpm disc that forced him to compress his work.

Through 1940 he made a number of outstanding recordings as part of the Goodman sextet (not including the numerous sides on which he played rhythm guitar with the larger orchestra). His solos in the sextet were breathtakingly consistent. He accompanied pop singer Eddy Howard on October 4, 1941 and just 24 days later participated in a unique ex-

periment. According to jazz authority Frank Driggs, Goodman had just lost Lionel Hampton, and decided to test out a group consisting of himself, Christian, Count Basie and Basie bandmembers Lester Young, trumpeter Buck Clayton, rhythm guitarist Freddy Green, bassist Walter Page and drummer Jo Jones.

The band never performed onstage, but Christian was clearly at home with the relaxed Kansas City rhythm section (virtually the same one with whom he'd played the 1939 "Spirituals to Swing" concert). His solo on "Wholly Cats," a Goodman sextet favorite, is brief but perfectly focused. On the minor-keyed "Charlie's Idea" he plays a solo that is the perfect complement to Lester Young's tenor saxbreak.

The Goodman sextet recorded a number of classic songs that would forever be associated with Christian, among them "Breakfast Feud," "I Found a New Baby" and "Gone With What Draft." One interesting variant was a February 5, 1941 session done with the Edmond Hall Celestial Quartet featuring clarinetist Hall with Christian, pianist Meade Lux Lewis on celeste and bassist Israel Crosby. On this date the producers, still dubious of the electric guitar, insisted Christian play acoustic. It might have inhibited a lesser musician. But Charlie acquited himself well, particularly on "Profoundly Blue." Here his solos, shorn of their amplified dynamics, stand strictly on their own: graceful, delicate, but without any loss of the blues feel.

On March 4, still at the height of his powers, he returned to the studio with Goodman to record the magnificent "Solo Flight," perhaps Christian's finest moment on record. The song, his collaboration with writer/arranger Jimmy Mundy, was built around Charlie's solo. Originally known as "Chonk, Charlie Chonk," it was given the more dignified title by Goodman. Christian is clearly in command on both takes of the number, though his solo lines change considerably from take to take. The solo lines are fleet and perfectly articulated.

Nine days later they were back in the studio, jamming. First pianist Johnny

Guarnieri got Christian into the key of B, where he improvised a delightful blues. Next they started playing over a relentless beat by drummer Dave Tough, both Christian and tenor saxophonist Georgie Auld tried out lines. Then suddenly Charlie fell into a riff that everyone else caught hold of. At that same session they recorded "A Smo-o-o-th One" that featured the exact theme Christian had devised during the jam session. Whether Christian composed the tune on the spot or stumbled onto a song they were planning to do anyway isn't clear, and the recorded "Smo-o-oth One" was considerably more arranged and slower than the jam. But some of the spontaneity did carry over to the sextet's formal recording (both the arranged tune and the jam—later issued as "Waitin' for Benny"—were in the key of G). The session ended with the classic "Airmail Special."

Christian was still working with Goodman, but had a new problem to contend with. As early as 1940 he had been diagnosed as having tuberculosis, but was simply advised to be careful and not overtax himself. Unfortunately, he didn't heed the advice. Goodman's orchestra was working around New York, and Charlie couldn't pass up the jam sessions at Minton's club in Harlem, where Kenny Clarke, Dizzy Gillespie, Thelonious Monk and others were fanning the first flames of bebop.

The solos recorded there by a collector named Jerry Newman were uninhibited and show Christian clearly assimilating bebop concepts into his music. His melodic lines are still long and graceful, but freer, in part due to the context in which he was playing. Kenny Clarke's drumming, the model of the early bop style, gave Charlie greater impetus than did the average swing band drummer. Clarke's rhythmic accents complemented Charlie's solo lines perfectly. Charlie's comping changes broke from standard 4/4 rhythm to the irregular accents of bop.

Christian continued working with Goodman until the summer of 1941, jamming in Harlem when he wasn't gigging. It all began to weigh on his already-fragile health, and in July he finally left Goodman to enter the Seaview Sanitarium on Staten Island. By late 1941 he seemed to be improving. But Christian wasn't helped at all by the well-meaning friends who spirited him out of the hospital to party. In February of 1942, a friend brought him a woman and some marijuana. For a man in Christian's condition the combination was too much. On March 2 he died.

Yet the repercussions of Charlie Christian's life continued. Around the country young guitarists like Barney Kessel and Herb Ellis strove to emulate him. Even in Nashville, two men later known as major names in country guitar—Billy Byrd and Harold Bradley—worked on learning Christian's solos. He had, in the end, the same impact Jimi Hendrix would have nearly two decades later; as a guitarist who made his own rules and was unafraid to take risks, whose sense of drive and daring would change the perception of guitar in America and provide the electric guitar with the credibility it needed to flourish in fields far beyond jazz. To say the Charlie Christian legacy affected jazz alone would be terribly shortsighted. He is one of a handful of musicians whose effect on guitar playing can never be overstated.

DISCOGRAPHY
Virtually all of Charlie Christian's material recorded with Benny Goodman is available on *Solo Flight: The Genius of Charlie Christian* (Columbia), as well as several live tracks cut in Minneapolis. His early bebop experiments, taped live at Minton's in Harlem by jazz collector Jerry Newman, comprise the entirety of *Charlie Christian* (Archive of Folk Music). Since this album is usually priced at or below $4.99, this is an excellent bargain. Two other Christian albums derive from material recorded with Benny Goodman. The best is *Charlie Christian with Benny Goodman and the Sextet: 1939-1941* (Jazz Archives). A second Jazz Archives album combines Count Basie material and Benny Goodman sextet material from 1930 along with rehearsals from a 1940 session featuring members of the Goodman and Basie bands (including Lester Young on sax). The title is *Lester Young and Charlie Christian: 1939-1940.*

TAL FARLOW

eclusiveness has long heightened the public's interest in musicians, particularly those involved in popular music, because it creates an aura of mystery. Certainly it did that for Elvis Presley, though his isolation ultimately helped to kill him. It did the same, less fatally, for Phil Spector. And the great Texas pianist Peck Kelley long enjoyed acclaim due, of course, to his prodigious talents, but also to his unwillingness to leave the area in which he lived.

It would be grossly unfair to refer to Tal Farlow as a total recluse. He does, after all, record often. He doesn't shun performing. However, after becoming disillusioned with the high-pressure world of the fulltime jazz musician, Farlow quit active performing for a number of years to work in the creative world of sign painting. Nonetheless, though he was prominent for only a few years, he left such an impression on jazz guitarists in that short time that he has to be considered a true genius of the idiom. And when he reemerged from obscurity he was greeted with unbridled en-

thusiasm, a measure of the depth of his contributions.

Though Farlow began, as did so many of his generation, under the sway of Charlie Christian, he, like Barney Kessel, moved out of swing (as Christian himself was doing before his death) into the music that became known as bebop. He did so with a sense of adventure, listening to the best the idiom had to offer: Charlie Parker, Dizzy Gillespie and their disciples, as well as Lester Young, whose tenor sax work originally inspired Parker. Like so many guitar virtuosos, Farlow isn't confined by the "proper" established approaches. He did not read music, and he has long been known for such characteristics as tapping the top of his instrument in a group without percussion to compensate, just as Eldon Shamblin played bass runs with the Texas Playboys to compensate for the weakness of the bassists. Tal has also developed a dizzying technique that is thoroughly musical and not used for mere showbiz effect.

Talmadge Holt Farlow was born in

Greensboro, North Carolina, on June 7, 1921. His family played hillbilly music, and by 1930 he was fooling with a mandolin. By the mid '30s, he'd moved on to playing a guitar that belonged to his father. His initial focus was pop music, but it changed when he first heard Charlie Christian, who inspired him to take a serious approach to the guitar. Certainly there were no real teachers for this new style, so Tal took lessons from the phonograph, playing Christian's solos on the Benny Goodman sextet and orchestra recordings over and over to glean every note and nuance. Listening to Lester Young with Count Basie's Orchestra also proved inspirational, as Tal found much to admire in Young's clean solo lines.

By World War II, however, he'd settled on a career painting signs, though music remained important to him. He often played around Greensboro, putting the lessons he'd learned from Christian and Young to good use. Ironically, the first professional gig he got was playing bass notes on the guitar for a bassless combo. He went on the road with them and wound up in Philadelphia, the band's home town. But he was not really a fulltime musician; his sign painting skills kept him from needing to scuffle.

In 1944 he arrived in New York, performing with pianist Dardanelle and a bassist (this drummerless piano/bass/guitar combination found favor during and after World War II, largely due to the success of Nat King Cole's trio). He gigged at the Copacabana with them, which brought him in contact with a number of other talented guitarists, among them Oscar Moore and Chuck Wayne. Tal began hitting the jazz clubs after work, where he absorbed the best music New York had to offer in the mid '40s, including that of Charlie Parker. As as he had with Christian and Young, Tal was soon attempting to transfer the brilliant, unpredictable lines of Parker's alto sax to the fretboard.

Leaving Dardanelle, he joined a group led by vibraphonist Margie Hyams (an early member of Woody Herman's memorable First Herd), then returned to North Carolina and sign painting for a time. He returned

north in 1947. He also was working with non-jazz commercial trios in the elegant environs of the Hamptons in Long Island, and it was there that he developed his unique percussive habit, compensating for drummerless groups by tapping the guitar's top. It was a skill he put to excellent use in the next couple of years.

After a 1949 stint with progresssive clarinetist Buddy DeFranco, Tal replaced guitarist Mundell Lowe in the chamber jazz trio led by famed vibraphonist Red Norvo. Norvo, whose roots were in the swing era, had made a surprisingly effective transition to more modern jazz. Not only had he recorded with Charlie Parker in 1945, but shortly after that he became a valued member of Woody Herman's First Herd.

It was a new world for Tal. Norvo liked to segue from slower tempos to fleet, rapid ones, and Farlow doubted his own ability to play at lightning-fast tempos. But he mastered them, and Norvo continued to bring out Tal's greatest assets. Farlow's harmonic sophistication, his unique technique and cleanly articulated lines all fit perfectly within Norvo's context. Another fortuitous development occurred when the trio's bassist Red Kelly quit in California and was replaced by Charles Mingus.

Between Norvo's beautifully textured vibes, Farlow's impeccable, adventurous solos and Mingus' solid, creative sense of dynamics on the bass, the band actually managed to sound larger than three pieces. Farlow played a vital role in this, serving as a rhythmic "bridge" between Norvo and Mingus. At times he tapped on the guitar; at other times he would stroke his choked strings rhythmically to add a brushed snare drum effect. He could give an amazing impression of bongos while still managing to sneak in a muted note here and there.

The early '50s recordings that the Norvo Trio made, originally issued on Albert Marx's Discovery label, constitute some of the finest small-group jazz of the period. It achieved critical acclaim for its combination of light, beautiful textures, solid, daring jazz improvisation and a truly cohesive sound. Those recordings feature Farlow in a highly sympathetic and advantageous environment. Their version of the bop classic "Move" is only one example. The melody is complicated, but Farlow and Norvo kick it off flawlessly in unison; when Norvo solos, Farlow jumps in behind him comping chords in just the right places. Tal's own solo is sparkling, playing off of Norvo's ideas but nonetheless revealing his own creative thought. At the end, Farlow states the melody in high harmony with Norvo instead of in unison, a surprise that enhances things and is a measure of Farlow's mischievous sense of humor, which also emerges in the Trio's interpretation of the standard "Little White Lies."

From 1950 to 1953 the Norvo group maintained incredibly high standards for small group jazz, and Farlow achieved great acclaim for his skill in executing technically difficult passages effortlessly (he also gained the affectionate nickname "Octopus"). Even when Mingus left in 1951 the quality continued. Farlow finally split in late 1953 (the equally talented Jimmy Raney replaced him) to join Artie Shaw's Gramercy Five. Shaw, a veteran bandleader, had led the smaller group within his orchestra, but now was concentrating on the Five itself. Farlow did well, but in 1954 returned to Norvo, with whom he remained until '55. He recorded with him again on the Prestige album, *Red Norvo with Strings* (the "strings" were Tal and bassist Red Mitchell) and showed himself as inventive and well-focused as ever. On the beginning of "Let's Fall in Love" he chimes the melody, and does so with such a natural feeling that it comes off tasteful and appropriate. He also uses the chimes to play harmony with Norvo on their enchanting arrangement of "Old Devil Moon," adding another tonal color in combination with the vibes.

Tal struck out on his own in 1955, beginning an impressive recording career for Norman Granz's Norgran label. As he'd won *down beat* magazine's New Star award in 1954, his reputation justified a solo career. With pianist/vibraphonist Eddie Costa and bassist Vinnie Burke, he formed his own trio; *Tal*, one of his first albums, showed him more than up to the leader's task. As he had with Norvo, he concentrated on pop standards.

He did a superb job with "Isn't It Romantic," featuring improvising that remains inventive though it never strays too far away from the melody. His tone retained a warmth and intimacy enhanced by the small-group setting. Again he chimed passages wherever he felt they fit.

In both 1956 and 1957 Farlow won the *down beat* Critics' Polls as best guitarist, and continued making outstanding records for Norgran. On *The Tal Farlow Album* he departed from the trio setting, with the legendary bassist Oscar Pettiford, rhythm guitar master Barry Galbraith and Dave Brubeck's drummer Joe Morello on three-fourths of the record using just piano and drums on the remainder. Freed from providing rhythm, Tal could concentrate simply on soloing, and again created awesome improvisations, expertly complemented by Galbraith's rhythm. As early as his Norvo days Farlow had picked up on the idea of playing with his right-hand thumb, something Wes Montgomery later excelled at. The thumb gave Tal a warmth of tone that he employed consistently and well. His ear for chordal melody was obvious on the exquisite introduction he essays unaccompanied at the beginning of "My Old Flame." Tal and Galbraith play excellent twin guitar harmony on Pettiford's "Blues in the Closet," and Tal's lower-register solos on "Lullaby of the Leaves" summon up a superb air of mystery.

When in 1958 the New York nightclub where he was engaged closed, Farlow, newly married, walked away from acclaim to paint signs, play New Jersey clubs and teach guitar at his home in Sea Bright, New Jersey. The business end of music had always made him uneasy, and unlike many jazz musicians, the idea of a day job never revolted him much. He seemingly had no interest in coming back, and for years the only thing that kept his name visible at all was the Gibson Tal Farlow model jazz guitar, introduced in 1962 (ironically, four years after his retirement). He performed irregularly at night spots near his home, but it wasn't until October 1967 that he was convinced to return to the big time. Feeling he had little new to say and not wanting to repeat himself, Tal reluctantly formed a trio that did so well at a Manhattan club that his three week engagement was extended to seven weeks. In 1969 he went back into the studio to record *The Return of Tal Farlow* for Prestige, an album that showed no dearth of creativity. His intricate solo on Thelonious Monk's "Straight, No Chaser" was but one example of his abundant talent; his sensitive interpretation of "Darn That Dream" was another high point.

His 1969, 1970 and 1973 appearances at the Newport Jazz Festival increased Farlow's visibility. He also showed himself open to electronic inventions such as the octave divider (then a daring new device). He recorded again in 1976, but pursued music sporadically, preferring to perform and record where and when he wished.

Nonetheless, the quality of Farlow's work never faltered. In 1977 he began recording for Concord Jazz, creating a fine body of work that attests to the timelessness of his playing. His first Concord effort, *A Sign of the Times* (punning on his alternate vocation), featured him in an intimate trio setting with bassist Ray Brown and pianist Hank Jones. He played some delightful harmony lines of "Fascinating Rhythm" with Jones. On "You Don't Know What Love Is" he picks a contrapuntal line behind Jones that adds color to the song before moving into a dusky, after-hours solo of his own. "Stompin' at the Savoy" takes on more menacing, bluesier flavors than in Tal's earlier renditions, with odd slurs and more complex harmonies than those normally abstracted from the melody. Farlow begins to tap the strings behind Jones' solo, then slaps the strings for the snare effect that's his longtime trademark. "Georgia on My Mind" becomes a playful romp for the trio.

Farlow has continued to perform occasionally, still amazing audiences with his harmonic depth and technique (and he still doesn't read music). He's cut other albums for Concord, and reunited with Norvo at the 1976 Concord Summer Festival. In 1980 filmmaker Lorenzo DeStefano, a former jazz guitarist, after several years of applying persuasion, began filming a documentary on Farlow, dealing with his past, his performing life today and his life at home in Sea Bright, N.J.

His recordings continue. His most recent, *Cookin' on All Burners*, is another outstanding effort. Playing this time with a rhythm section that includes a drummer, Tal makes music of undiminished beauty.

On "If I Should Lose You" he pops off octaves as well as he did nearly thirty years ago. He treats "I Wished on the Moon" with pleasant, lyrical lines and does the same, flashing his legendary speed, on "I've Got the World on a String." Cole Porter's rarely heard "Why Shouldn't I" gets a lavish chord treatment leading into Tal's solo. "Just Friends" almost veers out of control on occasion, but Tal holds it together.

There is little doubt that Tal Farlow now has the music business on *his* terms. An acknowledged jazz guitar master, he has the best of both public and private worlds. The acclaim is there every time he performs and each time a new Farlow album (or a reissue of old material) hits the record bins. Yet his personal life has remained centered in a small seaside town that seems to recharge his creative batteries. Perhaps his reclusiveness has enhanced his legend, but nothing changes the fact that his music has remained constant, his sense of adventure, fire and creativity as pure—and exciting—as it was in the '50s.

DISCOGRAPHY

In Tal Farlow's case, the amount of his best material that's still readily available is somewhat surprising in view of his years out of the spotlight. His early, reputation-making material with Red Norvo and Charlie Mingus is available on *The Red Norvo Trio* (Savoy). Some later material, produced not long after he left Norvo, is available on *Guitar Player* (Prestige). Two early Norgran albums recently reissued in the original covers as Japanese imports, *The Tal Farlow Album* and *Tal* (Verve Japan), are available in most larger record shops, not just from import specialists.

For Concord Jazz he's recorded *A Sign of the Times, Tal Farlow '78, Chromatic Palette, Onstage* and *Cookin' on All Burners* in recent years.

BARNEY KESSEL

In Charlie Christian's wake came dozens of newly-amplified jazz guitarists, all doing their level best to emulate the sophisticated improvisations and harmonies of Christian himself. Many did a respectable job; some got little acclaim. When Christian died in 1942, just as he was beginning to explore the harmonic concepts soon to become known as bebop, he left a seemingly unfillable void.

But Barney Kessel filled that void. A disciple of Christian's who had received the master's stamp of approval while still working in Oklahoma City bars, Kessel had the same marvelous melodic inventiveness, and an unyielding swing comparable to any other guitarist of the time. It's not altogether surprising, as both men grew up in Oklahoma, and had been exposed to the great territorial bands and jazz legends (Lester Young, Count Basie, etc.) that emerged from that part of the nation. Indeed, it seems that many of the true greats of jazz guitar have emerged from the Texas-Oklahoma region.

Kessel had a number of advantages. For one thing, he was not locked into the Eddie

Lang/Carl Kress styles, which were based on either European harmonic concepts or (in the case of Kress) on banjo techniques developed before the guitar asserted itself as a rhythm instrument. Still a teenager when first touched by Christian's style, Kessel was able to develop his style in the midst of the new ideas being advanced by Christian and other progressive swing musicians.

More importantly, Kessel was unafraid, as were many swing musicians, to move into bebop when it developed into the modern jazz idiom of the '40s. By his own admission, he had difficulty understanding it at first and it took time for him to appreciate its value. Yet when he did, he took to it as he had to Christian, acquitting himself superbly on an all-star Charlie Parker session in 1947 and on numerous live performances with the leaders of the bop revolution. Yet Kessel's solid sense of swing remained.

From the time he first recorded under his own name (he did some early sides for small Los Angeles labels like Atomic), Kessel has been a model of consistency. At least part of this consistency can be traced to Kessel's personal life. In a world of music where drugs and alcohol are ubiquitous, Kessel ignored their temptations, debunking the myths that musicians need them to play better. Ironically, jazzman Charlie Parker, whose alcoholism and drug abuse did him in at age 35, sometimes preached against overindulgence but couldn't follow his own advice.

Today, in his early sixties (but looking younger), Barney Kessel is an acknowledged master of jazz guitar. He has not moved into fusion jazz or jazz-rock, and has successfully resisted the sort of commercial temptations that derailed George Benson's jazz career. Yet he has a solid understanding of the commercial, something he gained over years in Hollywood's sound studios, recording with pop, jazz and rock performers. In his jazz career, both solo and with the Great Guitarists (fellow masters Charlie Byrd and Herb Ellis), Kessel has maintained a loyal following both among older fans and with younger guitarists, including many rock players.

Barney Kessel was born in Muskogee, Oklahoma, on October 17, 1923. The city contained a unique cultural mix of oil workers, blacks, cowboys and American Indians, and territorial bands regularly played in the area. By the time Barney was 12, though his parents had definite doubts, he was expressing strong interest in playing guitar, and saved his earnings from a paper route to buy his first one. He began his career playing in a hillbilly duo over KBIX radio in Muskogee. But jazz, it seemed, was all around him. He was moved by the music of Count Basie and other swing musicians, and began gigging in clubs in the area, cutting his musical teeth by interaction with other players, not by studying lesson books.

Most types of popular music held interest for him. He picked up music from movie soundtracks, learning some of the devices and techniques that would later help him when doing soundtrack sessions in Hollywood. In addition, he grew up in the heart of western swing country. When he was a teenager Bob Wills and his Texas Playboys virtually dominated Oklahoma music and radio. Wills'

noontime radio show, broadcast over KVOO in Tulsa, was at the peak of its popularity. And since Wills often featured the electric steel guitar of Leon McAuliffe (and after 1937 the superb lead and rhythm guitar work of Eldon Shamblin), they, too had an impact on Barney's musical roots.

Jam sessions stood him in good stead, and by 1937 he was playing with a black band in Muskogee in which his was the only white face. Naturally, he had come under the influence of the pioneering recordings of Charlie Christian with the Benny Goodman Sextet. Christian, who'd joined Goodman in August 1939, had already recorded such classics as "Rose Room," "Seven Come Eleven," "Gone With 'What' Wind" and "Air Mail Special" with Goodman, set the standards that Kessel strove to emulate. He learned Christian's solos off of records, and one night in October, 1940, while playing with a regional band called the Varsitones in Oklahoma City, met a black waiter at the club who praised his playing and promised to call Charlie Christian, who was back in town to visit his family.

Kessel soon found himself under Christian's admiring glance, and the next day was in the unimaginable position of jamming with his idol. Writing in *Guitar Player*, Barney said "I'm sure I probably repeated a lot of his own [solo] lines back to him. But because of that experience I made up my mind that from then on I would actively and consciously seek to find my own approach, my own style... I decided that no matter how much I liked Charlie Christian or anybody else, they would remain only influences."

There were indeed other fine guitarists, known and obscure, who also influenced and inspired him. Among them were Oscar Moore, with the Nat "King" Cole Trio; Teddy Bunn, with the Spirits of Rhythm; and Anthony "Bus" Etri, a brilliant and sadly unheralded guitarist with Charlie Barnet's orchestra, whose approach to both chords and single-string electric solos was advanced and somewhat different from Christian's (Etri's solo on Barnet's 1940 "Tappin' at the Tappa" is a minor classic) and would have gone far had he not died in a 1941 auto accident.

In June 1942 Kessel, not out of high school, moved to Hollywood. His meeting with Christian had only strengthened his intent to turn professional. Not surprisingly, he washed dishes at first, then joined an orchestra led by the Marx Brothers' Chico Marx, and then a group led by veteran bandleader and drummer Ben Pollack, who had a knack for picking out good musicians (Benny Goodman once worked in Pollack's band). In the void left by Christian's death, Barney's playing shone through and earned him considerable respect among the Hollywood jazz cadre. In 1944 he was the only white musician to appear in the highly respected jazz film *Jammin' the Blues*, which featured Count Basie alumni Lester Young and Jo Jones as well as bassist Red Callender and trumpeter Harry "Sweets" Edison.

That same year he was working with two of the finest jazz orchestras in the country: Charlie Barnet's through the summer, and Artie Shaw's after that. With Barnet, he played mostly rhythm, though he was featured on the band's arrangement of "Blue Skies," doing a brief, swinging break. Shaw featured Kessel both as a soloist in the orchestra and in the smaller Gramercy Five. He acquitted himself superbly in both contexts. His solo on "Jumpin' on the Merry-Go-Round" with the full orchestra featured a Christian-influenced, bell-toned sound that contrasted with the ensemble, and on "September Song" he played some beautiful, Etri-flavored chord work.

With the Gramercy Five he was featured more, shining brilliantly in the company of Shaw, trumpet legend Roy Eldridge, and the superb pianist Dodo Marmarosa. On the minor-keyed "The Grabtown Grapple," Barney plays flawlessly in the ensemble and contributes an acerbic solo not unlike the pre-bop work Charlie Christian did at Minton's, as well as a tight, economical break on "The Sad Sack." "Scuttlebutt," a riff number, had the flavor of the best Goodman-Christian sextet sides, while "The Gentle Grifter" was more introspective.

Barney spent 1945 and '46 working in Los Angeles, playing in big-name bands visiting the area and doing radio shows, before moving into the hardcore jazz scene. Bop did not have an immediate effect on him, but he was too musically astute not to eventually notice its appealing qualities. A 1945 jam session with alto saxophonist and bop pioneer Charlie Parker in a Los Angeles club began to change his mind. Certainly bop guitar was a new area to explore, though Arv Garrison had recorded some bop in 1946 with Parker. Kessel began showing up at more bop jam sessions, and saw the adventure and excitement that music held. He won the respect of the boppers, and at Parker's behest, was called upon to record with him for Dial Records in February, 1947—Parker's first formal session since his release from Camarillo State Hospital following a drug-induced psychotic episode.

Among those on the date were Barney's old Artie Shaw partner Marmarosa, bop trumpet virtuoso Howard McGhee and tenor saxophonist Wardell Gray. Parker, in good physical condition, was in a near-ideal setting, and it brought out the best in Kessel as well. His brief break in "Relaxin' at Camarillo" is outstanding. His rhythmic chord punctuations in "Cheers" and "Carvin' the Bird" added an appealing contrast. Both breaks display his considerable humor. On "Cheers" he quotes from "I Can't Get Started."

If Kessel had any remaining misgivings about bop, they were quickly stilled. His superb bop composition "Swedish Pastry," a variation on "Carvin' the Bird," remains a minor bop classic, and Swedish clarinetist Stan Hasselgard's 1947 recording of it, with Kessel and vibraphonist Red Norvo, is ample proof of Kessel's solid command of bop. That year he also jammed with top Los Angeles bop exponents Wardell Gray and fellow tenorman Dexter Gordon. One session, at the Elks' Club on July 6, 1947, is documented. And though Barney was tentative and repetitive on "Disorder at the Border," he hit his stride on "Cherokee" with a burning, extended break. The Gray-Gordon chase choruses kept the excitement at fever pitch and on "The Hunt," Barney was clearly playing superb bop.

That same year he found the perfect vehicle for his playing when he joined promoter Norman Granz's Jazz at the Philharmonic touring ensemble, accompanying a variety of musicians from Ben Webster and Parker to Lester Young. The high visibility of JATP also figured in boosting Kessel's reputation, bringing his virtuosity to thousands and establishing him as one of the preeminent modern jazz guitarists of the time.

In 1952 he joined pianist Oscar Peterson and bassist Ray Brown in the first Oscar Peterson Trio, a drummerless group modeled (as were many similar units) on the King Cole Trio, but concentrating on high levels of instrumental sophistication. Among the more interesting recordings the group did, augmented by drummer Alvin Stoller, tenorman Flip Phillips and trumpeter Charlie Shavers, was a trilogy of albums backing Fred Astaire as he sang a number of pop songs given solid jazz arrangements. Barney played brief, vibrant solos on the vocals, but truly glowed on instrumentals like "Jam Session for a Dancer," two takes of "The Astaire Blues" and "Stompin' at the Savoy." He played with unparalleled drive and inventiveness, never repeating himself, and it is sad that these recordings have gotten so little notice as part of his repertoire. While touring with Peterson in March 1953, Kessel was able to meet Django Reinhardt in France, just two months before Django's death.

He was working with former bandleader Bob Crosby's Los Angeles-based TV program when he signed with Contemporary Records in the fall of 1953. His first album, released as *Easy Like* early in 1954, was a truly stunning debut, a mixture of originals and standards that featured Bud Shank's superb flute work. The overall sound combines the blues and swing music that Barney absorbed in Oklahoma with bop and the cooler sounds of the West Coast. Kessel's "Easy Like" is a playful, inventive number, while "Tenderly" and "What Is There to Say" reveal a gift for chord melody clearly inspired by George Van Eps (with creative use of harmonics). "Lullaby of Birdland" and Kessel's own "Bernardo" feature swinging, Latin-flavored lyricism. "Salute to Charlie Christian"

spotlights Kessel's interpretation of his mentor's style, within a minor-keyed swing context not unlike Christian's "Till Tom Special." "I Let a Song Go Out of My Heart" is easy and mellow, and "Vicky's Dream" is a bop variant on "All the Things You Are."

By the time the album was issued, Kessel had returned to freelancing in the Los Angeles area, doing film and TV soundtracks and playing on recording sessions in addition to club dates; he played the rich accompaniment to Julie London's 1955 hit "Cry Me a River." He also continued recording for Contemporary, with his excellent *Kessel Plays Standards* and *To Swing or Not to Swing*, done in 1955. The latter was an outstanding effort, featuring a large group that included trumpeter Harry "Sweets" Edison, tenor saxophonist Georgie Auld, studio veteran Al Hendrickson on rhythm guitar and drummer Shelley Manne, among others. The emphasis this time was less on bop and more on straightforward swing, reflected in titles like "Indiana," "Moten Swing" and "Louisiana." Kessel was full of ideas for this set, his tone mellow and creativity as fluent as ever. His originals, "Happy Feeling" and "Wail Street" continued in that vein, with the latter conjuring up strong Basie-esque or Kansas City Five/Six impressions. "Embraceable You" again reflects Van Eps.

By the mid '50s Kessel was also doing his share of artist and repertoire work, moving into areas far beyond jazz. He did a good deal of work for Verve Records, including the lead guitar work on Ricky Nelson's first 1956 hit single "I'm Walkin'," and as rock music grew he played on rock sessions as well as taking other studio assignments. Also in 1956 came the first of the Poll Winners LP series, featuring Barney with drummer Shelley Manne and bassist Ray Brown, all of whom had won the *down beat*, *Metronome* and *Playboy* jazz polls on their respective instruments. The records were pioneering efforts in themselves, with Kessel's guitar as the only lead instrument. That he managed to keep things flowing without a hint of boredom was a tribute to his preeminence on the scene. There were four albums in all, including *Exploring the*

Scene!, a group of 10 numbers done by top jazz composers. Barney was also appearing on TV at this time, as part of the regular group on the *Johnny Staccato* TV series about a jazz pianist/cop.

He continued working in the studios, recording for a variety of labels for another decade, before leaving the lucrative work to concentrate solely on his jazz career and on teaching. Kessel wrote *The Guitar*, a comprehensive look at career development for the aspiring professional guitarist. He recorded a superb album with Stephane Grappelli titled *Homage to Django* in 1969. There was no attempt by Kessel (nor should there have been) to imitate Django, but instead he tried to evoke the fire, creativity and passion that Reinhardt exemplified. Barney's original "I Remember Django" was an eloquent dedication to Reinhardt's spirit, as were his renditions of other Reinhardt-Grappelli standards like "Honeysuckle Rose" and "I Found a New Baby." Kessel's round tone—the result of his use of an original Charlie Christian pickup—was far more in his own style (with Christian overtones) than Django's, but the concept worked.

Kessel continued his activity into the '70s, and one new facet to his performing came in 1974 when an Australian jazz promoter came up with the idea of Kessel, Charlie Byrd and Herb Ellis working in that country as the Great Guitars. The trio succeeded, and soon the three were doing selected dates together in addition to their own solo appearances. They began recording for the new Concord Jazz label, owned by auto dealer and jazz promoter Carl Jefferson of Concord, California, and soon Kessel began recording as a solo artist for the label. His newer music retains its beautiful consistency, clearly on a par with his best work for Contemporary. His first set for Concord, *Barney Plays Kessel* cut in 1975, is a compelling collection of original numbers recorded with a large group. From the bop-orientation of "Sea Miner" to the soulful beauty of "For My Love" and "I'm On My Way," a delicate, good-natured bossa nova number, Kessel plays with finesse and sensitivity throughout, and is particularly adept in handling the Latin tunes. "Brazilian Beat" in particular features some wonderfully lyrical lines and pleasing interaction with vibraphonist Victor Feldman.

Kessel's career on the road, including his guitar seminars and other recordings for Concord Jazz, have continued unabated for a decade. He's recorded two other high quality solo LPs for Concord, plus three with Ellis and Byrd as the Great Guitars that have reflected well on the three individually and as a unit.

In 1983 Concord released Kessel's most ambitious effort yet. *Solo*, recorded in 1981, places him in one of the most challenging contexts for any jazz guitarist: playing unaccompanied, without a rhythm section to kick things along. Generally this is a feat that can be performed only by the greats of jazz. Jimmy Raney, Eddie Lang, Django, Bucky Pizzarelli, Joe Pass and just a handful of others have really pulled it off over the years. Barney, not surprisingly, proved more than up to it. His good-natured, effervescent rendition of "Brazil," Les Paul's old hit, is surprisingly effective. And even such overdone cocktail lounge favorites as "People," "Alfie" and "You Are the Sunshine of My Life" take on new depth in his hands. His own compositions, such as the funky blues "Jellybeans," also work well, losing none of the rhythmic drive needed.

Barney Kessel now lives in Oklahoma City. Having shunned the fast life, he is still playing at the top of his form. He is not totally in love with all of the trends in music today, and has written intelligently and incisively about the senselessness of musicians who attempt to substitute form and flash for substance. Considering the legends with whom he has worked—Charlie Christian, Charlie Barnet, Artie Shaw, Lester Young, Charlie Parker, Ben Webster, Billie Holiday, Oscar Peterson, Anita O'Day, Pete and Conte Candoli among others—it's understandable that he holds dear the high standards he has set for himself, and all jazz guitarists. It is safe to expect him to hold to those standards for the remainder of his career.

DISCOGRAPHY

Barney Kessel is fairly well-represented on records. Though not all his LPs for Contemporary are in print, several of them have been reissued in their original covers. The four *Poll Winners* LPs—*Ride Again, Exploring the Scene!, Poll Winners* and *Straight Ahead*—are all available, as is his outstanding *To Swing or Not to Swing* and *Let's Cook!* with saxophonist Ben Webster.

Of course, Concord Jazz details Kessel's output of the past ten years, and he's amassed a substantial catalogue, including *Barney Plays Kessel, Soaring, Poor Butterfly, Jellybeans* and *Solo.* With the Great Guitars, he's done *Great Guitars, Great Guitars II, At the Winery, At Charlie's Georgetown,* and *Straight Tracks.*

EDDIE LANG

eneralizations about music are risky; inevitably, invariably there comes the exception. But I'm going to take a chance and make one anyhow: there was no real jazz guitar before Eddie Lang, at least none that amounted to anything. Lang created the entire idiom almost singlehandedly, setting many of the precedents that jazz guitarists follow to this day.

Like so many other musical innovators, Lang had to carve out his own niche; his work bears almost no resemblance to any predecessor. Some critics consider the great blues guitarist Lonnie Johnson a jazz guitar pioneer, and cite him as a major influence on Lang. But that's a shaky premise. Johnson was not really working in the jazz idiom most of the time, and nothing he played during the time he and Lang recorded together indicates any major influence. If Johnson was a true master of blues guitar, Lang was the same in jazz. Their collective brilliance permitted them to create some incredible jazz-blues duets; but they were working in related, not identical, styles.

Lang was also the first true studio guitarist. Indeed, some of his finest moments occurred while he accompanied other performers, among them his longtime friend and partner jazz violin innovator Joe Venuti, as well as cornet genius King Oliver, the Mound City Blue Blowers, Paul Whiteman and his orchestra and Bing Crosby. Lang's sense of taste and polish enabled him to accompany all of these artists—and others—with almost intuitive, highly sympathetic backing.

Lang also created a sense of style and image for the jazz guitarist. His pioneering use of the Gibson L-5 f-hole archtop guitar set a precedent that has been followed by jazz guitarists from George Van Eps and Freddy Greene to Charlie Christian, Barney Kessel, Herb Ellis, Bucky Pizzarelli and Joe Pass. The traditional archtop model, though often amplified, remains standard apparatus for all but a handful of mainstream jazz guitar players nearly 60 years after Lang first came into the public eye.

Lang possessed many strengths as a soloist. Not only could he create sparkling, precise and complex single-string solos, he also injected humor where appropriate. More importantly, he demonstrated an impeccable sense of taste; when you listen to any Lang recordings, it is clear that he did not know the meaning of the word excess. Every note rings clearly and conveys the intended mood. His arpeggios added harmonic richness every time he used them. The bass runs he utilized so often worked well in a music that had not yet fully accustomed itself to the use of string bass and often relied on tubas. He could choke a string with the exact amount of tension needed.

Eddie Lang's impact on jazz guitar is immeasurable. It is entirely possible the idiom would have developed anyhow, but it wouldn't have grown precisely the way it did without Eddie Lang. Consider his huge influence on Django Reinhardt, and the fact that the violin-guitar ensembles that Reinhardt created with Stephane Grappelli were admittedly inspired by Lang's recordings with Joe Venuti, though Reinhardt certainly was no mere imitator. Yet, like so many great jazzmen, Lang died young, a death made all the more tragic by its accidental nature—unlike the deaths of so many later jazz greats.

Today there can be no question that Lang advanced not only jazz guitar, but guitar in general a quantum leap forward. Where tenor banjos dominated jazz orchestra rhythm sections in the past, Lang—himself a former banjoist—almost single-handedly made banjos obsolete in that context. He advanced the guitar as a solo instrument outside classical music as no other instrumentalist before him had, and established protocols for accompaniment that hold up well to this day.

His real name was Salvatore Massaro, and he was born into a musical family on October 25, 1902 in Philadelphia. His father came from Naples, Italy, and made fretted instruments by trade. Beginning his musical career on a specially crafted miniature guitar, Salvatore began studying violin at age seven and played around the Italo-American enclaves of south Philadelphia. Somewhere along the line he met a young Italian immigrant named Giuseppe "Joe" Venuti, who also

was studying the violin. In their spare time they began playing duets together—Lang using his guitar while Venuti played ethnic music on the violin.

Sometimes they even jazzed the music up a bit, improvising on the time-honored melodies and laying the groundwork for the guitar-violin synergy that would make them legends by the late 1920s.

At age 17 Eddie got his first orchestral job playing banjo with the Charles Kerr Orchestra of Philadelphia. He impressed everyone who heard him. By 1922 he and Venuti were both playing violins in the Bert Estlow dance band in Atlantic City. Though they were tightly confined to playing acceptable ballroom dance music, they started jamming between shows (Reinhardt and Grappelli began playing jazz together in the same way nearly a decade later, ironically).

By 1923, the Kerr band was at Atlantic City and Kerr, who'd been impressed by Lang in Philadelphia, brought him back into the band as a banjoist. Then, in late 1923 or early 1924, Eddie caught on with a northeastern Pennsylvania band known as the Scranton Sirens which featured Tommy and Jimmy Dorsey. But though he was gaining a reputation among fellow musicians, he was still relatively obscure. That summer, back in Atlantic City, he played his flattop guitar with the popular novelty trio known as the Mound City Blue Blowers, who at the time had a hit recording of "Arkansaw Blues." The group, basically a skiffle or jug band, had no bass support; it was dominated by kazoo, banjo and harmonica. Lang balanced the Blowers' sound, so they hired him as a permanent member. Their recording of "Tiger Rag" proved that Lang added sophistication.

The job with the Blue Blowers was a fortuitous move for Lang. Their popularity on the theater circuit brought him into theaters and recording studios for the first time, and people began noticing his superb playing. The group toured England and wound up back in Atlantic City by the end of 1925. At that point Lang decided to move on.

His reputation was now his calling card, and by early 1926 he was doing numerous recording sessions in New York with everyone from Al Jolson to the mysterious Emmett Miller, who would have a definite influence on country music (he recorded the original "Lovesick Blues") and particularly on the western swing music of Bob Wills. Lang and Venuti continued working closely, on sessions and occasional live appearances.

Around this time he and Venuti also began an on-off relationship with Jean Goldkette's orchestra. The pair was in heady company, as the band contained not only Bix Beiderbecke, the famed cornetist who was making his own impact on jazz, but also boasted Frankie Trumbauer, whose C-melody sax work left repercussions a generation later (Lester Young was a great Trumbauer admirer).

Yet it was as a team that Lang and Venuti had some of their greatest moments. Their 1926 recording of "Stringing the Blues" had a robust ebullience that exemplified the two at their wildest. Venuti's violin work reflects his mischievous, raffish personality. The stop-time arrangement adds excitement, and Eddie's beautiful, rich (and swinging) chord textures provide the perfect rhythmic vehicle. It is quintessential Lang-Venuti.

In 1927 Eddie and Joe cut recordings with the Goldkette orchestra that contained some of Beiderbecke's greatest moments, among them "I'm Comin' Virginia," which featured Lang's skillful support to Bix's now-classic solo. That year Lang also began making records under his own name, including "Eddie's Twister" and "A Little Love, a Little Kiss." And if anyone had any doubts as to his abilities with more complex music, he also recorded "Prelude" by Rachmaninoff, reflecting his early classical training. Jim Ferguson's August 1983 Guitar Player story on Lang revealed (for the first time anywhere that I know of) that Eddie also was a dedicated admirer of Andres Segovia—not surprising considering his background.

1928 saw more equally superb Lang recordings, including his stinging, lucid "Church Street Sobbin' Blues," issued under the pseudonym "Blind Willie Dunn." Though more polished here than on the sides he did with Lonnie Johnson, Lang showed a precise

and firm attack, with every note clearly articulated. He bent notes as Johnson and others did, and did it with equal resolve. His eclecticism was demonstrated still further in his March 1928 recording of "Rainbow Dreams." With only pianist Frank Signorelli, who often backed him, Eddie created a stately, rich melody not terribly close to jazz but appealing just the same, and featuring an example of his skillful use of harmonics.

"Church Street Sobbin' Blues" had been recorded November 5; on November 8, he entered the studio again, this time with the fabled blues guitarist Lonnie Johnson. The tracks they recorded, "Two Tone Stomp" and "Have to Change Keys to Play These Blues," document Lang primarily as an accompanist to Johnson's muscular, articulate 12-string lead guitar. The two masters of their respective styles complement each other beautifully, with Eddie's solid, melodic rhythm work and timing the perfect frame for Lonnie's soloing. On their 1929 recording "Bull Frog Moan," Lang demonstrates his humor with the loping bullfrog sound and odd syncopated figure he plays behind Johnson's bluesy solo.

In 1929 Joe and Eddie connected with Paul Whiteman's Orchestra and remained with it, going to Hollywood to film the now-classic film King of Jazz. Whether Whiteman was ever really a jazzman is a subject to debate, but undoubtedly one of his greatest contributions was his featuring of great jazz artists in commercially acceptable pop settings, giving them a chance to make adequate livings without extreme musical compromises. During their stay with Whiteman the duo found a new friend in the band's vocalist, Bing Crosby. Crosby was to figure prominently in the last years of Lang's life.

By 1930 Crosby, Lang and Venuti were all out of the Whiteman organization. Lang went on to make some superb recordings with Venuti's band, the Blue Four. He also continued freelancing in New York. One example of his driving guitar is on the Smith Ballew Orchestra's version of "I Got Rhythm," which features his L-5 cutting through the orchestration to dominate the rhythm of the band.

Venuti's 1930 version of "I've Found a New Baby" features an excellent Lang solo, buried somewhat by the other instruments.

In 1931 he continued recording with Venuti, doing outstanding work on "Beale Street Blues," which also featured Benny Goodman, trombonist/vocalist Jack Teagarden and his trumpeter brother, Charlie. Lang played rhythm, but again held the group together. In addition to recording, Lang also began working on Bing Crosby's radio show. The Lang-Crosby friendship had developed steadily after they had left Whiteman's band, and Crosby's vocal style at the time was light years away from "White Christmas" or any of his later hits. Bing then sang with a strong jazz orientation.

Both men were featured in the film *The Big Broadcast of 1932*, and also did a brilliant recording of "Some of These Days," in which Bing tears through an impressive scat chorus, followed by Lang's single-string solo, modeled somewhat on Bing's scatting. Lang also recorded two classic jazz duets with guitarist Carl Kress. Kress was known for his chord solos, which reflected his days as a banjoist. As he had Lonnie Johnson, Lang complemented Kress. On "Pickin' My Way," the two support each other so closely they seem to be thinking out of the same head. Lang's beautifully crafted solos were well set forth by Kress' chords. Conversely, Kress' rich chord solos were ably underpinned by Lang's outstanding bass lines. They switch into a minor key and achieve the modulation so skillfully any guitarist would find the passage worth studying.

By this time Lang was at the top of his profession, with his recording and performing bringing him phenomenal income for the era. With Venuti he continued doing peerless rhythm work on such numbers as "Vibraphonia" and "Hey! Young Fella." The latter tune, recorded on February 28, 1933, was among his final recordings with his friend.

The Lang-Crosby relationship was blossoming in mutual benefit, as Bing, about to make a movie, wanted Eddie prominently featured in a minor role with a few speaking lines. Lang had been having problems with his tonsils and Crosby suggested that he have them removed. There was risk in such operations on an adult at the time; on March 26 Lang had the surgery, but an embolism (blood clot) formed in his lung during the operation and he never regained consciousness. Crosby and Venuti were as devastated as Lang's widow, Kitty.

At the time of Eddie Lang's premature death, other guitarists were just beginning to follow in his footsteps—Kress, George Van Eps, Dick McDonough and Django Reinhardt would pick up his flame, adding their own ideas, projecting Lang's legacy far into the future. Regrettably, few guitarists today attempt to play in his style. Nonetheless every jazz guitarist, whether or not they realize it, carries a bit of Eddie Lang in every solo they play.

DISCOGRAPHY

The most essential Eddie Lang package, featuring excellent examples of his work in a variety of contexts (including performances with both Bing Crosby and Joe Venuti), is the two-record *Stringing the Blues* (Columbia Special Products). Almost equally important is *Eddie Lang: Jazz Guitar Virtuoso* (Yazoo). Two Australian LPs with various examples of the Lang-Lonnie Johnson duets are also available on the Swaggie label through Down Home Music.

WES MONTGOMERY

Musical compromise in the jazz field has always bred controversy. Commerciality has always been looked upon with suspicion and even outright contempt. And there is certainly something to be said for the assumption that jazzmen who enjoy financial success, if they weren't born into money (and most weren't), either have a lucrative studio career or have subjugated much of their musical integrity in favor of formulas guaranteed to sell huge numbers of records. Either way to wealth has its pitfalls. Studio work pays incredibly well, but can get boring and is fraught with politics. Casting aside integrity in favor of hit records subjects the jazzman to being abandoned or harshly criticized by some of those who loved one's music in the past.

Wes Montgomery had to face this kind of criticism when he became the most popular jazz guitarist of the mid '60s, recording a steady stream of simplistic hit instrumentals that stylistically and esthetically were miles from the brilliant, exciting jazz he had been playing just a couple years earlier. Amid pseudo-jazz arrangements, he played songs that had previously been rock hits or pop standards. Suddenly you could hear Wes all over AM radio; he sold millions of his versions of "Windy," the vacuous 1967 hit by the schlock-rock group the Association, and Hoagy Carmichael's "Georgia on My Mind." Wes, who was making a living and little more (having to support a wife and six kids on his earnings) during the periods of his greatest acclaim for jazz, was unexpectedly enjoying the sort of financial success most jazzmen only dream of.

It was not so much that jazz fans turned on him as it was that they felt let down by his new approach. And certainly Montgomery himself felt plenty of conflict, torn between his newfound good fortune and his own creative juices. It was not as if he'd signed on with Lawrence Welk, but his change of direction was a departure from the pure jazz he'd played with his brothers in the Mastersounds and the uniformly superb albums he'd recorded for the Riverside label, when he was consistently winning every jazz popularity poll and was rightly cited as one of the most vibrant, inventive guitarists to emerge since Charlie Christian.

In any case, Wes didn't live long enough to resolve his conundrum; he died of a heart attack in 1968 at the peak of his popularity. Ironically, since his death, and most notably in recent years, there appears to be a strong revival of interest in his earlier work, with numerous reissues of the late '50s and early '60s recordings that helped make his reputation. Some have even been released with their original jackets and liner notes duplicated. His pop albums are all still available as well. Like Charlie Christian, Montgomery's influence will probably never wane regardless of future trends.

Most of the guitarists in this book fell in love with their instrument early in life. But John Leslie Montgomery, born in Indianapolis, Indiana on March 6, 1923, never touched a guitar until he was 19 years old. Charlie Christian had been dead two years by that time, but after hearing Christian's recording of "Solo Flight" with the Benny Goodman orchestra, Wes, a working man, bought himself a Gibson electric guitar, an amplifier and as many of Christian's records as he could lay hands on. Every night when he got home from work he would sit down with his guitar and a pick and the records, and learn them note-for-note. He took no formal lessons and never learned to read music.

Any beginning guitarist can be excruciating to listen to; a beginner using an electric guitar is often worse than excruciating. It wasn't long before the neighbors started complaining about Wes' noise. And it was directly because of their complaints that he came upon the style that set him apart from all other Christian-based guitarists. He set his pick aside and began striking the strings with his thumb. The sound was less harsh, its tone pleasing. Never again did Wes use a pick. The neighbors' complaints ceased. He caught on to the instrument relatively quickly, and soon had devised the "octave" style of playing for which he became well known. This octave style was distinctive; it gave his sound even more smoothness. Tal Farlow occasionally used his thumb,

and Django Reinhardt had used octaves as early as the mid '30s, but often used them to play his loudest passages. Wes combined both ideas into his own cohesive style.

He was also learning to create single note improvisations by studying Christian's solos, and though many of his pop fans never realized it, his jazz reputation was built not on his octaves or his use of the thumb, but for those adventurous, superbly crafted, improvised lines. Wes always had enough taste to incorporate the octave work into the context of what he was playing. It was never a gimmick, and he never used it where it was inappropriate.

He made phenomenal progress in just six months, and was hired by a local band to play his note-for-note versions of Christian's solos. But gradually he began to assert his own concepts, listening to other musicians and devising his own ideas. He continued playing local clubs until he joined Lionel Hampton's big band in 1948. He was not a featured soloist; that was left to Hampton and his stars. Wes generally confined himself (on records, at least) to fills and rhythm work. He was his own man offstage while with Hampton, shunning liquor and earning the affectionate moniker "Rev" (for Reverend). He left Hampton in 1950.

Montgomery's stint with Hampton, surprisingly enough, did not whet his desire to play jazz fulltime. He had a family to consider, so he held down a fulltime day job with a radio parts manufacturer in Indianapolis. His desire to play music, however, was strong. His shift was from 7 a.m. to 3 p.m.; he'd rest for a while, then play at the Turf Bar from 9 p.m. to 2 a.m., moving to a second gig at another club, the Missile Room, from 2:30 to 5 a.m. It could be said that he had two fulltime jobs, and this regimen continued for six years. But it gave him an education that well prepared him for what was about to happen.

His brothers, bassist Monk and pianist/vibraphonist Buddy, were members of the Indianapolis musical scene, and in 1955 they joined Wes to record. Their efforts were recently reissued on Columbia, but they tell us little about what Wes was doing at the time.

By 1957, Wes was added to the Mastersounds, Monk's and Buddy's chamber jazz group which recorded for World Pacific records. Wes did his first substantive recording sessions with them for World Pacific in late '57 in Indianapolis. These recordings didn't get much attention, though the musicians played quite respectably. "Fingerpickin'" is an early, imperfect example of Wes' use of his thumb and octaves. It lacks the authority he later had, and is too abrasive and repetitive in places, yet it clearly defines a very distinctive approach. Several local hornmen, including a very young trumpeter named Freddie Hubbard, were added for several other songs, including the original version of the Monk Montgomery blues standard "Bock to Bock" (named for producer Dick Bock). Wes' lines here have a clear authority about them, and some excellent harmonic ideas, though they lack the fluency of his later work. And he plays with great fire and passion on a furious rendition of Charlie Parker's "Billie's Bounce."

The Mastersounds continued with minimal success. Wes recorded with them (on the 1958 King and I album) and without them for World Pacific. In April of that year the Montgomerys, along with tenor saxophonist Harold Land, recorded some fine material. On tunes like the medium-tempo "Far Wes," it becomes clear that Wes is more comfortable with recording than previously. The annoying string-snapping that marred his Indianapolis sides is replaced with a more confident, darker-hued tone and still more fluent, even eloquent, improvisations that reach their peak on an austerely moving version of "Old Folks." Wes acquitted himself equally well on "Hymn For Carl," Land's minor key musical tribute to his former partner pianist Carl Perkins, who'd just recently died. On the King and I album, Wes contributed a beautiful unaccompanied intro to "Baubles, Bangles and Beads."

Meanwhile, Wes was continuing to work clubs in Indianapolis with his trio (an organist and a drummer). In September of 1959, at saxophonist Cannonball Adderley's behest, Riverside Records' Orrin Keepnews traveled to Indianapolis and, sufficiently impressed, recorded Wes and his trio in New York City in October. The first album, The Wes Montgomery Trio, puts Wes up front and permits him to stretch out. His lines truly stand on their own, with skillfully applied elements of both humor and drama. On "Round Midnight" he alternates between single lines, octaves and chord soloing. With the organ and drums restrained, his use of octaves to provide depth and color to his lines is all the more impressive. He built single string lines, took them into octaves, added to their intensity but not their volume (unlike Django, who did both). Montgomery's original compositions, such as "Missile Blues," show a true command of the funky sound then popular in jazz.

Even more stunning was The Incredible Jazz Guitar of Wes Montgomery, recorded in New York in late January of 1960. With a top-flight rhythm section of pianist Tommy Flanagan, bassist Percy and drummer Albert Heath, Wes swung the album from start to finish. Sonny Rollins' "Airegin" crackles with the fire of Wes' creative concepts; "D-Natural Blues," a Montgomery original, becomes an archetypal blues for jazz guitar, performed in octaves. "Four on Six," another original, is an awesome piece of improvisation. Side two contains still more. There is the original version of his epic "West Coast Blues," in which Wes' solos are bursting with ideas, leading up to a compelling octave statement. The Latin flavored "Mister Walker" showed him in a percussive, but no less inventive, mold. The album received considerable critical acclaim, and though the down beat readers' and critics' polls were often at variance with each other, in 1961 and 1962 Wes topped the guitar category in both polls.

The Mastersounds had disbanded, which meant the Montgomery Brothers—Wes, Buddy and Monk—occasionally reunited for performances and recording. Buddy and Monk became a remarkably cohesive unit over the next several years, providing outstanding accompaniment for Wes. In the fall of 1960, they recorded several numbers in San Francisco and several more in a club in Vancouver, Canada, for two albums, The

Montgomery Brothers and *In Canada*. The former featured memorable performances of Carl Perkins' haunting "Groove Yard" and "Lover Man." The latter album boasted a shimmering interpretation of Claude Thornhill's "Snowfall" and several other excellent efforts.

Early in 1961 they recorded a fine remake of "Bock to Bock" and a blues-drenched "Groove Yard" constructed around Wes' crisp octave work and some clean, precise doubletiming. Buddy Montgomery, who doubled vibes and piano, did a fine job. On this number in particular, Wes' memorable solo lines were compositions in themselves. His muted version of "If I Should Lose You" had a purple-hued beauty and stateliness that made it one of his most moving performances. This material was issued as *Groove Yard* on Fantasy.

Wes did a lot of recording in '61, including an album with vibraphonist Milt Jackson in December and, within days, another featuring the Montgomerys with pianist George Shearing. The latter is an engaging, relaxed record that clearly reflects Shearing's love of Wes' playing (he insisted that Capitol, his own label, permit him to record with Wes). One often-used trademark of the Montgomery Brothers that Shearing catches on to and employs well is their tendency to play the theme of a song in unison—Wes and Buddy sounding like one. Shearing fits right into this, and they merge with distinction on the Latin-flavored "Stranger in Paradise." They also, in the tradition of Charlie Christian, utilize a recurring riff throughout the number that makes it infectious, even danceable.

By this time Wes had gained the eminence due him in the jazz world, producing a steady, high-quality level of music regardless of the context. His flow of ideas, soulful articulation and effortless technique confronted other influences. The direction of John Coltrane had a certain impact, but Wes retained his own ideas in whatever he did. In 1962 he cut a fine album with pianist Winton Kelly's trio in a Berkeley club, issued as *Full House*.

By 1963 Montgomery was trying out new concepts; one experiment was an album titled *Fusion* that featured him with such fine jazzmen as Kenny Burrell (on rhythm guitar) and bassist Milt Hinton, backed by a string orchestra. It was a harbinger of things to come, though nobody realized that at the time. Wes made the best of it, though his performances were certainly not among his most distinguished. He also returned to his old Indianapolis setting, reuniting in 1963 with organist Melvin Rhyne for two albums worth of material that vacillates between merely acceptable and occasionally brilliant (such as "Fried Pies" and the jazz waltz "Besame Mucho"). Certainly considering the contexts in which Wes had been playing over the past couple of years the organ trio idea was a bit old. But Wes was comfortable with it.

The results were mixed, but the best was good indeed. "The Breeze and I" was light and airy, and the musical telepathy between the musicians was evident, as Melvin set up Wes' solos. It was even more apparent on the arresting "Freddie the Freeloader," a Miles Davis composition featuring straight single string passages. Wes may sometimes have been concerned that his thumb technique inhibited his speed, but the passages he executes here, though difficult, are played with perfection. Barry Harris' "Lilita" returns him to a Latin groove, on which his octave work was always effective. "Blues Riff," (two takes [one previously unissued] are included) is repetitive, but the longer take is downright hypnotic.

By 1964 Riverside Records had been sold, and Wes signed with Verve, the prestigious jazz label founded in the '50s by promoter Norman Granz. And it was here that to many jazz purists and Montgomery fans alike, the stubborn integrity of his music began to unravel. It would be unfair to state that this occurred all at once. He did some more fine small group recordings with Wynton Kelly's combo, but by 1965 he was being eased into a more conservative, orchestrated sound by a&r men Creed Taylor and Esmond Edwards. At first it wasn't that bad. His 1966 album *Tequila* had a title track which Wes handled well, though he relied too much on rhythmic riffs, flourishes and his famous octaves, which were being pushed as his obvious selling point. He was using them far more than in the past, often to the exclusion of any single-string work at all.

The album had its moments, however. Even Claus Ogerman's orchestrations weren't all that schmaltzy. Wes did manage to play some sparse single-note passages in "Little Child," and on "What the World Needs Now," the Burt Bacharach composition—but they were weak, often simplistic and secondary to his dependence on octaves. Even his original tunes were inconsistent. "Bumpin' on Sunset" was pretentious; "How Insensitive" was dull Latin schmaltz and "Midnight Mood" was pointless. Only "The Thumb" showed any of the humor and jazz values that had been so much a part of him in the past.

To say this was a total disaster doesn't paint the entire picture. For one thing, Montgomery's onstage performances were for the most part as jazz-oriented as ever, with Monk and Buddy providing excellent backing. In addition, his new approach was giving Wes exposure to audiences who paid him little mind in the days when he was recording for Riverside. But jazz critics who had praised him in the past were disappointed, often despondent, over his bows to commerciality. And when Wes moved to A&M Records in 1967 he continued his climb towards mass acceptance, having a huge hit with the frivolous "Windy." With Creed Taylor guiding him, it seemed Wes was headed for the sort of financial success that only one other jazz guitarist—George Benson—has enjoyed. And unlike Wes, Benson had to sing before widespread popularity came his way.

The criticism bothered Wes. In several interviews he was downright defensive about it. "It doesn't matter how much artistry one has," he told down beat's Bill Quinn in 1967. "It's how it's presented that counts." And his financial rewards can't be ignored. Jazz musicians who remained incorruptible often made mediocre livings; Wes had six children. So he continued to record "Georgia on My Mind," "Where Have All the Flowers Gone" and "A Day in the Life," giving them an unmistakable jazz flavor, often wringing out much of his sub-

tlety but reaping the sort of success that he should (but never could) have achieved back in the early '60s when he did his best work.

One wonders what would have happened eventually. Would Wes have continued recording easy listening material forever? Or would he have played the game long enough to assure his financial security, then returned to jazz? Certainly Stan Getz managed to enjoy his pop successes and retain his jazz identity. It's conceivable that Wes could have alternated MOR releases with the unadulterated jazz he was still playing in the clubs. As a star, however, he had to be paid far better by the clubs—and all he had to do was play a few of his hits. Then he could play what he wanted.

We'll never know what might have been, for on June 15, 1968, at age 45, Wes Montgomery died of a heart attack in Indianapolis. His records, of course, remain, and it appears that the ones with the greatest effect will be those with the most jazz content. Pop fans will be able to buy his hits forever. But it is the jazz albums—most of them reissued at budget prices—that will be analyzed and studied, and that will have the most impact upon young guitarists and jazz students.

DISCOGRAPHY
A wide variety of Wes Montgomery material has recently emerged. His pop vehicles are all easily found, including *The Best of Wes Montgomery* (Verve). In the jazz area, *Small Group Recordings*, a double set, is available. From the Verve Japanese reissues comes *Bumpin'* and *Tequila*. His A&M albums, *Down Here on the Ground, A Day in the Life* and others can be easily found.

Much of his top-flight material is also available. Fantasy Records has reissued several of his Riverside discs in beautiful, $5.99 packages identical to the originals, including *Wes Montgomery Trio*, and *The Incredible Jazz Guitar of Wes Montgomery*. Also, Milestone Records has released a number of great double LP sets, including *The Alternative Wes Montgomery* (alternate takes), *Wes and Friends* (with Milt Jackson and George Shearing), *Groove Brothers* and *Yesterdays*.

LES PAUL

Les Paul, to many of his fans, would not be thought of as a jazz guitarist. Indeed, many of his greatest contributions to the guitar were technological as opposed to musical. His pioneering experiments with amplification techniques, with the concept of a solidbody electric Spanish guitar, with multiple recording, echo and (after tape recorders became available) overdubbing have been unmatched. Likewise, his development of the classic Gibson Les Paul series of guitars alone could sustain his legend.

Certainly Les is not a jazz guitarist in the same sense that Barney Kessel is and Wes Montgomery was, though there's little doubt he could have been. Indeed, he was not often one for extended improvisations; his records were huge pop music hits, palatable to millions. Many were Tin Pan Alley ditties that were hackneyed when he recorded them in the early '50s.

But it would be unfair to denigrate the considerable jazz values in his music. For one thing, his technique and musical concepts are solidly rooted in the styles of Eddie Lang and

particularly Django Reinhardt. And though Les' records enjoyed solid mainstream pop acceptance, there weren't safe, down-to-earth efforts aimed at giving the listener music of bland predictability. He created cascades for solos, shimmering, rippling curtains of tasteful electric guitar that tested the limits of electronic technology and blazed new trails. If the music Les made was highly commercial, his means of creating it were anything but that.

What made all of this more than amazing is the American public's conservative attitude toward popular music in the early '50s, when Les and his wife Mary Ford had their greatest successes. It might have been just that their records were refreshingly different in a pre-rock world dominated by Johnnie Ray and Margaret Whiting; they certainly sounded futuristic enough then. But Les' sense of good taste always governed his experiments. Radical as many of them were, it could hardly be said that he did anything for mere shock value; taste undoubtedly helped guarantee his success.

The influence of Les Paul can't be fully

measured and evaluated in anything less than a full-length book. One can hear a bit of him in every experimental or innovative guitarist. Many of the effects used by contemporary guitarists are perfected versions of ideas Les was tinkering with in his workshop-studio 30 years ago. So many jazz, rock and country guitarists were inspired by his Capitol recordings that it would be impossible to list them here. But his sound can be heard particularly in the playing of Chet Atkins, whose brother Jimmy worked in Les' early '40s trio. Jimmy Page of Led Zeppelin has cited Les as a major inspiration when he was starting to play. And even tunes like the Yardbirds' "Jeff's Boogie," featuring Jeff Beck on lead guitar, have strong overtones of the man known as the Wizard of Waukesha.

Waukesha, Wisconsin was where Lester William Polfuss was born on June 9, 1916. In 1925, when he was just nine, he heard a sewer worker playing a harmonica on the street and stared at him for so long that the worker gave him the instrument. He also listened intently to the early Grand Old Opry over the next few years, and perfected his harmonica abilities to a point where he could play for money on the streets of Waukesha.

Such activities for one so young required a fair amount of guts and aggressiveness, and these traits were ones that would give Les a huge advantage throughout his career. He was never a timid person, and took a direct and straightforward approach to everything from learning to play guitar to designing the various devices he's pioneered and building a professional career. When he was 11 he started playing a Sears Roebuck guitar. A good example of Les' drive concerns his learning to play an F chord. Gene Autry was playing in Waukesha, and in the dark theater, Les was trying to watch Autry's hands when he played an F. He used a flashlight, turning it on each time Autry hit an F chord to see which strings he was fretting. Autry finally became disturbed enough to mention it to the audience, but as Les put it, "I confessed, and he called me up onstage and asked me to play my guitar and sing..."

It also took a lot of nerve to fool with electro-

nics and, particularly in the late 1920s-early '30s, to design things for the guitar few had yet dreamed of. But Les did, developing the interest that would serve him so well later on. He studied the basic theories of electronics in books before embarking on his earliest efforts to amplify his new Gibson L-5. His ideas were certainly creative. One time he jammed the needle of his mother's phonograph into the top of his guitar to acoustically amplify it.

Nor was that the only experiment he initiated. He jazzed up the music on his mother's player piano by punching additional holes in the rolls to augment what was there. Another invention, involving the use of radios as multiple voice and guitar amplifiers, may have been the first prototype of the concept of stereo. By the time Les was 12 he'd built his first recording machine.

Throughout this time he was playing around Waukesha, using a variety of pseudonyms. He joined a country music band that came through town and featured singer/guitarist Joe Wolverton. He toured with Wolverton in the summer of 1929 before returning to school, and then linked up with him again in 1930 in Springfield, Missouri. Dubbing themselves "Sunny Joe and Rhubarb Red," the duo became popular in the Midwest, and though Les wasn't permitted by Wolverton to indulge his taste for amplified guitar, he did permit him to put together a public address system for their stage shows. Les also learned about showmanship and handling audiences.

They stayed together until 1933, and separated in Chicago. Les' interest in jazz was piqued, and the music of Eddie Lang had a profound effect on him. So he remained in town, performing as Rhubarb Red over WJJD radio and also leading a jazz band under his own name. He wound up on the famous WLS National Barn Dance in his Rhubarb Red guise, and managed to get away with playing his L-5 amplified guitar, which may make him one of the first—if not the first—country performers to use an amplified guitar. He also did some recordings as a sideman, using his own name, with blues singer Georgia White.

His new ideas didn't stop through this period. He had a special guitar designed for him in 1935, with a heavy maple top, marking the beginning of his experiments with solid-bodied instruments. But in the meantime jazz absorbed his attention. The early records of Django Reinhardt had a profound effect upon him; he drank in the fluent, impassioned music of Django and by 1936 abandoned his Rhubarb Red persona to plunge head-on into the jazz field. The boldness of his music made him a favorite as he jammed with people like trumpet virtuoso Roy Eldridge and others in Chicago clubs. Les then formed his own group, the Les Paul Trio, with Jimmy Atkins and bassist Ernie Newton.

The group went to New York in 1938 and appeared as a featured act on Fred Waring's NBC radio show. Though Waring has always been a relatively conservative musician, he encouraged Les' use of amplification, even though the initial response from listeners was somewhat unfavorable. Les continued his experimentation, creating his own radio station in the apartment building known as the "Boger Brothers Broadcasting Company." The hot jazz jam sessions the station featured were favorites in its area, but interference with aviation radio put a swift end to the station once the federal authorities caught onto it.

His trio stayed with Waring until 1940, when Les left to return to Chicago, to work on radio and play with Ben Bernie's orchestra. He also resumed his solidbody guitar designing, having Epiphone build him what became known as "the Log," an instrument made of solid wood with a wing on either side to give it a guitarlike appearance (it's now in the Country Music Hall of Fame in Nashville). By 1943 he and Ben Bernie traveled to Los Angeles, and Paul's professional reputation continued to flourish as he formed a new trio, which did extensive radio work. The draft caught up to him, but he was placed in Special Services and worked with his trio in Hollywood doing special radio shows and recordings. He also reasserted his abilities as a jazz guitarist by performing in a Jazz at the Philharmonic program with Nat "King" Cole as pianist. His Reinhardt-based improvisations left little doubt of his formidable abilities in jazz, and had he opted to continue in that idiom alone he undoubtedly would have done well.

Les preferred working in a variety of contexts, and his association with Bing Crosby proved especially beneficial. In 1946 he and his trio recorded "It's Been a Long, Long Time" with Crosby for Decca. Bing, whose special love for fine guitars went back to his close association with Eddie Lang, undoubtedly heard Lang's ghost in Les' poignant, lyrical guitar playing. There is little question that Paul's playing was unique on this recording. Guitar amplification at the time tended to produce a thick tone, yet Les' playing has balance and warmth and a glistening edge obtained through the use of echo. The sparse instrumentation of the trio provided great intimacy for Crosby's vocal, and Les' arpeggios and obbligatos enveloped him, as an orchestra would, even though he was not yet overdubbing. Led Zeppelin's Jimmy Page has singled out this recording, calling it "fantastic."

Crosby encouraged Les to take his multiple recording experiments even further and to build his own recording studio. Paul put it in his garage, designing and constructing most of the equipment himself in between jobs with his trio. He built his own recording lathes and began experimenting with recording in multiple parts, laying down lead guitar, rhythm guitars, and bass to the extent of creating—through much trial and error—what amounted to self-contained orchestrations, his guitar piled in layer upon layer to achieve his end.

By 1948 he'd completed multiple recordings of "Lover" and "Brazil," which were released by Capitol Records and remain classics. By speeding up certain parts on tape to give them an ethereal feeling while his arpeggios swirled, Les began "Lover" at waltz tempo, with daintiness before moving into a hard-driving mode, again with speeded up guitar parts counterpointing his solo. Its effect at the time must have been riveting—after all, barely a decade before Les had been catching hell for even using an electric guitar. "Brazil," another classic, was given a similar complex treatment, but Les never forgot to add humor. His best recordings are always laced with musical jokes, be it a jazzed-up quote from another song or a weird lick of some sort. He experimented with an aluminum-bodied guitar on these tracks as well.

Capitol realized that it had something unique, and even billed the records as "The New Sound of Les Paul." Another aspect of even his most unorthodox sides was the fact they always swung. Les was not one to push aside a solid rhythmic foundation to indulge himself in technological gimmickry.

But a devastating auto accident nearly cost him everything in 1948. His car skidded on an icy bridge, then plunged 50 feet into a snowbank. He lay for eight hours before anyone found him. When they did, he was riddled with broken bones, including his right arm, which was shattered almost beyond repair. Amputation was considered, and only the intervention of a doctor who was a fan of Les' music saved the arm. Instead of being amputated, it was set in guitar playing position, and though Les was sidelined for nearly two years, as soon as he could he was back in his studio making records. His strength of character probably kept his career alive.

Late in 1949 he married Colleen Summers, a former western singer who became his performing partner as well. Recovered and working as Les Paul and Mary Ford, the duo began to find success beyond any Les had enjoyed in the past. Les continued recording solos, including his first hit, a version of the standard "Nola," which reached number eight on the pop charts in 1950. He also did a weird version of the old tune "Goofus," slowed down far beyond its usual upbeat tempo. The duet's first hit was a cover of the 1948 top seller "Tennessee Waltz," featuring double-trackkd vocals which permitted Mary to harmonize with herself. As early as '49, Les was working closely with the Ampex tape recorder company, and had one of its early four-track recorders. The "sound on sound" idea, now a routine recording technique, was Les' baby, though he never took out a patent on it.

Some of the Les Paul-Mary Ford material was terribly corny pap, particularly

"Mockingbird Hill," their 1950 number one hit. What set it apart from the schlock of that era were its musical richness and adventurous electronic effects. And not all their pieces were without real excitement. "How High the Moon," their 1951 number one recording, was solid and swinging, with Les playing bluesy overtones on the leads while his own rhythm tracks backed him. Some of his licks predict of late '60s rock guitar cliches. Les alone had a number 12 instrumental hit in 1951 with "Josephine," featuring tape delay on the lead guitar tracks. The song itself was nothing, but his incredible precision was something to marvel at in and of itself.

"The World Is Waiting for the Sunrise" was a number three hit for the duo in 1951, but featured Mary more than Les, whose playing was relatively restrained. Les dominated the flipside, "Whispering," which featured clever multiple cascades of speeded up passages and rhythmic, subtle pizzicato lines which gave the accompaniment to his solo a percussive edge. His 1952 recording of "Carioca" is one of his more elaborate efforts, with layer upon layer of parts, both normal and speeded up, to the point it sounds totally and thoroughly orchestrated.

One of Les' wildest solos appeared on the duo's 1952 recording of "In the Good Old Summertime." While Mary sings a rhythmic fragment of the song, Les cuts loose with playing that sounds as if it was recorded straight, without overdubs. He again essays bluesy phrases that anticipate future rock solos, snapping the strings and doubletiming with great skill. He got off equally pungent solos on the pair's 1952 recording of "Bye, Bye Blues," again played straight. Their biggest hit came in the summer of 1953, when "Vaya Con Dios," which was built around Mary's plaintive vocal, achieved number one. It was conservative by their standards, but Les was always smart enough not to let his techniques use him. Their late 1952 single, "My Baby's Comin' Home," for example, featured minimal overdubbing. Paul was especially careful to be sure that he tailored his arrangements to the song and not vice versa.

By 1953 Les Paul and Mary Ford had sold

millions of records. They had their own TV program sponsored by Listerine, and Les had designed his famous Les Paul solidbody guitar for Gibson, the company which had ignored his previous experiments with solidbody instruments and so been beaten to the punch by Fender, which introduced its Broadcaster guitar in 1948. Gibson had already designed a solidbody guitar, and Gibson's president Ted McCarty met with Les and Mary to draw up an agreement concerning the guitar that would bear his name. Les worked on the tailpiece and various other aspects of the design with Gibson. The Les Paul line grew and thrived until Les parted with the company in 1962.

It was somewhat ironic, considering Les' impact on rock and roll, that the popularity of rock brought to an end the career of Les and Mary. They had toured throughout their most successful period, with Les' electronic gadgetry permitting them to reproduce some of their complex material onstage. Les even had Gibson design a miniature guitar tuned an octave higher so he could recreate the speeded up, high-pitched parts onstage. But it didn't matter. They moved to Columbia Records, but by the late 50s, the hits were past. By 1964 Les and Mary had quit touring and were divorced. Les moved back to Mahwah, New Jersey, outside New York City, where he continued working on ideas and inventions. He didn't record at all commercially. Gibson stopped producing its Les Paul guitars, but when blues-rock players like Duane Allman, Eric Clapton, Mike Bloomfield, Jeff Beck and Jimmy Page began featuring them, and rock guitar became a virtuoso's craft in the late '60s, Les Pauls suddenly became collectors' items. Gibson had produced its SG series of double cutaway guitars after Les refused to endorse them with his name, but in 1968 the company resumed production of the original Les Paul designs with some modifications, and the line has continued with infinite variations (and Les' resumed input) ever since.

He recorded an album titled *Les Paul Now!* for London in the late '60s, and had never been totally out of touch. He'd heard Jimi Hendrix, for example, playing a New Jersey roadhouse in 1966, and tried to get hold of him only to find Jimi and his band had been fired from the club for their unorthodox sound. By 1970, however, Les was out of commission with inner-ear problems that sidelined him for several years. He decided to return to performing in 1974, bringing with him vastly improved effects devices (including his Les Paulverizer tape echo device) and his new guitars with low-impedance pickups.

In 1976 he and Chet Atkins got together for the *Chester and Lester* album. Chet and Les had been friends since Chet's brother worked with Les in his trio. With just a spare rhythm section, the two greats fooled around with a bunch of old standards and their loose, wisecracking interplay resulted in a Grammy in 1977. They won yet another Grammy in 1978 with *Guitar Monsters.* Les' technique hadn't changed much from the days of his million-sellers; though he wasn't creating the elaborate multi-tracked sounds, he was still able to suggest enough of them to remind you of the old Les Paul. And though any knowledgeable guitarists could see the contrasts in their styles—Chet often relied on his classical guitars—there were many points where their playing seemed to merge, a measure of their mutual respect. Les created some fine moments, especially his octave passage on "Meditation."

Today Les Paul is an elder statesman of the electric guitar, yet age hasn't slowed his creativity. He recovered from open-heart surgery several years ago, and has continued to work on a variety of ideas. In 1982 he was featured on a live TV concert with Jeff Beck, and though he seemed stylistically out of place, he wasn't intimidated. After all, much of what Beck was up to had its roots in Les' playing. And in an era when people are working with guitar synthesizers and briefcase-sized cassette recorders with mixing boards and overdub capabilities on board, it's comforting to know that Les Paul, the man who made all of that possible before anyone else ever heard of a transistor, is still at work.

DISCOGRAPHY

Quite a number of Les Paul's recordings are available. "It's Been a Long, Long Time," with his original trio, is available on MCA's *The Best of Bing* (though it's the only such track on the album; the rest is pretty schlocky). Some of his late '40s trio material is available on *Les Paul Trio* (Glendale).

Much of his best Capitol material is available. *The New Sound of Les Paul* is a reproduction of a 1950 LP, while *The World Is Waiting for the Sunrise* is an excellent single-disc sampler of the best Les and Mary Ford material. *Early Les Paul* deals with the best of his pre-Mary instrumental numbers, while the 3-LP box *Their All-Time Greatest Hits* (Murray Hill) includes just that, with excellent discographical data (though one wonders why the classic "Brazil" is on none of these collections).

Paul's late '70s albums with Chet Atkins, *Chester and Lester* and *Guitar Monsters*, are still available, the former as a budget-priced LP.

JIMMY RANEY

Like Tal Farlow, Jimmy Raney has a reclusive nature; unlike Farlow, Raney has never walked away from the music business for any prolonged period. From the limelight, yes; from performing and teaching, not at all. In many ways staying out of the limelight is appropriate for Raney, one of the most sensitive, introspective guitarists in modern jazz and one of the few truly skilled bop guitarists.

Like Barney Kessel and Tal Farlow, Raney was one of the wave of post-Charlie Christian guitarists who came up in his shadow, only to become enchanted with bop and begin moving in that direction. When Raney first emerged in the late '40s he was one of a very exclusive fraternity. Only Kessel, Farlow, Arvin Garrison, Billy Bauer and Chuck Wayne were truly in the forefront of modern jazz guitar at the time.

Like Kessel, Wayne, Bauer and Farlow, Raney cut his teeth in some of the finest modern jazz units of the postwar era: Woody Herman's Second Herd, Artie Shaw's new, more progressive 1950 orchestra, Buddy De-

Franco's combo and the pioneering small group of Stan Getz. In those bands he first came to the attention of audiences who were universally impressed with his creative, beautifully articulated and harmonically advanced single-note playing. There was little brashness to Raney's solo approach. Then as now, he tended to understate his attack, giving his sound a "cooler" approach appropriate to the music and anticipating the cool style of the '50s.

Raney's gift for lyrical phrasing has left its impact on other guitarists, among them Pat Martino and Wes Montgomery. Though he remains low profile, he still records regularly with his son Doug, and has managed to grow harmonically and professionally while spending much of his time in his native Louisville, Kentucky.

James Elbert Raney was born in Louisville, Kentucky on August 20, 1927, the son of a popular local sportswriter. The guitar first impressed him when he was ten, and his mother's relatives were all amateur mountain musicians playing a music Jimmy quickly grew to despise. His mother gave him his earliest instruction, after which he studied with a Louisville classical guitar teacher, A.J. Giancolla.

His interest in jazz flourished around 1940, when he began to study under jazz guitarist Hayden Causey. Causey opened up an entirely new world to Raney. He began listening to Oscar Moore (whose influence can be heard clearly in some of Raney's early work), George Barnes and Django Reinhardt. But when an acquaintance played him Charlie Christian's recording of "Solo Flight" with Benny Goodman's orchestra, as with so many other aspiring jazz guitarists, Raney's direction was set.

He began working with other teenagers in small local bands, and by World War II was a full-fledged union musician. As he'd learned to read music under Giancolla's tutelage, he had little problem handling professional jobs. In the meantime, his studies with Causey began to pay off in more ways than he'd expected. Causey had left Louisville to go to New York, where he worked with bandleader Jerry Wald, a clarinetist in the Artie Shaw vein. Causey left Wald in 1944 to join Harry James' orchestra, and recommended Raney as his replacement.

Jimmy arrived in New York at an exciting time. Bebop was just beginning to emerge as a potent new mode of jazz expression, and Raney was able to absorb it firsthand. An added advantage was that one of his fellow Wald sidemen was pianist Al Haig, known for his work with Charlie Parker. As he and Haig began playing together, Raney saw bop's potential, and after leaving New York to return to Louisville he immersed himself in Parker's recordings.

Six months after returning home he moved to Chicago, another hotbed of musical activity. Bop was influencing musicians there, too, and Raney continued to study the music as he performed in the area through 1946 and 1947. Drummer Tiny Kahn knew of Raney's work, and in 1948 his recommendation propelled Raney into the forefront of modern jazz

at the time: the Woody Herman band. At the time, Herman was making jazz history with his legendary Four Brothers saxophone section of Stan Getz, Al Cohn, Zoot Sims and Serge Chaloff playing their incredible ensemble work. Bop now surrounded Raney, permitting him to delve even deeper into it.

In October of '48, he made his first recording session with Getz, Al Haig and a rhythm section, contributing brief choruses on "Interlude in Be-Bop" and "As I Live and Bop." At the time Raney's soloing was tight, still echoing Oscar Moore's concise approach, but his harmonic concepts were solidly implanted in bop. His overall sound had some similarity to Arvin Garrison's. In May 1949 he recorded again with a fragment of the Herman band (Getz, Cohn, Sims, trombonist Earl Swope and bassist Mert Oliver) plus bop pianist Duke Jordan and drummer Charlie Perry. The sound was a variant of Herman's, but Raney got off fine, if brief, solos on "Stan Gets Along" and "Slow." He also recorded with Haig and saxophonist Wardell Gray.

He moved next to Buddy DeFranco's progressive group, doing some lyrical, cerebral solos on recordings that became a part of DeFranco's classic *Crosscurrents* material for Capitol. Leaving DeFranco in late '49 Raney joined Artie Shaw's orchestra, where his technique began to jell even further on songs like "Foggy, Foggy Dew" and "I Get A Kick Out of You" with the full orchestra and "The Shekomeko Shuffle"—with the Gramercy Five. Though his solos were brief on these numbers, he played with great confidence and showed his marvelous phrasing off to good effect.

Jimmy moved to another small group, this one led by vibraphonist Terry Gibbs, before joining Stan Getz in 1951 for some of his most memorable work, preserved in their live recordings (with old friend Al Haig on piano) at the Storyville jazz club in Boston. Raney's original compositions "Signal" and "Parker '51" were but two examples of his great contributions to the Getz combo. Getz and Raney formed a unique musical relationship that drew upon mutual virtuosity and understanding, culminating in Raney's becoming musical director for Stan Getz before he left in 1953 to replace Tal Farlow in the Red Norvo Trio. He remained with this group for nearly a year, until Farlow returned.

Raney recorded extensively over the next three years in a variety of contexts (little of which is currently available, or could be reviewed for this essay). His reputation had grown to such heights that he won *Down Beat*'s critics' polls in both 1954 and '55.

By that time he'd joined pianist Jimmy Lyon's trio in New York, with whom he would stay for the next six years, playing jazz and lounge music as well as serving as a backup unit for club acts. Raney continued with the group until 1960, but his visibility on the New York jazz scene began to wane. Part of it was his strong distaste for traveling. In '60 he started working as a Broadway musician, doing shows including *A Thurber Carnival* and *The Nervous Set*. The music was far from jazz, and though Raney continued doing jazz sessions as a sideman, and worked for a time with vibist Gary McFarland, he had immersed himself in substantive musical studies, starting in 1959 with cello and composition.

In 1964 he decided to return to Louisville with his family to teach and perform, returning to New York only occasionally. Like Tal Farlow, Raney found offstage pressures of the music business alien to his nature.

By the late '60s, however, he began to reemerge, albeit gingerly, recording an album, *Momentum*, with a trio in Germany in 1969. Raney did a highly acclaimed performance at the 1971 Newport Jazz Festival, and began working in New York City again, playing as well as ever (in fact he'd never laid his guitar down as Farlow had). Another excellent recording that shows him in masterful form is *Strings Attached*, from 1975. His long, sinuous solos, exquisitely phrased and harmonically adventurous, but still highly introspective, are intact; and reunited with Al Haig he produced fresh, marvelous music, revitalizing older tunes like "Invitation," soloing with the warm, smoky tone that characterizes his sound. On "Out of Nowhere" Raney was assisted by his son Doug, at age 19 a former

rock guitar player who turned to jazz and, under his father's tutelage (with help from Tal Farlow and Barry Galbraith), showed strong potential as a jazzman in his dad's style, though he would need time to grow and mature.

Around that same time a reissue LP, Strings and Swings, was issued, combining live 1969 recordings from Louisville with some unique material Raney wrote for jazz guitar and a string quartet. He signed with producer Don Schlitten's Xanadu Records in 1975, commencing a series of outstanding new albums. *The Influence*, recorded that year with only bass and drums, was a stunning, even inspiring album that demonstrated all that is great about Raney's artistry. Every note exudes the most tasteful, polished attack imaginable. Even his chord flourishes on his bluesy version of "Body and Soul," combined with his use of octaves, were superbly articulated, giving the song a Reinhardtesque flavor. Raney's rich harmonic concepts took this shopworn jazz standard into an entirely new dimension.

He likewise gives the pop standard "It Could Happen to You" a spirited reading, moving into highly involved, complex improvisational lines and dazzling double-time choruses. His comping behind Sam Jones' bass solo smacks of George Van Eps. "Suzanne," an original composition, features overdubbing. It is a highly complex number played precisely, featuring unorthodox harmonies played with a precision and discipline reflecting Raney's classical music studies. It doesn't swing at all but is nonetheless an enthralling number, exemplifying Raney's sense of daring. Cole Porter's "Get Out of Town," (also overdubbed) is a beautiful latin-flavored performance featuring warm, joyful solo lines and some finely textured rhythm comping. His unaccompanied version of "End of a Love Affair" is entirely self-contained, and he manages to keep chords flowing so smoothly (again reminding one of Van Eps' influence) it's hard to believe it's *not* overdubbed. *Live in Tokyo*, also recorded in 1975, is an equally fine set.

Solo, his 1976 album, features Raney

alone, using overdubbing and an F-guitar tuned to F7, pitched a fifth lower than standard tuning. The lack of a rhythm section means nothing, for Raney selects his material carefully. His opener, "The Fugue," is a complex original; Raney states in the liner notes that it "was inspired by the Bach two-part inventions for keyboard." Yet the jazz influence is clear; at times the lines come together in harmonies reminiscent of the Woody Herman "Four Brothers" sax sound he knew so well. The contrapuntal sound again reflects his classical discipline, however. "New Signal" is a revisionist approach to the song Raney made famous in 1951 with the Getz combo. His use of contrasting block chords with free-form, single-note lines gives the song considerable density. "How Deep Is the Ocean" is eloquently stated, with the F guitar giving the song a bass underpinning. "The Way You Look Tonight" gets a spritely, almost playful treatment while Jimmy turns "Wait Till You See Her," the Rodgers and Hart standard, into a delicate, appealing jazz waltz.

More recently, Raney has recorded two impressive sets of duets with his son Doug, who shows even more signs of being the keeper of his father's flame.

It is sad that, in a field where a fine guitarist like George Benson—now only peripherally involved with jazz—is considered a virtuoso for his pop records and where fusion jazz fans listen primarily to the hot acts of the moment, Jimmy Raney's work is so neglected. But then Raney has never been a self-promoter. So he continues to live quietly in Louisville, teaching but traveling for performances and still recording. His approach has been without compromise, and his intellectual, yet emotive playing has the beauty, integrity and impact of fine artwork (in fact, both "Signal" and "Parker '51" were named for a painting and an artist, respectively). Even if Jimmy Raney continues to perform for small but admiring audiences, he is still setting the standards for any serious jazz guitarist.

DISCOGRAPHY

Luckily, right now there's probably more Jimmy Raney material available on record than ever—though much of the older material on which his reputation is based is out of print. Some of his early material with Stan Getz before 1950 is available on *Opus De Bop* (Savoy). His stint with Artie Shaw is represented on the double album *The Best of Artie Shaw* (MCA). The Getz Quintet material is out of print. His first solo sessions can be found on *Early Getz* (Prestige).

Raney's later recordings are far easier to find. *Strings Attached* with Al Haig (Choice), *Momentum* (Pausa) and *Strings and Swings* (Muse) are all '60s works while *The Influence, Live in Tokyo,* and *Solo* (all on Xanadu) are easily found. His duet LPs with Doug, *Duets* and *Stolen Moments* (both on Steeplechase) are also available.

DJANGO REINHARDT

Thirty-odd years have passed since a stroke ended Django Reinhardt's life at age 43, yet the repercussions of his music have never ceased. Indeed, his music seems more alive than ever. The massive 20-disc set *Djangologie*, issued by the French Pathe label (and containing a substantial chunk of his recorded legacy), remains a best-seller. Numerous other single and multiple discs of Django material, including live shows, proliferate around the Western world.

His admirers stretch across the entire musical spectrum, from classical (violinist Yehudi Menuhin, guitarist Julian Bream), jazz (pianist John Lewis, guitarists Barney Kessel, Larry Coryell, Les Paul, Joe Pass and many more), country (steel guitarist Joaquin Murphey, guitarists Chet Atkins, Don Gibson, Hank Garland, Grady Martin, Eldon Shamblin and Willie Nelson), and rock (Carlos Santana). Reinhardt was a direct influence on the "new acoustic music" of the late '70s—a fusion of jazz, bluegrass, classical and ethnic forms—that was pioneered by mandolinist David Grisman.

Unlike many jazz guitar pioneers, Django not only lived to see his music appreciated but also enjoyed a level of adulation in France that few jazzmen anywhere have equaled. Why? Perhaps it was not so much a French love of pure jazz as it was that he spiced an American music with the sounds of his gypsy culture, giving it a distinctly European flavor.

That may have helped attract more Europeans to his music—ordinary people beyond the hardcore European jazz fanatics, people who normally would have paid jazz no mind. Django's playing reconciled old with new, creating music of breathtaking beauty. That novelist James Jones devoted a passage in *From Here to Eternity* to Django, that teenager guitarist Bireli LaGrene today plays so hauntingly like him, are but two more measures of the impact Django Reinhardt has had on popular culture.

There is a certain amount of romanticism in all this, of course. The image of the brilliant, egocentric, eccentric, volatile Belgian-born gypsy entrancing thousands with his stunning guitar work certainly has a universal appeal.

And to some extent this has made it difficult to place Django in perspective. Oscar Aleman, the Argentine jazz guitarist who technically was *every* bit Reinhardt's equal, has only recently been recognized as the virtuoso he was, and he was dead by the time this happened. During most of his life, he was doomed to exist in Django's shadow.

Yet Django's fame also transcends his image, for he fought for both his music and for the right to keep one—or both—feet planted in the gypsy lifestyle that nurtured him. He could be one *tough* bastard. When his hand was so severely burned he was never expected to play again, he struggled back to play better than he had before the injury. When tied into contracts or engagements where he felt his name was slighted, he blew up (reflecting his infinitely large ego), yet he was also lackadaisical about money. And it took years to get him to settle down; faced with playing a club or partying with his gypsy "cousins," he chose the latter through much of his life.

There's little question that Django's musical roots were in both the gypsy and classical music around him, and in the jazz of the '20s and '30s. In the latter area Louis Armstrong and Duke Ellington were particularly strong inspirations, but Eddie Lang was undoubtedly Django's major guitar influence. Lang's impact on Reinhardt's style is often overlooked or taken for granted, though it was considerable. One can often hear Django bass lines or improvisations that echo something Lang had recorded years earlier. And, in fact, the famous Quintet of the Hot Club of France, featuring Django and violinist Stephane Grappelli, began as the two tried to imitate the famous Lang duets with jazz violin pioneer Joe Venuti. Also, Lang was trained in European classical music of a sort Django would have heard, making him in many ways the ideal role model for the gypsy.

Jean Baptiste Reinhardt was born January 23, 1910, at Liverchies, Belgium, not far from the French border. At the time of his birth his mother, LaBelle Reinhardt, traveled with a gypsy caravan. His musical talent was perhaps inherited from his probable father, Jean Ve'es, who had lived with Django's mother.

Ve'es was a combination comic and musician. However, he played a minimal role in his son's life, leaving everything to LaBelle. In the best gypsy tradition, school was of minimal concern, meaning Django grew up illiterate and was only able to write his name after considerable instruction once his musical career had begun in earnest.

Most of Django's early life consisted of traipsing across Europe in caravan with his baby brother Joseph before settling, after World War I, just outside Paris. Since he didn't attend school, Django acquired skill first as a billiards player. But music crept into his life by the time he was ten, and he was soon begging his mother for a guitar. He wound up with a banjo-guitar, with which he became obsessed, practicing it in marathon sessions that laid the groundwork for the brilliance that was to come. He listened to gypsy music, and by 1923 was good enough to play low-level Paris dancehalls. He continued improving, and by March, 1928, had done his first unexceptional record date as a sideman. British bandleader Jack Hylton heard him and wanted to sign him to appear with his orchestra; Django agreed.

But on November 2, 1928, Django and his first wife were preparing for bed in their caravan (a wagon) which was loaded with celluloid flowers to be sold at a nearby cemetery. Hearing a rustling noise, Django, without thinking, lit a candle. He burned himself with it and when the candle fell into the flammable flowers, found himself engulfed in flames. While protecting himself with a blanket, his left hand, exposed to the fire, was seared. He was severely burned on the lower right side of his body as well. For a time doctors considered amputating his right leg, but Django's stubbornness prevented that.

Yet his left fretting hand appeared to be destroyed. The ring finger and little finger were fused together, paralyzed and useless, and the rest of his hand was also severely deformed. Only his index and middle fingers were even partially usable. The doctors decided his guitar might boost his morale, and it was this recommendation that he play it for therapy that revived Reinhardt's career.

It took him eighteen months to recover enough to function alone; strengthening his left hand took even longer. Struggling to relearn his instrument, Django had to find his own method. That he did so with such incredible finesse remains a miracle. His new fingerings were unorthodox, as was his approach to chords. Yet he allowed himself no breaks; he employed no compensatory tunings or other shortcuts. Most amazing was his speed. With only two fingers, Reinhardt managed to attain tempos that many guitarists with four good fingers could never master. His willpower and determination that made this possible remains an inspiration to any guitarist facing physical impairment.

By 1930 Django was playing well again. He had heard his first jazz when he met an artist in Toulon, France who played him Eddie Lang and Joe Venuti 78s as well as those of Duke Ellington and Louis Armstrong. Armstrong's *Dallas Blues* had such a powerful impact that Django sobbed, overwhelmed with the beauty of Louis' music. He soaked up the music in his friend's record collection, but did not jump right into playing jazz. Insted he joined a pop dance band led by bassist Louis Vola in Cannes. By this time he was already pulling his famous no-shows, a measure of his capricious attitude to performing.

Vola's orchestra returned to Paris in 1932, but Django bummed around Paris with his gypsy friends, playing when he wished to, usually in backstreet dives but occasionally in better clubs as well. He signed on in 1933 with Andre Ekyan's group and made one trip to London. After that he re-joined Louis Vola in Paris; he had a large band with two violinists, one of whom was Stephane Grappelli. On breaks, Django and Stephane fooled around, eventually latching onto the Lang-Venuti model, playing their own interpretations of songs like "Dinah." Soon other musicians, including guitarist Roger Chaput and Vola himself, were sitting in. And the nucleus of one of the greatest jazz groups of all time was formed, with Django's brother Joseph signing on.

The Quintet of the Hot Club of France, an extension of a jazz club, became their names, and throughout Django's career it was the group most associated with him, the one in which he made much of his finest, most enduring music. The witty, elegant swing of Grappelli, with the daring, uninhibited improvisations of Reinhardt, was a potent combination. But Joseph Reinhardt also deserves credit for his buoyant, driving rhythm guitar work, and Vola for his consistent bass playing.

They had difficulty getting a recording contract, with many French companies considering them too modern or unorthodox to achieve any commercial success. But they did begin to record, in December 1934, and the success of these recordings made legends of both Django nd Stephane. Django continued working as a sideman, but until August, 1939, when World War II split up the Reinhardt-Grappelli team, the Quintet defined jazz to many listeners in Europe and also found fans on the other side of the Atlantic. The interplay of the musicians, driving yet delicate, lyrical yet hard-edged and dominated by Django's unending flow of ideas, has held up to this day. Admittedly, some sides were weaker than others (the 1935 cuts featuring mediocre vocalist Jerry Mengo aren't terribly distinguished), but the Quintet nonetheless achieved a rare level of consistency among jazz units for the period, and despite its tentative start, its earliest records for the small Ultraphone label attracted a strong following.

With the Quintet Django called the shots, and the band's high points were many. Its 1935 recordings alone prove this. "I Got Rhythm" features a superb Django solo full of puckish humor; "Limehouse Blues," one of the numbers most associated with the Quintet, is more graceful, played at medium tempo. "St. Louis Blues" offers not only an introspective introduction from Django, but also some early examples of his use of octaves, which would be widely copied by others in later years. "China Boy," a most exciting side, contains many of the best-remembered attributes of the Quintet. Grappelli careens through the melody, while Reinhardt hits sharp rhythmic accents to punctuate the tempo; both essay intense solos that weave in and around each other.

The Quintet's accomplishments continued throughout the remainder of the decade. There was the ethereal beauty of "Oriental Shuffle," and some pleasant material with expatriate American vocalist Freddy Taylor including "Nagasaki." It was, however, in April 1937 that it did some of its most enduring work. By then the ensemble's sound had not yet jelled, was anything but predictable. An engaging version of "Exactly Like You" was followed at the same session by a wildly uninhibited version of "Charleston," an exciting rendition of "Hot Lips," a pungent, spirited "Rose Room," and an "Ain't Misbehavin'" dominated by Django. "Body and Soul" featured a unique introduction in octaves. Also recorded at this time was Django's superb interpretation of "Liebestraum," "Mystery Pacific," a swirling original "train" number showcasing some of Django's most intense guitar work, and "The Sheik of Araby." Grappelli was equally outstanding; these sessions exemplify all that was wonderful about the Quintet.

It would wax other superb sides. Its 1937 original of the now-classic "Minor Swing" featured an interesting role reversal, with Grappelli playing with total abandon and Django playing with unusual restraint. Also cut then were memorable versions of "Honeysuckle Rose" and "Them There Eyes," another example of Django laying out while Stephane rushed through the song. If this group were never to have recorded again, these songs alone would have sealed its reputation.

Of course, Django did other recordings during the '30s, such as his passionate "Parfum," recorded alone, and "Alabamy Bound," featuring him and Grappelli *sans* Quintet, in the Lang-Venuti style. He also did a number of dates with American jazzmen, including Coleman Hawkins, Benny Carter and trumpeter Bill Coleman. Though he often simply played rhythm, there were notable exceptions. On the '37 "Hangin' Around Boudon"

with trombonist Dicky Wells, Django's opening solo gave interesting contrast to the gutbucket blues of the tune. He and the legendary American jazz fiddler Eddie South recorded "Sweet Georgia Brown" together, and recorded some jazz and classical tunes with Grappelli, too. In 1938 Reinhardt did a fine solo and some effective, rhythmic octave work on "I'm Comin', Virginia" with multi-instrumentalist and arranger Benny Carter and French sidemen, and added slashing, rhythmic chord embellishments on "Farewell Blues" at the same session. That year Django and the Quintet met American harmonica virtuoso Larry Adler in some effective recordings, though they lacked substantive jazz value.

In August of 1939, with the war ominously approaching France, Reinhardt and the Quintet were in London for recording sessions and concert appearances. However, in September, Reinhardt hastily returned to France, while Grappelli opted to remain in England. The German invasion of France, ironically, helped make Django a god in his own country. The deterioration of freedom in France under Vichy made anything that even hinted of individuality and self-determination—American characteristics—highly attractive to the masses. Among those things was jazz.

Django, as France's premiere jazz musician, suddenly found himself worshipped. Jazz became a code word for freedom. He replaced Grappelli with clarinetist Hubert Rostaing, giving the Quintet a decidedly European sound, perfect for the French flavored jazz compositions Django relied upon. Among them was "Nuages," originally recorded in 1940, a melancholy, delicate tune that remains among his most enduring. The band sold out everywhere it played in France, with its records popular throughout the nation, too. Original compositions or retitled American standards were the order of the day, the German occupation forces frowning upon overtly American music. Some superb music came out of this, including big band arrangements of original Reinhardt pieces like the mischievous "Belleville" and the furious "Feerie." The "swing" element in many of these numbers was minimal (and nothing comparable to American orchestras of the time). Packaged and released as "Django's Music" and similar titles, they fueled hope among the French in a dark period.

Django's reputation continued to spread in America and elsewhere, despite at least one rumor of his death. And when Allied forces recaptured France, he found himself the object of adulation and curiosity among many jazz-loving American soldiers and soldier-musicians. In 1945 he recorded with the American Air Transport Command Orchestra in Paris, a relatively sophisticated unit, and acquitted himself brilliantly on big band arrangements of pre-war numbers like "Swing Guitars" and "Djangology."

Reinhardt and Grappelli reunited in 1946 in England, recording in the Quintet context using British sidemen, and the old blend was restored. Though not all his original collaborators returned to the fold, Django had new opportunities open to him. Interest in him among American jazz musicians was such that in the fall of 1946 he made his first—and only—trip to the U.S. to tour as a featured soloist with the Duke Ellington Orchestra. The tour was to be Django's triumphant debut in a country about which he had fantasized for nearly two decades. His confidence was so high that he even left behind his Maccaferri guitar, long his signature instrument, anticipating American guitar makers would fall over themselves to present him with their models.

That didn't quite come to pass, nor were many of Django's other dreams about America fulfilled. The tour with Ellington was not as successful as everyone had hoped. He wound up playing an American electric guitar whose design differed from his Maccaferri, making him uncomfortable. Though Django himself impressed audiences everywhere, his two scheduled Carnegie Hall appearances were problematic. The first night went well; the second was derailed by the same wanderlust that caused Django to miss shows in France. Ellington had to apologize for his absence, after which Reinhardt showed up,

hastily closed the show, and explained that a cab driver had gotten his directions crossed. The entire affair left a bad taste, however, and he spent the remainder of his stay in America playing in a New York jazz club, disillusioned and homesick for France.

One style of American music that captured his fancy was bebop, and this made him somewhat anomalous among musicians of his generation, many of whom derided it as "Chinese music" (Cab Calloway's description) or worse. Django, however, like Ellington, Basie and other true jazz greats, found much in bop to interest them, and soon Django was assimilating bop into his improvisational lines with surprising ease.

After the war he worked only in Europe in a variety of contexts. His recordings were also a mixed bag. He recorded with Rostaing and the wartime version of the Quintet, but also with Grappelli and his brother Joseph in the pre-war Quintet style. He began creating his own bop numbers, such as "Babik," named for his young son. However, the bulk of his post-war recordings were remakes of his earlier songs. Gradually his more modern numbers began to take a greater role, among them the darkly textured "Diminushing," first recorded with Grappelli in 1947 and featuring some hypnotic unison playing by the duo and an elegant, lyrical solo from Django that contrasts with the air of French mystery the piece conjures up. "Mike," an uptempo bebop rampage recorded in 1948, shows Grappelli was beginning to grasp the style, though far less firmly than Reinhardt, who creates a superb solo using his famous staccato picking to good effect at strategic places.

In early 1949 Django and Stephane recorded 68 numbers in Rome with an Italian rhythm section that could serve as a retrospective of their years together. A number of tunes, among them "Djangology," "Swing 39," "Swing Guitars" and "Liza," all long associated with the Quintet, were recorded. But the modern rhythm section and the consistent brilliance of both guitarist and violinist made this far more than a trip down Memory Lane preserving pre-war swing. It placed them in a more modern context. These were the final significant recordings that Reinhardt and Grappelli did together.

By 1951 Django had a solid command of bop, and was playing an amplified Maccaferri that gave his sound a more modern edge. He was delighted to have made the change, but according to his biographer Charles Delaunay he still held pride in his older work and style, though jazz in general was moving away from his music. Reinhardt once complained of the younger musicians he worked with, saying, "These little kids... think it's all happening, that we're no good anymore, that we're finished. But one day I got angry; I began to play so fast they couldn't follow me! And I gave them some new numbers to play, with difficult sequences. And there again they were all at sea! They've got some respect for me now!"

Nothing bothered him when he played. He could break strings and compensate as if nothing was amiss. Married life and a family had also settled him. He lived near Samois, France, and fished in his spare time (when he wasn't playing billiards, long a favorite hobby). He continued performing and recording, and though a comparative veteran stylist, kept his music interesting. In February 1953, he had the opportunity to jam with a longtime idol, Dizzy Gillespie, proving himself able to hold his own with the boppers. In April '53, he made his final commercial recordings, turning in a performance on the original "Deccaphonie" as good as that of any bop guitarist.

Then, on tour of Switzerland, Django was plagued by headaches and numbness in his fingers, telltale portents of blood pressure problems. Friends urged him to get medical help, but Reinhardt, who feared doctors, refused. His physical symptoms continued, and on May 15, 1953, while at home in Samois, he was talking with acquaintances at a local cafe when he collapsed, the victim of a severe stroke. Finally a doctor was called. Despite hospitalization, Django died at the relatively young age of 43, in a Fontainebleau hospital.

Django Reinhardt achieved a status that virtually no other European jazz musician has even approached. In a uniquely American form of music his name is justifiably mentioned in the same breath as Armstrong, Ellington, Charlie Parker and Art Tatum. Like that of those men, his music remains a constant source of inspiration and ideas. The fact that his erstwhile companion Stephane Grappelli—still youthful in his late '70s—keeps Django's music before the public is almost anticlimactic.

DISCOGRAPHY

More Django albums are available than there is space to list them. ut the most essential collection is *Djangologie*, volumes one through twenty, on French Pathe. This material is generally available either in a boxed set (available through Blue Angel—1738 Allied St. Charlottesville, Va 22901) or as separate volumes through Down Home Music. German Teldec has available some of his hottest early material for Decca in two packages: *The Very Best of Django Reinhardt* and *Django Reinhardt and Stephane Grappelli*. Each are two-record sets and despite being in electronic stereo, cover some valuable ground that the *Djangologie* collection misses. Also important is the three-LP *Django Reinhardt* boxed set from RCA France (available from either Down Home or Daybreak Express).

American Django LPs are also plentiful. GNP Crescendo currently offers much of the Decca material, and other Django material for a total of seven LPs. The budget Everest label also has four volumes of Django's music.

GEORGE VAN EPS

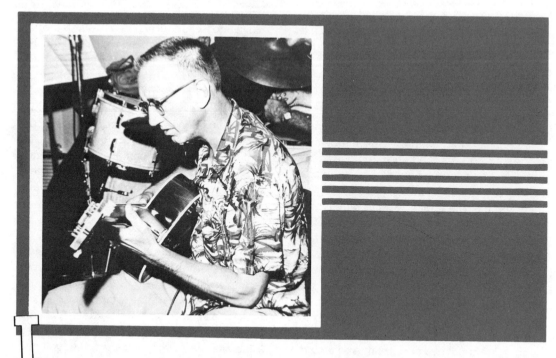

It is sadly ironic that while Charlie Christian, Eddie Lang and Django Reinhardt have rightfully achieved legendary status, an artist who has performed with consistent brilliance for over half a century, whose genius and artistry is a foregone conclusion among jazz aficionados, has remained obscure to the public at large. But such is the lot of George Van Eps.

There are any number of reasons for his relative obscurity. For one thing, Van Eps has never been a self-promoter. It appears that his quest for beauty and musical excellence has held sway over ambition for commercial success through much of his career. He has never really been in many high-visibility situations, never having worked with a truly hot orchestra or in a commercially favorable context, and so he has lacked the exposure needed for stardom in the jazz field. He has never gone in search of a hit record, preferring instead to play his music without facing the inevitable compromises that come with stardom.

Nonetheless, among those familiar with jazz guitar, Van Eps is a distinguished elder states-man, respected for the harmonic beauty that he brings to the instrument and for the innovative musical concepts that permit his music to take on a richness comparable only to that of Art Tatum on the piano (Van Eps himself considers his style to be "lap piano"). The Van Eps style—his skillful arpeggios, his flawless voicings, his chord melodies with so many incredible colors and counter-melodic shadings—has been arrived at through intense study and trial and error.

Van Eps largely created his own style. There were undoubtedly influences, but most of it was of his own making. He designed his seven-string guitar, adding the low seventh string to create richer, piano-like bass lines that made his playing literally self-contained. He also designed a string damper that helps eliminate feedback on amplified instruments. This device may not mean much to most guitarists, but among jazz guitarists like Herb Ellis, the Van Eps String Damper is an essential accessory, and since they were commercially available for only a brief time, they are treasured and protected.

Listening to Van Eps for the first time offers

a revelation. Few other guitarists—even other virtuosos—convey such a thorough sense of life and exhilaration in their music. His touch is so sure, so *right*, that there is no question of the depth of his skill or vision. At times, it is difficult to imagine that he's doing it all himself; such depth and textures seem impossible for one guitarist. Yet gentle, good-natured humor comes through as well. For all Van Eps' musical complexity, he does not articulate his music with stony dignity, as a classical musician might. There is an appealing element of wit in his music that makes it all look easy, but also a deep, obviously emotional involvement.

And however modest, Van Eps has inspired an entire school of guitarists who look to him for inspiration, seven-string players whose roots he's so strongly shaped. Bucky Pizzarelli, Howie Collins, Lenny Breau, Jerry Case, John Pizzarelli and other seven-string players have had to steep themselves in his music before they could create their own. However, Van Eps' touch can also be heard in that of any other jazz guitarist playing unaccompanied. Each strives to create that same aura of self-containment that Van Eps achieves. Listen to Jimmy Raney, Johnny Smith, Barney Kessel playing unaccompanied; you'll hear the distinctive qualities of each, but also echoes of George Abel Van Eps.

He was born in Plainfield, New Jersey on August 7, 1913, the youngest son of classical banjo virtuoso Fred Van Eps. George's three older brothers and his mother all were active musicians. In 1923 George began playing banjo and within a year—at age eleven—was a card-carrying member of the Plainfield Musicians' Union. George's musical interests leaned to pop and jazz. Eddie Lang was a major influence and in 1929, at age 16, George joined the orchestra of Smith Ballew, a bandleader who also employed both the Dorsey Brothers and Glenn Miller early in their careers. In 1931 he joined Freddy Martin's orchestra. Both of these units were respectable dance units, but hardly oriented to hardcore jazz. He joined Benny Goodman's orchestra in 1934, but left before that band was to give mass popularity to the big band

era (peerless rhythm guitarist Allan Reuss replaced George).

By 1936 Van Eps had joined the dance orchestra of Ray Noble, and Noble gradually began to feature him soloing on specific numbers, including "Dinner for One Please, James." He stayed with Noble's organization for five years, and moved to Hollywood with the group in 1938.

It was about that time that the idea of the seven-string guitar hit him. The potential of an instrument that could include the bass lines a conventional guitar could not reach, giving him greater freedom, fascinated him. Epiphone agreed to build it to Van Eps' specifications. After he began using the seven-string, his musical direction was never the same.

He began freelancing in Hollywood, doing recording sessions and working on radio. Van Eps also taught guitar and assembled his first instruction book rather hastily. Interviewed by Ted Greene in *Guitar Player Magazine*, he explained that word filtered back that one of his former pupils was planning to write an instruction book based on what he'd learned. With help from Epiphone, George got his book out in an unbelievable seven weeks. World War II sent him back to Plainfield briefly, but by 1944 he'd returned to California and picked up his freelance career.

Part of his time was spent with Noble, and with Paul Weston's orchestra as well. But Van Eps spent most of his time in recording and broadcast studios, either as a sideman on other artists' recordings, working in radio network staff bands or on movie soundtracks (including a number of Westerns). He also made television and film appearances.

Some of his first recordings on his own were done in 1949 with former Bob Crosby saxophonist Eddie Miller and pianist Stanley Wrightsman, and these early recordings exemplify the musical direction Van Eps would take on his own recordings. It's hard to define just what kind of music this was; it was not hot jazz in the traditional sense, being more restrained and introspective. Perhaps the term "chamber jazz" is as good as any.

On June 13, 1949, with bassist Jack Ryan and veteran swing drummer Nick Fatool, Van

Eps recorded four numbers. "Kay's Fantasy," written in honor of his daughter, is celebratory and uptempo, featuring complex melodic lines and simultaneous moving chords, with occasional nods towards bop. "Tea for Two" emits a totally new intimacy, as Van Eps totally recasts the melody, excising the song's inherent snappiness in favor of a bluer, introspective flavor. His version of "Once in a While" is warm, reassuring and vibrant, his impressive, rapidfire solos played with simultaneous perfectly placed rhythmic punctuation. "I Wrote It for Jo," an instrumental dedicated to his wife, is ballad-like, stately and rich with unusual chord choices, all beautifully articulated.

With Miller and Wrightsman Van Eps became more rhythmic, compensating for the absence of a bassist and drummer. He did this quite successfully while still contributing subtle tonal colors behind Miller's saxophone on "Ain't Misbehavin'," and takes a delicate, unaccompanied solo break featuring skillful variations on the melody. "Stomp, Mr. Henry Lee" is New Orleans-flavored swing that shows Van Eps in a more clearly defined accompanist's role to Miller and Wrightsman. Yet again he strums subtly, as if emulating drumstick brushes. "Love is Just Around the Corner" features a fluent, delicate and complex opening by Van Eps; Miller states the melody before returning it to George, whose solo is packed with brilliant ideas.

Amazingly enough, 35 years later, though Miller's Coleman Hawkins-styled saxophone sounds thoroughly dated, Van Eps' playing sounds vital and modern, a tribute to his advanced concepts in that period. And color itself is often suggested by his phrasing and his harmonies, as Van Eps himself believes. "B has a very brilliant sound to me," he told Ted Greene, "a light color. But C-flat is a dark brown."

In the '50s Van Eps began to work with amplification. His 1958 recording sessions yielded *Mellow Guitar*, his single album for Columbia. Using a recording technique involving a self-designed pickup connected directly to the mixing console, with a second microphone picking up his acoustic sound, Van Eps made marvelous, highly romantic music on this album, mostly delicately arranged pop ballads with the most uptempo tune being a hip, swinging version of "I Never Knew." It remains one of his finest moments. Unlike the recordings he had previously done with Paul Weston's orchestra, he had only drummer Fatool and bassist Morty Corb backing him, which enhanced the intimate feel.

In these years he also devoted time to operating a model shop, and didn't resume active play until 1966, when he signed with Capitol. He recorded three superb albums for that label: *My Guitar, George Van Eps' Seven-String Guitar* and *Soliloquy*. All of these albums leaned toward popular standards, played in the intimate settings that seemed to bring out his best. *Seven-String Guitar*, for example, comprised an appealing "Satin Doll," a cool, exquisite version of "A Blues Serenade" and a stately, elaborately embellished rendition of "The Very Thought of You." Embellishments can be tiresome and even annoying if overdone, but Van Eps is never obtrusive, enhancing the melody without obscuring it.

He was also using a different guitar by this time, a seven-string double pickup electric model designed to his specifications by Gretsch (although he continued to play his original Epiphone seven-string as well). Gretsch produced the Van Eps models for over a decade, a measure of the instrument's popularity.

Through the early '70s little was heard of Van Eps. He had other interests, among them model building. He was featured on some late '60s recordings released on the Blue Angel Jazz Club's own label, featuring him in the heady but entirely appropriate company of such jazz legends as Jess Stacy, Joe Venuti, Matty Matlock and Johnny Guarneri.

Van Eps' failure to perform regularly is explained in part by his efforts to elucidate his musical concepts in a trilogy called *Harmonic Mechanisms for Guitar*.

Happily, it appears that his long absence from recording may be coming to an end. A new record company has announced plans to release recent recordings from him. His itch to perform has resurfaced. With relatively few

Van Eps recordings to begin with—only two of his best in print as of this writing—it certainly seems that such a consummate artist owes his admirers (and himself) a more substantial documentation. In an age of expedience, George Van Eps stands almost alone as a musician who carved out a niche totally through his own hard work and genius, singlehandedly creating an entirely new guitar style in the process.

DISCOGRAPHY

Sadly, little of George Van Eps' material is currently in print, but there are some things available. His early recordings, alone and with Eddie Miller and Stanley Wrightsman, are available on a Jump album, *George Van Eps*. Bandleader Paul Weston's Corinthian label recently leased *Mellow Guitar* from Columbia, a welcome addition. None of the 1960s Capitol albums is currently in print. Several albums from the Blue Angel Jazz Club feature some fine Van Eps material, largely in the context of late '60s/early '70s jam sessions on *Don't Call It Dixie*, a fine two-LP set.

SECONDARY ESSAYS

Larry Coryell

If any one guitarist can be credited with paving the way for most of the popularity of the so-called jazz-rock fusion music of the '70s, it's Larry Coryell. Coryell has taken the best from several musical genres to create a style that in his case is innovative and never less than interesting. If jazz-rock tends to become excessive and unlistenable in the hands of certain guitarists, Coryell is one notable exception.

Born in Galveston, Texas, in 1943, Coryell grew up in the Pacific Northwest and began playing rock guitar around 1957 before taking instruction from a local teacher who introduced him to the recordings of Barney Kessel and Johnny Smith. He was hooked, and went on to study the entire spectrum of mainstream jazz guitar. Playing took up an increasing amount of his time and became so all-consuming that he left the University of Seattle in his senior year to move to New York.

His relative youth left him open to the increasingly progressive sounds of rock music, and in 1966, when rock bands flourished, he and several other jazz-oriented players formed the Free Spirits, a band which recorded one unsuccessful album. He moved through a variety of gigs before settling into vibraphonist Gary Burton's quartet. Coryell and Burton tried many innovative techniques, mixing rock ideas with jazz with the result that they became favorites at such prestigious rock venues as the Fillmore Auditorium in San Francisco. Coryell's deft mixture of rock, jazz, and even Indian ragas (he listened to sitarist Ravi Shankar long before George Harrison made it fashionable to do so) gained the group considerable interest.

Leaving Burton in the late '60s, Coryell played in an array of contexts, organizing his own rock fusion band, the Eleventh House. When that group split up, he continued playing and recording in a variety of contexts, from electric solos to acoustic albums with Steve Khan, John Scofield, Joe Beck and Philip Catherine.

Coryell continues to record and perform extensively.

DISCOGRAPHY

Unfortunately, all of Larry Coryell's innovative collaborations with Gary Burton, including *Lofty Fake Anagram*, are out of print. *The Essential Larry Coryell* (Vanguard), sums up his work for that label. *Young Django* (Pausa) features his collaboration with Stephane Grappelli, and his talents on both acoustic and electric guitar are prominent on *Guitar Player*, a jazz/blues jam session featuring Coryell, Barney Kessel, Herb Ellis, B.B. King, Laurindo Almeida and Irving Ashby (MCA).

Herb Ellis

Though not a true innovator, Herb Ellis continues to be among the most entertaining and creative jazz guitarists of the day. Ellis, a member of the post-Charlie Christian school, has distinguished himself not only with his solid sense of swing, but with the country and blues influences (not surprising for a native of Texas) with which he colors his technique.

Mitchell Herbert Ellis was born just outside Dallas in 1921. His first instrument was banjo, but by age eleven he was playing guitar. A plethora of influences surrounded him, including blues and western swing, both of which were extremely popular in Texas during the late '30s. One of the first electric guitarists he heard and enjoyed was Muryel "Zeke" Campbell, the pioneering lead player with the Light Crust Doughboys. It was while Ellis attended North Texas State College in the early '40s that Charlie Christian first moved him and helped him delineate his own direction. He attended school for two years, then entered into professional music with Glen Gray's Casa Loma Orchestra, and in 1945 joined the Jimmy Dorsey organization, where he was featured soloist on such tunes as "Perdido" and "J.D.'s Jump."

Herb left Dorsey in 1947 to form a vocal/instrumental trio known as the Soft Winds, modeled after the "King" Cole Trio. The band stayed together five years, but never did as well as it should have, considering its engaging music. Barney Kessel, a close friend and at that time guitarist with Oscar Peterson's trio, recommended Herb as his replacement. For the next five years Ellis worked with Peterson, who was creating complex, beautifully articulated instrumental music within the trio framework. Herb began his solo recording career during this period for Verve.

His warm, buttery tone, shot through with elements of blues and country, clearly made him an engaging and accessible guitarist. Among his most interesting and enjoyable trademarks is an ability to transform shopworn folk songs like "John Brown's Body" or "Darling Nellie Gray" into astonishingly potent vehicles for jazz improvisation.

By the early '60s, Herb had entrenched himself in the A-team of Hollywood studio musicians, working soundtracks, recording sessions and making television appearances. He was featured occasionally in the Don Trenner Orchestra, which appeared on Steve Allen's syndicated early '60's TV show, and also on the Merv Griffin Show with Mort Lindsey's orchestra. However, like Barney Kessel, Herb began to emphasize his own live performances and solo recordings in the late '70s, undertaking a series of consistently fine recordings for Concord Jazz, including solo gigs and appearances with Charlie Byrd and Barney Kessel as the Great Guitars. His playing, adventurous but with the familiarity of an old shoe, remains among the finest in jazz today.

DISCOGRAPHY

Herb Ellis had been well-represented on recordings for years, though certain of his early albums, are difficult to come by. One early Verve LP *Softly...With Feeling* was reissued by Japanese Verve a couple years ago, along with two albums featuring him with the Oscar Peterson Trio: *Live at the Stratford Shakespearean Festival* and *At the Con-* *certgebouw,* recorded live in Amsterdam, Holland. His later material on Concord Jazz includes the label's first LP, *Jazz/Concord,* along with *Rhythm Willie* (with the legendary jazz rhythm guitarist Freddie Green), the Great Guitars series (with Barney Kessel and Charlie Byrd) and *Triple Treat.* Ellis records prolifically, so this list will undoubtedly get longer.

Dick McDonough

Until Eddie Lang died, Dick McDonough stood in his shadow. Like Lang, he'd been a banjo player (though he'd played mandolin before that). Born in 1904, McDonough, a native of New York City, grew up in a comfortable home with music surrounding him. He attended Georgetown University in Washington from 1921 to 1925, and played banjo in the orchestra there. Back in New York, he gigged on banjo with several pop music groups, and commenced his brief career as a studio musician.

It was in the fall of 1925 that he started playing guitar, backing novelty singer Cliff Edwards (known as Ukelele Ike and later the voice of Walt Disney's character Jiminy Cricket). Guitar continued to be McDonough's main instrument for the next thirteen years. Much of his work was in radio and recording studios, backing jazz and pop music acts of all varieties; he never really had any interest in traveling on the road with an orchestra.

McDonough's technique was rich and fully developed, and that, combined with his ability to read music, gave him a polish that few other jazz guitarists had at the time. There are similarities to McDonough's technique and Lang's, but McDonough tended to alternate between chord and single string passages, integrating both into an immensely appealing style, which was not spontaneous, usually being fully arranged (about the only way his sort of precision could be attained).

Tunes like his 1934 "Chasing a Buck" feature his chord melody on a minor keyed composition. He played unaccompanied, creating lines that were complex even by today's standards. Equally impressive was his unaccompanied, relaxed version of "Honeysuckle Rose," recorded at the same session. His duets with Carl Kress, which commenced in '34 and continued almost until his death, were models for jazz guitar duets for years.

But McDonough, though he was playing better than ever and making a good living in the studios, faltered due to a drinking problem that grew increasingly worse. Studio musicians, then as now, were counted on to be reliable. Those who weren't could count on losing work. That's what happened to McDonough, and his career became shakier as his drinking worsened. It finally caught up with him on May 25th, 1938 when he collapsed at the NBC studios. Despite emergency surgery, Dick McDonough died, the victim of a ruptured ulcer.

DISCOGRAPHY

Regrettably, nobody has seen fit to dedicate an entire album to reissuing McDonough's work. However, he can be heard in random cuts on *Pioneers of The Jazz Guitar* and *Fun on the Frets* (Yazoo) and on *The Guitarists* (Time-Life Giants of Jazz series).

Oscar Moore

Oscar Moore is one of the least-celebrated but most important jazz guitarists. Best known for his tasteful backing work and economical soloing as part of the original Nat "King" Cole Trio, Moore was one of those guitarists whose impact was subtle and who never really got the credit he deserved during his life. He's been cited, however, as an influence by a variety of jazzmen, and even by B.B. King.

Oscar Fred Moore was born in Austin, Texas in 1916, and got some of his first experience in 1934 playing with his pianist brother Johnny. He joined Cole in September 1937, and played on nearly all of Cole's earliest hits, from "Sweet Lorraine" on. Working in the drummerless trio, Moore had a unique and difficult role to fill, and he did it superbly. While Cole sang, Oscar would strum rhythm chords on his electric guitar, or play tasteful runs. His comping was excellent, and helped to provide a sense of harmony and movement. Instantly he could switch to fleet, tasteful solos, generally brief but astonishing in their effect. On occasion, such as their 1940 recording of "Honeysuckle Rose," he would play single notes in ensemble with Cole.

The color he added to the "King" Cole Trio, and the warmth of his tone were the perfect complements to Nat's singing and Fatha Hines-based piano style. Initially, Oscar was overlooked in the flurry of attention Charlie Christian received, but as Cole's star began rising during World War II, numbers like "Straighten Up and Fly Right" gave Moore greater exposure. Still, he did not leap into a career of his own, instead remaining with Cole until 1947, playing on such hits as "Route 66" and "For Sentimental Reasons." Irving Ashby, an equally fine guitarist, replaced Moore when he left Cole in '47.

Oscar then joined his brother Johnny's band, the Three Blazers, where he remained into the '50s, working out of Los Angeles. He recorded after that, but his level of activity diminished. He died in 1981.

DISCOGRAPHY
Recordings by the "King" Cole Trio are available in various incarnations. Some of its earliest work featuring Oscar Moore is documented on *From the Beginning* (MCA), an anthology of early trio sides for Decca. The Capitol years are excerpted on *The Best of the Nat "King" Cole Trio, Volumes 1 and 2* (Capitol). Equally impressive, though more vocal-oriented is *20 Vocal Classics* (Australian Capitol), featuring Moore in a supportive capacity. Hard to find, but worth it, is an all-instrumental collection *Trio Days* (Capitol Jazz Classics). A fine, and comprehensive Trio set combining vocal and instrumental material is *Classics*, a 3-LP set on French Pathe records. Two excellent collections of radio transcriptions featuring Moore with the trio are *The "Cool" Cole* (Sounds Rare) and *The Forgotten Years* (Giants of Jazz).

Joe Pass

Many jazzmen with Joe Pass' background—talent, drugs, and prison—never fulfill their potential. Pass, however, was luckier than many. He came through his rough times and went on to become one of the most respected and acclaimed jazz guitarists of any period.

Joseph Anthony Jacobi Passalaqua was

born January 13, 1929 in New Brunswick, New Jersey, but grew up in Johnstown, in the mountains of western Pennsylvania. It was coal and steel mill country, but Joe's father, Mariano, decided early on that his son would take guitar lessons and strictly supervised Joe's daily—and lengthy—practice periods. Though it bothered Joe at first, he gradually became very interested in playing, and began pushing himself. He gigged in the Johnstown area, then moved to New York just in time for the bebop revolution of the late '40s.

Jazz became his major obsession. Unfortunately, he also was caught up in the hard-drug epidemic that gripped many of bop's finest artists, and was dogged by drugs through most of the '50s, winding up in a Texas prison. Released by 1960, but convinced he had hit bottom, Pass entered the original Synanon therapy program and regained his health. His musical abilities re-emerged, and in 1962 he recorded *Sounds of Synanon* with a number of other musicians in the program. By 1963 he had licked his drug problem and gained the attention of Pacific Jazz Records' a&r man Dick Bock. His technique had begun to jell, and Pacific Jazz albums like *For Django*, a Re-

inhardt tribute done with fellow guitarist John Pisano, showed Joe's formidable range and scope. His technique is graceful and lyrical, his tone marked by a warmth and density that enhances his rhythmic, swinging solos. Another album, recorded live in Los Angeles in 1964 (but not released until 1981), was the outstanding *Joy Spring*, which revealed the depth of his abilities in a loose, jam session format.

Pass spent the rest of the '60s working studio jobs, but eventually returned to jazz, touring with Norman Granz's jazz shows, and making an impressive series of albums for Granz's Pablo label, which he records on today.

DISCOGRAPHY
The list of Joe Pass recordings is entirely too large to be included here. However, *For Django* and *Joy Spring* have both been reissued, and his more recent sets for Pablo Records includes numerous collaborations with Stephane Grappelli, Niels Henning Orsted-Peterson, Oscar Peterson, Ella Fitzgerald and others, and solo albums.

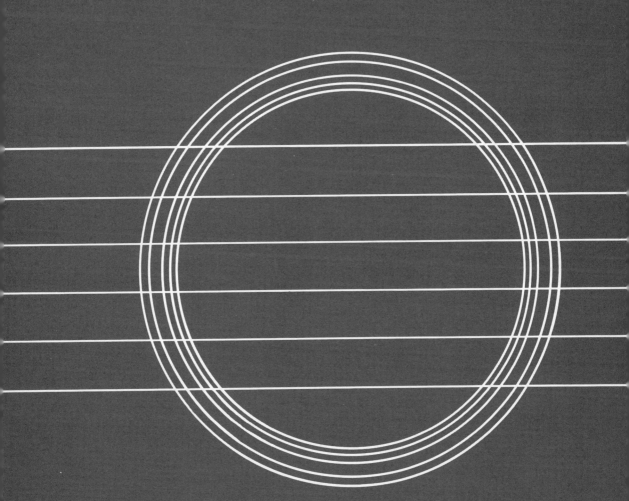

ROCK

DUANE ALLMAN

Everyone, it seemed, was playing the blues in the mid '60s, grabbing the Chess albums by Muddy, Wolf, Sonny Boy and Little Walter, scouring the stores for OJL, Arhoolie and Yazoo reissues in order to glean every nuance of every guitar lick played on every record. The problem was that for every Eric Clapton, Michael Bloomfield or Jeff Beck who used the blues as a jumping-off point for their own musical visions, there were a dozen guitarists who simply learned to copy each lick note-for-note. They revered the masters' music—but nine times out of ten their versions stunk, for they couldn't capture the feel of the original records if they tried for a lifetime.

Duane Allman was smart enough to avoid that cul-de-sac. As leader of the Allman Brothers Band, the flagship group of the so-called "Southern Rock" movement of the early 1970s, he created some of the most powerful, moving blues-based rock music ever heard. Allman used the blues as a reference point for his own ideas, and to a lesser

extent picked up ideas from country and early rock guitarists as well.

Though the Allmans in their heyday exemplified the wild, booze-and-roar southern lifestyle, Duane Allman's guitar music always reflected an unmistakable sense of taste and discipline that placed him head and shoulders above many of the groups who came after the Allmans. These qualities came, in all likelihood, from his years as a studio guitarist in the rarefied atmosphere of Muscle Shoals, Alabama, where he recorded with a wide variety of artists and where versatility and discretion went hand-in-hand with creativity. The sterility that can often creep into the playing of studio guitarists never appears in Allman's work. Duane put great passion into all his playing, whether he was plucking straight single-string leads or slide guitar.

Slide guitar, a black blues guitar technique that originated in the late nineteenth century and has African roots that go back centuries earlier, was Duane's forte. Son House, Kokomo Arnold, Bukka White, Tampa Red,

Casey Bill Weldon and Robert Johnson played great country and blues slide; Muddy Waters, Earl Hooker and Elmore James each played inspiring amplified slide through the 1940s and '50s. But Duane Allman surpassed all of them. Using their records as reference points, he created a fiery, dynamic approach of his own, inspired by but not imitative of the great slide players.

When Duane picked up the Corcidin pill bottle that served as his slide, what often emerged were smoothly articulated passages with the sting of a bullwhip, or crying, voice-like sensitivity and tenderness. When he played leads in tandem with fellow Allman lead guitarist Dickey Betts, the effect was arresting, creating excitement both among audiences and musicians alike.

Whereas the deaths of Jimi Hendrix and so many other rock legends were not unexpected considering their reputations as drug consumers, Allman's death in a 1971 motorcycle accident was a first-class tragedy and shock. Only 24 at the time, he was just beginning his career and already at the top of his profession. That his legacy is carried on by a number of fine southern guitarists—including Dickey Betts—is clear. Though there's not yet been a real revival of interest in Duane's playing, the sustained popularity of the blues through white southern guitarists such as the Fabulous Thunderbirds' Jimmy Vaughan, his younger brother Stevie Ray Vaughan, George Thorogood and others make the prospect of revived interest in Duane's playing likely.

Howard Duane Allman was born in Nashville, Tennessee on November 20, 1946. Brother Gregg, with whom he performed most of his life, was born December 8, 1947. Tragedy entered their lives early; their father was murdered in 1949. After a stint in military school, the boys with their family moved to Florida, and in 1957 Gregg began playing guitar. In a disturbing omen of the future, Duane wrecked his first motorcycle and swapped its parts for a guitar of his own. The two Allman brothers started playing together.

The blues became a formidable influence early in Duane's musical experience. B.B.

King and Robert Johnson had a particularly strong impact on his direction. Rock guitarists were also appreciated, however, particularly Chuck Berry and Jeff Beck. Duane liked to listen to jazz guitar as well. He and Gregg started playing in bar bands around Daytona Beach in their free time in high school, and after graduating in 1965 formed the Allman Joys, a low-echelon unit that played throughout the south during the acid-rock era. Duane's interest in the blues put him in good stead in the south, considering the impact B.B. King and other bluesmen were exerting on the guitar styles of the period. They did some recording in 1966 that went nowhere (until the Allmans became a hot property a few years later), and the Joys split up the following year.

Another band followed, and this time they were in the right place at the right time. Rock music was becoming a blue chip commodity, and any band with enough guitars could get a recording contract with half an effort, talent or not. The new Allmans' group was clearly a cut above the crop, and wound up in Los Angeles in 1967 as a Liberty Records' act dubbed the Hourglass.

An important concept for late 1960s rock bands was creative control, with the artists determining their producers, the material they'd record and even what would appear on their album covers. But Liberty Records didn't see things that way, and the Allmans were tied up with people who were bent on creating an image for them—even though it didn't reflect the personalities of their band. The results were two wretched examples of corporate psychedelia that deservedly sold little, while the band, increasingly frustrated, stewed in California, playing few jobs.

That the band had potential is without question. They recorded in 1968 without Liberty's interference in Muscle Shoals, creating the undeniably exciting "B.B. King Medley"—a fusion of King's "Sweet Little Angel," "It's My Own Fault" and "How Blue Can You Get," songs that had become cornerstones of his repertoire. The track reveals a powerful, thick-toned and inspired blues-based style, and an uninhibited approach far superior to the Liberty material. It was as if all the pent-up frustration was emerging from Duane through his blues playing, which included phrasing much like that he would use with the Allman Brothers Band. The gospel-tinged "Been Gone Too Long" was also far better than anything they'd done in Los Angeles. It was hardly encouraging when their manager rejected this material. Liberty put enough money into the band to hold it to a contract, but it was too much for Duane. Showing the singleminded determination he possessed throughout his life, Duane went to Jacksonville, Florida, while Gregg and the others remained in California to work off the contract.

Duane had met Dickey Betts in Florida and found a kindred spirit and highly compatible guitar partner. In the fall of 1968, Muscle Shoals producer Rick Hall, who'd been impressed with Duane's playing on the earlier Hourglass session there, asked him to do a session with r&b singer Wilson Pickett for Atlantic Records. This was the start of Duane's studio experience, a period that would spread his reputation and develop his playing further. Pickett's version of the Beatles' "Hey Jude" became a million-seller, and it spotlights Duane almost as much as Pickett. As he played graceful little fills behind Pickett's vocal, he gave the Memphis-styled r&b arrangement a new freshness with his trebly slide. Duane's tone was pinched compared to his later work, but it stood out among the bottom-heavy bass, organ and horn arrangements.

Certainly Allman was unique in Muscle Shoals, his shoulder-length hair and clothes much flashier than what the 1968 deep South preferred (*Easy Rider* was a year away). But none of that mattered in the studios, where his playing was widely respected. He had the opportunity to work with many artists there, from Aretha Franklin and King Curtis to Arthur Conley and Herbie Mann. He played really promising slide work on John Hammond's 1969 Atlantic album *Southern Fried*, doing some smoothly articulated, screaming fills and solos on "Shake for Me," "Cryin' for My Baby," "You'll Be Mine" and "I'm Leavin' You." His slide playing was evolving

and improving, his phrasing becoming more articulate and fluid. Allman helped to make *Southern Fried* one of Hammond's better (if least heralded) albums. On *Ronnie Hawkins*, another Atlantic album, and on Boz Scaggs' debut album for the label, Duane played sensitive, pleasing dobro and feverish lead (on Scaggs' "Loan Me a Dime"). On the Hawkins album he also essayed some mad, uninhibited slide on "Matchbox," "Down in the Alley" and rhythmic, lightning-hot licks on "Who Do You Love."

Regular studio work wore Duane down after a year or so, though he didn't totally give it up until late 1969. He preferred playing on the road. He went back to Jacksonville and jammed with Betts, bassist Berry Oakley, drummers Butch Trucks and Jai Johnny Johanson. In March 1969 Gregg, free of the Liberty obligations, returned to find a band ready and waiting to begin. They woodshedded until September, when they began recording their first album for Capricorn Records of Macon, Georgia. Since Capricorn was distributed by Atlantic Records, they had some formidable weight behind them.

The Allman Brothers Band, released in early 1970, was not, in retrospect, up to the standards of their later work. They were still in the process of developing a cohesive identity, but had come a long way toward achieving it. In an era of psychedelia, of cosmic and other assorted pretensions, the experience of the Hourglass may well have soured them on that entire direction. Instead, their driving, high-volume sound drew on a range of genres, from Stax-Volt r&b to country music and, of course, blues. And Duane, playing solo and together with Dickey Betts, was responsible for many of the album's finest moments. While Gregg's organ, Oakley's bass and the two drummers, Johanson and Trucks, maintained the rhythm, most of the band's instrumental signature came from the guitars. The industrial-strength twin-guitar introduction (played in octaves) to "Don't Want You No More," which kicks off side one, was but one indication of what was to come.

Muddy Waters' "Trouble No More" features another Allman-Betts octave hook at the beginning with some perfectly-placed, rhythmic slide interjections from Duane. The two play searing solos together on "Every Hungry Woman." Yet without question "Dreams," a Gregg Allman composition, marks Duane's finest moment on the album. Using both his slide and feedback (probably feeling Jeff Beck's influence) he plays a delicate, exploratory solo that grows in power and authority as it goes along. There is nary a moment of excess; every note is tasteful and clean. It was, in light of all this, strange that the debut record wasn't a huge seller.

The Allman-Betts team was one of the first, if not the first, truly cohesive and credible twin guitar teams in rock at the time. "Lead" and "rhythm" guitars were a part of rock bands since the days of Elvis, Scotty and Bill. But twin leads were another matter altogether. Twin lead guitars had been used in jazz in the '20s and '30s (Eddie Lang-Lonnie Johnson and Dick McDonough-Carl Kress are notable examples). And in western swing, steel guitarist Leon McAuliffe and standard guitarist Eldon Shamblin had started experimenting with twin leads in the late '30s as part of Bob Wills' Texas Playboys. In 1944-'45 Wills also featured twin lead guitarists Jimmy Wyble and Cameron Hill. In the late '40s Zeb and Zeke Turner were doing twin leads on country recording sessions in Nashville and Cincinnati, occasionally going for three-way leads with steel guitarist Jerry Byrd. The precedents were there, but it was Allman and Betts who changed the context.

Their second album, *Idlewild South*, reflected even greater strength from the band as a whole and from Duane and Dickey. Their rhythmic twin intro to "Revival" set the tone for the remainder of the album. Duane played tense, chilling slide on "Don't Keep Me Wonderin'," soaring over the band and created a roaring finale. His acoustic playing—minus his slide—established the rhythmic pulse of their classic "Midnight Rider." "In Memory of Elizabeth Reed," a minor key, jazzy instrumental, featured more restraint and control from both Allman and Betts, with twin harmonies (again, *sans* slide) and meaty solos from both. Their creative juices were flowing, and the pair turned in furious guitar free-for-alls on "Hoochie Koochie Man" and "Leave My Blues at Home."

Duane spent most of his time working with the band, though he did do some work on Delaney & Bonnie Bramlett albums in 1971, his best being some beautifully articulated acoustic slide guitar on their all-acoustic *Motel Shot* album, contributing tight, colorful solos on "Going Down the Road Feeling Bad" and using an amp for "Sing My Way Home."

The Allmans were a rising force in rock at the time, but Duane attracted as much attention for his awesome, passionate slide playing with Eric Clapton on Derek and the Dominos' 1971 *Layla* LP. Clapton had heard the Allmans in Florida, where he was recording, and invited Duane to guest on his session. It was a smart decision on Clapton's part, for the two perfectly complemented each other. Clapton played some of the finest, most individualistic guitar of his career. Not surprisingly, the blues tunes were the strongest. On "I Am Yours" and "Nobody Knows You When You're Down and Out" Duane interjected slide comments behind Clapton's vocal, as he would have in a Muscle Shoals studio. But on "Key to the Highway" the pair outdid itself. Clapton played wrenching lines on his Fender Strat, and sang a verse. Then Duane cut loose. His intonation was perfect and his choruses grew ever wilder before Clapton cut back in (it was, after all, his album), played himself, and handed it back to Duane.

The rest of the album maintains that high level. "Why Does Love Have To Be So Sad" features a guitar duel of arresting, unrelenting ferocity that builds to fever pitch; it remains some of the finest rock guitar ever recorded, bar none. On "Have You Ever Loved a Woman," Duane creates beautifully-articulated slide phrases, solidly rooted in blues but imitative of no one. "It's Too Late," the old Chuck Willis tune, gets a similar treatment. "Layla," however, has an inner strength that transcends any idiom. As Clapton plays churning licks, Allman again soars, offering seemingly impossible soprano slide figures on the absolute upper register of his fretboard, sounding as if he's going off the neck altogether. Never once does his intonation falter. *Layla* remains a classic album in the discographies of both guitarists, and one of the finest rock guitar albums. The pair also recorded an acoustic version of Little Walter's tune "Mean Old World" without other accompaniment, Duane playing delta-style slide—and even here, the two manage to continue their teamwork minus their amps. This track didn't emerge until after Duane's death.

The Allmans, in the meantime, were about to achieve the highest level of success. On March 12 and 13, 1971 they played Bill Graham's Fillmore East, and with tape recorders running captured the excitement of their onstage performances. *The Allman Brothers at Fillmore East* (Polydor) is one of the finest live rock albums ever pressed, and Duane is on throughout. Both alone and with Betts, a steady flow of ideas courses through their Les Pauls, whether they use slides or not. They turn "Statesboro Blues" into an arresting number, with Duane at his wildest. "Hot 'Lanta" and "In Memory of Elizabeth Reed" are equally brilliant. There is absolutely no sense in describing these performances; they must be heard to be believed.

Predictably, the album became a massive seller and gave the Allmans the success they'd struggled years to accomplish. They'd begun their fourth album, *Eat a Peach*, in the fall of 1971. Duane had worked on three of the tracks. "Stand Back" features some soaring double-barrel twin lead guitars from Allman and Betts, with a pungent solo break from Duane. He played lyrical lead on "Blue Sky," a country number with another impressive twin-lead passage from Allman and Betts. "Little Martha" is an ethereal acoustic guitar duet—and one of the few pieces Duane wrote—with a lofty, folk music air as he and Betts show their considerable fingerpicking skills and what is apparently a meticulously arranged duet.

The momentum was building for southern rock, and the Allman Brothers in particular. Duane was becoming prominent as a major

force in rock guitar, and the future held potential that apparently was unlimited. The band decided to take a breather in October and went back to Macon. On October 29, 1971, Duane was riding his motorcycle, a habit he'd never shaken since he'd smashed up his first one. Soon after he made a social stop at Berry Oakley's house, a truck pulled out in front of him; Duane swerved his bike, went into a skid and crashed. After being extricated from the wreckage he was rushed to the Macon Medical Center. Three hours of surgery couldn't undo the damage and he died that evening.

After a huge performance-funeral, during which the band and other friends offered their own musical eulogies, Duane Allman was interred in the Rose Hill Cemetery, a hangout for him in the Band's earliest days in Macon. But the tragedy didn't stop there. The band decided to carry on after Duane's death, but Berry Oakley was killed in a hauntingly similar motorcycle crackup in November 1972. But the group's high musical standards, in part Duane's legacy, remained. With Gregg Allman and Betts at the helm, the Allman Brothers Band went on to other phenomenal successes, both musical and commercial before splitting, and reuniting again.

One feels the loss of Duane Allman as keenly as that of Eddie Lang. Both men were on the verge of greater commercial acceptance and acclaim. More importantly, neither had reached his peak. Since Duane accomplished so much so quickly, one wonders what else he would have contributed had he lived longer. For a 24 year old, Duane Allman had enormous depth; he understood musical forms beyond blues and rock. His integrity and vision would undoubtedly have carried him far. Nonetheless, in the brief time we had him, his soulful virtuosity had an undeniable—and indelible—impact on the development of many future great guitarists.

DISCOGRAPHY

The demise of Capricorn Records a few years ago transfered much of the Allman Brothers' catalog to Polydor, including *The Best of Duane Allman*, a single LP drawn from

Duane Allman: An Anthology (volumes 1 and 2). The first two Allman LPs are available as *Beginnings*, a double set. *Live at Fillmore East* and *Eat a Peach* are also still available. His performance on "Hey Jude" by Wilson Pickett can be heard on *The Best of Wilson Pickett* (Atlantic). Of course, Duane's work with Clapton is on *Layla (RSO)*.

JEFF BECK

Any question of Jeff Beck's importance to the rock guitar's development and
growth was answered long ago. Aside from
Hendrix, Clapton and Bloomfield, nobody
has been important. Indeed, the roots of not
only much of the rock of the early seventies,
but also of today's Heavy Metal sounds, are
directly traceable to the guitar work Beck was
doing back in the 1960s. As Bloomfield was
creating lengthy instrumental jams, and Clapton was building his own virtuosity out of the
blues, Beck, using the same reference points
and roots, was building daring new sounds for
the electric guitar. Jimi Hendrix's dominance
of the late sixties got much of the attention,
but in fact before Hendrix was well-known
Beck, as a member of the Yardbirds (Clapton's replacement, in fact), was blazing new
trails with his use of feedback, fuzztones and
impassioned, stops-out guitar battles. He may
have even influenced Hendrix; it wouldn't be
surprising.

Beck would be important for that alone, but
that doesn't nearly cover it. His first solo band,
organized in 1967, was the model by which
many top rock bands of the 1970s were measured. The lineup of vocalist/lead guitar/bass/
drums was, of course, nothing new; the Who
used it since their inception. The difference
was that Beck's band—vocalist Rod Stewart,
bassist Ron Wood and drummer Mick Waller—had much the same sound, blues-based
and largely built around the guitar, that begat
Led Zeppelin, Bad Company, Free, Queen,
Ted Nugent, Rush and Van Halen among
others. All of these bands have identical lin-
eups, and in many ways Beck originated the
concept.

That, too, underscores Beck's importance,
but doesn't completely define it, for around
1975, this father of Heavy Metal and guitar
raveups took a dramatic 180 turn into jazz
rock fusion with his superb and much acclaimed 1975 *Blow By Blow* album, a natural
evolution, but one reflecting a growing
musical maturity and sophistication. It
brought him new appreciation, and proved
him unwilling to be bound by his work of the
past. It would have been simple enough for
him to coast on his Yardbirds/Jeff Beck Group

reputation. It is a tribute to his musicianship that he refused to accept such constrictions.

Beck's evolution can be easily traced on record from his first primitive recordings in the 60s as part of a British band recording blues informally (with the results later released, to everyone's consternation). His growing abilities and self-confidence can be heard through his work with the Yardbirds, where he first came to public attention, first on his own, then as part of a twin-guitar team with Jimmy Page within the group. From there Beck's career generally, but not always, moved on to higher levels of achievement.

This is not to say that Beck, particularly in the days of the Yardbirds and the Beck groups, didn't have some substantial limitations. He was initially a weak improviser in both bands. In the original Stewart/Wood Beck group he tended to rely at times on hoked-up and tinkered-with blues cliches. He was, of course, hardly alone. Many guitarists never did evolve beyond regurgitating old B.B. King and Muddy Waters licks.

Beck the musician has generally approached his music with great integrity, refusing to move in any direction he couldn't embrace wholeheartedly. The idea of going for a commercial hit at the expense of producing good music has never been Beck's style. He has, of course, had lapses in some dreadful solo recordings that brought commercial success, but those have been aberrations, not the norm. The quality of his most serious work has not always been consistent. Still, his achievements and high points remain as vital and exciting as when he first recorded them.

Jeff Beck was born in Wallington, Surrey, England, on June 24, 1944. He spent his childhood in private schools, and until the advent of rock and roll his only real musical experience was the church choir. By the late 50s he'd become taken with Buddy Holly and began his rock experience by learning the instrumental introduction to "That'll Be the Day." He built the first electric guitar he owned, and it soon became the driving force in his adolescent life. Though he went to art school, at 18 he was alternating between art, odd jobs, and music. He'd soaked up every

guitarist who mattered back then—Eddie Cochran, James Burton, Cliff Gallup (Gene Vincent's lead guitarist) and, of course, Chuck Berry.

It was only a short step from those players to the blues, and by 1964, when he was working with a London band known as the Tridents, he'd begun immersing himself in the music of Muddy Waters, Buddy Guy and other Chicago bluesmen. Since the Tridents' music was in the same mold, he had little problem developing an ersatz blues style within the group.

He'd also become interested in slide guitar, and around the same time he was working with the Tridents he became friendly with Jimmy Page, then beginning his career as one of London's top studio guitarists. Through this same period Beck jammed with a number of other London musicians at Page's house. Beck did one such session with a band known as the All Stars, formerly led by the late British blues harpist Cyril Davies. The recordings weren't very good, but they do give some indication of where Beck was at musically. "Steelin'," a bottleneck tune, is pretty much in the mold of Chuck Berry's "Deep Feeling." Beck's touch and intonation with the slide are pretty tentative. And on several other tracks he plays busy, rather insignificant solos that reflect Berry's influence.

It was, in fact, his relationship with Page that led him to replace Eric Clapton as the Yardbirds' lead guitarist in March 1965. And it was obvious, despite Clapton's tremendous abilities, that Beck was more than up to the task. His harsh, fuzztone solo on "Heart Full of Soul," issued in 1965 (it was a hit both in Britain and America), showed a dramatic new approach for that time. "Steeled Blues," the flipside, showed he still had a ways to go, however. It just wasn't terribly different than "Steelin'."

His buzzing, roaring sounds, played on a Fender Esquire, gradually became an integral part of the group. On "Shapes of Things," recorded in 1965, he made brilliant use of feedback and distortion in his solo. The song itself was trite (as were many of the Yardbirds' numbers), but Beck more than compensated for it. He showed still greater confidence on their remake of Johnny Burnette and the Rock and Roll Trio's "The Train Kept A-Rollin'," playing a slashing, vicious solo. "I Ain't Done Wrong" featured more confident slide work, done in the Elmore James style with one of the band's famous doubletime "raveups" at the end of the number. "Over Under Sideways Down," another mediocre number, was also a Beck tour-de-force as he played his fuzztoned, laced, sitarlike runs throughout the song (similar to those he'd played on "Heart Full of Soul").

Beck's work in the Yardbirds marked the true beginning of his musical maturation, and the experimental nature of their sound gave him—and the world—the first real indication of his potential. If Paul Butterfield was influencing guitar-oriented psychedelia in America, then the Yardbirds were doing likewise in Britain, making an impact on both sides of the Atlantic. He was, perhaps, best featured on the Yardbirds' *Over Under Sideways Down* (issued as *Yardbirds* in Britain), which features his still-exhilarating "Jeff's Boogie." Though the theme is basically Chuck Berry's 1958 "Guitar Boogie," Beck makes it his own with flashes of fuzztone and humor (he quotes from both "Merrily We Roll Along" and "Alfie" during the stop-time portions of the song. Two version of of "What Do You Want," as included on this album, have been issued (one on a more recent compilation of Yardbirds material). One, without a vocal track, features some vicious, muscular playing and shimmering slide while the completed vocal version on *Over Under*, more disciplined, features effectively-used feedback and an uninhibited solo that in many ways exemplified all that was great about the Yardbirds.

In June 1966, when bassist Paul Samwell-Smith left the band, Jimmy Page was added as bassist, occasionally playing twin leads with Beck while rhythm guitarist Chris Dreja played bass. The results were fiery, as you can hear on the brilliant single recording of "Happenings Ten Years Time Ago" b/w "Psycho Daisies" and "Stroll On," featured in the film *Blow Up*. The Yardbirds had a sort of

identity crisis constantly being hounded by their management to play teen-oriented pop when in fact they were doing well with blues-oriented rock. Beck finally left in November 1966.

After a brief time in inactivity, Beck began recording again. With Jimmy Page on 12-string guitar, John Paul Jones on bass and Keith Moon playing drums he recorded "Beck's Bolero," an extraordinary piece of music at the time, with Beck's finely crafted lines floating over the churning rhythm track. It was far better than "Hi Ho Silver Lining" which was the flip side of the single, which was issued in 1967. In February of that year he began organizing the Jeff Beck group, going through several musicians before settling on Rod Stewart as vocalist, Ron Wood, formerly of the Creation, as bassist and Aynsley Dunbar, ex-John Mayall Bluesbreaker, as drummer. In the fall of 1967, Mick Waller replaced Dunbar. It was this group, with a bit of outside help, that recorded *Truth*, released in 1968.

Truth was, in fact, one of the most important albums of the era. Listening to it, and then listening to Led Zeppelin's debut album, released in early 1969, there can be no question of the formidable influence it had on Jimmy Page and his vision of Zeppelin. But in addition, it featured a superlative blend of talent, even though they never became close personally. Beck's tight, well-disciplined solos on "Let Me Love You" showed him developing and polishing the distorted sounds he'd used with the Yardbirds. Their version of Willie Dixon's "You Shook Me" (recorded by Muddy Waters in the 1950s) featured forceful lines behind Stewart's vocal, with feedback and occasionally a harsh, percussive picking that gave his playing a violent edge. The song also showed up on Zeppelin's debut album.

There were some fairly mundane blues numbers such as "Rock My Plimsoul" (a barely disguised version of B.B. King's "Rock Me Baby") and "Blues DeLuxe," featuring more B.B. King style playing. And his playing on Howlin' Wolf's "I Ain't Superstitious" sounds a bit dated now. Nonetheless, it firmly established Beck, though at the time he was certainly eclipsed by Hendrix and, unfortunately, by Zeppelin as well. The album remains a classic today.

The band expanded with the addition of former studio player Nicky Hopkins on piano for the 1969 album, *Beck-Ola.* The focus here was more dissipated than on *Truth,* and as a whole it didn't measure up, though Beck himself played well on "Plynth." More interesting was the Beck group's backing on Donovan's 1969 recording of "Barabajagal," a nonsensical lyric but featuring some searing guitar work from Beck.

The group was in shambles by the fall of 1969. Beck and Stewart made plans to join with bassist Tim Bogert and drummer Carmine Appice, both of whom were members of the American psychedelic band Vanilla Fudge. The idea faded, though, and in April 1971 Beck formed another short-lived group that recorded two albums, both mediocre. In the summer of 1972 Beck finally got together with Bogert and Appice for some of the least inspired music of his career. The album *Beck, Bogart and Appice (BBA),* issued in 1973, was one of Beck's worst efforts. By 1974 they had disbanded.

Meanwhile, Beck himself was absorbing new musical influences, among them the jazz fusion material of Mahavishnu Orchestra pianist Jan Hammer. With Max Middleton, keyboardist from Beck's post-Stewart Beck groups, he entered a London studio in October 1974, and with George Martin producing recorded *Blow By Blow.* Late that year he nearly joined the Rolling Stones, but considering the success he was about to have it was well he didn't.

Blow By Blow remains a stunning album, a case study of a virtuoso redefining himself. Released in April 1975, it had little connection with the heavy metal music he'd pioneered. It instead showed Beck's solid command of the jazz-rock-fusion concept. He now played lyrical, intricate improvisations with clear confidence, while Middleton and two studio musicians created swirling, rhythmic backing for him and Martin added intermittent, tasteful string orchestration totally in sympathy with Beck's playing. While "You Know What I

Mean" was riff-oriented, Beck's version of the Beatles' "She's a Woman" featured his use of a "talk box," which permitted vocal phrasing, or a "talking guitar" sound, a device with a tube placed in his mouth. Though it impressed many fans, there was nothing particularly new about this. Pop steel guitarist Alvino Rey had employed it decades earlier; Chet Atkins used it in the '50s and steel guitarist Pete Drake had a hit with "Forever" using the same device in 1964.

"Air Blower" featured the familiar, fuzz-oriented Beck sound, but here it was more developed, as were the double-tracked lines he played. He created a variety of moods throughout the album, going from harsh figures to more fluent, displayed improvisations. "Scatterbrain" in particular reflected this. It was jazz-rock-fusion at its best, without the sense of excess that often stigmatized it. The album became a huge hit in America.

The new direction seemed to revitalize Beck as well, for his next gambit was to record and tour with Jan Hammer in his group. They produced (in 1978) *Wired,* an even more jazz-oriented album, based largely on Hammer's compositions. Hammer also asserted his musical personality more than Beck on the album, creating a fundamental conflict. Nonetheless, Beck did some outstanding work here, particularly on his interpretation f Charles Mingus' "Goodbye Pork Pie Hat." A live album followed that was equally impressive. In November 1978 Beck formed a band that included Stanley Clarke for a Far East tour. He recorded *There and Back,* another jazz-oriented album, in 1980. In mid 1984, he began touring with former bandmate Rod Stewart, but quit after a dispute over his onstage role.

Jeff Beck has proved himself to be a guitarist with considerable courage. To have distinguished himself in one style—a style he played a major role in formulating and that had a far-reaching effect on rock music—and then to move on to something he felt better expressed his current thinking took a great deal of bravery. Many musicians do well financially by remaining with one popular style, whether because they excel at it, or because their limitations prevent them from growing. Beck has been fortunate in this respect. His talents have evolved dramatically from those early days with the Yardbirds. Yet his early material has worn well over the years. With Beck there is clear cause for optimism about his future.

DISCOGRAPHY
The earliest Beck music available is on the *White Boy Blues* anthology (Compleat) album, with material from Clapton and Page as well. Several Yardbirds albums (some budget sets) also feature Beck prominently, including CBS package titled *Yardbirds*.

Most of the Jeff Beck Group material from CBS/Epic is still around, including a nice double album repackage of *Truth* and *Beck-Ola*. Several of the later albums can be found, and *Blow By Blow* and *Wired*, both on Epic, are easy to find even in fairly modest record departments, as is most everything he's done since then.

CHUCK BERRY

huck Berry was the first true rock guitar stylist, the first to come up with an instantly identifiable sound of his own. His playing included elements of blues, jazz and even country, but they were melded together so skillfully that it was not often possible to pick out specific stylistic characteristics from other players.

Berry's impact on the idiom has been massive and long-lived. It can still be said that the essence of Rolling Stone Keith Richard's guitar playing was learned directly from Berry classics like "Johnny B. Goode," "Carol," "Maybelline" and "Around and Around." Younger fans of the Stones often fail to realize that the group began in the early '60s by copying not only bluesmen like Muddy Waters and Howlin' Wolf, but also by immersing themselves in Chuck Berry's music. His influence has not waned twenty years later.

Berry's infectious guitar style has been frequently imitated by legions of guitarists of minimal competence to the extent that specific licks, such as his slashing instrumental

intro to "Johnny B. Goode," have become instantly recognizable cliches. Listen, for example, to the Beach Boys' "Surfin' U.S.A.," one of the better known incarnations of Berry's "Sweet Little Sixteen."

Certainly Berry has his limitations as a guitarist. Extended jamming has never shown him in a strong light. One notable example is an eight-minute version of his own "Rockin' at the Philharmonic," retitled "Rockin' at the Fillmore" and recorded (backed by the Steve Miller Band) live at San Francisco's Fillmore Auditorium in 1968. It's certainly entertaining enough, yet Berry exhausts all his ideas in the first couple of minutes and has to start back at the beginning before segueing into "Everyday I Have the Blues."

But long jam sessions tend to reveal weaknesses in nearly all rock guitarists. It isn't surprising that forty-minute guitar duels didn't survive much beyond the mid '70s, when even hardcore jammers like Eric Clapton abandoned the concept. Berry's strengths have always been most effective in the brief solos on his records, where his use of shuffle rhythm and choked double stops provide guts and excitement.

Berry's guitar style was pretty much formed at the time he began recording. It hasn't evolved much, and he has wisely resisted the temptation to tinker with electronic effects or otherwise alter his sound, which remains as powerful and pungent as ever without seeming dated.

Of course, much of Berry's career has been built on his reputation as a master American pop songwriter with his finger on the consciousness of both sock-hop and American culture after three decades of performing. That aspect of his career in and of itself justifies an entire book. Also, Berry has had problems with the law; that, combined with his intensely private nature, makes the idea of a definitive biography difficult at the very least. He has not, to my knowledge, ever spoken at length about his playing technique, choice of instrument strings, or amplification aside from the most general comments. In this essay his playing itself is of primary interest.

Charles Edward Anderson Berry was born in San Jose, California, probably in 1926. His family later moved to St. Louis. Both his parents sang in a church choir and all three of his sisters had musical backgrounds. He remained in St. Louis through high school, and first became interested in performing while attending Sumner High. He'd sung in the choir at the family church, but by high school he'd gotten deeply interested in the blues. Though it was highly unorthodox to sing blues in school programs at the time, he sang a rendition of the hit "Confessin' the Blues" at a men's musical revue and was so impressed with his accompanist, a guitarist named Tom Stevens, that he determined to play himself.

Berry's musical influences are among the few things about which he's been candid. Charlie Christian had a profound influence on him, and one can hear bits of the Christian technique, particularly in some of Berry's single-string work. T-Bone Walker, the father of electric blues guitar, had an equally powerful influence that's quite notable in Berry's

blues playing, though he rarely imitates Walker.

Yet if any one guitarist is heard in Chuck Berry's playing it is, by his own admission, Carl Hogan. Hogan, longtime guitarist in singer/songwriter/saxophonist Louis Jordan's band the Tympany Five, was playing Christian-inspired licks in the late '40s and early '50s that incorporated doublestops and string bending similar to what Berry would later use. Hogan never became well-known, and Berry is one of the few who have named him as an influence, which may explain why his own technique never seems baldly imitative of Christian and Walker. Les Paul had his impact on Chuck, too, though to a lesser extent.

Louis Jordan himself was a major influence on Berry's songwriting. His wit and humor were the precedents for Berry lyrics like "You Can't Catch Me," "School Days" and "No Particular Place to Go."

But Berry wasn't immediately ready for a musical career. In 1944, a scrape with the law landed him in reform school for three years. Berry was released in 1947, and after working in an auto plant he took up cosmetology and hairdressing, married and began a family. But music still interested him, and in 1952 he formed the Chuck Berry Combo to perform around St. Louis, concentrating on the blues. As money from his engagements supplemented his beauty shop income his interest in playing grew, and he began gingerly moving toward a musical career.

Finally in May 1955 he decided to go to Chicago to meet one of his idols, blues singer Muddy Waters. Muddy, who was performing at a Chicago club, permitted Berry to sit in. Impressed, he suggested Berry see Leonard Chess, co-owner of Chess Records, Muddy's record company and one of the leading independent blues labels in the country. Berry did so the next day, and Chess was impressed by a tape he'd made which included Berry's version of "Ida Red," an old country fiddle number popularized by Bob Wills and his Texas Playboys, among others. His shouted, breathless vocal and unrelenting drive stirred something in Chess (in fact, it sounded much like what became rockabilly). Though another song, the bluesy "Wee Wee Hours," was Berry's favorite. Chess recorded both of them, changing the title "Ida Red" to "Maybelline."

With the staunch support of disc jockey Allan Freed, "Maybelline" wound up a top five pop hit and a number one rhythm and blues hit. Berry's guitar playing on "Maybelline" is brash, distorted and uninhibited. With Johnny Johnson's piano providing a tinkling counterpoint in the background, Berry's guitar is important in building excitement. His solo features snappy staccato notes and abundant string choking that gives one pure, unbridled thrills. "Thirty Days," a virtual clone of "Maybelline," has an extended break with a high-register crescendo that takes on a life of its own. "Thirty Days," too, was a top r&b hit.

Berry began to create unique, infectious figures, such as the introductory lick of his December 1955 recording "You Can't Catch Me" (which doesn't feature a guitar solo). "Too Much Monkey Business" and "Brown-Eyed Handsome Man," cut in February 1956, both offer distinctive guitar breaks. The former uses fragmented phrases against a boogie-woogie beat; the latter has an infectious opening figure. During his vocal, Berry strums swirling arpeggios for a percussive, flamenco-styled effect. "Roll Over Beethoven," another classic, was his first song to feature the famous "Johnny B. Goode" riff. The Beatles' 1964 cover repeats every lick Berry played on the original, with George Harrison playing them note for note.

Within a year Berry had become one of the premiere artists in rock 'n' roll, playing Allan Freed's Paramount Theater shows in New York City and touring the country. He did a little more recording through 1956, but in January 1957 cut a number of tracks, including "Deep Feeling," obviously utilizing a lap steel guitar to create a languid, after-hours, Hawaiian-flavored blues. Recorded at the same session was "Blue Feeling," an anthology of blues licks clearly inspired by T-Bone Walker and Carl Hogan. Actually, two versions of the tune were released on the LP One

Dozen Berrys; a slower version was titled "Low Feeling," with one stanza removed. "School Days," an original number out of the Louis Jordan school of songwriting, featured Berry singing a stanza, echoing his vocal with a guitar lick throughout the song (its melody and structure surfaced seven years later in "No Particular Place to Go"). "Oh, Baby Doll," recorded in May '57, reprised more Hogan guitarisms.

There were some occasions when Berry placed the guitar in a strictly secondary role, among them "Oh, Baby Doll" and "Reelin' and Rockin'," two tunes on which he doesn't even solo. However, on his February 1959 session, guitar playing was quite prominent. He recorded two instrumentals: "Rockin' at the Philharmonic," an infectious r&b jump tune with Count Basie overtones, and "Guitar Boogie," a straightforward rave-up that was ventured in 1966 by the Yardbirds (featuring Jeff Beck) as "Jeff's Boogie." Also from Berry's '59 session came the classic "Johnny B. Goode," which has been the archetypal rock guitar anthem for a quarter of a century now.

At a 1958 session Chuck recorded an underrated instrumental titled "In-Go," a shuffle that clearly delineated T-Bone Walker's influence on his playing. He tried a steel guitar number, "Blues for Hawaiians," as well as "Around and Around," one more classic boogie-woogie with a solo based on the guitar figure in the Champs' hit instrumental "Tequila." Berry was in an experimental mood at another 1958 date when he created "Jo Jo Gunne," overdubbing much as his hero Les Paul had earlier. Berry separates each verse with echo-laden, stabbing guitar licks, including a quote from the Gillette "Look Sharp" razor slogan, another from Lionel Hampton's jazz standard "Flying Home" and one from the "Dragnet" theme. "Memphis, Tennessee," which may well have been overdubbed with multiple guitar parts, was cut at the same time.

By 1959 Chuck's singles didn't reach as high on the charts as they once did, and he himself was headed for a world of trouble. He met a woman in El Paso, Texas whom he hired to work as a hat check girl in a club he owned in St. Louis. She turned out to be a youthful prostitute, an Apache Indian fluent in Spanish (Berry said he wanted her to teach him the language), and he ran afoul of federal authorities for taking her across state lines. He went to trial in 1960, and the proceedings were so burdened by racial slurs and innuendo that a second trial was ordered. But the second verdict remained the same. Berry headed for a two-year prison term. His sex-related offense proved the danger of black-based music to conservative white Americans, and rock music did not recover from this charge until the Beatles; Berry and other rockers were replaced on the charts by the emasculated, white, pop-oriented croonings of Neil Sedaka and Frankie Avalon.

Prison had a doleful effect on Berry. His marriage foundered, and his two years in jail (1961-'63) left him bitter and distrustful. However by early 1964, with the Beatles and Rolling Stones recycling his music for a new generation, the charts were again safe for Chuck Berry. "Nadine," which didn't feature much substantive guitar, became a respectable top twenty hit, as did the superb "No Particular Place to Go" (a remake of "School Days") and "You Never Can Tell." Berry became a tough businessman, unwilling to accept verbal contracts or any performance deal that didn't seem correct. He also began to duck the press, often baring considerable hostility to potential interviewers.

In 1966, after 11 years with Chess, he left for Mercury Records, which paid him an astronomical sum. But in 1969, his contract nearly over and a series of undistinguished recordings under his belt (many of them remakes of his past hits), he was back with Chess where he returned to form, singing "Tulane," which captured the essence of the head shop ethos as succinctly as Berry had perceived '50s high school culture. In 1972 he had yet another big hit with "My Ding-a-Ling," a childish but enormously popular piece of raunch that he'd done for years onstage.

Since then, he's continued to record albums, some of them excellent (like his 1979 Atco LP *Rockit*), others mediocre. But his problems with the law hadn't yet ended. He was charged with income tax evasion and wound up back in prison, despite the fact other performers have committed similar offenses and gotten off far easier. Berry bounced back to the concert circuit, as a living symbol of an era; now in his mid fifties, he's still able to entertain.

Berry's use of the guitar as a visual tool shouldn't be discounted. His famous "duck walk," a hunched-over amble across the stage, has been one of his greatest crowd-pleasing devices through much of his career. And his guitar sound always has a density that makes it recognizable, partly due to his technique and partly due to his constant use of Gibson hollowbody electric instruments with pickups capable of giving a full and rounded tone.

If Chuck Berry never again picked up a guitar, his place in the pantheon of rock guitar legends would be safe. His playing style is at one with his songs. One cannot play "Johnny B. Goode" or "School Days" without using some variant of his original licks; the songs just wouldn't sound right without them. His ability to meld composition and technique into a cohesive whole is as substantive a contribution to rock 'n' roll as his wonderful gifts for songwriting, and shall endure long after the man himself has gone.

DISCOGRAPHY

If you can afford only one Chuck Berry album, make it *The Great Twenty-Eight* (Chess). It is the best single compendium of Berry classics ever compiled, in pristine mono sound as good as and in some cases clearer than the original Chess singles. A number of his Chess LPs have been reissued with their original covers in France, though their availability in the U.S. may be limited; these include the three double albums of the *Golden Decade Series, Two Great Guitars with Bo Diddley, After School Session,* and *One Dozen Berrys.* As imports tend to fluctuate in availability, check with Down Home Music before ordering. His 1979 *Rockit* album (Atco) is probably his best recent effort.

MICHAEL BLOOMFIELD

Like so many of the bluesmen he admired, Michael Bloomfield's impact on music derives from a relatively small group of recordings, released over three years. Nonetheless, the effect his blues-based virtuosity had on the course of rock guitar was profound and long-lasting. The concept of extended solos, of a guitarist taking more than a mere chorus or two can be traced directly to Bloomfield, more specifically to his 1965-'66 recordings as lead guitarist with the Paul Butterfield Blues Band, one of the most influential bands of the progressive rock scene.

Certainly Bloomfield was not the first young white to gravitate to the blues; musicians had done the same thing for decades. But for the most part his predecessors admired the music from a distance, while Michael inserted himself directly into the blues atmosphere of his native Chicago, learning by playing with that city's legendary bluesmen. Part of a cadre of like-minded young whites, Bloomfield went on to establish that music with a new audience, giving some of the bluesmen he admired overdue recognition for

their achievements among audiences that had previously ignored them. In at least one case—that of B.B. King—Bloomfield's professed admiration helped revitalize a career, bringing the Mississippi-born bluesman exposure that raised him to an entirely new level of success in American music. With such an impact, Bloomfield himself might have become a major rock star. Everyone from the Grateful Dead's Jerry Garcia to Carlos Santana to former Jefferson Airplane guitarist Jorma Kaukonen cite him as a major influence. The Butterfield Blues Band had such a huge impact on the entire San Francisco music scene of the late 1960s that without them, the musical atmosphere of that city during those years would have been very different.

Sadly, Bloomfield was dormant through much of the '70s, the result of a variety of personal problems, that ranged from insomnia to overindulgence in alcohol and hard drugs. Mike has never regained his momentum. Indeed, he appeared to have turned away from anyyrock star aspirations. With his great personal wealth, he rarely, if ever, had to worry much about the basics of economic survival.

Michael Bernard Bloomfield's roots were hardly in keeping with his chosen music. Born July 28, 1943 in Chicago, he was the eldest son of Harold and Dorothy Bloomfield. Unlike the families of many of the guitarists in this book, his wasn't particularly musical. His father owned a prosperous restaurant supply firm, and was among Chicago's wealthier manufacturers. His mother, a former actress, was a bit more open to art-oriented pastimes like music.

Around 1953 Michael began to realize there was more music around than the bland stuff his parents played on their hi-fi. According to Ed Ward in his excellent book *Michael Bloomfield: The Rise of an American Guitar Hero*, an AM radio Michael received as a bar mitzvah present turned him around. Chicago was big on ethnic programming at the time, the city being a veritable melting pot of blacks, transplanted southerners, Germans, Irish, Eastern Europeans, Italians and other groups. Chicago radio then had enough ethnic programming on its many stations to satisfy all of them. Bloomfield zeroed in on the blues, r&b and hillbilly programs, drinking in all of it. By 1956, he'd decided to play guitar.

This didn't please his father, who undoubtedly had hopes of ensconcing Michael in the family business someday. The combination of his weird listening habits and his guitar at a time when Elvis Presley had made the guitar a tangible symbol of youthful rebellion caused conflict between father and son. Soon Mike was taking guitar lessons from his mother's hairdresser, an amateur who taught him the rudiments of the instrument. The rest he would learn on the job.

During Mike's adolesence he was obsessed with the guitar, practicing every chance he got and playing with a variety of groups. His love of the blues had crystallized, and he began sneaking down to Chicago's south side, where Muddy Waters, Howlin' Wolf, Little Walter and other blues legends held sway. He played in rock and roll bands and just about anywhere else where he could get experience. Gradually he became a fixture at the south

side bars, and the black regulars at these places accepted him; the musicians were first amused and then respectful of his sincere attempts to learn to play the blues. He would jam with any blues artist who would let him onstage. Up until the early 1960s he worked with rock bands and experimented with acoustic folk blues as well, but eventually he phased out his rock and roll gigs to concentrate on learning acoustic guitar and the blues styles associated with it.

By 1963 he was managing a Chicago folk music club, booking folk artists and local bluesmen like Big Joe Williams, who taught him much about the earlier country blues forms and the pre-World War II blues scene in Chicago. But soon Michael returned to the bars and to electric music. He turned another bar, Big John's, into an important gathering place for the young whites who were coming to the blues, among them harmonica players Charlie Musselwhite and Paul Butterfield and singer Nick Gravenites.

In 1964 Bloomfield's guitar playing came to the attention of Columbia Records producer John Hammond, discoverer of Count Basie, Charlie Christian, Billie Holiday, Aretha Franklin, George Benson, Bob Dylan and Bruce Springsteen (and most recently white blues guitarist Stevie Ray Vaughan). Hammond liked what he heard, and signed Bloomfield to the Epic label. Mike had recorded acoustically with blues mandolinist Yank Rachell and again with veteran country bluesman Sleepy John Estes in 1963, but for this session returned to electric guitar. His group, by today's standards, wasn't terribly cohesive, but Bloomfield's playing on "Got My Mojo Working" showed real promise.

In the meantime, Paul Butterfield had formed his own blues band, using another aspiring white bluesman, Elvin Bishop, on lead guitar. Butterfield's band attracted the notice of Elektra Records, and was signed to the folk-oriented label as its first electric band. Early in 1965, Butterfield asked Bloomfield to join him. They were to record in New York City, but had considerable trouble doing what Elektra producer Paul Rothchild wanted. Some of their earliest material was never released. However, it's fairly certain that several tracks appeared on a 1966 Elektra blues-rock anthology entitled *What's Shakin'* (also featuring Eric Clapton, Steve Winwood, Tom Rush and the Lovin' Spoonful) since keyboardist Mark Naftalin, who appeared on the band's first album, is not present on the earlier tracks.

The four tunes include a straightforward reading of Howlin' Wolf's "Spoonful," which seems to feature Bishop more than Bloomfield. "Off the Wall," the Little Walter instrumental, features no prominent guitar playing. "Lovin' Cup," however, presents the gnashing, screaming high-register leads Bloomfield became known for, with some but not all of the edge he'd later develop. "Good Morning Little Schoolgirl" sounds like a primitive, late '40s Chicago blues side, with no audible bass, a churning rhythm laid down by ex-Howlin' Wolf drummer Sammy Lay and some barbed-wire guitar licks by Bloomfield. "One More Mile" displays the Bloomfield of legend; he did some of his finest early work on its elongated, slashing solo break.

Butterfield's band generated enough interest to secure a booking for the 1965 Newport Folk Festival. Little did Butterfield, Bloomfield and company realize they were heading into a veritable hornet's nest. The controversy over electric instruments among folk purists was nearly as intense as it had been among country performers in the early '40s. When folk idol Bob Dylan released his *Bringing It All Back Home* album in early 1965, with a clumsy but clearly amplified band of New York studio players backing him on most of the tracks, the controversy grew even more heated. Into this walked the Butterfield band, playing authentic south side Chicago blues complete with amplifiers and drums. Some folkies, obsessed with their own simplistic perceptions of what was and wasn't folk music, were upset. It actually wasn't anything new. Muddy Waters took plenty of flak when in 1958 he brought an electric guitar on his first trip to Britain. Ironically, when he returned on a second tour with his acoustic guitar, audiences by then accustomed to amplified blues wanted him to play electric.

So things were tense at Newport. Noted folklorist Alan Lomax introduced the Butterfield group with thinly veiled skepticism, but the band proved itself with a tough, sharply honed set. One sample of the 1965 Newport performance, "Mellow Down Easy," shows how the sound has coalesced. Butterfield's harmonica phrasing has a lyrical integrity and control built of many nights of jamming in the south side clubs. Bloomfield has every phrase under control, throwing white-hot, whiplash riffs out around Butterfield's vocals. It went over with the audience better than anyone expected, and it was little wonder that Bob Dylan, who shared a manager (Albert Grossman) with Butterfield, asked some members of the Butterfield band to back him that night.

They did, and controversy swells to this day as to whether Dylan was roundly applauded or booed for his heresy in using amplified backing in that performance. In any case Dylan, who had met Bloomfield back in his folkie days in Chicago, was impressed. Following Newport, the Butterfield Band went to New York, where it was to take a stab at recording again. This time it worked.

The result is one of the classic albums of American blues/rock fusion. The Paul Butterfield Blues Band remains in print nearly 20 years after being issued in October, 1965. In an age of heavy metal its significance may seem questionable, but in the context of the times it was a compelling record, although so alien to Elektra's acoustic music tradition that a note on the album cover suggests it be played at "as high a volume as possible."

The band had come together musically at last. From the opening bars of Nick Gravenites' "Born in Chicago" came heated, passionate music oozing with the flavor of the south side. Bloomfield was playing extraordinary guitar here; his Telecaster rang out like gunfire. His slide work cut julienne strips through the boogie beat of Elmore James' "Shake Your Moneymaker." He contributed steely but well-articulated single-string work to Little Walter's "Blues with a Feeling" and showed his mastery of the B.B. King/T-Bone Walker shuffle styles on "Thank You Mr. Poobah," engaging Butterfield in some exciting call-and-response work. His opening riff on Muddy Waters' "Got My Mojo Workin'" was his only significant addition to the song, but it sets the tone for the entire performance. He punctuated "Mellow Down Easy" with piercing rhythmic phrases and an undermixed solo that created an urban cacophony appropriate to the lyrics.

Nobody in the band let their guards down on side two. "Screamin'" is a riff-oriented instrumental with Butterfield revealing his total command of his harp and Bloomfield slashing his way through his solo with searing, lean phrasing. He plays a supportive role to Butterfield's vocal on "Our Love Is Drifting," but his solo has such blazing, demonic intensity that it takes on a life of its own independent of the 12-bar context. Junior Parker's "Mystery Train," ironically, has much in common with Elvis Presley's cover version on Sun, but it, too, is dominated by Butterfield, Bloomfield and Sammy Lay's unrelenting percussion. Bloomfield's rough phrases, played with a slide, counterpoint Lay's drumming. He plays a more supportive role on Little Walter's "Last Night," sung by Butterfield, but "Look on Yonder's Wall" is a revelation. Bloomfield plays screaming single-string leads for a supercharged version of the famous Elmore James riff.

Though some blues purists may dispute it, *The Paul Butterfield Blues Band* is a perfect album. There was never any pretense of doing "new" music, but the effect it had on many aspiring young guitarists—including acoustic players—was immediate. Suddenly the potential of amplified guitar was clear; the album became a classic of the blues-rock genre, one whose influence has yet to ebb.

Late in 1965 Bloomfield got a call from Bob Dylan, who was recording what would become *Highway 61 Revisited*. He wanted Bloomfield on the album, cautioning him against playing "any of that B.B. King shit." Bloomfield's work on *Highway 61* wasn't quite as well focused as his things with Butterfield. He was still using his Telecaster, but rock was still not as close to him as the blues. He crosspicked a sparkling little figure behind Dylan's vocal on "Like a Rolling Stone" while

Al Kooper, who later became Bloomfield's performing partner and had crashed the session, faked his way through on organ. Mike was somewhat more at home on "Tombstone Blues," playing raw, modal phrases with overtones of Hubert Sumlin, Howlin' Wolf's lead guitarist. His work on "Just Like Tom Thumb's Blues" was in the mold of gospel guitarist Pop Staples.

Dylan wanted to take Bloomfield on the road, but Michael opted to remain with Butterfield. It was a fortunate decision, opening the way for the group that became The Band to join Dylan, and for Bloomfield to cut a record that had an even greater effect than the first Butterfield band LP: *East-West*, its second album.

It was far different than the straightahead Chicago sound of the first album, and oddly enough *East-West* lacked a clearcut focus. One attempt at top 40 success, "Mary, Mary," is a total waste of time. Robert Johnson's "Walkin' Blues" contains a fair Bloomfield solo, but Elvin Bishop asserted himself far more on this album than the first one. Bishop, the band's original lead guitarist, had been eclipsed by Bloomfield and resented it. Bloomfield soloed less on the shorter tracks, though he was exemplary on "I Got a Mind to Give Up Living," and "Two Trains Running," an adaptation of Muddy Waters' "Still a Fool."

But two extended instrumentals—Cannonball Adderley's "Work Song" and the original composition "East-West"—boldly broke new ground in rock music. These jazz oriented tunes couldn't be considered traditional blues. "Work Song" runs for nearly eight minutes. Butterfield opens up, stating the theme on his harmonica, followed by a radically new solo approach from Bloomfield. No longer is he ripping hard-edged blues from his Telecaster—he now creates innovative melody lines, sharply phrased, lyrical improvisations unlike any others in rock, from his Gibson Les Paul. He invokes Wes Montgomery with a passage in octaves. Butterfield takes it back with a saxophone-like harmonica break before turning it over to organist Mark Naftalin. Bishop's solo is clearly inferior to Bloomfield's, though his improved phrasing shows he's been listening to Michael. The two guitarists work out a fiery three-way call-and-response with Butterfield that's really exciting before returning to the melody.

"East-West" is another matter. It's clear that Bloomfield had studied the Indian music of sitarist Ravi Shankar and the "new jazz" exponents like John Coltrane, and that their effect on him was nearly as strong as that of Hubert Sumlin, Big Joe Williams and B.B. King. The result is thirteen minutes and ten seconds of sheer brilliance. Bishop, playing better than ever, phrases the opening with far more finesse than he showed on "Work Song." Butterfield follows with a voice-like harmonica solo, then Bloomfield enters. He plays like a sitarist, buzzing strings to create sympathetic tones while burning up the fretboard with flurries of notes to a crescendo. He plays with more economy after this climax, smoothing out the jagged textures of his earlier solo while Naftalin offers gentle counterpoint. Mike moves into a boplike line, repetitive yet building upon itself; at one point he constructs harmonies from a single bass note, then advances a repeating, playful phrase, countered by Bishop, both in the upper registers of their instruments. The two come to a second crescendo, Bishop holding the rhythm while Bloomfield freaks out. The song ends abruptly.

"East-West" and "Work Song" wrote the book for the late 1960s "psychedelic" jam sessions and rock solos of the Jefferson Airplane, the Steve Miller Band, Santana and the Grateful Dead. If the rest of *East-West* is uneven, even mediocre in places, these two numbers marked a turning point in American rock music.

All of this should have put the Butterfield Blues Band and Michael Bloomfield at the top of the heap; it didn't. He found, despite the acclaim the group received, that he despised the road. He was listening to different forms of music that gave him other ideas, and at the end of 1966 Bloomfield left Butterfield's fold. He did session work for a time, then began to gather the Electric Flag, a group designed to cut across all barriers and run the gamut of

American music, from blues to jazz to rockabilly to country. His friends singer Nick Gravenites and organist Barry Goldberg were involved, and soon Bloomfield had a band complete with horn section and r&b drummer Buddy Miles. Mike moved north of San Francisco to Marin County and began rehearsing. His reputation had spread by then; he was America's first real guitar legend, not a Duane Eddy or Lonnie Mack, but a serious soloist, accorded the same reverence by fans and critics as a Miles Davis or Charlie Parker.

The Flag debuted at the Monterey Pop Festival, and got a good reception; but *A Long Time Comin'*, their Columbia debut album, didn't come off. Though Mike played some fine solos, he remained strongest with the blues, most notably on his version of Howlin' Wolf's "Killing Floor," his jumping solo on the Stick McGhee favorite "Wine" and his beautiful, fluent blues fragment "Easy Rider," at the end of the album, played alone on electric guitar. It remains a great, albeit brief, moment in Bloomfield's musical legacy. The Flag didn't really jell as he had hoped, and the use of heroin by several members, combined with the pressures of being so highly touted, sunk the band by the end of 1967.

Next came one of Bloomfield's worst records, *Super Session*. He teamed up with organist Al Kooper and a rhythm section for what was little more than pointless, formless jamming, for Bloomfield almost a self-parody. It was a million-seller in jam-crazy 1968, but it was certainly not Bloomfield's best work. A live LP from the Fillmore Auditorium in San Francisco, *The Live Adventures of Mike Bloomfield and Al Kooper*, was even worse.

Through 1969 into the '70s, Bloomfield backed away from the spotlight. He and Gravenites did some production work together, and Michael played on other peoples' albums. He recorded another pointless jam at the Fillmore, backed Gravenites on his own solo album, and gigged locally. He recorded a mediocre solo album, *It's Not Killing Me*, which did his reputation little good. Much of the problem was traceable to his use of heroin. He sloughed off work much of the time, sitting in front of the TV and not touching his instrument. Occasionally he recorded—once with jazz bandleader Woody Herman. In 1973 Bloomfield, pianist Dr. John and blues singer John Hammond, Jr. recorded a nondescript effort titled *Triumverate*. In 1974 he mistakenly tried reviving the Electric Flag with a wretched LP on Atlantic. In 1975 he was pushed into a "supergroup" titled KGB with old friend Barry Goldberg that disbanded after one album.

Bloomfield did film soundtracks, but remained out of the spotlight while Carlos Santana and other admirers gained prominence. Then in 1976 he created, for Guitar Player Records (a subsidiary of the magazine) *If You Love These Blues, Play 'Em as You Please*, on which he delivered suggestions on playing and brilliant recreations of the styles of blues guitarists who'd influenced him. Other records followed, but this one—nominated for a Grammy—was his final acclaimed effort. Alcohol was taking its toll on him. He tried to clean up, and by 1981 it appeared he had. Then on February 15, 1981 he was found dead in a car in San Francisco. The coroner's autopsy revealed he'd ingested cocaine and methamphetamine. In an era when Stevie Ray Vaughan, Johnny Winter, the Fabulous Thunderbirds and other blues-flavored bands continue to make an impact, Michael Bloomfield, the man who in many ways started it all, is remembered only by hardcore fans old enough to recall him at his peak. He deserves better.

DISCOGRAPHY

Most of the essential Bloomfield sides are still available, including the first Paul Butterfield album and *East-West*, as well as a greatest hits anthology titled *Golden Butter*, all on Elektra. The Electric Flag album *Long Time Comin'* is out of print, though *Super Session* with Al Kooper can be easily found. Bob Dylan's *Highway 61 Revisited* boasts some excellent Bloomfield playing. Also, several later albums on Takoma and other labels are still around. And following the appearance of Ed Ward's biography, Columbia released *Bloomfield*, a two record anthology of material ranging from his 1964 Columbia session through Butterfield, the Flag and other, later Columbia material. Some of the tracks are great, others are only fair.

ESSENTIAL READING:

Michael Bloomfield: The Rise and Fall of an American Guitar Hero, by Ed Ward

JAMES BURTON

It is routine today for a rock guitarist to exclusively associate himself with one brand of guitar. Eric Clapton favors Stratocasters, as did Jimi Hendrix. Michael Bloomfield generally used Les Pauls; Lonnie Mack has been forever linked with the Gibson Flying V. Duane Eddy and Eddie Cochran both favored Gretsch Chet Atkins models, as does former Stray Cats lead guitarist Brian Setzer. And in many cases each guitar's unique qualities become intertwined with the musician's sound. The raw, thick tones of a Les Paul could be heard in Bloomfield's work with the Butterfield Blues Band (on its classic F202East-West album); the Strat's unique tonal configurations and vibrato mechanism were crucial to Hendrix's playing throughout his career.

If one man pioneered the idea of a rock guitarist building his sound on a particular instrument, James Burton is that man. Burton and the Fender Telecaster are so closely tied together that it's difficult to picture one without the other. Other guitarists have forged similar ties with Telecasters, among them

Roy Buchanan, Albert Lee, bluesman Albert Collins, Roy Nichols of Merle Haggard's Strangers and Waylon Jennings. But without a doubt, Burton is the founder of Telecaster rock. Beginning with his growling, blues-influenced lead guitar work on rockabilly Dale Hawkins' 1956 recording of "Suzie Q," Burton, more than anyone else made the Telecaster integral to rock and roll, creating a role for it that hasn't diminished in nearly three decades.

In the process Burton has become one of rock's most revered guitarists. Countless rock stars of the 1960s and '70s cite him as a major influence. Of course, Burton had his share of breaks along the way. His work as Rick Nelson's lead guitarist, with Rick's weekly performance on the popular *Ozzie and Harriet* TV series, did much to increase his visibility and promote his talents. Burton's work on such early rockabilly classics as "Suzie Q" and Bob Luman's "Red Hot" also enhanced his early reputation, but it was the Nelson show—and Rick's personal appearance tours—that cinched Burton's fame.

Burton was smart enough to take advantage of that exposure. After leaving Rick in the early 1960s, he plunged into the busy Hollywood studio scene, recording with countless rock, country and pop artists, playing on soundtrack sessions and doing occasional TV work (most notably as leader of the red-hot Shindogs, the house band on ABC's popular *Shindig* TV program). Sessions were a way of life for him; performing onstage became secondary until he joined Elvis Presley's backup band in 1969, remaining until Presley died in 1977, the sole remaining rockabilly touchstone in Elvis' music. Between tours he was hired for sessions with country and rock artists ranging from Emmylou Harris and Gram Parsons to Singing Cowboy Jimmy Wakely. Since Presley's death, his schedule has continued unabated, most recently as lead guitarist for first John Denver and then Jerry Lee Lewis.

Burton's style, aside from special requirements of individual producers on studio dates, is a crackling, decidedly hard-edged sound. The Telecaster, originally introduced by Leo Fender under the name "Broadcaster" in 1949, was, by just about everyone's estimation, the first commercially successful solidbody electric Spanish guitar. Though other companies had their own models out in the 1930s (most notably Rickenbacker's Electro model), the Telecaster made the first substantial impact. It had a unique sound, created partly by its pickups, the density of its body and by the fact that like a steel guitar, its strings were anchored within the body, not in a tailpiece. This gave the "Tele" a strength and a cutting tone that emphasized its highs and gave the bass strings a "twang" unlike any other instrument at the time. First favored by west coast country performers like guitarist Jimmy Bryant, the instrument subsequently became a favorite among country players everywhere, rivaled in 1952 by the first Gibson Les Pauls. Even today, few guitars can slice through a band with the finesse and sharpness of a Telecaster.

Burton's style involved a technique known by some as "chicken pickin'," a percussive gesture that employed both a flatpick and one fingerpick. It's a well-articulated, crisp attack that takes advantage of the Telecaster's natural treble to pluck the strings cleanly but harshly, enough to produce a stabbing sound that could turn into a scream if Burton bent strings into the upper register. He also played two strings at once, deadening one while striking the other one clearly to give the precussive edge. Though he originally developed it within the rockabilly context, it was accepted to the point that it became an integral part of country music by the mid '60s, particularly influential on the "Bakersfield sound" pioneered by Buck Owens and Merle Haggard. Telecasters were not only standard equipment among country bands there, but the players (Phil Baugh and Roy Nichols, among others) derived styles similar to Burton's. Burton, in fact, had a hand in their development; it was he who played on some of Merle Haggard's early hits like "Strangers."

Burton's versatility was a distinct advantage. Aside from the fact that he could double on dobro, he could elicit different sounds with his guitar, imitating a pedal steel guitar effortlessly, before the famous Parsons-White string-bending devices were designed to be built into Telecasters for steel guitar effects. His sense of taste was formidable, as was his ability to tailor his licks to a given context. Onstage, Burton has always formed his solos for maximum excitement, taking the spotlight for a moment but never intruding on a vocalist. This he learned to do early on; self-indulgence has never been part of the Burton style.

James Burton was born in Shreveport, Louisiana, on August 21, 1940. Guitar interested him as a child, though he didn't really start playing until around 1953 (the ages of 12 and 13 seem to be crucial launching years for many of our best-known guitarists, regardless of style). After trying a couple of models, he wound up with a Tele, a guitar with which he almost immediately felt comfortable.

The influences on Burton's early playing aren't really surprising. He listened to the radio, picking up on country performers like Chet Atkins, Lefty Frizzell, Hank Williams, Carl Smith and their sidemen, such as guitarists Sammy Pruett (with Williams and Carl Smith), Zeke Turner (with Red Foley and Williams), Hank Garland (with Foley and Eddy Arnold, among others) and Grady Martin (with Foley). But r&b music and blues were equally important. He was particularly fond of Chuck Berry. Burton, however, does not credit any one player as his major blues influence.

He practiced—and listened—sufficiently to meld his own technique from his influences. His first substantive job came around age 15, when he recorded with Louisiana-based rockabilly Dale Hawkins, who was working the Louisiana Hayride. Burton played behind other artists, too. Sometime in 1956, along with Hawkins and some other musicians, he wrote (and, at the KWKH radio studios in Shreveport, recorded) "Suzie Q," a song Hawkins had based on a blues number by Howlin' Wolf. Burton never got a cut of the song's royalties, but the 1957 hit recording, released on Checker, a subsidiary of the Chicago-based Chess label, showed a budding virtuoso.

Two takes of "Suzie Q" have been issued—one alternate take, the other the released version. They reveal some contrasting sides of Burton's playing. The first, faster take features handclapping and cowbell-dominated percussion, as well as the rolling, low-register riff that gave the song its musical identity. This same riff had a variety of other incarnations, including Burton's playing on Rick Nelson's recording of "Milkcow Blues Boogie" and, eleven years later, Creedence Clearwater Revival's successful remake of "Suzie Q." Creedence leader/lead guitarist John Fogerty clearly loved it, for he also incorporated a variation into his 1969 recording "Green River." But on the first version of the song Burton flies through his initial, rhythmic solo, then takes a second break dominated by single string passages, played with less assurance than on the finished version.

The final, slower tempo version of "Suzie Q" shows us Burton in all his glory. He is in total control, playing the rhythmic licks of the first solo with complete ease, creating music of

pure, purple menace. Scotty Moore tried doing the same thing on the 1955 Sun version of "Good Rockin' Tonight"; good as it was, he came nowhere near Burton, whose solo had all the relentless fury of a Louisiana thunderstorm.

James wasn't with Hawkins long when, in 1957, he joined the backup band of Bob Luman, a Texas-bred country singer who'd turned rockabilly after seeing Elvis, himself a *Louisiana Hayride* regular, on tour in Texas. Now Elvis was a star and Luman was on *Hayride*. Luman wound up with an Imperial recording contract and Burton distinguished himself with two brief, punchy chicken pickin' solos on a dynamic cover version of Billy Lee Riley's Sun recording "Red Hot." Luman's popularity was sufficient to get him an appearance in a 1957 film, *Carnival Rock*.

What happened when Luman and Burton went to Los Angeles to make an interesting movie? They wound up joining the Los Angeles-based *Town Hall Party*, an Opry/Hayride-based show that featured some of the top country music talent in the nation. There are many stories recounting how Burton ended up with Rick Nelson. Some claim Rick, then enjoying his first rockabilly-inspired hits ("I wanted to be Carl Perkins," he once said), came into a studio where Luman and company were recording and decided to try to hire his band (Burton, bassist James Kirkland and drummer Butch White). In another telling, *Town Hall Party* performer Joe Maphis, then one of the top country guitarists, who worked at some of Rick's early Imperial sessions (including "Be Bop Baby" and "Waitin' in School") and live appearances, insists that he introduced Rick to Burton and Kirkland. The studio scene may have happened after this; in any case, by 1958 Burton and Kirkland were the nucleus of Rick's touring and performing band.

From that time on Rick Nelson made some of the finest rockabilly records around. Despite the bland TV image he projected on the Ozzie and Harriet series, his records rocked, largely due to his own affinity for hard-edged music and Burton's raw, driving lead guitar. Burton's work played a major role in giving Nelson's records the credibility they needed. At that time, in fact, only Paul Burlison, lead guitarist with Johnny Burnette's Rock and Roll Trio (and a fellow Telecaster user) was playing anything even remotely similar to Burton.

"Believe What You Say," recorded in 1958, is an example of Burton at his best. His solo is filled with screaming crescendos and contrasting passages on the bass strings. The Telecaster lets his lines cut right through the band. On "Shirley Lee" he plays a fluent break that provides nice contrast to Nelson's screaming, barely controlled vocal. Ricky was more restrained on his cover of Jerry Lee Lewis' "Down the Line," but Burton was ready with a driving rhythmic break to complement the chugging, pumping beat of the song. Nelson's version of Hank Williams' "I Can't Help It If I'm Still in Love with You" features Burton mimicking a pedal steel guitar. He creates a bluesy pastiche of licks for Rick's cover of Fats Domino's "I'm In Love Again," with stinging bent notes. "My Babe," the Little Walter blues (a variant of the old "This Train" folksong), gets a malevolent treatment combining a variant of Burton's "Suzie Q" riff with some harsh, foreboding playing. In his obsession with Elvis, Rick also covered "Milcow Blues Boogie," but Burton put a far different stamp on the song, relying on his "Suzie Q" style instead of aping Scotty Moore. The result is a powerful performance, not necessarily superior to, but certainly different than Presley's.

Burton was on virtually all of Nelson's hits during this period, and he and his Telecaster were prominently featured on Rick's obligatory musical performances on the Ozzie and Harriet shows. James' hands were sometimes shown in closeups. Ozzie Nelson was no great shakes as a bandleader, but his understanding of how to present music on the then-new medium of TV was more innovative than most people realized. And Burton knew how to vary his playing. He came up with his own interpretation of the Travis style for Rick's hit recording of "Hello, Mary Lou."

Burton remained with Nelson for nearly a decade, even living with the Nelsons in the early days. But by the early '60s gradually he began feeling constricted as the Nelson organization wanted him on an exclusive basis and discouraged him from doing outside work. Since Rick wasn't always recording or touring, and the TV show was out of production several months at a time, James began chafing at the bit. Finally, in 1964 he left to begin his studio career.

James Burton's pop, rock and country recording work during the next several years is impossible to document in full. He worked with Elvis Presley on film soundtracks and was featured on the Everly Brothers' classic Warner Bros. LP *Roots*. Also, in September of 1964, he became prominently featured on the ABC rock TV show *Shindig*, as part of the show's house rock band, the Shindogs, whose appearance and occasional tours boosted his visibility even further. The sessions he did varied widely, depending on an artist's needs. At times he doubled on Dobro. He contributed superb Tele support on Merle Haggard's 1966 hits "Swingin' Doors" and "The Bottle Let Me Down," playing incisive leads on both numbers along with a steel guitarist (probably Ralph Mooney, one of the cornerstones of the "Bakersfield sound" made popular by Capitol Records in the late '60s).

Around 1967 Burton and Mooney did an album together for Capitol. *Corn Pickin' and Slick Slidin'*, now a collector's item, was a shimmering example of guitar/steel synergy. Working in a straight country context (unlike many guitar/steel teams, who concentrated on jazz or western swing), they crafted energetic performances best exemplified by "Texas Waltz," dominated by Mooney's steel and featuring Burton on wah-wah guitar.

The progressive rock scene of the mid-to-late 1960s also brought James much work. He played dobro on the country-oriented "Child's Claim to Fame" on Buffalo Springfield's 1967 LP *Buffalo Springfield Again*, on former Monkee Mike Nesmith's solo effort *Wichita Train Whistle* (1968) and (that same year) on Judy Collins' album *Who Knows Where the Time Goes*. There were also more hits with Merle Haggard, including his classic

"Mama Tried" (in 1968), featuring an economical riff and a tight solo break on Telecaster. In fact, both Burton and Phil Baugh had much to do with putting the Telecaster in that sound; later on Waylon Jennings, a longtime Telecaster user, brought Ralph Mooney into his band, the Waylors, which has preserved the Bakersfield sound in country music (since both Haggard and Buck Owens have moved away from it somewhat).

In 1969 Elvis Presley, in the wake of a highly successful TV special, decided to return to live performing. Scotty Moore was so busy working in Nashville as a recording engineer that he couldn't go on the road. But Burton was available, and played a major role in assembling the nucleus of Elvis' touring band. He was first captured on record with Elvis in the documentation of his first Las Vegas appearance, and James' playing enhanced the excitement of the occasion. Burton was not Moore, but he needed only to be himself, quoting Scotty only on some of Elvis' older Sun material (it's a tribute to the timelessness of Scotty's work on those tunes that virtually no other solos would ever quite work as well—and Burton knew it). But on the other numbers, the chicken pickin' came fast and furious. He was particularly outstanding on "Johnny B. Goode" and a"Mystery Train" on which he combined Scotty's old licks with his own to create some of the most underrated—and exhilarating—guitar ever played behind Elvis Presley. It is little wonder that Burton remained with him a total of eight years.

By the early 1970s, the legacy of James Burton was returning in the form of Creedence Clearwater Revival, which racked up a phenomenal body of top ten hits between 1968 and 1971, all of them featuring John Fogerty's excellent lead guitar. In an age of self-indulgent half-hour long solos, Fogerty's tight leads recalled the durability of Burton's music. Meanwhile, Burton himself was recording a solo album for A&M Records: The Guitar Sounds of James Burton. It was not one of his better efforts, however. For one thing, it was a last-minute production, for another, Burton wasn't able to sustain musical interest through the entire album, a problem

common to some of the best studio musicians. What sounds great on a solo break or backing doesn't always translate into an entire LP of instrumentals.

Between tours and sessions with Elvis, Burton's studio work continued much as before. Though in areas such as Nashville studio musicians who weren't always available because of their touring often found themselves losing work, this didn't seem to effect Burton, who remained in demand. Among the records he worked on during this time were Michael Nesmith's Nevada Fighter (1971), Joni Mitchell's For the Roses (1972) and Phil Everly's Star Spangled Springer (1973). Also, in 1972 he began working with Gram Parsons, the former Byrd and founding member of the Flying Burrito Brothers, who was embarking on a solo career. Parsons' knowledge of traditional country music was considerable, and played an enormous influence on the Byrds when they waxed their 1968 Sweetheart of the Rodeo album. After leaving, he recorded the superb Flying Burrito Brothers, and after leaving the Burritos established himself as a solo artist.

But Burton began working with Parsons between Elvis' tours, on his first, outstanding Grievous Angel (1972) and GP (1973), playing dobro and Telecaster. Much of what Burton played was straight out of his sessions with Merle Haggard, particularly on "Kiss the Children." He also essayed some shimmering, rhythmic chord punctuations on Gram's mournfully evocative ballad "She." On the r&b flavored "Cry One More Time" James played a pungent solo that crossed T-Bone Walker's playing with his own style, and he attacked his solo on "Big Mouth Blues" with muscular ferocity.

Amid critical acclaim for Grievous Angel, for Gram's backup vocalist Emmylou Harris, and with good things ahead, Parsons pushed his drug use too far while out in the California desert and died in September 1974 of a drug overdose. The shaken Harris emerged as the musical focal point, and Burton, between tours with Elvis, joined Parsons' former band, soon to be dubbed the Hot Band. He worked on Emmylou's superlative 1974 album Pieces of the Sky, playing one of his most beautiful solos on her waltz-time ballad "Too Far Gone." His Elvis commitment finally forced him to leave the Hot Band, but he had established the Telecaster sound there, and that continued as Albert Lee, Frank Reckard and Barry Tashian followed in Burton's place.

He remained on the road with Elvis, and as drug addiction took its toll on both Elvis' body and his performances, James became one of the few constants, his crackling guitar breaks impressive even when Elvis himself was not. Burton was in Maine with the rest of Elvis' group, waiting for Elvis to fly in for a show, the afternoon the star died. Though the death devastated James, he plunged back into recording with Jesse Winchester on his *Nothin' but the Breeze* album (1977), with vocalist Nicolette Larson (1978) and with former Hot Band bassist/songwriter Rodney Crowell. He toured and recorded with, of all people, John Denver, and continued working on Emmylou Harris' albums.

Today, James Burton still divides his time between touring and session work. He and some of the members of Presley's TCB Band (Taking Care of Business—a Presley organization motto) have recorded, in some cases backing Elvis-inspired artists, and in 1984 Burton joined forces with rockabilly legend Jerry Lee Lewis.

James Burton has inspired an entire generation of rock and country-rock guitarists, ever since he ripped those nasty riffs out of his guitar on Dale Hawkins' "Suzie Q." His playing sounded 20 years ahead of its time in 1955, and the consistency of his musical vision in such disparate contexts over nearly 30 years is a tribute to the solidity and inventiveness of the original Telecaster wild man.

DISCOGRAPHY

Regrettably, James Burton's early work with Dale Hawkins (including both takes of "Suzie Q") is available on *Dale Hawkins* (Chess). However, much of his best recording with Rick Nelson is available on *The Ricky Nelson Singles Album* (British United Artists), *Rick Nelson* (Legendary Masters Series-Liberty), and *The Decca Years* (MCA). He can be heard particularly well on Elvis Presley's *In Person at the International Hotel* (RCA), recorded in 1969, and on all Elvis' albums from 1969 to 1977. His solo albums are out of print, but he can be heard on the Emmylou Harris albums mentioned in the essay. In truth, one could fill an entire book on the albums—in and out of print—that he played on. The Burton/Ralph Mooney *Corn Pickin' And Slick Slidin'* has recently been reissued by French EMI.

ERIC CLAPTON

At the same time Michael Bloomfield was flattening listeners with his work on the first Paul Butterfield Band album, Eric Clapton, a young British guitarist who had absorbed America's blues was doing the same thing in England as lead guitarist with John Mayall's Bluesbreakers. If Bloomfield shrunk from the spotlight following the internal problems that ruined his Electric Flag in 1969, Clapton's influence and stature were only beginning to grow.

In Britain, it became routine to find "Clapton Is God" graffiti around London, and though guitar stars were nothing new in England (the Shadows' Hank B. Marvin had enjoyed popularity for years), with Clapton the adulation was serious, on par with bebop fans' love of Charlie Parker. Clapton's reputation began to spread across the Atlantic to the U.S., but his most enormous impact came not with Mayall but with Cream, the so-called "supergroup" that rocketed him to international fame. He became the first Guitar God of Rock, followed soon after by Jimi Hendrix.

That Clapton himself never felt comfortable with this role became clear, particularly after Cream disbanded and Blind Faith, an even more eagerly awaited "supergroup," flamed out amid hype and unrealistically high expectations. Though his status remained considerable, Clapton began to withdraw from the rarified atmosphere he was in, trying to reaffirm his love of working in a band as opposed to dominating one.

It seemed that the minute expectations were lowered Clapton played music with more substance and creativity, for some of his most enduring work came in the post-Cream/Blind Faith period. This isn't to say he was totally successful during that time, however. A severe problem with heroin nearly wrecked him in the 1970s before he pulled himself out of it. However, in the end Clapton triumphed, and though his later music has lacked consistency, he has become a better rounded performer, capable of sustaining interest on more than one level. He's also become an effective vocalist, while retaining his outstanding guitarist touch. Clapton's most recent music remains rooted in the blues, which is a touchstone that revitalizes him.

Stylistically, Clapton has taken much of his inspiration from the T-Bone Walker-B.B. King school of blues guitar, and at Eric's best echoes of Freddy King and Otis Rush (particularly the former) can be heard. But Hubert Sumlin, the late Howlin' Wolf's longtime guitarist, has also exerted a profound influence on him. Though Clapton could recreate various blues solos almost note-for-note, it's to Clapton's credit that he uses them primarily as a jumping-off point, unlike so many foreign guitarists who slavishly imitated their favorite bluesmen (one such extreme example was former Fleetwood Mac guitarist Jeremy Spencer, an immensely talented musician, who spent several years in his early career copying Elmore James' solos, to the point where he even learned how to play James' fluffed notes). Clapton never fell into this rut. If he had, it's doubtful his career would have reached the heights it has.

Clapton today can be disappointing; several of his more recent albums have missed the boat. Yet his place in rock and roll is secure, and along with Paul Butterfield and Michael Bloomfield, he deserves credit for readily acknowledging the bluesmen who inspired him. In some cases this gave them much needed financial help (Clapton, while with Cream, made sure country blues legend Skip James got much-needed songwriting royalties from "I'm So Glad" before his death) or recognition that energized their careers. Freddie King, for example, found his audiences expanding beyond the chitlin circuit into progressive rock clubs, as did B.B. King, Albert King, Otis Rush, Muddy Waters and many others following the young, white guitarists' attentions.

Born in Ripley, Surrey on April 30, 1945, Clapton seemingly had no special interest in music until he first heard Chuck Berry when he was 17. From there Eric embraced Buddy Holly, and gradually immersed himself in rock and roll. He gradually expanded his interest to the blues while he attended Kingston Art College (art school has been the first stop for a surprising number of rock stars). He took the guitar seriously enough to move towards music in 1963 with a band known as the Roosters. That August he joined another blues-oriented group called Casey Jones and the Engineers. Within a month or two he'd joined the Yardbirds, then the replacement band for the Rolling Stones at the famous Crawdaddy Club in London.

In 1964 the Yardbirds began recording for England's Columbia Records, and along with two singles came *Five Live Yardbirds*, a live recording done at London's Marquee Club. If Clapton showed any promise, it wasn't apparent on this material. He appeared to be an overeager, sloppy amateur, with little understanding of the soloist's role. The few breaks he took were immature and pointless, more appropriate for a 12-year-old garage band guitarist than a professional rocker. His solo lines were ill-defined, limited to disjointed hot licks that reflected no coherent musical vision and much awkwardness.

However, Eric was delving deeper into the blues at a time when the Yardbirds were moving towards greater pop involvement. Eric was drinking in B.B. and Freddy King and Robert Johnson. The Yardbirds' new commercial direction clearly displeased him, and though he played on the band's hit single "For Your Love," he was out of the group by March 1965. Within two weeks, bandleader John Mayall offered him the lead guitarist's slot in his band the Bluesbreakers.

Mayall's recording history was as spotty as Clapton's at that point. His first album, *John Mayall Plays John Mayall*, issued in 1964 with lead guitarist Roger Dean, was American frat house rock rather than blues. Clapton stayed with Mayall for four months, took a brief leave, then returned. And the Clapton/Mayall combination finally began to jell. Clapton's playing had taken a 180-degree turn. Though he was playing carelessly with the Yardbirds, he now showed incredible confidence and true emotional commitment to his music. This was obvious not long after Clapton rejoined Mayall, when they recorded some casual numbers for the Immediate label. Produced by Jimmy Page, the tracks revealed a strong musical partnership; Clapton contributed unison riffs behind Mayall's vocal on "I'm Your Witchdoctor." But his growth was even more evident on "Telephone Blues," where his Freddy King-styled solo carried real authority, and his sense of phrasing was definitely improved over his Yardbirds period (even if it *was* still developing). Some other tapes, done with no intention of releasing them, featured Clapton and Page together, along with Mick Jagger on harmonica, Bill Wyman on bass, a drummer and the Rolling Stones' road manager Ian Stewart on piano.

These tapes show Clapton's increasing mastery of several blues styles. "Snake Drive" is a copy of Chuck Berry's "Deep Feeling"; "West Coast Idea" features Freddie King's concepts, while "Tribute to Elmore," a Page/Clapton jam, offers some ill-conceived James licks and some more Freddy King ideas. Page also produced a better-than-average "Sittin' on Top of the World" with Mayall and Clapton—not the blues classic, but a rock number with some interesting use of feedback by Clapton, anticipating some of his work with Cream. The pair also recreated a late '40s Chicago blues sound with "Bernard Jenkins" and "Lonely Years," though both were somewhat contrived.

The other Clapton-Page tracks are of peripheral interest compared to the first Clapton-Mayall collaboration, *Bluesbreakers with Eric Clapton*.

Clapton's development as a guitarist had been nothing short of amazing, as he proved with his stunning work on Otis Rush's "All Your Love." Rush clearly inspired him, but the power and conviction in his solo was his own. He followed with a supercharged version of Freddie King's instrumental "Hideaway." Though Clapton often copied King's lines, the fire and passion of this recording was anything but contrived. And it continued through his thick-toned (he was using a Gibson Les Paul) solos on "Double Crossing Time" and his exquisite work on "Have You Heard," a B.B. King-style slow blues written by Mayall. Clapton slid up and down the neck, playing jarring, vibrato-laden licks behind the vocal and letting loose with a cathartic, occasionally busy but nonetheless com-

pelling solo. He also performed a low-keyed solo version of Robert Johnson's "Ramblin' on My Mind," featuring his first, shyly sung, solo vocal. "Steppin' Out," the James Bracken number, demonstrates Clapton's gift for making a song his own. His furious, driving lines are virile, and the song became one he would play into his days with Cream.

Onstage with Mayall Clapton was thrilling audiences, and "Clapton Is God" was being written on walls. Some April 1966 live tapes, issued in the late '70s as one side of a Mayall album, display a white blues soloist rivaled only by Bloomfield. Clapton, despite having heard relatively little blues live, had an understanding of the idiom that translated into an individual style. He made creative use of feedback before Jimi Hendrix became widely known, substantiating that he was not interested in becoming merely a good copyist. His playing on "Have You Ever Loved a Woman" (another song that remained in his repertoire) and Muddy Waters' "Hoochie Koochie Man" remain valid nearly two decades after they were first recorded. Clapton was becoming famous, but three months later, in July, he left Mayall. Former Mayall bassist Jack Bruce and former Graham Bond Organization drummer Ginger Baker united with Eric in a blues-oriented trio to further explore the music. They dubbed their group Cream and began to attract interest almost immediately.

Cream's first recording had its share of problems. There were tunes like "I Feel Free" and "Dreamin'" that had no tangible purpose for being (though the former became a top-20 hit in Britain). It appeared from the wretched material that dominated *Fresh Cream*, their first album (on Atco), that the band had little going for it—except for two tracks that delineated its future: "Cat's Squirrel" and "Rollin' and Tumblin'." The former tune, originally done by bluesman "Dr." Isiah Ross, featured an unrelenting modal sound consisting of two chords, some driving guitar choruses from Clapton and harsh harmonica from Bruce. "Rollin' and Tumblin'" was based on a 1929 Hambone Willie Newburn blues that had figured in a number of bluesmen's repertoires, but Cream's version was clearly based on a 1950 rendition by Chicago bluesman Baby Face Leroy with Muddy Waters on guitar. Though Clapton solos little, he evokes Waters' slide guitar savagery with astonishing accuracy.

Still, *Fresh Cream* showed little evidence of their improvisational gifts. The second album, 1967's *Disraeli Gears* was another matter entirely. Here the band had become a cohesive whole, and Clapton's playing achieved a smooth flow and tonal qualities that made it as flexible as a voice. Though he had to overdub on many of the tracks, the album fulfilled Cream's initial promise. "Strange Brew" was one example; though Clapton's solo bears the clear imprint of Albert King (particularly in his string-choking) his sound is now his own, with blues at its root. On "Sunshine of Your Love" Clapton devised a highly commercial riff (that subsequently became a rock music cliche) around which the song was constructed. Clapton also was working with electronic effects such as wah-wah pedals that no self-respecting bluesman would have used at the time. Some of the songs were trendy and lightweight, such as Clapton's own "Tales of Brave Ulysses"—he did get off strong solos—still, the blues content remained heavy. "Take It Back" was based on the famous Elmore James riff, and "Outside Woman Blues," though it began with Clapton playing the well known lick from Wilson Pickett's hit "Funky Broadway," was otherwise based on Delta bluesman Blind Willie Reynolds' 1930 original (titled "Married Man Blues"), right down to the guitar riff at the end of each stanza. Clapton was amplified; that was the only difference.

Disraeli Gears established Cream, and became one of the symbols of the psychedelic era which was then in full bloom. The band became legendary for its 20-plus minute onstage jams, dominated by Clapton's freewheeling improvisations, now played on a rainbow-hued Gibson SG Standard. In 1968 came an unprecedented double album, *Wheels of Fire*, that supplemented studio cuts with live recordings. The studio tracks had their moments, but were often mediocre com-

positions, made worse by Jack Bruce's pretentiously melodramatic vocals. Clapton did manage some respectable solo work on the blues-oriented tunes. Cream's version of Albert King's "Born Under a Bad Sign" proved just how closely Eric had listened to Albert, as well as B.B. and Freddy—not to mention Wolf's guitarist Sumlin. But it was on the live stuff, especially "Crossroads" (which became a classic), and "Spoonful" that his onstage improvisational abilities came through. Not all of it holds up well today, but the best of *Wheels of Fire* solidified Clapton's reputation on both sides of the Atlantic.

Unfortunately, there were conflicts in the band. Baker and Bruce had a contentious personal relationship, and when *Rolling Stone* magazine's senior critic Jon Landau referred to Clapton as "a master of the blues cliches of all the post World War II blues guitarists" in the May 11, 1968 issue, Clapton was devastated by the comment and realized the group had to end. That November, after an unsatisfying album titled, appropriately enough, *Goodbye,* Cream disbanded.

Clapton, always a sensitive person, agonized through a reappraisal of his music. He disliked the virtuoso guitarist label intensely, and had been inspired by The Band's *Music from Big Pink* album. He wanted to see himself less as a virtuoso and more as a member of a cohesive unit. In early 1969 Clapton, Baker, keyboardist/vocalist Steve Winwood and bassist Rik Grech formed another "supergroup" to be known as Blind Faith. They raised fans' expectations, but split up by early 1970 after one American tour despite a promising debut album, in part because the excess hype made them all uncomfortable.

Session work had also taken up some of Clapton's time through the Cream-Blind Faith period. Around 1968 he contributed a wrenching solo on Aretha Franklin's "Good to Me as I Am to You" on her *Lady Soul* LP. He also played on "While My Guitar Gently Weeps" on the Beatles' *White Album*, and on Jackie Lomax's first Apple single. Late in 1969 he traveled to Canada as part of John Lennon's Plastic Ono Band for the Toronto Peace Festival. On the album *Live Peace in*

Toronto Clapton played spirited solos on "Blue Suede Shoes" and "Yer Blues." But he still was looking for a situation with less pressure to be a virtuoso.

Delaney & Bonnie and Friends provided him with that respite. In January, 1970 Eric began working with the Memphis r&b styled group after enjoying the Bramlett's company on the Blind Faith tour. Under the influence of Delaney Bramlett, Clapton began taking singing more seriously. With this aggregation, he appeared on a live set, *On Tour*, that featured little truly impressive music. Bramlett also produced *Eric Clapton*, the guitar hero's first solo album, dominated by Clapton's guitar and vocals in the soul/gospel context favored by Delaney and Bonnie. Eric's guitar was secondary, though the instrumental "Slunky" is a tight, well-focused piece of rock and roll. One cut from the album, "After Midnight," became a hit single.

In May 1970 Clapton decided to head his own ensemble. He took organist Bobby Whitlock, bassist Carl Radle and drummer Jim Gordon from the Bramlett's Friends band to form Derek and the Dominos, which recorded that summer in Miami. Part way through the sessions Clapton met the then-ascending Allman Brothers Band. Eric and Duane Allman got along so well that Duane was added to the sessions, and their music was awesome. Allman's knifing articulate slide guitar created a synergy between him and Clapton that built to a fever pitch. *Layla*, among Clapton's (and Allman's) finest moments on record, was the result.

Playing in top form on the double album with Duane's brilliant assistance, Clapton found his own voice, as a singer, songwriter and guitarist. Though his licks were blues-inspired, they could no longer be traced to individual old blues records. "Anyday," "Why Does Love Have to Be So Sad?," "Tell the Truth," "Key to the Highway" and "Have You Ever Loved a Woman" all burned from start to finish. And the title track, "Layla," remains one of the finest creations in early 1970s rock, a beautifully crafted piece in which impassioned vocal and flawless guitar merge to become truly moving music. It was Clapton's own, deeply personal blues, which many analysts have related to his deep feelings for George Harrison's then-wife, Patti.

The Dominoes' potential was tested no further, however. In April, 1971 they split, and except for two isolated appearances, Clapton retreated into himself. His well-documented dependency on heroin sent him into a tailspin from which he nearly didn't recover. It wasn't until January 1973, with the help of the Who's Pete Townshend, that Eric returned to the stage. *Eric Clapton's Rainbow Concert*, featuring a backing band of Steve Winwood, Townshend, Ron Wood and Jim Capaldi among others, had more good intentions than good music. By 1974 Clapton was ready to try again, and came out with *461 Ocean Boulevard*. Eric was leading a tight new band but was no longer dependent solely on his guitar legend to carry things along. Blues forms still mattered (he reprised gospel and r&b tunes including "Motherless Children" and Johnny Otis' "Willie and the Hand Jive"). His wide-angle rendition of the reggae tune "I Shot the Sheriff" hit number one on the American charts.

Other albums followed, some excellent, some off the mark or with only a couple of excellent guitar tracks. His fluent dobro work on "Jesus Coming Soon" marked the 1975 *There's One in Every Crowd* (Clapton declared he was a Christian during this period). *E.C. Was Here* was a throwback to guitar-oriented music, with some of the most intense blues playing he'd recorded since his days with Mayall. "Have You Ever Loved a Woman" was an exhilarating performance as Clapton and his regular second guitarist George Terry traded choruses. "Rambling on My Mind," the Robert Johnson tune he did with Mayall, was reconstructed in a deeper, darker mold than it had in 1965. Though his calling out of key changes was somewhat distracting, Clapton was playing so well it didn't really matter. If putting his guitar out front had previously bothered him, it didn't seem to here. However, little that Eric played reflected any tangible growth or change, fine as his guitar was.

Inconsistency remained characteristic of

him. *No Reason to Cry*, his 1976 effort, was mediocre despite the presence of Bob Dylan and three members of The Band. *Slowhand*, released in 1977, was just the opposite, featuring such material as a tight, well-honed version of J.J. Cale's "Cocaine" that had some well-controlled guitar. "Lay Down Sally," the Don Williams number, got a sparse rockabilly arrangement (it hit number three in America late that year). "The Core" also featured driving guitar work from Clapton and Terry. *Backless*, issued in 1978, was of only minimal interest.

The Clapton band, which had remained static for several years, began to evolve. Albert Lee, Emmylou Harris' formidable guitarist, joined up, which provided Clapton with an equally established partner to play off of. The first album with the newer group (with former Joe Cocker Grease band member Chris Stainton on keyboards) was *Just One Night*, a 1980 double LP recorded live in Japan. Though Lee and he did well, Clapton was not quite up to standard. *Another Ticket*, released in 1981, was somewhat improved. There were country tunes ("Black Rose" by Troy Seals) and blues (a stomping version of Muddy Waters' "Blow, Wind Blow") with some pleasant, if not exactly startling guitar work. "Catch Me If You Can" and "Rita Mae" offered similar instrumental interaction. Clapton's most recent set, *Money and Cigarettes*, issued in 1983, is another lukewarm effort.

For the moment, it seems that Eric Clapton has backed out of the spotlight as a guitarist. Perhaps he'll emerge again in the future and achieve some sort of preeminence, but there's no guarantee of that. He has, after all, left a body of work of considerable size behind him, the best of which has had a dramatic effect on rock music. Aside from interesting more young white rock fans in the blues, he helped make the rock guitarist an artist worth taking seriously. The concepts he worked with in Cream inspired similar rock power trios (some good—most not so hot) and even heavy metal. Whatever happens from here on with Eric Clapton's music, his importance is beyond debate.

DISCOGRAPHY
Some of Clapton's early work with the Yardbirds is available on a variety of inexpensive budget albums (too many to list here). The essential material from the British blues anthologies is available on the *White Boys Blues* double LP (Compleat). John Mayall's *Bluesbreakers with Eric Clapton* has been reissued on London, and another album, *Primal Solos* (London), includes some stunning live material with Mayall.

All of the Cream LPs are available on Polydor at this time, including two post-breakup sets: *Live Cream* and *Best of Cream*.

Likewise, all of his solo albums as well as *Layla* are easily found on the RSO label, including *History of Eric Clapton*, an overview of his career from the mid '60s to his early solo efforts, which are *Eric Clapton, Derek and the Dominos in Concert, Eric Clapton's Rainbow Concert, No Reason to Cry, 461 Ocean Boulevard, There's One in Every Crowd, E.C. Was Here, Just One Night, Another Ticket*, and *Money and Cigarettes*.

JIMI HENDRIX

Jimi Hendrix's impact on the electric guitar, and rock guitar in general, can only be compared to that of Charlie Christian's upon jazz guitar in the early '40s. Where other players took conservative approaches to their instruments, using only a fraction of the guitar's capabilities, Hendrix wrung every sound imaginable out of his Fender Stratocasters. He coaxed seemingly impossible sounds from them. In the process, he expanded everyone's perception of the instrument; after Hendrix, it was never again simply a vehicle for straight melody and rhythm work. It was the transcendant rock instrument, capable of just about anything.

Hendrix understood the sounds he could create, and rarely used them as mere gimmicks. Every effect he used was aimed at enhancing and deepening the mood or imagery of his songs.

Amazingly, he never relied on effects, and many amateur guitarists who use racks full of accessories get only half the results he did with just a fuzztone, a stack of amps and a device to simulate a rotating Leslie organ speaker.

Many of Hendrix's most impressive sounds were done merely with his fingers or through the manipulation of his Strat's vibrato mechanism (which many contemporary guitarists call the twang bar).

John Morthland, in *The Rolling Stone Illustrated Encyclopedia of Rock and Roll*, writes that Hendrix "simply redefined how that instrument could be played." That is of course correct, but further, Hendrix symbolized both the best and the worst of the '60s, of the so-called Flower children, and of the guitar style known as "psychedelic." In fact, re-listening to many of the guitarists of that era, only a handful—Clapton, Beck, Page, Bloomfield, Allman, Hendrix and a couple of others—hold up after nearly two decades. Looking back, much of the playing during that time was sloppy and self-indulgent. It lacked finesse and often made up in volume what it lacked in musical value. Hendrix, on the other hand, still sounds relatively fresh and only rarely dated.

One of the great problems with Hendrix's sadly brief period at the top is that much of his most beautiful music was eclipsed by his flamboyant image. People saw a wildly dressed, blatantly sexual black man on stage. "Psychedelic badass" was only one of the images created for him. His actions in performance, from burning his Strat at the 1967 Monterey International Pop Festival to jamming his guitar between his thighs like a grossly exaggerated phallus, certainly confirmed the role. Later on, he became disillusioned with this kind of grotesque theater. Yet in his greatest period of popularity it was a drawing card, even though such antics were mere window dressing having little relevance to his music.

The truth is that music was one of the few constants in Hendrix's life; it vitalized and defined him. His obsession with the guitar started early, as it did for so many of the others in this book; his roots were in '50s rock and roll and '60s rhythm and blues, two styles that remained important to him throughout his career. Bob Dylan became his hero, as did practically every bluesman of any consequence. Their work all showed up in his repertoire at one time or another. And some aspects of the r&b tunes he played with the Isley Brothers, Curtis Knight and others remained with him through his greatest music, in form if not actual songs. Regardless of how far into new territory Hendrix journeyed, he never repudiated or denied his past, but instead integrated roots and new concepts into a cohesive whole.

The tragedy, of course, is that Hendrix didn't live long enough to grow into greater things. His indulgences were legendary; booze, drugs, women—he overdid them all, creating incredible music in spite of it, just as saxophonist Charlie Parker had done 25 years before anyone ever heard of Hendrix. What would have become of him is a matter of debate to this day, and nobody can ever say for sure. But like Django Reinhardt or Charlie Parker, the legacy of Jimi Hendrix has yet to fade, and the ideas in his music will be explored, imitated, juxtaposed and analyzed in as many different ways as there are people to play guitar or listen to him.

Johnny Allan Hendrix was born in Seattle,

Washington on December 27, 1942, the son of Al and Lucille Hendrix, professional tapdancers. Al was in the service at the time of his son's birth, and Lucille left the boy with relatives in the San Francisco area. Hendrix separated from his wife and by 1946 altered his son's name legally to James Marshall Hendrix, in honor of the elder Hendrix's deceased brother.

When he was seven, James Hendrix was sent to live briefly with relatives, while his parents attempted a reconciliation. Al Hendrix tried his best to keep his family together on very little money (Lucille died in the late '50s). In the mid '50s Jimmy began playing a ukelele and graduated to guitar, which he played left-handed. As he got interested, his dad scraped enough money together to buy him an electric. He had started playing at an opportune time; rock and roll was surging in popularity in the wake of Elvis Presley, and both rock and rhythm and blues were as near at hand as the radio. Jimmy took in both styles, and was soon playing with other kids in smalltime rock bands.

Somebody stole his first guitar at a gig, so he had to borrow instruments, and according to Jerry Hopkins in *Hit and Run: the Jimi Hendrix Story,* Jimmy borrowed guitars strung for normal right-handed playing. He learned to play right-handed instruments left-handed, and did so for the rest of his life. He played through high school, but discovered another pastime: breaking into stores with friends. He graduated from that to joyriding in "borrowed" cars. He was arrested once, in May of 1961 when he was 18, for such an incident, then was nailed by the Seattle police four days afterward for a similar offense. The judge who handled the case was taken aback by this record, and not wanting to send him to jail, made the then-common suggestion that Jimmy join the service as an alternative. Hendrix agreed, and was in the Army within a month.

The Army did his free-spirited attitude little good, particularly since he chose the paratroopers as his goal. It was something he clearly wanted, but he was also obsessed with his guitar (by then he'd adopted the Fender

Strat) and spent every bit of spare time playing it, which made him an oddball among his peers. Though he made it in the paratroopers he broke his leg in 1962, which prompted his early discharge. He was free to return to music, which is precisely what he did. Along with bass player Billy Cox, discharged at the same time, Hendrix began working around central Tennessee with r&b groups.

He moved around the U.S. with a variety of low-budget groups, dressed in a flashy short dinner jacket, looking like other musicians except for the right-handed guitar he played left-handed. By 1963 he was working with the legendary singer/pianist Little Richard, one of the most important rock performers of the era. Hendrix's pay was lousy, but certainly he was impressed by Richard's flamboyant, explosive style and his ability to excite an audience.

Eventually Hendrix freelanced with many other r&b performers. There was no glory in this, just the opportunity to play music. He listened to the blues players he heard on the r&b package tours, many of whom were fading at that time but still capable of making music rich with ideas that he could work into his own musical vision. He worked with the Isley Brothers, with Solomon Burke, and by 1965 had joined r&b artist Curtis Knight in New York City. Jimmy cut his first recordings in Los Angeles in 1963, and was taped with Little Richard and the Isley Brothers; his extensive recordings with Knight hinted at his developing style. Many of these recordings came back to haunt him after he became famous, but he was kicking in licks of his own—the rapidfire flurries of notes and feedback that were to become his trademark can be heard on them.

Hendrix was listening to Bob Dylan, and was inspired to try singing. Les Paul and his son heard him in a New Jersey club, but were unable to track him down when they returned there. It turned out Jimmy had been auditioning but given his wildly unorthodox style (he was playing guitar with his teeth on that occasion) and high volume, hadn't made the cut. For his part, he was tiring of playing such joints anyway. Under the pseudonym Jimmy

James he formed a band in New York City known as the Blue Flames and managed to get a job at the Cafe Wha? in Greenwich Village. He hung around the Village through 1965 and '66, finding refuge in its free-spirited atmosphere. And he didn't have the Cafe Wha? job long before he met white blues singer John Paul Hammond Jr., the son of the discoverer of Charlie Christian, Dylan and many other jazz and rock legends. Hammond recognized Hendrix's potential; after some interim jamming, he was added to Hammond's backup band as lead guitarist. Hammond's reputation being respectable, Hendrix suddenly became the guitarist to hear in the Village. Even Michael Bloomfield, himself becoming a legend, heard Hendrix play with Hammond and was floored.

Among others who caught Hendrix with Hammond were members of the Rolling Stones and the Animals. A woman named Linda Keith, who traveled in the social circles surrounding the Stones and who'd previously met Hendrix, brought Animals bassist Chas Chandler to hear him. Chandler instantly saw the potential that many of the r&b performers had been blind to.

Chandler immediately made plans to get Hendrix to England, but spent time determining Jimi's current contractual obligations and obtaining the necessary information to get a passport. In September 1966 both men arrived in London, and Chandler began building an image for Hendrix. Guitar heroes were becoming fashionable in the wake of Bloomfield, and Cream was just getting started. Chandler's understanding of coming trends was crucial in introducing Hendrix at the optimum time.

His first appearances in London were impromptu, as he had no work permit of any sort. During September and October he showed up with his guitar at the right clubs until his reputation had spread throughout London. Nobody—not Clapton, not Jimmy Page, not Jeff Beck—was doing anything even remotely like him. By that time, his name had been shortened to "Jimi." Auditions were held for a backing band to consist of only bass and drums, the better to highlight

Hendrix's playing. Noel Redding was selected as the bassist, in part for his abilities to work with Hendrix (a guitarist himself, Redding understood Jimi's playing) and Mitch Mitchell was hired as drummer. There followed a slow period, but by late 1966 the group known as the Jimi Hendrix Experience had a recording contract and was beginning to assemble an album. Hendrix's first single was a demo of "Hey, Joe," a modest hit for a California band called the Leaves. Where the Leaves' version was frantic, Hendrix slowed it down, giving it a bluesy edge not apparent in their recording and playing up the inherent violence of the lyrics. His guitar, however, dominated the record (it took him a while to gain confidence in his singing), even though his brief solo was relatively conservative compared to his later work.

Polydor Records thought little of the single it issued in early 1967, but in any case Hendrix had a recording contract with the Who's label, Track Records. "Hey Joe" became a top ten hit in England, and as Chandler had hoped, Hendrix's reputation began to take off. His first album, *Are You Experienced?* released that spring, was a far better measure of Jimi's abilities. From the first notes of "Foxy Lady," its feedback embellished by Hendrix fretting his strings without picking them and leading into the power chords of the song, it was clear that his approach to the guitar was total. The album was a revelation—here was a guitarist with a solid command of the blues idiom, but who chose to take it to new, undreamed-of dimensions. He was brash, yet at the same time was rife with subtleties, such as his unison licks at the beginning of his solo on "Manic Depression."

"Red House" underscored his authenticity as a bluesman. A pure blues, it had all the flavor of those late '40s recording sessions featuring Baby Face Leroy, Muddy Waters and Little Walter that helped define the postwar Chicago sound. From Jimi's opening riff this was as honest a performance as was ever recorded. His playing was based on Muddy's and B.B. King's and Otis Rush's styles, yet it was seamless and beautifully articulated. Even after a decade and a half, the track rings

with a timeless quality that could have placed his lyrics back in the Mississippi delta of the '30s. Surprisingly, this track was left off the U.S. release of *Are You Experienced?*

He created undulating guitar textures on other numbers, among them "Love or Confusion" and "I Don't Live Today." "Fire" sounded like a leftover from his r&b days, and he was beginning to develop his badass image through spoken asides ("Comin' to *gitcha!*" on "Foxy Lady"). But the substance was clearly there. "Third Stone from the Sun" remains a sublime piece of modern jazz, with Jimi playing in octaves a la Wes Montgomery before moving into free improvisations and oddly appropriate snippets of spoken verse. His use of feedback bespoke his remarkable sense of control.

Shortly after the album was released, Hendrix returned to America with the Experience to participate in an event that was to become a watershed in American music: the Monterey Pop Festival. The Beatles' *Sgt. Pepper's Lonely Hearts Club Band* album had just been released; San Francisco was gaining prominence as a counter culture center and rock, for the first time, was being taken seriously as an art form. It was an exciting period in American music, with many bands—the Byrds, Canned Heat, the Electric Flag, Big Brother and the Holding Company, the Jefferson Airplane and others—at the peak of their powers. Hendrix performed on the final night of the festival—June 18, 1967—dressed in a far wilder outfit than in his days on the r&b circuit. He played across the spectrum—B.B. King's "Rock Me Baby," "Can You See Me" from the first (British) Experience album, then an awesome performance of Bob Dylan's "Like a Rolling Stone" and finally the Troggs' hit "Wild Thing," with its power chords a totally appropriate ending. The crowd was ecstatic, and Jimi demonstrated his showmanship by pouring lighter fluid on his Strat, lighting it and smashing it on the stage, a stunt he'd pulled in England.

Still, he got a mixed reaction. Critics disliked what they felt was hamboning, though Hendrix's show solidified his reputation in America. *Axis: Bold as Love*, his second album, was highly uneven. Jimi had a command of the wah-wah pedal, as he proved on "Up from the Skies," letting it ripple behind his Mose Allison-styled vocal. "Little Wing," which remains one of his most beautiful and enduring ballads, had simple, unencumbered guitar chords reminiscent of Curtis Mayfield framing Hendrix's vocal. Yet there was also much pointless material. "EXP," the opening dialogue, was silly. "You Got Me Floatin'" was trite and "If Six Was Nine" was simplistic '60s foolishness that doesn't hold up well. Still, *Axis* became a massive hit when it was released in early 1968.

Hendrix's star rose as it became clear that he, more than any other rock guitarist at the time, was blazing some radical new trails on the guitar. Clapton, Jeff Beck, and Bloomfield all were important, but none was as daring as Hendrix. If his psychedelic act had its share of affectation, his playing did not. His image would eventually get to him, to the point he began toning it down in favor of his music. But that did not happen yet.

In September came *Electric Ladyland*, Jimi's most ambitious effort. The album itself took months to assemble, in part due to what Jimi was trying to accomplish, in part due to his increasing abuse of liquor and drugs.

Though it, too, had its pretentious moments, much of the *Ladyland* album revealed his ability to use the studio as an instrument, in the same manner as the Beatles had done with *Sgt. Pepper*. Again, the mix of gutty blues, r&b, psychedelia and driving rock resulted in some incredible performances. There was "Voodoo Chile," a song based on Muddy Waters' "Rolling Stone" (a structure Hendrix borrowed more than once). With Steve Winwood playing tasty organ fills and Jack Casady playing bass, Jimi brought the dark delta malevolence into the '60s, punctuating it with an effective vocal and stunning, fluid guitar. He reached into his r&b past for Earl King's "Come On (Part 1)." He played many flashy, dizzying runs, but his two-chord strumming built the excitement as much as anything, proving he didn't have to rely on flashy technique for effect.

Hendrix's overdubbing helped him to create great textures, playing some lines in harmony, others with heavy fuzztone or with no effects. "Little Miss Strange," featuring a wretched Noel Redding vocal, is saved by Jimi's technique. "Gypsy Eyes" is a solid rocker; though he kicked it off a la Muddy Waters' "Rollin' and Tumblin'," it also featured a doubletracked vocal recalling John Lee Hooker. His version of Bob Dylan's "All Along the Watchtower" featured more memorable guitar work and became better known than Dylan's own version. He played too repetitively on "Still Raining, Still Dreaming," an in-studio jam, but the overall effect was nonetheless exhilarating because of the vocal sounds Hendrix could elicit from his instrument enhanced by wah-wah. "Crosstown Traffic" was largely a rhythm number, as was "House Burning Down," which had a fair amount of "Foxy Lady" in it. The album may have been pasted together, but it managed to function as a cohesive whole and established Hendrix as the pre-eminent rock guitarist of the period.

Hendrix's new-found stature brought with it problems. A label he'd signed with before meeting Chandler issued some of his material with Curtis Knight. After court fights it turned out Hendrix owed the production company another LP, so he didn't record for nearly a year.

Early in 1969 Jimi recorded his outrageous version of "The Star Spangled Banner" (later released on *Rainbow Bridge*), a performance that exhibits the totality of his playing. He created unheard-of effects—the sounds of bombs, tanks and aircraft seemed to roar out of his guitar. He piled up layer upon layer of effects that reflected his own version and vision of America. At the time the Vietnam war had polarized the nation, and this was perhaps as definitive a musical protest as anyone could have created.

Meanwhile, Hendrix had other problems. On May 3, 1969 he was arrested in Toronto, Canada for possession of heroin, found on him by Mounties called in by customs officers (he beat the charges that December). There were a variety of professional difficulties, too. He restructured his band, replacing Noel

Redding (now working with his own band) with his old army buddy, bassist Billy Cox; former Wilson Pickett and Electric Flag drummer Buddy Miles replaced Mitch Mitchell.

Hendrix also spent more time at a Woodstock, New York country retreat where he jammed with musicians through the summer, trying to create what he called an "electric sky church," which would feature players of varying styles behind Hendrix's musical visions. It was a good idea, but the only place he got to put it to use was at the Woodstock Festival that August, when he closed the weekend-long show on a Monday morning with a second (and still legendary performance) of "The Star Spangled Banner."

Gradually, he decided to return to a trio format, using Cox and Miles; they debuted on New Year's Eve at New York's Fillmore East. The concert was taped to fulfill the one album still owed under Jimi's old recording contract. His group, the Band of Gypsies, did a decidedly mixed show. Their leadoff, "Who Knows," was apparently marred by a badly out-of-tune guitar, and was next to useless. Hendrix's next number, "Machine Gun," was far improved, and, in fact, is one of his most memorable performances. The blues form was still there, and as Miles pounded away, Hendrix played smoldering guitar behind his own vocals and a riveting solo rife with tracer bullets, screams, musical explosions—all live, with nary an overdub, a measure of the music he could create at his best. The song projected anguish, violence and a chilling sense of rage, clearly a protest number even more arresting than the national anthem had been. The remainder of the Band of Gypsies album (on Capitol) was fine, but anticlimactic in the wake of "Machine Gun."

Through 1970 Hendrix did many recordings at his new Electric Lady recording studio, an expensive, self-designed, state-of-the-art facility where he could record whenever he wished in New York City. After Jimi's death, several albums of this material were released that included much excellent music. War Heroes featured "Bleeding Heart," a blues with some of his most passionate and furious flurries of notes. "Highway Chile" was

also based on blues, but was primarily a rhythm track. "Tax Free" featured some impressive multi-tracked lines, while "Peter Gunn Catastrophe" was simply the old "Peter Gunn" TV show theme as a brief jam that deteriorated into mere futzing around. "Stepping Stone" was another rhythm track with some beautifully crafted guitar lines in the opening, and "Beginning" had some wonderfully intense, unrelenting solo work.

There were certainly weak spots in much of this stuff. Hendrix favored the same rhythms throughout his career, as if he was uncomfortable with anything else than the beat behind "Purple Haze" or "Foxy Lady." On another later album, Loose Ends, he plays "Blue Suede Shoes" to this same repetitive rhythm. Nonetheless, on occasion he did deviate, as on his steaming "Jam 292" which combines the blues guitar principles of T-Bone Walker with feedback and screaming crescendos, alternating with grunting rhythm licks that still sound fresh. Jimi's version of Muddy Waters' "Hoochie Koochie Man" is credible, though marred by an improvised, comedic vocal. The live Hendrix in the West was a more consistent posthumously released album, with a sharp version of "Johnny B. Goode" and a stops-out rendition of "Voodoo Chile." Also interesting is a bizarre "God Save the Queen" recorded live at the 1970 Isle of Wight Festival and an extended "Red House."

Jimi recorded through the summer of 1970, creating what would be his final formal studio album, The Cry of Love. This time, he brought in more outside musicians (among them Stephen Stills and Steve Winwood) than he'd ever used before. The music, all recorded at Electric Lady studios, was fine enough, with some impressive and well-conceived, almost symphonic-sounding layers of guitar on "Night Bird Flying." "My Friend" returned Jimi to the blues form in a loose, live setting. "In from the Storm" featured some chilling guitar that conveyed all the fury of thunder and lightning.

Hendrix's final important recording was done live at Britain's Isle of Wight pop festival on August 30, 1970. Though there are some fine extended improvisations on "Foxy

Lady," accompanied by Billy Cox and Mitch Mitchell, the set was inconsistent. "All Along the Watchtower," for example, was far less effective than it had been on *Electric Ladyland*. Jerry Hopkins, in *Hit and Run*, chronicled some of the problems Jimi had onstage there, including the festival security police communications that suddenly blasted over his amplifier. The set was tepid at best.

After another disastrous appearance at a German rock festival, he settled in London, and was clearly at a crossroads. Much of the hamboning of his earlier days was gone; he was beginning to tire, as had Eric Clapton and Michael Bloomfield, of the "guitar genius" nonsense that attended him. It could have been the start of a dramatic new direction for Hendrix, one that would have permitted him to transcend all of the hype of rock and move toward achievements in other fields. Miles Davis had expressed admiration for Jimi, and it's not impossible that he could have taken jazz guitar in a totally new direction.

But Hendrix, like saxist Charlie Parker, had a compulsive personality. He seemingly had to have drugs and, considering his prodigious appetite, it was inevitable that they would finally catch up with him. It happened on September 18, 1970, when he died of a barbiturate overdose, strangling on his own vomit in the London apartment of a girlfriend. He was buried on October 1 in Seattle. A London coroner's investigation found a variety of drugs and some alcohol in his system, hardly a surprise to those who knew him.

After Hendrix's death, producer Alan Douglas took possession of hour upon hour of unfinished tapes Jimi had been working on at Electric Lady studios. Douglas overdubbed other musicians on this material, and though the results were at times interesting, none of it can compare with any of the material Jimi completed, even his music with Redding, Mitchell, Cox and Miles that was issued after he died.

Jimi Hendrix's impact on the rock guitar has yet to be thoroughly defined. Some guitarists have become obsessed with carrying on his vision, among them Robin Trower and Frank Marino. Some guitarists even tried to impersonate Hendrix for a time, but that was to be expected. Hendrix extended the possibilities of what a musician could do with an electric guitar, how a guitarist could use effects as tools and not just to produce weird sounds or cover up one's shortcomings. Like Charlie Christian, Jimi Hendrix created an entirely new sound for the electric guitar, gave birth to several styles (including heavy metal) and gave guitarists of the future something to aspire to. It may be that no one will ever match him.

DISCOGRAPHY

There appear to be at least a dozen albums of early Hendrix material from his r&b days on the market, often packaged with low-budget covers. Most are a waste of money.

However, all the classics are still available on Warner Bros., as well as some later live concert material, *The Jimi Hendrix Concerts*. *Band of Gypsies*, at last report, was still readily available on Capitol.

ESSENTIAL READING:
'Scuse Me While I Kiss the Sky, by David Henderson
Hit and Run, by Jerry Hopkins

LONNIE MACK

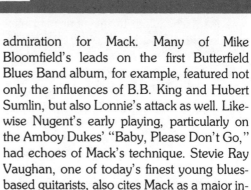

Walking away from success is something few musicians would dare to consider. Lonnie Mack has done it twice. A guitarist for whom the love of music, not success, was paramount, Mack has never really felt comfortable with the business end of his art. Like Tal Farlow, he has had few reservations about hibernating when things got to be too much for him. As a result, Mack has remained a cult figure, known primarily by guitarists who remember his biting, enduring 1963 hit instrumental of Chuck Berry's "Memphis," recorded at the end of someone else's session, which skyrocketed him to prominence.

In fact, Mack bridged the considerable gap between the rock guitar stylists of the '50s—Scotty Moore, Chuck Berry, James Burton and Duane Eddy—and the progressive rock guitarists of the late 1960s. His solos, rooted in the blues, contain much of the cutting tone and screaming upper-register crescendos later used by Michael Bloomfield and such others as heavy metal guitarist Ted Nugent, who has frequently professed his admiration for Mack. Many of Mike Bloomfield's leads on the first Butterfield Blues Band album, for example, featured not only the influences of B.B. King and Hubert Sumlin, but also Lonnie's attack as well. Likewise Nugent's early playing, particularly on the Amboy Dukes' "Baby, Please Don't Go," had echoes of Mack's technique. Stevie Ray Vaughan, one of today's finest young blues-based guitarists, also cites Mack as a major influence.

Lonnie McIntosh was born in 1941 in Harrison, Indiana, in the southeastern part of the state across the river from Kentucky and not far from the Ohio border and Cincinnati. His parents named him for the fabled country harmonica player Lonnie Glosson, then a favorite in their region. His parents played instruments, and Lonnie grew up immersed in the country songs and artists of the day. With Cincinnati radio stations like WCKY and WLW specializing in country music, he was able to absorb plenty of ideas. His mother taught him banjo and his father taught him guitar, but Lonnie's first real inspiration came from a blind guitarist named Ralph Trotto who specialized in gospel.

Lonnie also heard the blues early on. This isn't surprising, for not only did Cincinnati have a black station (WCIN), it also was home to King Records, one of the top independent American record labels, which recorded blues and country artists extensively from 1943 into the '60s. So Lonnie was exposed to both blues and country pickers, from Merle Travis to T-Bone Walker and Zeke Turner, and it was from their traditions that his later style emerged.

While a teenager Lonnie formed a band and started playing joints in the south and midwest with a repertoire combining blues, country and rockabilly tunes. Returning to Indiana, he took over a band called the Twilighters on the Indiana club circuit. Bassist Troy Seals (later a fine Nashville songwriter) managed to land the Twilighters a contract with King in 1963, and took them into King's Cincinnati studios for a session that took less time than scheduled. In the remaining minutes Lonnie and the band took off on their version of "Memphis."

It was magical. Mack, playing a then-new Gibson Flying V, began with two chords, battering the silence. As the rhyyhm section kicked in behind him he began to rip out some of the most awesome tones ever committed to tape. They were full, rich and harsh, no fuzztone, no effects at all (there were none except tremolo, tape and reverb at the time). Each crackling note was loaded with the jagged tension of a lightning bolt. He choked strings so hard it was a miracle they remained intact. Bloomfield later played hauntingly similar licks on Bob Dylan's "Tombstone Blues."

Suddenly the Fraternity label of Cincinnati picked up on "Memphis," released it and sent it to the top of the pop music charts. This was all a shock to Lonnie, whh'd expected little of the single when it was released. He was getting top billing, and in fall went back in the studios to record The "Wham" of That Memphis Man, a classic guitar album packed with the sort of gutbucket, rhythm and blues-

based rock one seldom heard outside of the south.

From start to finish, Lonnie's exhilarating guitar dominated the LP—from the churning ferocity of "Wham" through an acid-toned version of Dale Hawkins' "Suzie Q" to the equally awesome "Chicken Pickin'," which featured whirlwind rhythm under Lonnie's machine-gun staccato. The Twilighters were so cohesive that they could do anything, and were further helped by Lonnie's outstanding country/gospel vocals best exemplified on his down home rendition of Bobby Bland's "Further On Up the Road" and the gripping, cathartic ballad "Why?" There were no phony black inflections, just beautifully clear, soulful, unaffected singing.

More fantastic—if unheralded—Fraternity singles followed; fantastic because of Mack's consistency, but unheralded because, less than a year after "Memphis" propelled him to stardom, the British invasion erased him from the public consciousness. Lonnie managed to continue touring; his high points in this period were many. There was an impressive, flashy instrumental cover of Ben E. King's hit "Stand By Me," the hard-driving "Soul Express" with its bows towards T-Bone Walker, and a rocking "Wildwood Flower" that worked surprisingly well, with a dynamite blues improvisation in its middle. Mack continued cutting instrumentals of hits such as Junior Walker's "Shotgun" and Wilson Pickett's "I Found a Love." In 1965 he updated Bill Doggett's "Honky Tonk" as "Honky Tonk '65," and did a credible job of it. "Lonnie On the Move" recaptured much of the guttiness of "Wham," while tunes like "Florence of Arabia" and "Men at Play" were jam sessions, the latter obviously an attempt to jump into the funky organ format then being popularized by Jimmy Smith. Lonnie played some excellent blues on the cut, with a more restrained attack than he normally employed.

But few heard this material at the time. "Memphis" got some attention as a mid '60s hit for Johnny Rivers, so Lonnie's version was relegated to "oldies" segments on rock radio stations. Ironically, changes in rock music were setting the stage for Mack's first comeback. Blues guitarists were gaining credibility through the advent of Clapton, Bloomfield and others; Lonnie's playing fit right in. In 1968 Alec Dubro, a young *Rolling Stone* reviewer, reviewed Mack's five-year old Fraternity LP, then out of print. At the time Lonnie was touring (with James Brown among others) and doing studio work around Cincinnati. The review and Lonnie's reputation among guitarists managed to spark some interest. Elektra Records signed him to a contract.

His first album for Elektra, *Glad I'm in the Band* (1969), was a near-perfect, slightly updated blend of his strongest attributes from the Fraternity sides. His jagged-toned Flying V was as good or better than the playing of many of the so-called guitar idols of the period. And his clear, pure vocal style was recalled by his strong performance on the country ballad "Old House." "Too Much Trouble" featured a guitar solo as relevant as anything on the charts at the time, and he managed to speak his piece in just seconds. The record wasn't a huge seller, but it did manage to garner glowing reviews, and Elektra offered him a position in its a&r (artists and repertoire) department in Los Angeles.

Lonnie did two more albums for the label, in 1970 and '71. *Whatever's Right*, brought him together with the Cincinnati crowd with whom he'd previously worked, and though he played as well as ever it was less disciplined than *Glad I'm in the Band*. His third Elektra effort, *The Hills of Indiana*, moved him closer to a country style, emphasizing his vocals. Though neither sold well, Elektra wisely decided to lease his first Fraternity album, issuing it as *For Collectors Only* in '71.

But the high-pressure L.A. music scene was getting to Mack, and after a blowup with an Elecktra executive he quit the job, grabbed what possessions he wanted from his residence and headed home to Indiana. He made the first few dates of an Elektra artists' tour that year, then decided he'd truly had enough and returned to southeastern Indiana, no less in love with music, but thoroughly burned out

and fed up with the affectations and bureaucracy that stood between music and its audience. Lonnie lived with his family in an idyllic rural setting and jammed with local musicians, creating the kind of natural, unforced music he preferred. Not that this period was totally placid. In Cincinnati in 1975 Lonnie got into a scuffle with an off-duty cop who shot and arrested him; he talked of suing the city. He saw this incident as an omen and moved to Nashville, where he pitched his original compositions and produced a demo tape that wound up being issued by Capitol as *Home At Last*. The songs weren't particularly imaginative, and there was precious little guitar involved.

By 1977 Lonnie saw Nashville taking on the phony affectations of L.A., and left. His one decent album for Capitol, *Lonnie Mack and Pismo*, featured more of his excellent guitar work, but lacked the power of his Fraternity sides or even his first Elektra album.

Heading west, he played a few jobs, and formed a group known as South, whose debut album has yet to be released. He went to Toronto and worked with rock legend Ronnie Hawkins, whose 1960s ensemble the Hawks later were better known—and acclaimed—as The Band. Then it was back to Indiana, where Lonnie remains today, working with a band led by Billy McIntosh, his brother (and a former member of Pismo). He's playing now on his own terms, doing local gigs and occasional out-of-town bookings like a 1984 show at New York's Lone Star Cafe. Most recently, he's been in Austin, Texas. A near-fatal illness behind him, he's most recently recorded a new album for the Alligator label of Chicago, produced by Stevie Ray Vaughan.

There is no sense in predicting Lonnie Mack's future, as he himself may not be terribly sure what the future holds. His playing remains compelling, inspirational and exhilarating. Success has little to do with financial gain to him, and his music has remained the liberating factor in his life. His achievements will stand, but it is clear that whatever happens will be on *his* terms.

DISCOGRAPHY

Virtually none of Lonnie's material, including the great Fraternity sides from the '60s, are commercially available. If you are very lucky, you might find a copy of *The Memphis Sounds of Lonnie Mack* (Trip), a collection of some of the more obscure Fraternity singles.

SCOTTY MOORE

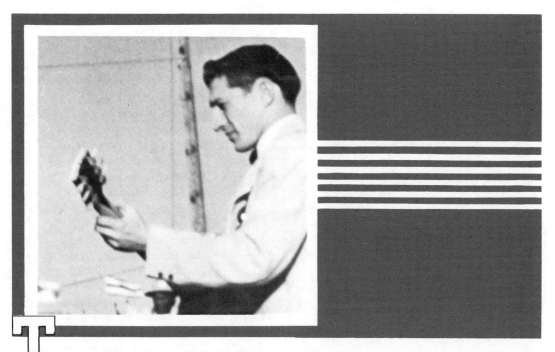

T he last thing Scotty Moore ever expected to become was a rock guitar legend. He probably figured that, like so many obscure country guitarists, he would wind up playing country music evenings after work and on weekends for beer money. But that's not how things turned out. He began picking Merle Travis-styled guitar behind a neophyte hillbilly singer named Elvis Presley, whose early expectations were as modest as Scotty's, and the chain of events that occurred after they met was bigger than either man. Elvis became a pop culture hero and Scotty became a rock guitar pioneer, both still revered thirty years after they first recorded together.

Elvis, of course, didn't survive these thirty years; Scotty, however, has held on nicely, and though he plays little today, he remains an important touchstone in the history of rock guitar, while producing and sound engineering have dominated his life in the past two decades. With the rockabilly revival of the 1980s the vitality of his early playing has again brought him attention and acclaim—from kids not yet born when he took up with bassist Bill Black and Elvis.

As a guitarist, Scotty was no grand innovator. Indeed, he had many technical limits that prevented him from ever becoming a studio player with the versatility of, say, Joe Maphis or James Burton. But like Ringo Starr's drumming with the Beatles, Scotty's work with Elvis fit perfectly within the musical context. His screaming, pulsating, silvery tones fell behind Presley's vocals with uncanny perfection, to the point where it is impossible to imagine any other guitarist on those Presley Sun recordings, or on his early RCA sides. Elvis used plenty of sidemen throughout his career, including some of the greats like Jerry Reed, Grady Martin and James Burton. But even with those fabled pros the Presley-Moore synergy was never really equalled. In 1968 when Elvis did the famous Singer TV special on NBC that reestablished his credibility, Scotty's guitar again provided continuity and familiarity to take a small but vital role in recreating Elvis' roots. It was as though Scotty had never left.

The licks he played from 1954 to 1961 have been stolen, recycled, rejuvenated and regurgitated by some of the greatest guitarists of rock. They inspired Jimmy Page and George Harrison; John Fogerty stole some of them note for note during the days of Creedence Clearwater Revival; the Stray Cats' former guitarist Brian Setzer constantly pulls a Moore-ism out of his collection. And for years the Rolling Stones' Keith Richard has been obsessed with Scotty's solo on Elvis' 1955 Sun recording "I'm Left, You're Right, She's Gone."

With that in mind, it might seem odd that Scotty largely abandoned the guitar in favor of working in the more technical end of music. But then one suspects that this gentle, self-effacing man, though clearly proud of his work and the adulation that made his name, realizes that there are relatively few contexts in which he could play so effectively. Nonetheless, within those contexts Scotty *burned*, and could still do so today.

Winfield Scott Moore III was born December 27, 1931, in Gadsden, Tennessee, not far from Jackson. Music, specifically hillbilly music, was important to the family; and his father and three brothers all played together. He pushed himself to learn the guitar to fit in with the family, and stuck with the guitar until he dropped out of school in tenth grade.

At age sixteen, two years premature, he joined the Navy, and it was there that his musical horizons expanded dramatically. He was able to listen to jazz guitarists, and became particularly impressed with Tal Farlow, then making a splash with the Red Norvo Trio, and with Barney Kessel, then working with Jazz at the Philharmonic. He also listened to blues and country players, including Merle Travis and Chet Atkins. He played with other musical sailors in Washington state before being discharged in 1952.

By that time he'd begun to develop a technique based mostly on the Kentucky fingerpicking style Travis and Atkins had popularized. Scotty moved to Memphis to work in a drycleaning business owned by his brothers, concentrating on blocking hats. In his spare time he assembled a hillbilly band to work wherever he could get hired. Known as the Starlight Wranglers, the band comprised bassist Bill Black, singer Doug Poindexter as front man, along with a fiddler and steel guitarist. By 1954 they were enjoying modest popularity in the Memphis area, and decided to approach Sam Phillips of the relatively new Sun Records about cutting a record. Phillips agreed, and on May 12, 1954 they assembled in his tiny studio to record "My Kind of Carryin' On," Scotty's first appearance on record. The song itself wasn't much, and Poindexter's vocal was reedy, as though he was consciously trying to emulate Lefty Frizzell. Scotty's guitar break had a primitive edge (far more pleasing than some of the cornball stuff played by the other musicians) with licks similar to those he'd later use with Elvis.

But the band wasn't going very far when Sam Phillips, who'd become friendly with Scotty, asked him and Bill Black to back up an aspirant named Elvis Presley, who sang everything from Dean Martin tunes to blues. Scotty and Bill began touring with Elvis. Depending upon whose account you believe, after several days, weeks or months (the truth is probably somewhere in between) they were getting nowhere, when on July 6, 1954, at the Sun studio, they were running through potential ideas and Elvis struck up fooling with Arthur Crudup's "That's All Right (Mama)." As Elvis played an airy bluegrass rhythm on his Martin guitar, Scotty jumped right in with some smoothly played, lightly picked Merle Travis licks. They worked out the kinks and recorded it, with Scotty adding a melodic solo peppered with Travis-style picking. "Blue Moon of Kentucky," recorded shortly after that, employed the same formula.

There were soon problems within the Starlight Wranglers. Elvis couldn't very well join that band, since his style was so different from that of the other members. Then Poindexter, who never felt comfortable or financially secure as a professional musician, quit the business (today he's a Memphis insurance salesman) and the Wranglers broke up. Elvis, Scotty and Bill found themselves stirring up increasing interest with the local success of "That's All Right," and they were soon working shows around Memphis.

It seems that the more the three played together, the better, more confident and adventurous Scotty's guitar work became. Some of the first evidence of his growth was his malevolent, slashing lead on "Good Rockin' Tonight," recorded in September 1954. The Travis style still remained at the root of what he did, but it took on a supercharged edge, most noticeable on "Milkcow Blues Boogie," where he kept dancing figures moving and played a smooth, clearly confident solo with a far stronger attack than he'd used on his first recordings. "Baby, Let's Play House," recorded in February 1955, showed off more of his choked, doublestop licks that gave the records their sharp edge. In addition, the pulsating bass figures he played, combined with Black's bass-slapping, were responsible for much of the rhythmic excitement of Elvis' Sun sides.

"Mystery Train," also taped in February 1955, took that to a higher level of art with Scotty playing a syncopated bass figure behind Elvis' vocal, as well as a stinging A7 figure taken directly from blues guitarist Pat Hare on Junior Parker's original version of the song. That the blues were having a positive effect on Moore's playing was proved by Presley's explosive July 1955 rendition of "Tryin' to Get to You," where Scotty played stinging, razor-sharp single-string leads behind Elvis and a simple but effective chord solo. With Memphis' drummer Johnny Bonero added on drums, much of the rhythmic responsibility was removed from Moore's shoulders, and he was able to cut loose as a lead guitarist.

There can be little doubt that his time on the road with Elvis helped Scotty's playing considerably. A late (but undated) Sun recording, only recently released, of Elvis performing Sun bluesman Billy "The Kid" Emerson's "When It Rains It Really Pours," shows Scotty playing with yet more confidence than before, even though after one false start, Sam Phillips tells him not to get too damn complicated." However, by late 1955, he still hadn't hit his peak. By January 1956, he was being heard to better advantage than ever. Not all of this was due to his technique improving; Elvis was now with RCA, recording in studios technically superior to Sun's. On their first RCA session, at the Nashville studio, obviously

Scotty mixed so his solos could be heard, and with Chet Atkins on rhythm guitar he was free to concentrate on his lead work. Travis was still a strong influence, as evidenced by Moore's playing on "I Got a Woman" and "Heartbreak Hotel." But on the latter tune he played a positively bone-rattling solo, possibly influenced by Elmore James.

Occasionally, his technical limitations showed through. The first part of his solo on "Money Honey" wasn't musically correct, but he resolved it so well the mistake had little effect on the song. Scotty's vibrant, echo-laden tone generally contributed to the excitement of Elvis' early RCA sides. His solo on "My Baby Left Me" is pianolike in places. Better yet was his fiery, staccato solo on "So Glad You're Mine"; he fell back into Travis patterns on "I'm Gonna Sit Right Down and Cry Over You" but played a loping, shaking break on Elvis' version of "Lawdy, Miss Clawdy," the thick tone of his Gibson L-5 complementing Elvis to a tee. "Shake, Rattle and Roll" found Moore playing mad, sputtering variants of the Sun licks he used on "Good Rockin' Tonight" with utter elan. The slurring he did on this track should be a lesson to every other guitarist trying to learn this skill. "Hound Dog," however, must remain Moore's greatest moment. His guitar crackles as Elvis sings "high classed!" echoing and punctuating the voice. His first solo, slightly distorted, is surpassed only by his second, in which his guitar screams, taking on vocal characteristics unlike any other break he'd recorded. If Scotty never cut another record in his life, this one, recorded July 2, 1956, would remain his finest hour. He'd obviously mastered his echo-equipped Ray Butts Echosonic amplifier, which gave his tone a shimmering edge.

Of course, that *wasn't* the end of him. He played a brief but pungent solo on the September 1956 "Too Much," and another glorious break on Elvis' version of Little Richard's "Ready Teddy." Elvis recorded plenty of other songs later, of course, and Scotty was there with excellent playing on many of them. Their rerecording of "When It Rains It Really Pours" shows how far Scotty's blues had come. His solo crackles and embellishes Elvis' vocal as authoritatively as any of the better Memphis blues guitarists (Pat Hare, Willie Johnson, Matt Murphy) could have. Moore's work on "Jailhouse Rock" was explosive.

But by fall 1958 the Moore/Black/Presley relationship was strained, due to problems with Elvis' domineering, frugal manager, Colonel Tom Parker. Parker's penny-pinching and tendency to treat everyone else around Presley like half-bright sharecroppers made him few friends. In September 1957, Scotty and Bill left Elvis' organization because of salary disputes, but continued working shows and sessions with him as freelance musicians. It mattered little by then. In March 1958 Presley was inducted into the U.S. Army.

At that point Scotty and Bill struck out on their own. Bill organized the Bill Black Combo, which did well until (and even beyond) Black's death in 1965. Scotty bought into the Memphis-based Fernwood label and in 1959 produced the million-selling Thomas Wayne single, "Tragedy." He worked for Sam Phillips in the early '60s, running Phillips' new recording studio in Nashville. He also did some recording with Chess rockabilly artist Dale Hawkins on tracks like the strange "Googlie Booblie," on which he did some interesting, unusual (for him) octave work.

In early 1964 Scotty made his only solo album. He'd done a couple of instrumental singles in the past, but this album, The Guitar that Changed the World (Epic) was designed to reprise some of the Elvis hits on which he'd played, but was less than successful. Scotty's strength, even in his days with Elvis, lay in his abilities as an accompanist; as a solo guitarist he was weak. Here he was reduced to blandly stating melodies, while a "Nashville sound" chorus cooed in the background. An intrusive saxophonist (probably Boots Randolph) did nothing to help the record. Only once did Moore rise to excellence, with his churning version of "Milk Cow Blues." He played with his old fire and intensity, showing that Nashville sound production techniques (which included fuzztone bass and vocal chorus) were superfluous. A small rhythm section would have sufficed.

Scotty hadn't ceased doing occasional sessions with Elvis. In the midst of his engineering work, he recorded with Elvis in 1966 on the How Great Thou Art album. In 1967 Scotty and Jerry Reed played lead guitars on "Guitar Man" (Reed's composition). Scotty attended the rest of that session as well.

Then in 1968 Elvis boldly moved to reenergize his sagging musical career with an NBC TV special. Producer Steve Binder decided to evoke Elvis' roots, and created a segment in which Elvis, playing rhythm while Scotty played lead, D.J. Fontana thumped a box, and crony Charlie Hodge shook a tambourine, sang some of his '50s numbers. It was the last time Scotty played with Elvis.

Around 1973 Scotty opened his own studio, Music City Recorders. Though guitar was less evident in his life, he still played occasionally. Moore does some fine playing on neo-rockabilly Billy Swan's 1976 recording "I Got It for You" on his Billy Swan album. Scotty is still as potent as in his days with Elvis, his technique and tone unchanged. Scotty has continued to work as an engineer, playing guitar only sporadically on recording if someone requests him.

There's little question that Scotty Moore was a stylist, that he had limits and that he never would have developed into a Tal Farlow. On the other hand, his impact as a guitarist has been more enduring than that of many technically superior jazz players. And his work on Presley's 1954-'61 records will stand as some of rock guitar's finest moments.

DISCOGRAPHY

Scotty's most essential material, of course, are the Elvis Presley sides. The Sun Sessions (RCA) features most all of Elvis' classic 1954-'55 Sun releases. Elvis Presley, Elvis, Golden Records, Vol. 1, Loving You, Christmas Album, King Creole, 50,000,000 Elvis Fans Can't Be Wrong and Elvis Is Back! (all RCA) feature Scotty. Elvis: The Early Live Recordings (The Music Works) features some of

Elvis' early Louisiana Hayride sides from 1954-'55 with Scotty audible in the background. Some heretofore unreleased examples of Scotty at his peak with Elvis are included in the six-LP box *A Golden Celebration* (RCA) which include Sun outtakes, Elvis' 1956 appearances on the Tommy Dorsey, Milton Berle, Steve Allen and Ed Sullivan TV shows as well as two complete performances in his hometown of Tupelo from September 1956. On these Scotty plays with greater fire than on any of Elvis' studio recordings.

Several of Moore's later recordings for Epic are included on *Rockabilly Stars, Vol. One* and several more on *Instrumental Country* (British CBS).

JIMMY PAGE

When compared with all the guitarists discussed here, Jimmy Page is somewhat of an anomaly. His entire approach to the guitar differs considerably from the others discussed in this section. Michael Bloomfield, Eric Clapton and Duane Allman approached the instrument with a passion born of their commitment to the blues; Jimi Hendrix created his own musical visions, combining his roots with his sense of adventure and emotional capacity. Chuck Berry's guitar playing was an integral part of his stage act. Indeed, of all the rock players covered here, Page's place is closest to that of James Burton.

It is not to imply that Page's guitar work, particularly with Led Zeppelin, lacked passion and fire; it certainly did not. But Page is by and large a product of the London studios, an A-team sessionman through the 1960s who was required to produce credible guitar work in a variety of contexts. Some producers let him work out his own arrangements, but others insisted that parts be played precisely as the arrangers had written them. It's the same in any studio situation: producers want

certain sounds and the musician has an obligation to give them what they want.

To some extent this necessitates a technocratic approach to the guitar. The player must know what effects, licks or picking techniques will produce the desired effects. This demands a willingness to experiment, and at the same time instills a sense of discipline in the player. While Page's approach has been highly technical, he has also developed a formidable sense of taste when recording. It is ironic that many of the heavy metal guitarists who were inspired by his work with Zeppelin failed to emulate that restraint and control, often taking their own playing to the point of wretched, unmusical excess. Page's work on Zeppelin's albums has always seemed wild and unrestrained, yet it never got out of hand. Everything was calculated, and like the master studio player he was, Page always knew when to pull back.

As for his roots, Page had much in common with other British rockers of his generation. He listened to American rock records, picked up on players like Scotty Moore, James Burton and Cliff Gallup, then moved into a period of studying the great American bluesmen like B.B. King, Elmore James and Matt Murphy; he was into rock bands, then into studio work. He ultimately became, like Clapton, a blues-based guitarist, yet he never limited his listening. His interest in creating new, unusual sonic aspects with the guitar naturally led him to great interest in the music of Les Paul.

All of this combined in one truly formidable rock virtuoso, a player who may not have poured out his heart and soul, but who used all his gifts to create different dimensions in his own playing and for the sound of Led Zeppelin. That he succeeded beyond his expectations was in part due to his knowledge, the talent of his fellow musicians (though their material was not always up to snuff) and his near-perfect timing in introducing Zeppelin to the world.

James Patrick Page was born January 9, 1944, in West London, and grew up in Surrey, outside the city. He was living there when the skiffle craze hit England, and when rock and roll, through Elvis, made its mark in 1956. He became taken with rock's idiom, and particularly with its lead guitarists, such as Scotty Moore. Scotty's solo on Elvis' 1954 recording of "Baby, Let's Play House," his pulsating bass notes and Travis-style licks filtered through slapback echo, enticed Page to play guitar.

He'd taken an interest in a guitar laying around his house early on, and began teaching himself. The basic, powerful playing of Moore and James Burton, short on frills and long on impact, were what drew him. He went through the usual run of cheap electric guitars as he progressed. Naturally, he also picked up some ideas from Britain's own star rock guitarists, Bert Weedon and the Shadows' lead guitarist Hank B. Marvin.

Page's first serious band was Neil Christian and the Crusaders, a fairly straightforward British rock and roll ensemble. Illness took Jimmy out of active playing for about two years, during which time he, like so many other aspiring British rockers, wound up in art school. Live performing had been adversely affecting his health. He subsequently returned

to music seriously, playing some club work, but eventually built up such a reputation among friends that he was recruited for session-work. It was partly a matter of his talent, partly a matter of a need; rock and roll session guitarists were few and far between in London.

Page's history as a sessionman has been marked by misinformation, controversy and speculation. One of the major bones of contention is whether or not he played on such Kinks' hits as "You Really Got Me" and "All Day and All of the Night." This situation has never really been clarified, but it appears he was *not* on these songs, but definitely was on other early Kinks' numbers. Undoubtedly some enterprising researcher will someday nail down just what dates he did work with them.

But Page was clearly involved with other hits that came in the wake of the 1964-65 "British Invasion." It's almost certainly he playing on "I'll Cry Instead," a 1964 cover version of the Beatles' hit by Joe Cocker, with nimble rockabilly-flavored guitar. His brittle-toned lead also dominated some of the early recordings by Them. It was Page playing the famous E-D-A chord progression on "Gloria" and the busy, barbed-wire guitar licks on "Baby Please Don't Go" as Van Morrison sang lead vocal.

Not all of his sessions were this rock-oriented, however. He also played on a number of lighter pop numbers by Donovan, Petula Clark and Val Doonican, and on Tom Jones' "It's Not Unusual." There were jazz dates, rock dates with the Stones and the Who ("I Can't Explain") and a variety of easy-listening deals, all of which conspired to help—and hurt—Page. Studio work instilled that strong sense of discipline and control that has marked his work ever since. But, as with many studio players, it also burned him out after a point. His strengths were as a rock player—and he did not always handle the jazz and easy-listening dates so well.

So in 1965 he recorded two instrumentals of his own, the heavily blues-flavored "She Just Satisfies" and "Keep Moving." Sometime during that year he and Eric Clapton recorded the jam session subsequently issued on the *History of British Blues* series (instituted by Immediate Records). The guitar duets hinted at the potential of both players, though Clapton's prowess was featured more than Page's. The tapes were not meant for release, but several members of the Rolling Stones were overdubbed, and much to Clapton's and Page's chagrin they were released. Page had also began dabbling in production at the time, producing three fine numbers by John Mayall and Eric Clapton for Immediate, as well as a single by underground singer Nico.

Page had been approached early in 1965 about joining the Yardbirds after Eric Clapton left the band, but turned them down. Jeff Beck got the job, but a year later, in June 1966, Page was asked again when bassist Paul Samwell-Smith left the band. This time, despite the high pay of studio sessions, Page accepted, doubling bass some of the time and, when rhythm guitarist Chris Dreja moved to bass, playing twin lead guitars with Jeff Beck.

The Page-Beck team recharged the Yardbirds, making their already musically excellent situation with Beck even better. The two were friends, and one regrets they only did three tunes, "Happenings Ten Years Time Ago," "Psycho Daisies" and "Stroll On," before Beck left the group that November. Page remained with them as sole lead guitarist until they folded for good in June 1968.

Page had continued to do sessions when not touring with the Yardbirds. He'd worked on Donovan's "Hurdy Gurdy Man" in 1968 as well as playing the intense 12-string rhythm guitar on "Beck's Bolero" (with a group that nearly became the basis for a renewed Beck/Page band). He received acclaim for his solo on Joe Cocker's 1968 hit recording of "With a Little Help from My Friends." He also did some impressive work on the final Yardbirds' LP, *Little Games*. His modal tuning on the Indian-flavored "White Summer" hinted at things he would do later with Zeppelin. The song "Tinker, Tailor, Soldier, Sailor" featured another Page innovation: his use of a violin bow on the strings of an electric guitar.

Clearly, by the time the Yardbirds split for the last time, the groundwork was laid for Page to move on to a musical unit of his own. His studio work and other creative endeavors had given him the solid reputation he needed. Originally, he planned on forming a band known as the New Yardbirds, and in fact that is how his ensemble was initially known. Working through friends and studio acquaintances he enlisted vocalist Robert Plant, drummer John Bonham and fellow studio player John Paul Jones on bass.

They settled on the name Led Zeppelin, and managed to land a contract with Atlantic Records, the first British band signed on that label (Cream and others had been with its Atco subsidiary). They commenced recording their first album (issued in 1969) which without a doubt was inspired by the Jeff Beck Group's *Truth*. The instrumental lineup was the same and the choice of material overlapped in the case of one song, "You Shook Me." The album reflected the band's distinctive style at the time: very dense, thick, tightly arranged and built around Plant's primal-scream vocals and Page's guitar textures, played on a Telecaster.

Page created a variety of aural images on the album, however, using acoustic guitar and pedal steel effectively on "Babe, I'm Gonna Leave You." Page had been deeply influenced by fingerpickers like British folk guitar virtuoso Bert Jansch, and could do a respectable job on an acoustic instrument. Yet here he utilized acoustic in a hard rock context just as he would on Zeppelin's classic "Stairway to Heaven" a couple of years later. He played acoustic with great clarity and precision, integrating it well into the heavier sound. "You Shook Me," the Willie Dixon blues number, was straightforward enough, with Page invoking the Muddy Waters signature riff at the beginning, creating several lead patterns behind Plant echoing his voice (with a powerful descending slur mimicking Plant's vocal slide), and offering a thoroughly simplistic, but effective, guitar solo before Plant came back in to finish the tune.

Page created symphonic guitar backgrounds on "Dazed and Confused" by using the bow, playing perfectly. He created an exciting, busy solo on the number, but again it was all meticulously controlled and arranged. "Black Mountain Side," built on the influence of Jansch and of Indian music, was an appealing contrast in the midst of all the unworldly, hyper-amplified guitars. But "Communication Breakdown" picked up the energy again, with some of the guitar sounding compressed as a result of special miking techniques. "I Can't Quit You, Baby," Otis Rush's 1956 release, was fairly faithful to the original (Page was a Rush fan), as Jimmy evoked the deep, dark emotional playing Otis was renowned for. "How Many More Times," a Howlin' Wolf number, featured more bowed guitar, with wah-wah chords emerging from both stereo channels. Though again Page played well, the whole performance was a bit too calculated, sterile and monotonous.

The album became a huge seller in America, but did less well in Britain, where Zeppelin never had as much success as it enjoyed in the States. The second album, *Led Zeppelin II*, released late in 1969, featured some of the group's best-known material, though some of it was mediocre. "Whole Lotta Love" became a heavy metal anthem for the '70s, spotlighting Page's explosive guitar sound and a Theremin (often used for those eerie, high-pitched sounds in horror films). Page worked out his solo for the song's middle before going into the studio, and added effects while recording. Plant's vocal worked, but was annoyingly contrived. "The Lemon Song" was even worse, built on lyrics (and music) from old blues (including Howlin Wolf's "Killing Floor" and Robert Johnson's "Traveling Riverside Blues"). Page inserted the famous guitar riff from "Killing Floor" in the midst of the song. Why Wolf and Johnson got no composer credit is beyond me.

"Heartbreaker" is far superior. Page thought up a tough, threatening and muscular guitar riff that gave the song backbone. He then played a savage, unaccompanied solo in the middle. The song shifts into high gear, with several guitar parts going all at once. It

changes moods again as it segues into "Livin' Lovin' Maid," which features a clever octave guitar riff. "Ramble On" has acoustic and electric guitars voiced like mariachi horns, and the song's vacillation between stateliness and tension made it more effective than the lightweight material that marred the album. "Bring It On Home" began as Zeppelin's tribute to Jimmy Reed, but was too gussied up to be believable, and Plant's line "Wadge da train go down the track" came off almost as a blues satire. The heavy metal finale made no sense, nor did the return to straight blues.

By this time the group was a major concert draw in America, and one amazing aspect of its live shows was Page's ability to recreate many of his studio tricks onstage, a token of his abilities both as guitarist and technician. The 1970 *Led Zeppelin III* was far weaker than the first two LPs, though Page played some interesting banjo on "Gallows Pole" and more electric pedal steel on "Tangerine."

Led Zepplin IV, issued in 1972, was somewhat improved over *III*. Page's riffing through "Black Dog" was nearly as strong as on "Heartbreaker." Jimmy was still experimenting, double-tracking mandolin on the medievally tinged "The Battle of Evermore," a superb number. But the album's showpiece was obviously "Stairway to Heaven." This song has become horriily oveeexploited. Yet at the time of the album's release, it was truly impressive, with itt flutes and sparkling acoustic guitar, gradually evolving into an electric tune as Page dubbed on electric 12-string to remake it in a rock context. It remains, despite its overexposure (it became a fixture on FM radio), one of Page's finest achievements.

Oddly enough, the song was never issued as a single; the band never liked singles anyway ("Immigrant Song" from *III* was their sole top five hit in America), preferring the extended time afforded by LPs. But *IV* contained other examples of Page at his finest. "Misty Mountain Hop" was dominated by crisply voiced, overdubbed guitars. The same level of quality was met on "Four Sticks," as Page's guitar masses as a rumbling, machinelike sound behind Plant's voice. "Going to California" featured the multiple fingerpicked acoustic guitars that became a leit motif occurring at least once on every album, contrasting with the heavy metal.

Houses of the Holy, Zeppelin's 1973 effort, was less impressive than *IV* had been, though it branched out on "The Rain Song" into pop music that almost could have made the easy listening charts—except for its occasional lurch into heavy metal. "The Crunge," Zeppelin's answer to James Brown, featured Page playing guitar in the classic Jimmy Nolen funk style (Nolen was Brown's guitarist for most of the years between 1965 and 1983).

By 1973 Led Zeppelin was among the top concert draws in the world, and its stature was sufficient to justify beginning its own label, Swan Song Records, which released *Physical Graffiti* in 1975 and *Presence* a year later. In '76 the soundtrack from Zepplin's film *The Song Remains the Same* appeared. It captured their stage act (at New York's Madison Square Garden) extremely well, documenting Page's ability to reproduce most of what he did live; "The Rain Song" fared particularly well in this regard. There were some self-indulgent points. A 26-minute version of "Dazed and Confused" was a bit too long, even though Page evoked many moods, bowing his guitar and coming dazzlingly close to equaling the sounds he produced in the studio. "Stairway" fared well in concert, too. The album's musical success, both as retrospective and live performance, was largely due to Page's arrangements and the cohesion that he, Bonham and Jones maintained behind Plant.

Due to a death in Plant's family the band went on a nearly year-long hiatus. Zeppelin reunited in 1978 and a year later released *In Through the Out Door.* Times were beginning to change musically, and Zeppelin's musical formulas were beginning to sound a bit dated; regardless, the reunion was short-lived. After an alcohol binge ended drummer Bonham's life in 1980 the band broke up. Page has moved into movie music, composing and recording the soundtrack to the film *Deathwish II* in 1982. In 1983 ex-Yardbirds Page, Clapton and Beck united for a special concert to benefit research into multiple sclerosis, a paralytic disease which affects former Small Faces bassist Ronnie Lane.

Page's future projects, given his consummate skills onstage and in the studio, might take him anywhere. Soundtracks, commissions, continued recording and any number of other opportunities abound for a musician of his stature. So far, he has created some outstanding, much imitated music. He has managed to create guitar music of high artistic value that works on a commercial level as well—no small achievement. Jimmy Page's musical spark and durability will create much of interest, though he could easily rest on his Yardbirds/Zepplin laurels forever. We have not heard the last from him.

DISCOGRAPHY

The earliest Page material available is on the *White Boy Blues* double album, (Compleat) taken from the Immediate sides originally issued in the 1960s where he backs Eric Clapton. "Happenings Ten Years Time Ago" and "Psycho Daisies" are on *The Yardbirds.* Of course, all the Led Zeppelin albums—*Led Zeppelin I, II, III, IV, Houses of the Holy, Physical Graffiti, Presence, The Song Remains the Same, In Through the Out Door* and *Coda*—as well as his soundtrack for *Deathwish II* are quite easily found.

CARL PERKINS

It has been said that Carl Perkins could have been a rock and roll star on a par with Elvis Presley back in the mid '50s; for a brief time he was just that. But for Perkins, stardom never lasted. As a musician he was more talented than Elvis—who was a guitarist of minimal abilities—and far more adept at songwriting. But Elvis had the image: the gleaming black pompadour, the sideburns, the Tony Curtis/ Valentino appearance, the moves and the sneer, not to mention eyeball-blasting outfits he regularly bought from Lansky Brothers in Memphis.

Perkins, on the other hand, was a married man when he achieved his first success. His hairline was receding and his ears stuck out, and he looked like the impoverished West Tennessee dirt farmer he once was. Just as it is hard to imagine adolescent girls swooning for excellent country boogie artists like Moon Mullican, the Delmore Brothers or Merrill Moore, all of whom were conventional-looking adults, it's difficult to conjure up visions of proper young ladies fantasizing about Carl Perkins.

Nonetheless, Carl enjoyed considerable success, on his own terms. His raw, lean singing style, with its razor-sharp inflections, was unfettered hillbilly, but never corny. He was not a hip shaker, but the music he and his brothers made could certainly inspire an audience to shake theirs. And his guitar—that magnificent, sputtering, ringing guitar that inspired so many (George Harrison, John Fogerty and Albert Lee among them), was—and remains—one of the most exhilarating sounds in any era of rock and roll. Combining blues and country influences into a cohesive whole, Perkins's playing held the excitement his stage persona lacked. The results were almost always more than gratifying.

But there has always been a melancholy aspect to Carl Perkins's music, coming from several sources: the mournful country music he grew up with, the unvarnished adversity of maturing dirt-poor in rural Tennessee, a father who was disabled while Carl and his brothers were still in their teens, a violent auto crash at the peak of Carl's success that nearly killed all three Perkins brothers, the untimely death of his brother Jay, Carl's hunting accident and severe bout with alcoholism that lasted nearly a decade. Even today in interviews, a certain wistfulness is apparent as he talks lovingly of the Les Paul goldtop guitar on which he recorded "Blue Suede Shoes" that now rests in his Jackson, Tennessee museum. He sees it as a person, occasionally playing it to let it know, as he puts it, "that I still care."

His pride in his achievements, his zest for performing, his many good memories and the acclaim he receives from rockabilly fans old and new keep him going. He continues to play superbly today. His musical faculties haven't diminished. With two of his sons backing him as his brothers once did, Carl Perkins, the Rockin' Guitar Man, has continued to rock on through the 1980s.

Carl Lee Perkins was born April 9, 1932, at R.D. 1, Ridgely, Tennessee, in the state's northwestern corner. The son of Buck and Louise Perkins, he also had two brothers: Clayton and Jay. The Perkins family was poor, to say the least. Their poverty was so stark that they listened to a battery-powered radio only on Saturday nights, when the Grand Ole Opry was broadcast over WSM in Nashville. Buck Perkins shut the radio off immediately afterward to preserve the battery; the family could afford a replacement only once a year when they were paid for their crops.

Carl had friends among the black sharecroppers with whom he worked, and it was here that he was initiated into the wonders and mysteries of the blues. Particularly important in this regard was John Westbrook, an elderly black man who lived down the dirt road from the Perkins House. Carl became so entranced by "Uncle John's" blues guitar playing that he was on Westbrook's front porch every chance he could get, watching the old man's fingers play his unique licks and taking impromptu lessons from him. This happened around 1937, and it's entirely possible he was hearing, through Westbrook, some of the ideas of the great bluesmen of the day—Lonnie Johnson, Robert Johnson and Scrapper Blackwell. In

any case, Carl was learning blues firsthand, though he still didn't own a guitar.

Then came a scene that could have come out of a film. Buck Perkins ran into Westbrook, who told him he wanted "Carlie" to have his guitar. The next day, Westbrook presented it to Carl; he died just a few days later. Carl was soon playing along with the Opry on Saturday nights, throwing in blues licks decidedly unlike those he heard the musicians on the radio playing.

The idea of whites playing black music was nothing new. Even in the 1920s, rural southern musicians, both black and white, were stealing licks and ideas from one another. A few rural musicians like the Allen Brothers and Dick Justice had a unique understanding of the blues. But Carl's sneaking blues licks into white music became the crux of his style. He loved the bluegrass of Bill Monroe, and by the late 1940s he also loved the boogie of bluesman John Lee Hooker, and he began mixing them up, combining Hooker's raw blues with the smooth churning rhythms of Monroe's bluegrass. He heard records of other musicians doing similar things, most notably guitarist Arthur Smith, whose 1946 million-seller "Guitar Boogie" had a major impact on Carl. The Delmore Brothers, a country vocal guitar duo whose music took on increasing black and boogie-woogie influences in the post-World War II period, were also a major influence.

Meanwhile, it seemed that the Perkins family just couldn't get ahead. They moved near Jackson, Tennessee, where Buck planned to try factory work, but the factory closed; they resumed sharecropping. Then in 1948 Buck's health failed, and the Perkins boys had to work to support the family. Their income wasn't good, and by 1953, looking to make some extra money, Carl, Clayton and Jay formed the Perkins Brothers Band. Their country music trio featured Carl singing and playing a cheap Harmony electric guitar, Jay on acoustic rhythm guitar and Clayton on standup bass—the same lineup Elvis Presley used a year later. They played country hits of the day in some of the wildest honky tonks in the area, where booze and blood flowed free. And though their music was often hardcore country, it was also quite unique. Carl kicked in blues and boogie-woogie licks, making their sound different from most other performers in the area. Around that time Carl married Valda Crider, who enjoyed music and encouraged him to develop his abilities. When he was laid off from a bakery job, he decided that playing music full-time might be a way out of the dead-end life of sharecropping and factory work.

At the time Elvis was just meeting Scotty Moore and Bill Black, Carl was making steady money from his bar bookings. A Jackson songwriter encouraged him to tape his music and send out audition demos. Then, in the summer of 1954, Carl heard Elvis's "That's All Right (Mama)." It was uncannily close to the music the Perkins Brothers had developed themselves, and it made clear to Perkins that he had a real shot at professional music. Sun Records—Presley's label—was obviously open to his sound. W.S. "Fluke" Holland was brought into the band as drummer, and Carl bought himself a new Gibson Les Paul goldtop.

By the fall of 1954 the Perkinses had worked up enough courage to see Sun's owner Sam Phillips. They didn't succeed at first, but in October they got a shot at an audition. Phillips liked what he heard, but naturally he didn't want to derail Presley whose music was so similar, so he encouraged the Perkins Brothers' hillbilly music, putting their rock tunes on the back burner.

The Sun Years, Charly Records' exhaustive compilation of virtually all of Perkins's released and unissued recordings for the label, permits us to chronicle his development as a guitarist from the time he auditioned for Phillips until he left Sun in late 1957. It's true that Carl emphasized their rockers at the first audition, performing the hard-driving "Honky Tonk Gal" laden with blues overtones. Carl's solos were fast and threatening, complemented perfectly by his Les Paul's thick tone. As Carl sings, he plays muted bass notes in the famous "dead-string" rhythm guitar style

pioneered by Zeke Turner on 1940s recordings of Hank Williams and the Delmore Brothers. Perkins scat sings at the end, just as Elvis did on "That's All Right (Mama)." He continues in the same vein on the more countrified "Movie Magg" (a tune he wrote while still a teenager). His superb single-string solo has elements of Hank Garland's fleet-fingered playing and a slurred chord clearly meant to imitate a steel guitar.

A January 1955 recording of both songs constituted Carl's first Sun recording (though it came out on Phillips's subsidiary label, Flip Records). His second single, "Gone, Gone, Gone" was recorded in July 1955 and featured a raw country blues vocal with a stinging guitar solo clearly patterned in the Merle Travis/Scotty Moore style, but played with considerably more finesse. Carl also punctuated his vocals with rhythmic "grunts" on his guitar. But through 1955, Phillips confined Perkins to mournful country tunes, which he executed extremely well.

Then, in November 1955, Elvis Presley's Sun contract was sold to RCA Victor, and Phillips was without his star. The answer was simple: let Carl Perkins record the type of music he'd originally wanted to play. It was a wise decision. Carl's first flatout rock session was on December 19, 1955. Carl and Johnny Cash (then a new Sun artist) had witnessed a kid at a Jackson, Tennessee, dance trying to keep his pair of blue suede loafers from scuffing. They talked about it, and Perkins wrote "Blue Suede Shoes." Perkins changed the words as he recorded it, as some recently rediscovered alternate takes prove. But the music itself never changed. His guitar solos, full of slashing blues runs and hammer-ons, were magnificent. The flipside of "Blue Suede Shoes," "Honey Don't," was another Perkins original, featuring some heavily strummed acoustic guitar from Jay Perkins. Carl's flowing boogie phrases behind his vocals were direct copies of Arthur Smith's "Guitar Boogie," and his solos were punctuated by high-register power chords.

"Blue Suede Shoes" was released in early 1956, just as Elvis was being promoted by

RCA. By March, Carl Perkins had a number one crossover hit—on the pop, country and r&b charts simultaneously. His appearance fees went up, and he got an offer to do NBC's "Perry Como Show" on March 27, but they never made it. On March 22, after triumphant appearances through the south, Carl and his band were totally exhausted, having trouble staying on the right route heading north, when their car rear-ended a pickup truck outside Dover, Delaware. The truck driver was killed; the Perkins band members were all seriously injured. Carl's skull was fractured, his shoulder broken; Jay was even more seriously injured. All did recover, though Jay never totally regained his health.

But they never made the Como show, and that impeded Carl's career.

Before the accident, Carl had been busy in the studio. In January 1956, he had recorded the outstanding "Tennessee," a musical tribute to that state's country performers featuring a freewheeling guitar break with tough single-string lines and hard-edged chords. It was too country to do well on the rock charts. Early in March, before the accident, he'd done another session, which produced the classic, boogie-based "Boppin' the Blues," again borrowing the "Guitar Boogie" riff. He'd also recorded "All Mama's Children," the frantic "Everybody's Tryin' to Be My Baby," and "Perkins Wiggle," a song obviously modeled on the Delmore Brothers' "Good Time Saturday Night" with a low-string riff taken verbatim from the Delmore recording.

On June 5, 1956, after recovering from the accident, Carl recorded "Dixie Fried." One of his best sides, it was an unvarnished original tale of honky tonk violence reporting what he'd seen in the bars where he'd begun. His lucid playing was most articulate. He also recorded the wild "Somebody Tell Me," (not issued until 1982), a track that features unusually harsh, fragmented guitar, and was clearly a demo to be worked out at a later session. Better was the chilling, bluesy "That Don't Move Me," dominated by a pulsing, hammered-on lick behind the vocal. It too was a demo, but an outstanding one loaded with raw power.

That December, Carl, Johnny Cash, Jerry Lee Lewis and Elvis Presley came together by chance in the midst of a Perkins session at Sun, and recorded the legendary Million Dollar Quartet sides. Carl's accompaniment on this impromptu session was outstanding. He plucked ringing Merle Travis licks behind tunes like "I Shall Not Be Moved" that proved his country playing as potent as any of his rock work (something that would help him later).

In January 1957 he did two sessions with Jerry Lee Lewis as pianist. They recorded a boogie version of Louis Jordan's "Caldonia" including Carl's unusual slapping of his guitar strings. "Her Lovv Rubbed Off," never released as a single, was an odd collection of ideas and guitar riffs. Perkins used his Bigsby vibrato bar on the Les Paul and Sam Phillips' famous improvised slapback tape echo system to create an otherworldly effect. His rocking version of bluesman Blind Lemon Jefferson's "Match Box Blues," retitled "Matchbox," was infectious, though it wasn't the hit "Blue Suede Shoes" was. "Your True Love" featured some tense chord crescendos which were given extra tension by Phillips speeding up the master tape. Perkins did a hard-edged, emotive version of the Platters' ballad "Only You" which featured a delicate chord solo. On March 28 he recorded the gutbucket "That's Right," another bluesy number of implied hillbilly violence. Perkins slaps his guitar strings in the intro, then picks an insistent guitar riff that underscores his proclivity for using the guitar for rhythmic punctuation as well as for leads.

Carl recorded three other excellent sides in December 1957 that put his guitar out front. One, "Lend Me Your Comb" had screeching single-string blues playing; another, the churning "Glad All Over," had tough Travis-inspired licks. The final tune, recorded on December 11, was "Right String Baby But The Wrong Yo Yo," inspired by the old country-pop number "Right Key But the Wrong Keyhole." It contained some fine country-rockabilly leads with a ragtime flavor and two exhilarating solos, beautifully phrased with just the right measures of excitement and finesse. It is easily one of his most underrated numbers—and the last he recorded for Sun.

In January 1958 both Johnny Cash and Perkins left the label to sign with Columbia Records.

Carl's peak period was over despite the move to a larger label, and things weren't all well. Jay Perkins, finally recovered from the crash, returned to the band on guitar in 1957, but died of cancer soon after. Jay's death sent Carl reeling and sparked his heavy drinking. He cut numerous songs for Columbia, among them "Pink Pedal Pushers" (which he'd tried unsuccessfully for Sun in 1957) along with "Pointed Toe Shoes," which offered some interesting staccato guitar licks, but his sound was somehow more constricted. He got off some occasionally vital ideas, but more musicians were added to the production, which took the edge off his sound. It wasn't the same creative atmosphere he'd found at Sun.

Carl Perkins's career was on the decline, exacerbated by his worsening alcoholism. His audiences dwindled; Elvis was in the Army and a softer form of pop music was gaining ascendancy. In 1960 Fluke Holland left to join Johnny Cash. By 1963 Perkins was a Decca recording artist, playing low-level joints and doing shows in Nevada casinos. The road was getting to him, though Carl did a British tour. The rockabilly-conscious British liked him well enough to invite him back the next year, when he met the Beatles, all of whom worshipped him (George Harrison even adopted the stage name "Carl" in those early days as a tribute). He jammed with them, and gave them his blessing to record "Matchbox," "Everybody's Trying to Be My Baby" and "Honey, Don't." Their recordings, though imitative, show clear affection for him.

Around 1966, after a hunting accident in which he was wounded by an accidentally discharged rifle, Carl joined Johnny Cash's touring show. Cash was fighting his own battle with amphetamines, and the two regularly got high together. Carl was recording for the Dollie label but his records went nowhere, though "Country Boy's Dream" was particularly outstanding. Around 1967 Cash conquered his pill habit and encouraged Perkins to ditch the booze. He did.

It was at this point that Carl Perkins began to revitalize himself. Columbia re-signed him,

re-recording all his Sun material and also some outstanding new country-rockabilly material. His 1968 "Restless" featured standard Nashville overproduction, but was one of his better singles, with a hard, smooth, but clearly Perkins-styled solo. Carl's songwriting improved, and Cash had a huge hit with his "Daddy Sang Bass." Late in 1969, Carl was paired with the band NRBQ for *Boppin' the Blues*, an album showing him very much at home with these young, longhaired rockers. He played as well as ever on "Sorry, Charlie" and a straight-on remake of "Boppin' the Blues." But perhaps the most revealing piece was "Just Coastin'," a low-keyed, rather reflective solo guitar opus with echoes of early Chet Atkins, on which Carl played in a soft fingerpicking style different than anything else he'd done on record.

Meanwhile, he continued to record under his own name, issuing the fine "State of Confusion," a song that was rockabilly-influenced and beautifully polished. He remained with Cash into the 1970s, before leaving to resume his solo career full time. In the late '70s he received much acclaim for his *Ol' Blue Suede's Back* album, which showed his grippto be firm. He also turned to religion, writing an autobiography titled *Disciple in Blue Suede Shoes*. Yet he did not adopt the anti-rock mentality of many born-again Christians. He built a museum near his home in Jackson, Tennessee, showing off many of the guitars he'd used during his Sun days. He also formed the C.P. Express, another family band, this time featuring two of his sons, Stan and Greg.

Carl Perkins' guitar playing has found new favor with the neo-rockabillies of the 1980s. It's doubtful he'll ever become the hit artist he once was, but he will continue to inspire. Carl has had a number of setbacks, but as quoted in the superb Colin Escott and Martin Hawkins book *Sun Records*, he's clearly not looking back. "I've never felt bitter," he insists. "Always felt lucky to be in the business. Most kids from my background never drive a new car."

DISCOGRAPHY

Absolutely essential to anyone interested in Perkins is the 1982 compilation *The Sun*

Years (Charly). This five-LP boxed set features virtually everything he recorded for Sun, including demos, alternate takes, even radio spots for his concert appearances in the '50s. It is a beautiful package with a superbly illustrated, annotated booklet. Charly has also issued a reproduction of his 1950's *Sun Dance* album. Still available in bargain bins are *Original Golden Hits Volumes One and Two* (Sun), which feature many of his essential Sun sides. Some of Perkins' Columbia sides are available on the three volumes of the *Rockabilly Stars* series on Epic.

SECONDARY ESSAYS

Steve Cropper

Like so many great rhythm guitarists, Steve Cropper's contributions are often overlooked except by those r&b and rock fans who recall his lean, perfectly conceived licks that set the groove for a variety of hits from Memphis's Stax studios in the late '60s. Those gritty little string-bends and that economical, brief solo on Booker T. and the MG's "Green Onions," that hard-strummed G-seventh on Sam and Dave's "Hold On, I'm Comin'," and those beautiful, jewel-like embellishments on Otis Redding's "(Sittin on the) Dock of the Bay" all came from the Fender Telecaster of Steve Cropper.

Influenced by r&b guitarists like the Five Royales' Lowman Pauling, Cropper headed for a musical career early on, achieving his first success in 1961 with the Mar-Keys, a white r&b band that achieved top five success that year with "Last Night." A year later, Cropper joined organist Booker T. Jones and drummer Al Jackson in Booker T and the MG's. Duck Dunn soon joined, replacing bassist Louis Steinberg. The band became a hit on its own terms with the 1962 "Green

Onions," and was also in great demand for its tight, yet easygoing musical backings on r&b records. Subsequently, it became the house band at Stax.

Cropper's strength as a guitarist was not in a virtuoso lead style. Indeed, he seldom played anything even remotely resembling lead ("Green Onions" and "Soul Dressing" feature two of his longest solos: a few raunchy notes and phrases). But he and Dunn were masters at setting a framework for a song, and with Booker's rich, funky organ and Jackson's subtle drumming they became one of the greatest rhythm and blues groups of all times.

When Cropper did contribute a lick, it meant something. His strong rhythm chording on tunes like the MG's "Boot-Leg" and Wilson Pickett's "Ninety Nine and a Half" helped make those songs as danceable as they are, and his simple three-note chord licks on tunes like Pickett's "Funky Broadway" and Sam and Dave's classic "Soul Man" became as critical to their success as the vocals. Of all the rock and r&b guitarists of his generation, Cropper was a true model of economy.

Since the MG's split up in the early '70s, he has largely gravitated to production. He did one album with Albert King and Pop Staples (Jammed Together—out of print) and a solo set for Stax (With a Little Help from My Friends), neither of which showed him in an impressive light. His is not the sort of style that can be captured on a solo album, for he simply is not a soloist. He did participate in an attempt to reunite the MG's in the late '70s, but achieved more fame as part of the famous Blues Brothers' band (with Dunn on bass) in those years, playing his old style.

DISCOGRAPHY

The essence of Steve Cropper has always been subtlety, specifically when he plays behind another artist. His best work with Booker T. and the MGs can be heard on the *Best of Booker T. and the MGs* (Atlantic). His work behind some of the best soul singers of the late '60s is available on *The Best of Wilson Pickett* (Atlantic), *The Best of Sam and Dave* (Atlantic), *The Best of Otis Redding* (Atlantic) and *Albert King's Laundromat* (Edsel).

Duane Eddy

Duane Eddy was the first substantive rock guitar instrumental hero. While Carl Perkins and Chuck Berry were singers who also played guitar, and Scotty Moore was primarily a sideman, Eddy was a master instrumentalist who created some of the most vibrant rock guitar instrumentals of the late '50s.

Though Eddy's roots were solidly country, there was nothing country about his best recordings. They were not wild, flashy numbers with flurries of difficult licks, but fairly simple numbers that any respectable rock guitarist could learn easily enough if he had a fair command of the first position of his guitar. Duane's famous "twangy" sound was the product of an amp equipped with both tremolo and echo, making him one of the first guitar soloists to utilize electronic devices as part of his musical identity. His style was always melodic, which undoubtedly gave his recordings a solid commercial hook. Yet he could play surprisingly dirty blues, as he did on his version of "Hard Times."

Duane Eddy was born April 26, 1938, in Corning, New York. His father played guitar, and Duane picked up on it at age five. The family moved to Arizona when Duane was in his teens, and he graduated to electric guitar. By 1954 he was working joints around the area while going to high school. But Duane's direction was determined a year later when he met pioneer rockabilly guitarist and pianist Al Casey, who worked with Eddy's band through their most successful period.

Eddy's listening habits were broader than one might expect. He was an admirer of Chet Atkins and Merle Travis, and could play their fingerpicked style surprisingly well. Later on, he became an outstanding blues player, earning the admiration of B.B. King. He also enjoyed jazz, including the playing of Jimmy Wyble, the former Texas Playboy who built a strong career in jazz. Around the same time he met Coolidge, Arizona disc jockey Lee Hazlewood, who had aspirations to produce records.

Eddy was far more country-oriented in those days, though it didn't stop him from playing excellent Travis/Atkins styled rockabilly guitar. But at Hazlewood's suggestion, he adopted a new style, concentrating on skeletal melodies played on the bass strings. Eddy worked it out and, with Hazlewood and Casey, created the fluid "Movin' and Groovin'." Though Bill Justis had emphasized a melody played on guitar's bass strings (played by Memphis sessionman Sid Manker) on his 1957 hit "Raunchy," the instrumentation on "Movin'" was far more austere, with only sax, bass, drums and guitar. Released in 1958, it was not a huge hit, but the followup, "Rebel Rouser," skyrocketed to number six on the pop charts. It had a country feel, but the stomping beat and handclapping made it the perfect party record; it had a sort of commercial, controlled raucousness that made it great for dancing.

Two more hits followed—"Ramrod" (1958) and "Cannonball" (1958), which had a strong country-rock flavor combined with a Buddy Holly beat and strategically-placed screams. Steve Douglas's Boots Randolph-styled saxophone was also a contributing factor to this and other songs, giving the band a voice in a higher register. "The Lonely One" (1959), had a strong western flavor to it. "Forty Miles of Bad Road" was a number 9 hit in 1959. There was always a formulaic aspect to Eddy's recordings, yet he managed to create respectable music within that context, and his popularity in both America and England was considerable. As time went on, he diversified somewhat, writing the title tune to the film The Quiet Three, a schlocky number complete with strings. Yet he hadn't mellowed out. "Yep," also released during the late '50s, was a wild guitar tour-de-force. His hits, though, gradually tapered off, one of his last being the rockabilly-oriented "Some Kinda Earthquake" which barely broke the top thirty. Eddy ended his career with Jamie Records in 1962 and moved to RCA. With RCA he and Hazlewood advanced to TV and film-oriented projects, managing one hit, "(Dance with the) Guitar Man" soon after signing with the label.

The British invasion put Duane's career in limbo; his style of music wasn't terribly fashionable, and he was unwilling to change for the sake of change. However, as rock has opened itself to both new and old sounds, interest in Duane has gradually returned. In 1977 he recorded an instrumental version of "You Are My Sunshine" that deserved more success than it got.

In the early '80s Eddy reunited members of his old Rebels band for a concert, and one suspects—and hopes—that the magnificent guitar of Duane Eddy, which influenced a myriad of "surf" guitarists, as well as the "twangy" guitar sound that was a staple of the Bakersfield school in country music, will not be forgotten again.

DISCOGRAPHY

The essential Duane Eddy material, originally recorded for the Jamie label, is not in print in America, but is in print on a number of imports from the German Line label. The best bargain, and the one with all of his best playing (including "Rebel Rouser," etc.) is $1,000,000 Worth of Twang (Line). This is actually a reproduction of one of the old Jamie albums, repackaged into a two record set with excellent liner notes by vintage rock authority Greg Shaw.

Jimmy Nolen

Like Steve Cropper, probably even more so than Cropper, the name of Jimmy Nolen is comparatively obscure. For unlike Cropper, with his numerous production successes, Nolen was primarily a sideman, and probably the finest rhythm guitarist in all of rhythm and blues. His style, featuring rapidly-strummed, usually ninth and seventh chords, is deceptively simple. In truth, it requires an exemplary sense of taste and timing. Nolen's most important work was done in his eight-year tenure with James Brown. Those crucial rhythm licks in "Papa's Got a Brand New Bag," "I Got You (I Feel Good)" and "I Got the Feelin'," among others, are Nolen's.

On the surface it never seemed like Nolen did all that much with Brown, but in fact the sheer repetitive nature of his playing was essential to the well-lubricated rhythmic groove Brown wanted behind him. In the process, Jimmy's playing wound up being far more influential than even he himself realized. Sly and the Family Stone's "Thank You Falettin' Me Be Mice Elf (Again)" features snappy ninth chords taken lock, stock and barrel from Nolen's music with James Brown. Indeed, the entire "funk" guitar sound has been largely built on the innovations of Nolen.

Jimmy Nolen was born April 3, 1934, in Oklahoma City, and began playing guitar as a teenager. T-Bone Walker first influenced him, but as time went on he developed his own style of playing the blues. By the '50s he'd moved closer to r&b and even to rock and roll. It was Nolen's guitar that dominated Johnny Otis's 1958 hit "Willie and the Hand Jive." He passed through a number of other groups, joining Brown in 1965. Though he left him from 1970 to 1972, he returned, and was still working with Brown, and laying down his tightly structured, arresting chord patterns, when he died late in 1983 of a heart attack.

DISCOGRAPHY

Jimmy Nolen did his most important work with Johnny Otis and James Brown in the 1950s and 1960s respectively. His early work with Johnny Otis is available on *Rock & Roll Revue* (Charly) which covers his 1950s material (Nolen did not play on all of it). Nolen's work with James Brown can be heard in any number of configurations. For the budget-minded, there's *The Best of James Brown* (Polydor), a single album with hits like "Papa's Got a Brand New Bag" and "I Got You." There are a number of imports also available, although these are often hard to find. One interesting collection is a reissue of all of Brown's mid-to-late '60s King albums with facsimiles of the original covers from France. Nolen can be heard all through these albums, but how long they will remain available is open to question.

Stevie Ray Vaughan

Certainly since the death of Jimi Hendrix, other guitarists have come along insisting they were ordained to maintain his legacy. In some cases the results haven't been bad, as with Robin Trower. It's questionable how effective some of the others have been. A white guitarist who is "recreating" Hendrix onstage, complete with Afro wig, is about as tasteless as Elvis impersonators.

But Stevie Ray Vaughan, among the most exciting new guitarists of the '80s, approaches Hendrix from a totally different angle. A guitarist deeply influenced by Jimi, Stevie Ray, the younger brother of the Fabulous Thunderbirds' guitarist Jimmie Vaughan, has also been deeply influenced by the blues—as Hendrix was. What he's created is his own style, with the fluency and creativity of Hendrix but with a bluesy edge born of his admiration for Albert King, Buddy Guy, Otis Rush and others. By not studiously trying to recreate Hendrix's music note-for-note and by infusing it with the blues spirit, he actually comes closer to its essence than many others who learn "Little Wing" and "Voodoo Chile" off the records by rote.

One can hear elements of a number of fine guitarists in Stevie Ray's playing: Hendrix, Lonnie Mack, Rush (his backup band is named "Double Trouble," after an early Rush hit), Albert and B.B. King, T-Bone Walker and Guy among others. Vaughan's style has a maturity and understanding of the blues far beyond his years. Born in Dallas, Texas in 1955, he developed his musical tastes by listening to his brother, picking up the music of Hendrix, Eric Clapton, Mack, Jeff Beck and all of the bluesmen previously mentioned. He began playing as a teenager and worked around Austin by the time he was 17. His act was caught in 1982 by producer Jerry Wexler, who got him on the bill at the Montreux

Jazz Festival that year. He was recruited by David Bowie to work on his *Let's Dance* album, but returned to Double Trouble rather than touring with Bowie, and, under the guidance of producer John Hammond (of Benny Goodman, Bob Dylan, George Benson and Bruce Springsteen fame), produced his outstanding debut album *Texas Flood*, released in 1983.

The album is near-perfect, playing up Vaughan's strengths as a bluesman, showing his debts to Hendrix and indicating the direction he may be going—integrating the best of '60s rock guitar with the greatest blues. Vaughan's future can't really be determined from one album, but in an era when high technology new wave music seems to dominate the airwaves, Vaughan may be the one to carry the guitar into the '80s, never losing sight of its roots. His second, *Couldn't Stand the Weather*, is earthy and workmanlike, if less earthshaking than the first. More recently, he has produced an album on his longtime idol Lonnie Mack.

Link Wray

Link Wray's 1958 recording of "Rumble," heard more than a quarter-century after it was recorded, still features one of the most menacing guitar sounds in rock music. Distorted and angry, with the pent-up tension of an approaching thunderstorm, it builds slowly, as the alternating two D chords, followed by a harshly strummed E chord, lay out the theme. It was a raw, primitive recording, technically and musically, even by the past era's standards, yet its power has remained an inspiration to many guitarists, including Pete Townshend of the Who.

Wray has been a consistent, if somewhat surprising, artist over the years. His records never lose that distorted edge, regardless of

the context in which he plays. He's also astute enough not to turn out scores of "Rumble" clones in the wake of the song's success. "The Swag" was, in its own way, nearly as good, though some of his Latin flavored tunes, like "El Toro" and "Tijuana" sounded as if they'd been inspired by the Champs' success with "Tequila."

Wray's sound was one of the most prophetic of the '50s. Numbers like "Jack the Ripper" were uncannily close to things the Yardbirds would record in 1966-'67. Everything was as it would become—the distorted guitar, the pounding drums and the pulsating bass (usually played by his brother Doug, who also doubled organ and horns). He continued recording through the early '60s. Some of his tunes were clearly derivative, such as "The Sweeper," based on "Wipe Out." Yet his guitar was never anything less than savage in its force and effect, even on 1965 tracks like "I'm Branded" and "Hang On," where he coaxed unwordly sounds from his instrument. This—before the psychedelic era began!

In 1971 Wray revived his career recording for Polydor. Much of his music was gospel-flavored hippie fluff, recorded in a studio he built in a chicken shack in Ackokeek, Virginia, south of Washington. But his raw guitar remained unadulterated. His Polydor career petered out eventually, but in the mid '70s he picked up his momentum again, working with neo-rockabilly Robert Gordon on two impressive albums, delving into rockabilly's past, his guitar as unbridled as ever. It was some of the better neo-rockabilly made, pre-Stray Cats. Link Wray, in his mid '50s, gives no indication of toning his playing down in the future, and that's somehow reassuring.

DISCOGRAPHY

Link Wray's most essential recording was "Rumble." That song and 16 other tracks dating from 1947 to 1965, many of them as good a "Rumble," are compiled on *There's Good Rockin' Tonight* (Union Pacific).

INDEX